Sovereign Virtue

ARISTOTLE ON THE RELATION BETWEEN
HAPPINESS AND PROSPERITY

SOVEREIGN VIRTUE
Aristotle on the Relation Between Happiness and Prosperity

Stephen A. White

Stanford University Press   Stanford, California   1992

Stanford University Press   Stanford, California
© 1992 by the Board of Trustees of the Leland Stanford Junior University
Printed in the United States of America

CIP data are at the end of the book

FOR MARY

οὕτω καὶ τοῖς φίλοις αἱρετώτατόν ἐστι τὸ συζῆν

Contents

x   *Contents*

Preface

THE CENTRAL subject of Aristotle's ethics is happiness or living well. Most people, in his day as in ours, eager to enjoy life, impressed by worldly success, and fearful of suffering serious loss, thought happiness depends most on achieving prosperity and avoiding misfortune. But Aristotle argues that virtuous conduct is the governing or "sovereign" factor in living well. Human life, he concedes, has other needs, and neither the blessings nor the afflictions of fortune are unimportant. On his own account, in fact, many of the aims and desires that differentiate the several virtues stem from concern for other people and things. Nonetheless, he maintains that, in any circumstances, the virtuous find life more satisfying than other people do, and, with only modest good fortune, they lead happy and enjoyable lives. In this book, I present a systematic reconstruction of Aristotle's defense of these bold claims. I try to show in detail how his general account of happiness is reflected in and supported by his analysis of individual virtues and specific ethical problems. After setting out the aims and method of Aristotle's inquiry, I sketch the literary and philosophical background to the problem of happiness and present his position in general terms. In the second half of the book, which focuses first on physical well-being and then on external circumstances, I examine how he tries to reconcile the competing claims of morality and fortune by showing how the virtuous view such widely valued goals as health, wealth, power, and honor.

This book is intended primarily as a study of Aristotle's ethics.

My principal aim is the analysis and exposition of his views rather than the elaboration of Aristotelian proposals of my own. We can better appreciate the importance of his problems and discern what is distinctive in his solutions, however, if we see how he develops his account in response to the worries and concerns of his predecessors and contemporaries. I therefore devote more attention than customary to examining the wider cultural background to Aristotle's inquiry and to indicating, by reference to literary and historical sources as well as to philosophical texts, the inherited values and traditional ideals that inform his discussions and provide some of the basis for his conclusions. My goal throughout, however, is not antiquarian but philosophical—not to dwell on obsolete views devoid of significance for modern life, but rather, by tracing Aristotle's attempts to accommodate and amend rival views, to state accurately and precisely his position on a number of questions of vital and perennial interest.

No one writing on Aristotle today can ignore the question of his philosopical evolution. The systematic aspects of his corpus, both in method and in doctrine, are manifest, but it is hazardous to assume that his views are wholly consistent even within one and the same work. Questions of chronology and change, however, are highly controversial and too complex to address here. I have drawn on a wide range of Aristotle's corpus, not in the belief that the works I cite can be harmonized on every relevant point, but to achieve a comprehensive study of questions he addresses in many works. Moreover, whatever the origins of his corpus, it seems foolish not to emulate the learned ancient critics who, to use Porphyry's maxim, endeavored "to clarify Homer out of Homer." An author's own works are not only indispensable but also essential both for interpreting his text and for understanding his thought.

The problem of development is especially acute for Aristotle's ethics. Three explicitly ethical works—the *Nicomachean Ethics*, the *Eudemian Ethics*, and the *Magna Moralia*—have come down to us under his name, and the composite origins of two closely related works—the *Politics* and the *Rhetoric*—remain extremely obscure. I think few would deny, however, that the EN and EE, which bear most of the burden of my account, show both a general conformity of viewpoint and doctrine and innumerable correspondences in detail. Even if the *EE* is the work of another mind, I would argue, it aims to expound and defend substantially the same views. My considered opinion, based on experience but not on thorough study, is that the *EN* is generally superior to the *EE* in argument, insight, and precision of expression. Further, as reflected in its greater length—notably, its treatment of the several virtues (*EN* 3.6–4.9) is over twice as long as the parallel treatment in *EE* 3—it achieves significantly greater breadth and detail of discussion. For these reasons, and because the *EN* also addresses more directly and more thoroughly the subject defined by my title, I have used it as the primary authority; I also refer to the three books common to both works as *EN* 5–7 rather than *EE* 4–6. However, I have also relied heavily on the *EE* and on other texts, especially the *Politics* and *Rhetoric*, occasionally as the principal sources for a topic, but repeatedly to explicate, elaborate, and elucidate the arguments of the *EN* and to corroborate my interpetations more generally. Finally, all who are interested, as I am, more in the views and arguments articulated in these works than in their authorship or authenticity may take the name "Aristotle" to designate not the son of Nicomachus but rather, barring a few exceptions I shall note in passing, the corpus transmitted under that name.

Every student of Aristotle owes an immense debt to the legions of philosophers and scholars who have made his corpus one of the most thoroughly studied and analyzed in any field. I do not pretend to have recorded every point at which I agree or disagree with other interpretations. But in addition to indicating my major debts to previous scholarship, I have tried to address the more significant points of controversy and, given the wide range of subjects I cover, to suggest where to find further information or discussion. I began the work that has resulted in this book six years ago as a graduate student in Berkeley, and I have learned much from the steady flow of new work on Aristotle's ethics. But in the words of the poet, *omnes eodem cogimur*. I have been able to take some account of the recent and important books by Terence Irwin and Richard Kraut, but I regret I can only mention another major study, Sarah Broadie's *Ethics with Aristotle* (Oxford, 1991), which appeared too late for me to address.

In writing this book, I have drawn on the insight and understanding of many people, especially in Berkeley and Austin. It is a pleasure to express my gratitude to the following teachers and colleagues for instruction and for criticism and encouragement of the present work: Julia Annas, Hayden Ausland, Tom Chance, Alan Code, Michael Gagarin, Don Mastronarde, Don Morrison, Alex Mourelatos, Chuck Young, the anonymous reader for Stanford University Press, and above all, Mark Griffith, Tony Long, and Gregory Vlastos—τιμή τ᾽ ἰσόρροπος οὐκ ἂν γένοιτο, ἀλλ᾽ ἴσως ἱκανόν. The work of revising this study for publication was supported by generous grants from the National Endowment for the Humanities and the Research Institute of my home institution, the University of Texas at Austin. Special thanks go to Julius Moravcsik for early and continued support of my project, and to the staff of Stanford University Press—especially Helen Tartar, who genially coaxed my manuscript to port, and John Ziemer, whose meticulous editing added clarity to every page—for providing a most agreeable introduction to the process of publication. Finally, I am happy to express my thanks to Mary Ingle, *compar vitae*, who by word and example has inspired much that is in this book and has for many years sustained me in my work as in all else.

S. A. W.

A Note on Citation

MODERN WORKS are cited in the notes by author and date of first publication; citations of works reprinted in collections follow the pagination of the collected work, except when the original pagination is reprinted. For full bibliographical information, see Works Cited, pp. 307–16. References to ancient works are collated under the authors' names in the Index of Passages Cited, pp. 317–31; information on abbreviations and editions is provided there. In consecutive references to the same work, I cite the author or title only initially; thus, "1.32" preceded by "Herodotus 1.31" refers to Herodotus 1.32. References to Aristotle's works follow the standard pagination of Bekker's 1831 edition but the English chapter divisions. In consecutive references to the same chapter or Bekker page of Aristotle's works, subsequent references abbreviate the initial citation; thus, "b10" preceded by "EN 1.10 1100b6" refers to *Nicomachean Ethics* 1.10 1100b10. I have consulted a number of translations of ancient works, but unless otherwise indicated, all translations and italics are my own.

I

A GOOD LIFE

Those who object that what everything aims at is not good surely have nothing to say. For what everyone considers good we affirm is good. Someone who destroys this conviction will not say anything at all more convincing.

—EN 10.2 1172b35–73a2

The Pursuit of Happiness

PROBABLY THE most distinctive and certainly the most widely shared feature of ancient ethics is the conviction that the fundamental questions of ethics center on how people can find satisfaction in their lives. The good life, it was agreed, must be one we want to live, and if that is to include acting for the good of others, then it must be shown how such action contributes to our own good. In this respect, philosophical ethics follows the path of traditional wisdom: ethical principles are thought to derive their legitimacy from the analysis of actual human capacities and concerns. Only those virtues that can be shown to foster and satisfy these personal attributes are considered ethically commendable; any alleged virtues that regularly threaten their development or expression are found wanting for that reason alone. Hence, virtually all parties approach the task of justifying ethical principles by way of our inborn desire to lead a life of *eudaimonia* or happiness.[1] Conceptions of what is involved in this life vary, of course, often quite drastically. But these differences reflect disagreement about the nature of happiness itself, not about its central importance: they are different answers to the same question, not different questions. The ideals of epic heroism, of archaic moralizing,

---

1. "Happiness" remains the best translation of *eudaimonia* in current English. Many of its allegedly misleading connotations (such as pleasant feelings, success, or transitoriness), though alien to most philosophical accounts of *eudaimonia*, appear in ancient popular usage; see Kraut 1979*b*, Dybikowski 1981, Vlastos 1984: 181–82, and II.iii below.

of sophistic revisionism, and of the schools of Classical and Hellenistic times all articulate what their proponents think reasonable people want most. Figures as diverse as Aristippus the Cyrenaic, who identifies happiness with the pleasant feelings of the moment, and Ariston the Stoic, who identifies it with devotion to virtue alone, can still agree that their accounts must be based on what human beings want to do; both assume that the practical goal of attaining happiness is the primary concern of ethical theory. By extension, any attempt to base an ethical ideal on standards entirely independent of the actual concerns of people would have been thought perverse. The view, for example, that ethics has nothing to do with happiness, or that virtue is constituted by its very independence from desire, would have struck even the most severe as absurd.[2] To be sure, some ancients propose radical changes in the normal pattern of life that would require us to abandon much we hold dear. But revisionism must be justified, it was agreed, on the basis of recognized human aims; reform must find its foundations in goals that people actually pursue.

It is against this background that Aristotle's ethics must be studied. Many of his questions are set by his predecessors, his basic principles are drawn from earlier thinkers, and even his method of argument relies heavily on their views. Indeed, so wide is his debt to earlier thought that he has often been criticized (and sometimes praised) for upholding conventional morality. But one line of argument in this book is that this inference is unsound. To be sure, Aristotle is no radical in ethics, and he typically approaches topics by reviewing prevailing views. Far from endorsing those views, however, his analysis regularly uncovers basic misconceptions in them. Similarly, while he refuses to ignore conventional views, his account also aims to incorporate insights from unorthodox positions, including the revisionist views of Socrates and Plato and even of the Cynics, who disdained normal practice. In short, the relation between Aristotle's

2. Some of the major differences between ancient approaches and later tendencies to divorce morality from happiness (exemplified by Kant) are summarized in Annas 1981: chap. 13. The Cyrenaic Hegesias is an exception who proves the rule (see D. L. 2.93–94): he denied that happiness is the aim of ethics only because he thought happiness "entirely impossible" and "non-existent," on the grounds that life causes us such pain that only temporary pleasure is ever possible. Such is the price, Aristotle might have retorted, of hedonism.

ethics and conventional ideals is more complex than his approach may suggest: he follows tradition in making happiness the basic subject of ethics, he maintains the close connection between the good life and our satisfaction and enjoyment, and he insists that virtues are the traits most conducive to happiness. He develops each of these basic elements, however, in ways that revise the popular ideals of his day, and often those of today. The principal basis for this shift is an analysis of the priorities among our pursuits. Most of us organize our lives around certain dominant and abiding concerns, and our pursuit of these goals subordinates some interests to others; by developing the implications of this practice, Aristotle tries to show how a life centered on a certain range of these concerns can satisfy people with apparently divergent interests. Hence, although his analysis starts from a discussion of actual human pursuits, it also establishes new criteria for evaluating them. It banishes few of the things people like to do, but it also argues for reordering our priorities in ways that often owe much to less orthodox views.

This hierarchy of ends provides the starting point for Aristotle's account of the special role played by happiness in human conduct.[3] First, he surveys the relations among our many pursuits in order to find which are the more important—or in his terms, which are the more final ends. Then, once he has characterized the notion of a supreme end, he develops the implications of this hierarchy for ordering each individual's own life. At the outset, then, the argument invokes examples from everyday activities, ranging from household crafts to positions of power and prestige. But Aristotle does not simply report and describe how people behave. His mundane examples serve to focus the discussion on a single aspect of these activities, the ends or goals for which they are performed, rather than on any procedures they follow.[4] Further, the opening discussion refers only to vari-

3. My focus in the following pages is the argument of the *Nicomachean Ethics*. My views about the relation this work has to Aristotle's other works are outlined in the Preface above.

4. For want of an entirely adequate translation for τέλος, I use both "end" and "goal." Although neither shows the connection with τέλειον ("final," "complete," or "perfect"), jointly they cover the range of Aristotle's term; cf. Hardie 1980: 364. Problems with this term are long-standing: Joachim Périon, at Basel ca. 1540, defends his varied translation of the term (not only *finis*, but *extremum*, *ultimum*, *summum*) by appeal to Cicero's practice (e.g., *Fin.* 1.11, 1.29, 1.42, 2.5, 3.26); see Schmitt 1979.

ous crafts and practices themselves, not to those who practice them or their psychological attitudes. To be sure, he later turns to an internalist perspective; but initially his aim is to characterize the ends inherent in various practices rather than what people want or perform them to obtain.[5] When we compare the ends of our several activities, we find them arranged hierarchically: crafts like bridle making are subordinate to the art of riding that utilizes them, and that art in turn is one of many subordinate to military command (EN 1.1 1094a10–16). Even if all artisans prefer to practice their craft rather than command, their work still serves the ends of other pursuits that rank higher on the hierarchy of ends.

The focus on hierarchy yields immediate dividends when Aristotle introduces the notion of a supreme end and characterizes it by reference to the ordering of ends found in political communities. There, he argues, the practice that has the supreme end as its special province is "politics" (1.2 1094a26–27).[6] The most "authoritative" (ἀρχιτεκτονική) pursuit in any system has the overall good of the system as its end (a14–16, a26–27), and as he shows by pointing to actual practice, politics is the most authoritative pursuit in any community. Appealing directly to social practices, he cites three empirical observations (what "we see"; b2). First, politics directs other pursuits in the community by regulating training and education (a27-b2; cf. Pol. 8). Second, even the pursuits "held in the most honor," including military command, business, and public speaking, are subordinate to politics, since it "uses" these and other disciplines in setting and achieving its own goals (1094b2–4). Finally, it has authority over all other activities, since all are subject to its rule (b5–6). In practice, then, politics is the "most authoritative" and "most sovereign" (κυριωτάτη) pursuit (a26–27).[7] Provided its supremacy reflects the su-

5. EN 1.1 makes no mention of people (note "everything," not "everyone," 1094a3), and apart from the first sentence in 1.2, that chapter continues in the same vein. There is an element of Platonism in this way of discussing crafts and activities abstracted from those who practice them; see Burnet 1900: esp. xxiv–v and 6–10. Only in 1.4–5 does Aristotle turn to views about what is best, and only in 1.7 does he analyze the role of a supreme end for an individual.

6. Although this rendering of πολιτική suggests the partisans known as "rhetors" (literally "public speakers"), it is preferable to "statesmanship" since Aristotle applies the term to all aspects of governing, from the day-to-day business of officials and jurors to the grand vision of statesmen; see EN 6.8.

7. This translation of κύριος is especially apt in the present context of politics; cf. Pol. 1.1 1252a5. For the role of this crucial term in other contexts, see II.iv n22

premacy of its end (a14–16), politics pursues the end that Aristotle seeks (b7).[8]

Does politics have any distinctive end over and above the sum of its subordinate ends? Or does it aim only to coordinate those ends in a comprehensive whole? Its end cannot be all-inclusive, for Aristotle's claim that its end "embraces the ends of the others" (b6) appears as an inference from the observation that in regulating and limiting other pursuits (b1–2, b5), politics forbids some (a28, b5–6). Indeed, if politics had to include every other end as its parts, then every society would have to find a place for all possible pursuits. The notion of inclusion operating here, then, is hierarchical: the end of politics is to oversee and coordinate the pursuit of a given range of other ends. But to do this, to set guidelines for other pursuits and to settle the problems that arise when competing interests collide, it needs a criterion or standard. The question then is how this standard is related to the several component ends: Is the end of politics to achieve some determinate end, such as a wealthy or educated society, or simply "good government," an efficient ordering of ends, no matter what the ends? By extension, since the best good is the end of politics, the question is whether this good is something single and determinate, such as wealth or power, or a systematic ordering of several determinate ends.

To judge from actual practice, it is often the former. Any number of political systems are centered on the pursuit of a single end. Aristotle, however, thinks the evidence shows that politics has a composite end, and his account of how other ends are subordinate to politics tells against at least some determinate ends. Consider the subordinate pursuits to which he refers: artisans live in political communities, and although decisions made by the military govern their production, they often participate in or

---

and II.v *n*19 below. For the place of economic and military ends in a good life, see IV.i and ii, respectively.

8. Cf. *Pol.* 1.1 1252a1–7, 3.12 1282b14–16, and *EE* 1.8 1218b11–16. But why should actual practice have authority here? As the *Republic* shows, political theory might equally reject established practice in favor of principles derived independently of ordinary life. The central point, made at the close of the *EN*, is that sound political judgment requires familiarity with the forms of human life (10.9 1180b28–81b23). Indeed, Aristotle criticizes the *Republic* at length, arguing not only that Plato's project is impractical but that it runs counter to the diverse concerns of political society (*Pol.* 2.2–5). Aristotle's regard for empirical data presumably inspired the collection of "constitutions" compiled at his direction, and its fruits appear in *Pol.* 4–6; see Irwin 1985c: esp. 160–65.

contribute to the political process that sets military policy. Far from threatening Aristotle's approach, this inversion underscores the primacy he gives politics, not only because he focuses on practices rather than on practitioners, but also because artisans end up superior to generals to the extent that they participate in the political process. Hence, compared with any other practice, politics has a wider end in view. If generals reign supreme in some societies, that shows not that the hierarchy of pursuits is purely arbitrary, but only that some want commanders to govern. But in that case, the generals acquire political roles: since they set policy for society as a whole, their end is actually comprehensive. Similarly, just as military tyrants engage in politics despite themselves, so politicians who aim only to foster economic goals thereby serve their vision of the highest good. Even those who use politics to seek their own advantage implicitly make their private good supreme. Outside political activity, by contrast, no members of society, whether corporate or individual, have a comparably general end, since their decisions govern only their private aims. Hence, politics is inherently more comprehensive, even when directed at a single end, since it coordinates the ends of the whole. Indeed, it is bound to include individuals' different priorities in a way that no individual can. The question is whether politics *should* center on promoting a single end or on coordinating a range of ends.

At one level, Aristotle claims that politics has a single end, which he calls "the best good" (1.2 1094a22) and "the human good" (b7).[9] By common consensus, this turns out to be nothing

9. Cf. "the best" (1.7 1097a28, b22, *EE* 2.1 1219a29, 34), "the highest of goods for action" (1.4 1095a16, *Pol.* 7.14 1333a30), "the good for action" (1.7 1097a22–23), "the greatest and best of human goods" (*EE* 1.7 1217a21–22; cf. "the finest life and the best living," 1.3 1215a5), "the best way of life" (*Pol.* 7.1 1323b40), and "the best living" (a23). The *EN* gives "the human good" a special status. Aristotle uses the singular at three crucial junctures: with his first mention of the best good here (1094b7), in the conclusion of the initial formulation of his own account (1.7 1098a16), and when he returns to explain its underlying psychology (1.13 1102a14–15). The term plays no such role in the other works: the singular is absent from the *EE*, although a class of human goods is implied by the "no happy horse" argument in *EE* 1.7, and the *MM* sets the central problem of clarifying the precise sense in which happiness is "the best" (see White 1990). It is not clear that the "human" good here is meant to contrast with a "divine" good, as politics contrasts with philosophy in 6.7 and 10.7; after all, Aristotle thinks promoting education is a task for politics (see *Pol.* 8), and politics could set philosophy as its principal end.

other than happiness (1.4 1095a15–19). But it is notoriously unclear whether happiness consists of one or several ends. Although Aristotle examines several determinate candidates such as honor and wealth, his own account refers more generally to a way of life—rational and virtuous activity—that integrates a wide range of ends. But that is getting ahead of the discussion. To judge by the discussion of politics, at least, the supreme end appears neither to be a single end separate from all others nor to include all others. Rather, it is distinguished formally by its relation to other ends. As Aristotle puts it, the human good is the best end in the precise sense that we want it only because of itself, whereas we want all other ends because of it.

If in fact there is some end among the things we do that we value because of itself [ὃ δι' αὐτὸ βουλόμεθα], whereas we value the others because of it, and if we do not choose all of them because of another one—for in this way [the series] will proceed indefinitely, so that our desire will be empty and pointless—then clearly this end must be the good and the best.

(1.2 1094a18–22)

A number of points here are obscure, not least the notion of valuing something "because of itself." The primary function of the notion is to mark the familiar contrast between wanting things because of some further end and wanting them regardless of anything else; the conclusion here is that the supreme end is of the latter sort. Aristotle adds that this end is our final reason for every choice (a19)—although not that it is itself something we always choose—but his formulation does not yet resolve whether this final end is a single item (or type) or something composite. Not original with Aristotle, this notion of a final end was often used of single uniform ends.[10] Eudoxus, for example, defended a form of hedonism by arguing that pleasure is the best good since it is "something we choose not because of something else nor for the sake of something else" (10.2 1172b20–22). As

10. See 1.6 1096b10–19, 1.7 1097b2–4, and the evidence collected in Rabinowitz 1961: 282 *n*9. As 1.5 shows, some thought one or the other of these final ends to be the supreme end, but each can be final and yet a *part* of the supreme end (e.g., pleasure: 1099a13–16, a24–29); see below. Thus, I take it that "and" in 1097b2 is conjunctive, not disjunctive: the point is that some if not all of us choose *all* of these for the sake of happiness, not that each of us chooses some *one* of them (note b3–4: "we would choose *each* of them even if nothing resulted"); see Ackrill 1974 and White 1990. For Plato on the final end, see Irwin 1977: 51–54 and chap. 7, and Vlastos 1984: 183–85.

evidence, he alleged that "no one asks further for what sake people enjoy themselves" (b22–23). Although this end may be final whenever we choose it, there is no claim that we always choose it. As Aristotle observes, Eudoxus shows only that pleasure is one good, not that it is the best good or the supreme end (b26–34). But the reference to asking for reasons indicates the primary application of the notion—to characterize the relation between reasons and action. Our ends, which we want "because of themselves," are the reasons we have for what we do. Thus, once we say we are doing something for pleasure, Eudoxus argues, there is no point in asking us for further reasons since we have no further reason. More generally, different people have different final answers or reasons for what they do, be it wealth, fame, the prosperity of family and friends, or anything else they want "because of itself."

The problem with Eudoxus' principle is that it captures only one side of the role played by the supreme end. What distinguishes it from other final ends is that we value "the others because of it" (τἆλλα δὲ διὰ τοῦτο, 1094a19). This might appear to imply that happiness is the only thing we value for itself. But as Aristotle later insists, it entails only that happiness is the only thing we want *solely* for its own sake (1097b1–6). Eudoxus is right: pleasure is something we seek because of itself (b2; cf. 1096b18). But it is also something we want "in the belief that we shall be happy through it" (1097b4–5). Nothing here implies that a desire for a single uniform end underlies all our other desires and explains our every action; rather, each of us has a supreme end that represents our reason for pursuing our several determinate ends but does not itself have any further end as its reason. That is not to say that we can offer no reasons for pursuing our ultimate end, but only that our reasons for pursuing *this end* are not limited to ends. Most of us can say something to justify our supreme end, but in so doing, we appeal not to the ends we seek, but to claims about how things are, be it human nature or the will of the gods.[11] To put the point in Aristotle's terms, we "value" (βουλό-

11. In identifying conceptions of happiness with a distinctive sort of reasons, my account resembles J. McDowell 1980: 364–67. But whereas he sees the distinctive feature in an appeal to human nature ("it is the sort of reason for which someone acts when he does what he does because that seems to him to be what a human being, circumstanced as he is, should do"; p. 364), I find it only in finality. Aristotle's argument about human nature is then an appeal outside "reasons for action" for theoretical considerations to justify a certain set of final ends

μεθα) happiness because of itself (1094a19) and we "choose" (αἱρούμεθα) it always because of itself and never because of anything else (1.7 1097b1–2), but we never "decide" (προαιρούμεθα) on pursuing it (3.2 1111b28–29). This implies that our desire for this end is not derived solely from *desires* for other ends (as in "decisions"), but it also implies that we *judge* this end to be good, and hence that we have *beliefs* as our reasons for pursuing it.[12] One's conception of happiness is not the source of all one's desires; rather, as the analysis of politics suggested, it governs and controls the pursuit of what one desires by coordinating one's various component and subordinate ends.

According to this initial sketch, the supreme end might be either single or composite. Although we all have several ends we choose "because of themselves," we might also choose each of them for some one of them that we choose *only* because of itself. Or this supreme end might be the set of those ends as an organized whole. In the former case, the hierarchy of ends resembles a pyramid with happiness a single end at the peak; in the latter case, it resembles a plateau with several ends joined to form happiness at the top. The question, then, is whether happiness is a life directed at a single activity such as philosophy, or a life organized around the pursuit of several ends. I cannot do justice to this question here, but it deserves brief discussion because it bears directly on all that follows.[13]

---

as the right ends for us to have; in short, Aristotle does not appeal explicitly to our *wanting* to be human.

12. Aristotle first identifies happiness as an object of rational desire, as something we "value" (βουλόμεθα, 1094a19). However, only ends are objects of βούλησις (3.2 1111b26–29, 3.3 1112b11–16, 3.4 1113a15), and "no one values anything except when they *believe* it is good" (*Rhet.* 1369a2–4); see White 1988: esp. 220 n19.

13. On the nature of happiness, I follow for the most part Ackrill 1974 and Irwin 1985d; for some qualifications, see White 1990. Kraut 1989 provides a thorough defense of the major alternative, intellectualism, or the thesis that intellectual activity is the sole component of happiness. He also distinguishes this "perfect happiness" from "secondary happiness," which rests on practical virtues. In each case, however, he counts virtuous activity as the sole component of happiness. I cannot do justice to his arguments here, but in White 1990, I offer reasons for resisting his arguments against "inclusivism" (see esp. his chap. 5), and in II.iv–v and IV.ii–iii below, I offer an alternative to one of the linchpins of his account, his claim that "perfect virtue" (τελεία ἀρετή) is intellectual wisdom to the exclusion of other rational virtues (see esp. his chap. 4 sects. 15–17). Irwin (1988a: 608 n40) states my position succinctly: Aristotle does not "identify happiness with contemplation"; rather, he considers intellectual activity "the most valuable single component of happiness."

First, Aristotle connects choosing something "because of itself" with choosing it "by itself" and "alone" (1096b16–19).[14] The
criterion for final ends thus resembles a realistic version of G. E.
Moore's "isolation test": something is a final end for someone if
that person values it—other things being equal—without regard
to other ends it may serve or to any consequences it may have
(1097b3–4).[15] Happiness is "the most final" or "unconditionally
final" end because "it is chosen by itself always and never because of anything else" (a30–34). Further, it is the only end that
"by itself makes life worth living" (b14–15). Aristotle thus relies
on a threefold classification of reasons for action: (1) some ends
(especially those of productive crafts) are instrumental and
sought only to serve further ends; (2) others are final and are
sought "because of themselves" and "by themselves," though
also because of happiness; and (3) the supreme end is sought
only for itself. Whereas the first are good only "conditionally"—
on the condition that they serve further ends—the second are
good "by themselves," even apart from anything else that may
result. Although we would do without the first if we could attain
our final ends without them, we do not want to forsake any of
our final ends. However, although final ends are *intrinsically good*
because they are sought independently of any further end, they
are not *unconditionally final* because each may on occasion—in
some conditions—yield to other final ends in the light of wider
considerations, namely the supreme end. Hence, not only is the
supreme end unconditionally final and *a reason* for pursuing the
other ends we pursue, but it is also *the reason* behind our choosing
among those ends whenever we must. Although Eudoxus was
right to observe that we do some things for pleasure, he neglected to explain either why we pursue *other* ends "by themselves" without any regard to pleasure, or why we sometimes act
in spite of pain. For that, a more comprehensive end is needed,
an end that gives pleasure a place but admits other ends as well.

14. For my translation of the crucial phrase καθ᾽ αὑτό, note μονούμενον
(1096b17), and see Vlastos 1984: n85.

15. On Moore's test and the differences between "intrinsic goods" and "unconditional goods," see Korsgaard 1983. The crucial point for my argument is
that "intrinsic goods" (which Aristotle calls "good by themselves") are valuable
in and of themselves, although not in all conditions; in various special circumstances, they are not desirable and it would be wrong to choose them. Hence,
they are "conditionally final" not in the sense that they are choice-worthy only
under *special* conditions, but in the sense that they are choice-worthy in *most but
not all* conditions.

Aristotle recognizes that happiness is not the only thing we want because of itself and that we do some things for pleasure or justice, each of which we value because of itself. But this is compatible with choosing them for happiness, provided we consider them parts of happiness (*EE* 2.1 1219b13, *Rhet.* 1.5 1360b6). To choose pleasure because of happiness is to choose it both because of itself rather than for any result and also as a part of happiness—as an element on the plateau of reasons that jointly constitute one's final reason for everything one does.[16] But this does not entail that we choose these parts only for their contribution to happiness, and Aristotle insists that we do choose them "because of themselves," though always within the limits set by our conception of happiness. As he puts it, we choose them "in the belief [ὑπολαμβάνοντες] that we will be happy through them" (*EN* 1.7 1097b5). Although he denies that we choose each final end *only* for itself, he sees this as compatible with choosing them as valuable *by themselves*, even in the absence of other valued ends. Indeed, his use of temporal terms suggests that he has in mind situations in which we must choose among our final ends. Our reason for choosing a final end is that we value it both for itself and therefore as a part of a good life. Rarely, however, can we pursue them all at once; there are many times we must decide which to pursue and which to set aside, and for that, our reason is our supreme end, our conception of the good life as a whole.[17] Since we have several ends that we value for themselves, we cannot pursue any of them constantly; although we pursue each final end whether or not it yields results, we also limit our pursuit of each of them to allow for pursuit of the others. In choosing love over health, for example, we would base our choice on our conception of the supreme end and choose love for its contribution to our overall good or happiness. Only this end is *unconditionally final*, because only it includes the other final ends we consider *intrinsically good*; only by appeal to it can we adjudicate among those often competing ends.

As it now stands, Aristotle's account of the supreme end is compatible with diverse views about the specific content of hap-

16. See Ackrill 1974: 18–22, Whiting 1986: 73–75, and White 1990. Although τέλειον does not *mean* "complete," any final end that one chooses because of itself counts as a part of one's conception of happiness.

17. Note "never" (1097a31, 33, b1) and "always" (a33, b1, b20). See Kenny 1966: 55; cf. J. McDowell 1980: 362–63.

piness, from those of voluptuaries or businessmen to that of philosophers. But before we ask which specific views are correct, it will be helpful to illustrate this general account. Consider Milo, the celebrated Pythagorean wrestler. The ends he considers intrinsically good include fine dining, wrestling, and mathematics, each of which he pursues for its own sake. To some extent, these ends can be harmonized: the heavy diet required for his wrestling encourages him to indulge his taste for roast beef, and the prizes he wins help support the community of scholars with whom he studies. So he has several ends that he would pursue "by themselves," although in fact they contribute to attaining other ends. Nonetheless, the more he studies, the less he can wrestle, and vice versa; and both his training and the rules of Pythagorean study prohibit some of his favorite dishes. So Milo chooses his ends not only for themselves but also for their place in his overall good as he sees it. When he chooses to study, he chooses that end over others both because of itself and because of the part it plays in his view of the good life as a whole. Further, even if he considers this end more valuable than every other single end, and even if he would forsake his other final ends if he thought them incompatible with it, on at least some occasions he limits his pursuit of it in order to pursue his other ends. It is a better life on the whole, he thinks, to wrestle, dine, and study— so long as he can do all—than to give up wrestling and fine food in order to maximize time for his studies. After all, his desire for these ends is not *based* on his desire for study, nor is study the only end he values because of itself; much less does he want to study all the time. Rather, he enjoys wrestling and good meals, and he thinks them good in and of themselves, not because they promote his studies. So while he governs and limits his pursuit of his other ends in the light of the single end of study, those other ends are still coordinate with it rather than subordinate to it; he pursues even his studies in the light of a comprehensive end that includes all of his final ends. In short, each of these ends is part of his supreme end, centered in this case on one end but embracing other ends as well.[18]

18. As will be apparent, my example touches on the debate whether Aristotle's theory of happiness is "intellectualist"; see *n*13 above. I offer the example not to refute that view, of course, but to illustrate where I stand on this important debate.

On this account, none of us pursues any final end only because of happiness, or only because of itself. Rather, we organize our pursuit of our usually several final ends in the light of our conceptions of a comprehensive end, and it is by reference to that supreme end that we arbitrate among our major concerns, since even our pursuit of the component ends is constrained by the demands of the overall pattern. Of course, it is possible that some of us may have only one final end, which we value because of itself and which we organize our entire lives in order to achieve. But even then, we pursue our single final end also because of happiness, "in the belief that we will be happy *through it*" (1097b5). Moreover, the pyramid view implies only that a single final end justifies or *governs* all our desires, choices, and actions, not that we *have* no desires for any other ends. In short, whatever one's view about the content of the supreme end, that view governs and limits one's pursuit of all determinate goals. Although different people have different supreme ends and think that happiness is found in different ways of life, each governs all their pursuits by that end. Thus, I interpret Aristotle as first defining happiness formally as a comprehensive end that is unconditionally final as well as intrinsically good (1097a15–b21) and then specifying a principle that organizes the pursuit of the several parts of the supreme end around a single "dominant" end, namely the activity of rational excellence or virtue (1097b22–98a20).[19] But since this formula provides only an "outline" (b20–26), he goes on to analyze its central terms and their implications (1.13–3.5), and to work out in detail the relations between this dominant end and our other major ends as they appear in the several spheres of human life—first generally (1.8–12) and then in greater detail (3.6–10.8). But before we look further at this account, a more general question must be raised.

What connection does this formal analysis of a supreme end have with happiness and a satisfying life? To this point, the supreme end has been characterized formally in terms of choice. This very characterization, however, connects it with what we

19. This principle and the crucial "function" argument on which it is based will be my focus in III.i below. Although this argument establishes the single most basic principle in Aristotle's theory, it remains neutral between a range of alternative theories, and only through extensive further analysis of its relation to other ends does Aristotle construct a determinate account of the good life for humans; see J. McDowell 1980: 366–67.

want and value, and that opens the way for Aristotle to give it more content. Nearly everyone, he claims, has some conception of an ultimate goal, since we all agree on a single name for it—happiness (1.4 1095a15–18). We also agree that this goal can be identified with living and doing well (a18–20). Beyond that, disagreement begins. Many think that the highest good lies in something obvious and at hand; some even identify it with satisfying their immediate inclinations or needs (a20–25; cf. EE 1.3 1214b29–15a3). But in fact, most people equate happiness with satisfying more sustained interests, the long-term goals around which they organize their whole lives. The age-old question of the best way of life, implicit already in tales about the judgment of Paris, had it that happiness lies in attaining some single end, such as power, beauty, or wealth, which can guide and limit all our other pursuits.[20] So by tying questions about happiness to the choice between lives, Aristotle puts a premium on reasoned choice, for it takes experience, reflection, and foresight to assess the advantages and disadvantages of different priorities.[21] Despite major disagreement, the question about lives indicates the way to characterize happiness: first, the discussion at this general level underscores the importance of hierarchy; second, it can embrace competing pursuits by coordinating them. The problem is not that only one thing is worth pursuing, but rather how to organize the several valuable pursuits in ways conducive to overall satisfaction. If that can be done, it should be possible to appeal to a hierarchy to resolve disputes about the content of happiness without disregarding the rich diversity of human life. In particular, although the correct supreme end may require adjusting many priorities, it is unlikely to rule out many pursuits altogether, for these are what give the system its starting points, its content, and its appeal.

Although it seems implausible for Aristotle to claim that everybody chooses happiness, his formulation is clearly meant to describe actual practice.[22] In parallel remarks in the Rhetoric,

20. See 1.4 1095a20–30, 1.5, 1.6 1096b17–18, 1.7 1097b2, 1.8 1098b22–26, and EE 1.1 1214a32–33, 1.2 1214b6–9, 1.4–5; I shall return to this traditional question in II.iii. For the history of the topic, see Joly 1956 and Spoerri 1958.

21. Cf. the notion of a "broad rational agent" in Irwin 1981: 211–13 and 1988a: chap. 15, esp. pp. 338–39.

22. J. McDowell (1980: 359–64) answers the doubts about an indicative thesis expressed in Kenny 1966. Plato shares Aristotle's view of the facts: cf. Symp. 205a, Euthyd. 278e, and Gorg. 467c–68c (499e has a normative element, δεῖν). The claim

Aristotle claims that nearly all of us, both individually and in common, do in fact aim at happiness in our choices of what to do or avoid (1.5 1360b4–7). But his claim is compatible with actual practice and the great variety of final reasons people have. Disputes about the specific character of happiness can be explained as the result of different people concentrating on different parts of the supreme end at the expense of other parts. Further, Aristotle's discussion of the topic elsewhere suggests that he has in view only adults who have the freedom, the physical capacity, and the psychological maturity to do as they choose. Thus, at the outset of the *Eudemian Ethics*, he says that "everyone who can live in accord with his own decision sets some view [τινὰ σκοπόν] of living well, be it honor or prestige or wealth or education, looking toward which [πρὸς ὃν ἀποβλέπων] he will perform all his actions" (1.2. 1214b6–9). For, as he goes on to say, "It is a sign of great foolishness not to organize one's life toward some end [πρός τι τέλος]" (b10–11).[23] Hence, his claim that nearly everyone aims at happiness applies only to mature adults who decide what to do on the basis of reasons and whose lives allow them opportunities to act as they decide.[24] Finally, Aristotle's claim is not that having an end in view provides the sole basis for our other pursuits, but that the lives of mature people are "organized" (συντετάχθαι, b10) around certain specific concerns. Just as politics is not the sole reason for everything else done in a society, neither is any single specific end the sole reason for everything anyone does. The pursuit of wealth, for example, does not underlie even the miser's every desire; it only governs and limits his other desires. This organized pattern of life, not a single end, is what we all pursue when we can under the name of happiness.

---

is clearly factual in the parallel phrasing of the conventional view that "the good is what everything aims for" (1094a2–3, 10.2 1172b9–15, *Pol.* 1.1 1252a2–3, *Rhet.* 1.6 1362a23).

23. The text of 1214b6–9 is problematic: "sets" in my translation stands for θέσθαι (b7); most manuscripts provide no finite verb, but some editors insert δεῖ in b6 to yield "should set" (manuscript support for this is very weak). As the following sentence (b10–11) shows, however, the claim has normative force: any who do not "set some view of living well" are "foolish"; see Cooper 1975: 94–97, and J. McDowell 1980: 363–64.

24. "Opportunities" refers to having options available, although we also need the rational capacity to "opt" if we are to exercise our options; prisoners and slaves lack the former, and children and "the childish" lack the latter. Cf. οἱ ἐπ' ἐξουσίας τυγχάνοντες (*EE* 1.4 1215a35–36; the participle acknowledges that fortune has influence here) and the note on "freedom" in Irwin 1985a: 403.

If Aristotle's argument is more plausible when restricted to free and mature adults, what sense is there to proving that a final end exists? To be sure, Aristotle introduces the supreme end in what is grammatically a conditional clause (*EN* 1094a18); but that serves only to mark the logical force of a premise, not to express doubts about its existence. First, he inserts an argument (1094a19–21) to support his premises.[25] Second, although the conclusion is presented in the optative, it is presented as established (δῆλον ὡς, a21), and the protasis itself is marked as an assertion (εἰ δή, a18).[26] Further, the existence of a supreme end is taken as established in the following lines: it can be known (a23), it can be described (a25), and it is the special object of politics (a26–27). Aristotle has more to say about the notion of a supreme end later in his argument (1.7). But if he meant this opening argument to be conclusive rather than hypothetical, is he guilty of the fallacy of inferring from "all chains [of reasons] must stop somewhere" to "there is somewhere where all chains stop"?[27] He would be if he had meant to prove the existence of a single end valued only because of itself. But a more charitable interpretation is possible. First, the references to ordinary activities, which both precede (a1–18) and follow (a27–b7) his claim, suggest that the argument is meant to explain normal practice, which, I have argued, fits the model of several ends on a plateau. So the argument shows not that all chains end in the *same* place, but only that chains must end; the set of places where they end can then be considered together as one composite end.[28] Moreover, if the conclusion is not that everybody has the same supreme end (which conflicts with Aristotle's recognition that different people pursue different supreme ends) but only that all mature adults

25. Ackrill (1974: 25) characterizes the logic of the passage as an argument "if p and not q, then r," in which Aristotle offers an argument for "p" by arguing for "not q," when "q" is the only available alternative to "p."

26. An optative apodosis following an indicative protasis underscores an inferential connection (hence my "must be" for 1094a22); see Smyth 1956: §2300a. The use of δή here marks the conditional protasis as the *assertion* of a premise; see Denniston 1954: 223–24, cf. 1101a28–34: εἰ δή . . . , συλλογιστέον δή. . . .

27. See Anscombe 1957: §21; Clark (1975: 147) suggests the related fallacy of inferring "if everyone had a father then there is someone who is everyone's father" (unlike Anscombe's model, the relation of paternity is not transitive).

28. See Ackrill 1974: 25–26: "Where there are two or more separate ends each desired for itself, we can say that there is just one (compound) end." For the argument to be sound, Aristotle must conceive of the supreme end as composite, as in 1097a22–24.

have *at least one* final end as their reason for what they do, then the conclusion is more plausible.[29] Finally, if the point is not to prove that a single end exists but only to show how life without any final end would be seriously deficient, then charges of fallacy are irrelevant.[30] Yet that seems to be precisely his aim: the necessity involved is not logical but psychological, and the inference stands. But what is this psychological necessity?

Aristotle claims that unless we have at least one end we choose solely because of itself, "our desire is empty and pointless" (κενὴν καὶ ματαίαν, a21). What consequences does he envision here? What do those who lack a supreme end experience, and what are those who have such an end spared? First, since Aristotle refers not to decisions but to values and desires, the problem is not that we could not *decide* what to do because our deliberations would be endless if we had no end we considered good by itself. Rather, we could never be *satisfied* in what we do. If we had no final end, we could still decide what to do on the basis of intermediate ends, but even if we attained each of these ends, we would never attain anything we valued simply for itself. Likewise, what will "proceed indefinitely" (a20) is not a process of deliberation, but the reasons we have for our actions and hence our pursuit of the ends we value.[31] Neither "choosing" nor "val-

29. I take it that τἆλλα(1094a19) may be either comprehensive (referring to everything else someone does, as in 1102a2–3) or relative (referring only to actions subordinate to a given end, as in 1097a18–22).

30. The assumption that Aristotle intends a deductive proof has inspired great ingenuity; see esp. the formal reconstruction in Williams 1962. But Aristotle's talk about ends implies a relation that, though usually asymmetrical, is reflexive in the case of final ends, including happiness; it is often but not always transitive, as when Milo follows a light diet for health but wants to be healthy for wrestling, even though his diet interferes with the weight he needs for wrestling.

31. The subject of πρόεισι is "our valuing and choosing" (understood from "we value" and "we choose"), and the regress envisioned is of our valued ends (implied by τἆλλα, a19), i.e., the reasons we have for acting as we do; cf. the helpful but dubiously Aristotelian Met. α.2 994a8–10. In his discussion of deliberation, Aristotle uses similar terms to describe a regress of deliberation (3.3 1113a2), but there the regress moves downward from ends to the specification of means, rather than upward to more comprehensive ends as here, and deliberation is not mentioned in 1.2; see Stewart 1892 on 1113a2. As for Aristotle's notorious denial that deliberation is about ends (3.3 1112b11–12), his point is not that a doctor, for example, never wonders whether to cure someone, but rather that any deliberation presupposes having some end in view. If consideration leads to modifying or even abandoning that end, it does so in the light of some higher end, something the deliberator considers more important (either in general or in the circumstances). Although this rules out deliberation about happiness, it does not rule out reflection about it; see Wiggins 1974: 233.

uing" requires any deliberation, and although deliberation presupposes a conception of some end, it does not always have recourse to final ends, much less the supreme end. Rather, since we do not always rehearse our reasons in advance, Aristotle's claim applies to all actions for a reason, not only to deliberated action. His point is that some of our desires are for ends and these are the reasons that explain our actions.

The basic problem, as Aristotle diagnoses it here, is that people who have nothing they consider good because of itself cannot find any lasting satisfaction, since any end they may achieve will turn out to be sought for some further end. Like children who quickly tire of their toys, they live on an endless treadmill of desire that never reaches a final goal, and they remain ever "empty," like the jars carried by the Danaids in Socrates' allegory of hedonism.[32] This is why their pursuits are random and "pointless"; their life has no end that gives them purpose and direction.[33] Thus, Aristotle does not pretend to deduce the existence of one supreme end shared by all. On the contrary, its existence is shown by the phenomena of human conduct: many people do pursue ends that give their lives point, and some do find satisfaction in their pursuits, so they must have final ends. Of course, having ends to pursue is no guarantee of satisfaction, and some pursuits are more liable to frustration than others. Nor is every conception of a supreme end sound; having enough sense to formulate priorities scarcely guarantees getting them right. Many of us organize our lives around the wrong ends and follow the wrong priorities. But before specifying what ends are final and showing how they fit together in the supreme end, Aristotle

32. See *Gorg.* 493 and 496d–e, where Socrates speaks of desire as "full" and "empty"; cf. *EE* 1.5 1215b17–18, where discussion of the good life leads to the question "What in life is choice-worthy [αἱρετόν], and what makes one's appetite fulfilled [πλήρη τὴν ἐπιθυμίαν]?" By contrast, desire is "empty" when denied satisfaction; for Aristotle's use of this terminology for appetites, see III.ii below.

33. This accords with Aristotle's standard use of the term: something is "pointless" if it does not achieve its end, as a morning constitutional is "pointless" unless it leads to "evacuation" (*Phys.* 2.6 197b22–27). Similarly in the *EN*, the young will listen to arguments about ethics "pointlessly," since they cannot achieve the goal, which is action (1.3 1095a5). It would be "pointless" to look into every view about happiness, since the aim is to find the truth and not all views have much to add (1.4 1095a29). If the postulation of a form of the good is supposed to explain why particular things are good, yet only the form of the good is good, then the form of the good is "pointless" (1.6 1096b20). A braggart's boasts are "pointless" if he has no reason for exaggerating (4.7 1127b11).

characterizes formally what sort of end prevents life from being "empty and pointless": the pursuit of happiness is the coordinated pursuit of the several ends we value because of themselves.

A full account of the good life must both define its parts and show how they form an integrated whole. The first task is simpler than the second, because there is general agreement about what a good life must include but wide disagreement about the relative importance of these ends. No one disputes, Aristotle claims, that external goods, bodily goods, and goods of the soul are necessary for happiness, "but they differ on the quantity and the priorities, for some think any amount of virtue is enough, and they seek an unlimited excess of wealth, property, power, fame, and all the like" (*Pol.* 7.1 1323a24–38). Aristotle, of course, argues that this gets the true priorities backward, and that happiness can be found only in organizing our pursuit of other ends around the dominant end of virtuous activity and in governing our lives by rational virtues (a38–b36). But although he reverses conventional priorities, he retains the conventional ends, and in developing his account, he relies heavily on the evidence of current and traditional views and practices. This respect for conventional values is based in part on Aristotle's naturalism and the principle that most things people want and do are good at least in some respects and on some occasions. The problem, he argues, is roughly that we must also become the sort of people for whom those things are regularly good—that to enjoy them and lead a happy life, we must be able to use them well—and this requires developing rational virtues. But his respect for received views and practices also rests on a complex view about ethical beliefs and argument. Before we look at those ideals and his response to them, therefore, we need to look at his method and standards of argument because, as well as setting his questions, they help justify his answers.

Reputable Views

IN ITS RESPECT FOR received views and actual practice, Aristotle's formal analysis of happiness as a system of ends exemplifies his approach to ethical problems: he starts from a survey of things people do and say, and his aim is to describe how to satisfy a range of existing concerns, not to prescribe wholly new concerns.[1] This charity toward the phenomena of human life is not unfounded. At the most general level, it is dictated by the nature of his subject: happiness is something we do want and pursue, and however confused or misguided our pursuit of it may be, our practices and beliefs provide important evidence of its content. It may take us long reflection and much effort before we can re-shape our lives around the pursuit of the supreme end as Aristotle characterizes it, but the prospect is real precisely because that end embraces the ends we already value. Similarly, given that happiness is not itself a determinate end but rather an ordered pattern of several determinate ends, it must be characterized in terms of the ends that we actually value and desire. Further, a happy life must be enjoyed (not just enjoyable), and al-

---

1. Note δοκεῖ (*EN* 1.1 1094a2, a26) and φαίνεται (a3, a28, b8; cf. b2); cf. the surveys introducing the topics of incontinence (7.1), pleasure (7.11), and friendship (8.1), and more briefly, voluntary action (3.1) and several of the virtues (e.g., 3.6, 5.1). My account of Aristotle's method owes most to Barnes 1980, which builds on Owen 1961; see also Nussbaum 1986: chaps. 8–10. Here I disagree with Irwin (see his 1980, 1981a, and 1988a: esp. chaps. 1–2 and 16), who argues that principles of human psychology and metaphysics are fundamental to Aristotle's method in ethics; see *n*18 below.

though we may later regret doing something we enjoy, we are rarely wrong about what we enjoy. We often mistake enjoyment for happiness, but no one can be happy without enjoying life. Hence, although *"eudaimonia"* does not have the connotations of contentment that "happiness" often has, Aristotle's insistence that it is intrinsically pleasant gives authority to what people say about the satisfaction they find in their lives.[2]

Aristotle might have asked other questions. But the consensus was that happiness is the central subject of ethics, and that requires examining the goals and aspirations people take happiness to embrace. To start from standards that are *independent* of actual values and practice would conflict with the internalism implicit in his subject: as the supreme end of actual pursuit, happiness is not only something we should want and pursue but also something we do want and have reason to pursue. Its constituents are ends that most of us either already want or at least can come to recognize as desirable. Hence, when Aristotle defines happiness as virtuous activity, he needs to show that virtuous activity is something we already have good reason to seek. His appeal to human nature as the basis for his account presupposes not only that this is an internal principle rather than an external authority, but also that it accords with what at some level we want and believe. While consistent with egoism, this approach does not entail either psychological or ethical egoism, for the claim is not that everything we want and pursue is or should be essentially connected to our own good but simply that we can recognize happiness as something we have reasons to pursue, whether or not those reasons are egoistic.[3]

Although this approach does not rule out revisionist claims, it does set constraints on the ways those claims can be defended. Aristotle may survey the popular and traditional ideals of material and social success briefly at the outset (*EN* 1.4–5), but they provide material for further analysis, whereas he dismisses the

---

2. A preliminary statement follows the function argument (1.8 1099a7–29); the claim is defended in 7.13 and reiterated near the end (10.5 1176a26–29).

3. See Vlastos 1984: 203 *n*14, Williams 1985: 32, and Kraut 1989: esp. chap. 2. Kraut points out that Aristotle never says explicitly that we aim primarily at *our own* happiness; but Aristotle frequently uses the verb "to be happy" (εὐδαιμο-νεῖν) with personal subjects (e.g., 1111b28, where the primary sense of "we want to be happy" is "each of us wants *oneself* to be happy"). I discuss egoism in IV.iv below.

Platonist theory of the good not only for its flawed metaphysics (1.6 1096a17–b8) but also for addressing the wrong questions (1096b30–97a14). Despite the "convincing" arguments offered in its support, this idealism can be rejected because it "contradicts" actual practice by implying that all disciplines study the same object (1097a4–13; cf. 1096a29–34). Unlike Plato's "idea of the good," the good that Aristotle takes as his subject is something people can attain in action (1096b33–97a1; cf. *EE* 1.7 1217a21–40). Likewise, knowledge of the good must be useful for action, but knowledge of the "idea" has no bearing on actual practice (1097a1–13; cf. 1096a29–34 and *EE* 1.8 1217b23–40, 1218a33–b6).[4] Plato deserves credit for distinguishing a class of things good "by themselves," but it is "pointless" to postulate a single "idea" separate from these goods because it divorces them from action and actual pursuits (1096b8–20).

The critique of Platonic method shows that the good is not *independent* of actual pursuits and desires, but it does not show that the good depends *only* on prevailing concerns. Aristotle's approach requires that he not reject every pursuit, but it does not require that he endorse them all. Although most ends are likely to find some place in the comprehensive end that is happiness, some may be rejected entirely if they turn out incompatible with essential or more important pursuits. On Aristotle's approach, then, the problem is to strike the right balance between criticism and charity. He must resolve disagreements about happiness and its components without undermining his thesis that most of actual practice at least aims at something good.

This approach faces serious obstacles, not least the great controversy surrounding views about what is good or valuable, as Aristotle emphasizes at the outset (1094b14–19). First, there is the threat of relativism if conflicting views of the good are allowed to stand. To be sure, just as he argues that the Platonic "idea" of the good is no better for being eternal (1096b3–5), so he rejects the absolutist demand, associated with Socrates and the Stoics, that

4. The details of these arguments are infamously obscure, but their general import is clear; for a methodical discussion, see Woods 1982 on *EE* 1.8. The *EE* inverts the order of the *EN* by introducing happiness at the start (1.1 1214a1–8) and identifying it as an end of action only after dismissing Platonist forms and universals (1.8 1218b7–27), but it too gives actual pursuits the priority they have in the *EN*, which it echoes in calling happiness "the greatest and best of the *human* goods" (1.7 1217a21–22); cf. I.i *n*9 above.

nothing is really good, regardless of what we think or want, unless it is *always* beneficial, *always* good for us.[5] But the resulting relativism—that different things are often good for different people or in different situations—is something Aristotle rightly considers innocuous. Provided he can find some regularity underlying this variation, it is compatible with realism about the good. Indeed, his concession that things that are good for most people can be bad for some people underscores his realism, for it implies that the components of happiness are not wholly determined by what anyone happens to want or believe. On the contrary, the goodness of human ends must have an objective basis if some things some people want are not good and if some things are good even for people who do not want them. The upshot is that, as Aristotle puts it, we must be the sort of people for whom good things really are good.[6] This relativism is far from subjectivism and the claim that *believing* something good makes it so. Although the truth of many ethical claims may depend partly on people's subjective states (including desires and beliefs), Aristotle denies it ever depends *wholly* on their *beliefs*. Still, there remains the obvious worry that, the more weight given to received views, the harder it will be to reconcile incompatible views. Aristotle's appeal to hierarchy can accommodate a number of competing ends, but it cannot preserve every view about what is best. Moreover, it will not do simply to eliminate differences of opinion. Consistency alone cannot guarantee truth or determine which views are correct, and if reliance on received views leaves little room for criticism, it may only enshrine conventional pref-

5. For Socrates, see *Euthyd.* 279–82 and *Meno* 87–88. For the Stoic thesis, see D. L. 7.102–3 and Long 1988: 165–71. If not circular, this thesis seems simply to postpone the question of what is good: if the beneficial is what leads to good results, we still need to know what results are good. The order of arguments against the Platonic "idea" suggests that Aristotle sees it as conflating "intrinsically good" and "always good" (cf. 1096b3–5, b8–14). Discussing ancient skepticism, Annas (1986: esp. 9–10) shows how relativism is incompatible with absolutism but not with realism.

6. For this central thesis, see esp. 5.1 1129b3–6; cf. 5.9 1137a26–30, 7.13 1153b21–25, 3.4 1113a25–33, and *Met.* Γ.5. Cf. the discussion of objectivity in Lear 1984: esp. 143–5; but Lear's "neo-Aristotelian" approach differs from Aristotle's in abandoning appeals to "human nature," as in his proposed solution to cultural relativity (pp. 167–70). The opening lines of *EN* illustrate Aristotle's rejection of subjectivism: he allows that (1) "the good is what [οὗ] everything seeks" (1.1 1094a2), not that (2) it is "whatever" (ὅτου) everything seeks; (1) only describes the good, but (2) purports to define it (cf. 1.6 1097a5).

erences and practice. So unless he can explain how so many views go wrong, his starting points appear not only inadequate but actually inimical to his inquiry. What basis is there for thinking the method can yield truth as well as consistency?

Aristotle seems especially liable to charges of relativism for relying on what he calls *endoxa* or "reputable views." As the term suggests, these are views with high social status rather than epistemic status: repute implies public approval, not truth.[7] If Aristotle's appeal is *only* to consensus and common beliefs, his starting points will be strictly conventional. But, as a familiar passage makes clear, the respect for established practices which it exemplifies is more complex: reputable views provide the materials— not the conclusions—for his analysis, and the crucial stage—the work that clarifies and resolves the disputes that face us at the start—requires working through puzzles and allows for significant qualifications.

As in other cases, we should set out the appearances, and after working through the problems, we should prove preferably all the reputable views about these experiences, or if not, the majority and the most sovereign views. For it would be a sufficient proof to resolve the difficulties and leave behind the reputable views.   (7.1 1145b2–7)[8]

Clear enough in outline, this passage raises two basic questions about Aristotle's method: Why should reputable views have a *favored* status, and why should removal of difficulties count as *proof*? To take these in order, the first point to settle concerns the scope of the reputable views. As Aristotle explicates the term, they are those held "by all or most people, or by the wise, either all or most or the most recognized and reputable among them" (*Top.* 1.1 100b21–23; cf. *Rhet.* 2.23 1398b21–25).[9] The first clause

7. Brunschwig (1967: 113 *n*3) observes that the term describes beliefs externally rather than epistemically, as *accepted* rather than *worthy of acceptance* because reasonable or true; but given Aristotle's background assumptions about the overall reliability of human judgment, repute provides prima facie warrant for beliefs. For the fundamental importance of this term and the significance of this translation, see Barnes 1980: esp. 498–502; cf. Burnyeat 1986. Barnes finds the "method of *endoxa*" equally suited for other subjects, but I aim to show here why it is especially suited to ethics.

8. On the importance of this passage, see Owen 1961 and Barnes 1980: 490–94. For a paradigm of the method, see II.iv below on Aristotle's analysis of Solon's maxim in *EN* 1.10.

9. Aristotle later adds the qualification that reputable views are not "paradoxes" (*Top.* 104a10–12). Incidentally, the following lines there cast doubt on Barnes's inclusion of "implicit beliefs" (1980: 501): all that Aristotle adduces are "de-

admits "popular" views held by nearly everyone. Despite what theorists like Speusippus say, for example, pleasure must be good because "everyone thinks it is" (*EN* 1172b35–73a4). To be consistent, Speusippus himself should agree, for he holds that something is good if everything seeks it (1172b36; cf. a10, 1094a1– 2, 1097a5), and all creatures seek pleasure (1172b10, 1153b25–26). But consensus is rare. As the case of pleasure shows, it is compatible with disagreement in detail and hence with partial error: everyone seeks pleasure, but often very different pleasures (1153b25–32).[10] So the method does not automatically validate everything said by "the many" (οἱ πολλοί). On the contrary, the popular view of pleasure needs revision because the only pleasures recognized by the many are physical (1153b33–54a1). But because their view has some truth, Aristotle endorses Hesiod's maxim that no opinion expressed by a multitude is "entirely lost" (*WD* 763–64, at b27–28; cf. Demosthenes 19.243); after all, physical pleasure does have a place in a good life (*EN* 1154a15–18). Finally, reliance on reputable views does not admit everything anyone says: Aristotle dismisses views as fickle (1095a23–30), insincere (1096a1–2; cf. 1153b19–21), or mindless and immature (*EE* 1.3 1214b28–34).[11] The implication seems to be that only the con-

---

nials of the contraries of reputable views," and he says only that they "appear" reputable (a15–33); in fact, he later disqualifies some of them (cf. esp. *Top.* 2.7 113a1–19). On the term "recognized" (γνωριμός), see *n*21 below.

10. Owen (1961) rightly insists on the continuities between Aristotle's use of "the phenomena" in science and in ethics, but it is remarkable that the three instances of universal consensus he cites (p. 90 *n*15) all concern ethical topics. Moreover, not one survives examination. One case is illusory (*EE* 1.6 desiderates consensus but mentions none). The other two (both concerning pleasure) each presuppose some dispute and survive only in qualified form. One (*EN* 7.13 1153b27) is merely a line from Hesiod, cited to confirm that pleasure is "in a way" the best; his claim is emended twice, first because not everything seeks *the same* pleasure (b30–31)—which implies only a rough consensus—and then because even if all seek the same pleasure, it is "*not* what they think or would say" (b31–32)—which implies explicit disagreement. The other (10.2 1172b36) aims to refute those who *deny* pleasure is good—which implies again that consensus is not universal. In short, consensus is initially never more than rough and vague. Thus, when Aristotle cites "beliefs held by us all" as "testimonies" to his outline of happiness (*EE* 2.1 1219b1), he means only that *most* would find *some interpretation* of each claim acceptable.

11. The following lines may add that opinions of "the many" can be neglected, because they "need feeling, not argument" (1214b34–15a3). But the text is problematic, and the point may be that popular views deserve to be dismissed only if they are "like" childish views. Only a marginal note in one manuscript adds that *only* the wise deserve consideration; see Barnes 1980: 504–5. Reputable views are held by "all or most" (*Top.* 100b21–22), and that is consistent with ex-

victions of mature and reasonable adults who reflect about how to live and who organize their lives accordingly deserve special respect (cf. 1214b6–11 and *EN* 1095a2–13).

None of this implies that all or any of Aristotle's starting points are immune to revision or that his aim is simply to isolate the maximal consistent set of pursuits. But his express aim is "to prove all or most of the reputable views" (1145b4–6); if widely shared views were all he had to start from, he would be unlikely to reach many unconventional conclusions. However, reputable views are not merely "common beliefs," and not all are widely held. On the contrary, as his explication adds, they include the views of "the wise" (*Top.* 100b22), many of whom are notorious for contesting conventional wisdom.[12] To be sure, their views often found expression in prevailing institutions and ideals, not least because poets and sages of the past exerted a continuing influence through education and public ceremony.[13] However, the wisdom of the past is no mere record of actual practice: "the ancients" (οἱ παλαιοί; cf. *EN* 1.8 1098b17, b27) include Hesiod, Homer, Theognis, and others whose works abound in sentiments that challenge actual practice and belief. Indeed, the customs and conventions (τὰ νόμιμα) they helped shape, like the laws (νόμοι) others left as their legacy, were often honored in public but disdained in private (*SE* 12, esp. 172b36–73a6, a27–30). Moreover, the wisdom of the past includes the social criticism of Solon and Euripides and the esoteric theories of Pythagoras and Anaxagoras, and revisionist arguments from Socrates and Plato crop up alongside more orthodox views.[14] Finally, even

---

cluding views held by "the many," who may be characterized as (for example) the untutored rather than the numerical majority: "the many" who are poor may *say* happiness is being wealthy (*EN* 1.4 1095a23–25), but if that view is not widely *respected* (because, e.g., its proponents are poor or fickle), it is not "popular." In any case, *EN* 1.5 and 1.8 do examine views ascribed to "the many" at 1095a23.

12. Irwin (1988*a*) regularly speaks of "common beliefs"; but see Barnes 1980: 503. As Cooper (1988: 549–51), emphasizes, the ranks of the "wise" are not limited to sages, savants, and intellectuals; on the contrary, they include anyone with special expertise, from artisans to poets and artists, and from legislators to natural scientists and philosophers; see 6.7 1141a9–b8, *Met.* A.1–2, *Rhet.* 2.23 1398b10–19 (from Alcidamas), *de Phil.* fr. 8, and Kerferd 1976; cf. *Apol.* 21–22.

13. See *Pol.* 8 and the analysis in Lord 1982.

14. MacIntyre (1981: 138) is wrong to assert that "the absence of any sense of the specifically historical—in our sense—in Aristotle, as in other Greek thinkers, debars Aristotle from recognizing his own thought as part of a tradition." I aim to show why Aristotle is, on the contrary, honest—though not *always* reliable—about the views of his predecessors; see also II.iii below.

unorthodox claims may win respect by virtue of their exponents, for on ethical questions, where confusion and dispute are rife, the character and reputation of a proponent can be "a most decisive source of conviction" (κυριωτάτην πίστιν, *Rhet.* 1.2 1356a4–13). On the topic of pleasure again, Eudoxus added credence to hedonism by his temperance, "since he was thought to argue not as a friend of pleasure, but because it was truly so" (*EN* 1172b15–18). Socrates, although condemned by many in his day as a radical critic, still won renown; some of his views have never been widely accepted, but they are widely respected, not least because he had the wisdom and courage to question orthodoxy. Of course, nothing guarantees that the views of the wise will stand, and consensus takes precedence even among the wise (*Top.* 104a10, cf. 100b23). In any event, the range of reputable views is much wider than the term might suggest, and Aristotle relies less on conventional attitudes than may at first appear. Although he dismisses few views outright, he endorses most only in part, since he finds by analysis that most are partly mistaken.

The first stage in this method serves two other functions: as well as providing the views to be analyzed, the survey of "appearances" locates problems and supplies the materials for their solution. Disputes indicate error and confusion, and the more comprehensive the survey of views, the more likely that inconsistencies will appear. Thus, when Aristotle tests his own account of happiness against "the things said" about it, he observes that "all the facts harmonize with something true, but they quickly contradict something false" (*EN* 1.8 1098b9–12).[15] Speed aside, the existence of more than one view on a topic entails that most if not all must be false at least in some respects.[16] But further, just as breadth brings puzzles to light, it also adds to the stock of insights. Indeed, "it is reasonable that neither the many voices of tradition nor the reputable few are wholly mistaken, and that each is correct at least on one point or even for the most

15. For the omission of τἀληθές in b12, see Barnes 1980: 506 n35.
16. I know of no explicit admission by Aristotle that the reputable views are ever mutually inconsistent; but the discussion of the different "lives" in *EN* 1.5 offers a clear example. The class of "apparent *endoxa*" makes room for some inconsistencies, and since no *endoxa* have "an entirely obvious appearance [φαντασίαν]" (*Top.* 100b27–28), they all need analysis. Aristotle implies that there are degrees of repute when, adapting his requirement that premises in demonstrative arguments have more warrant than the conclusions, he insists that dialectical premises be "more reputable and recognized" than their conclusions (159b8–23); but see Barnes 1980: 503 n29.

part" (b27–29). If most views have at least some basis in fact, then objections lodged against them should serve not to refute them outright but to indicate where they need amendment or qualification. It is not the reputable views, then, but the problems they raise that need to be resolved; or as Aristotle puts it, "refutations of the objections are demonstrations [ἀποδείξεις] of the opposing views" (*EE* 1.3 1215a5–7). But this recalls the other basic question about his method: refutation may reinforce *belief* in the reputable views, but what license is there for thinking that the removal of difficulties offers any *proof*? In particular, why should Aristotle expect *truth* rather than mere consistency from this method?

One way out of this seeming circle would be to rely on broader philosophical theories. Terence Irwin, for example, argues that Aristotle makes his metaphysics and psychology bear "the main weight" in justifying his ethical theory.[17] But Aristotle explicitly disavows this appeal. To be sure, he sometimes invokes discussions from other works or views more fully defended elsewhere. But mentioning a view defended elsewhere is not the same as relying on that defense, much less the same as arguing for the view. To introduce his outline of happiness, for example, Aristotle appeals to considerations about the human soul and human activities (*EN* 1.7 1097b33–98a18) that he analyzes at great length elsewhere. However, he does nothing here to defend them, he prefaces them with a virtually Socratic analogy to crafts (1097b24–33), he maintains a frustrating degree of simplicity throughout, and he concludes by explicitly denying any need in ethics for the kind of explanation appropriate in strictly theoretical studies (1098a26–b6). Although he later concedes that ethical theorists need to know something about the soul, he adds that they "should study it for the sake of their subject, and [only] as much as they need for what they seek" (1.13 1102a23–27).[18] Aris-

17. See Irwin 1988a: chap. 16, esp. 358–59, and chap. 1–2 on what Irwin calls "strong dialectic," which differs from "pure dialectic" in justifying the first principles ("fundamental" beliefs) that it uses to resolve conflicts among the received views.

18. I have not noticed any mention in Irwin 1988a of these two explicit rejections of psychological theory; but see his 1980: 50. Irwin concedes that the evidence for strong dialectic is "relatively unobtrusive in the *Ethics*" but claims that it is "unmistakable in the *Politics*" (1988a: 358). However, 7.1 1323a21–23 relies on results from ethics, not from psychology or metaphysics. As I understand it, Aristotle's method in ethics comes closer to what Roche (1988) calls "autonomous dialectic."

totle could have constructed a deeper defense of his theory, as Irwin does for him, but he instead argues throughout from reputable views appropriate to his subject and denies that metaphysics is appropriate. Thus, I would characterize his method of reputable views in ethics as stronger than what Irwin calls "pure dialectic," not because it invokes first principles or principles from other domains (as Irwin's "strong dialectic" does), but because his account has—and he is aware that it has—explanatory power: his procedure not only removes disputes, it also clarifies and explains them.

The justification of Aristotle's ethical theory rests on his epistemology. Although he fails to provide a continuous and comprehensive account of the nature of ethical knowledge, a number of passages show both that he is aware of the problems he faces and that he has the resources to solve them. First, as scattered remarks indicate, he has good reason to think that our judgment in ethics is generally reliable. To defend the art of rhetoric, for example, he claims that "people are by nature adequately [ἱκανῶς] suited in regard to what is true, and they mostly [τὰ πλείω] do get the truth" (*Rhet.* 1.1 1355a15–17). This claim applies explicitly to the audiences judging speeches in court, in assembly, and at festivals, but it also has implications for ethical judgment. As Aristotle sees it, each of these three branches of oratory has ethical issues as its primary subject: forensic oratory addresses questions of justice, deliberative oratory explores how to achieve the goals of the state, and "display" oratory praises personal excellence (cf. 1.3 1358b20–29). If the people in these audiences are generally reliable, then their ethical judgments are likely to be so as well. No one is infallible, and people sometimes make serious mistakes. But it is unlikely that many of their judgments are wholly wrong, and if most have some truth, that is enough for the general accuracy Aristotle claims for reputable views.

All too many of us are confused about our own and others' good. But just as the survival of the species justifies confidence in the overall reliability of our cognitive capacities, at least for the needs of daily life, so the persistence of various practices argues for the presence of at least some good in most if not all of them. There would be something radically wrong with us if things that most of us want or admire were not good at least in some respects—in Aristotle's terms, our nature does nothing wholly in vain. And given that natural affairs occur "for the most part," as he is wont to say, then widely shared ends and ideals have a strong presumption of being natural and serving some good. In short, even if some human pursuits are bound to be bad, it is reasonable to expect most to aim at *some* good. Granted, this "soteriological epistemology" has its limits: like any "naturalized" theory of knowledge, it makes a theory of truth problematic, it does not rule out the possibility of systematic error, and it has to explain the existence of major disputes.[19] But in ethics, where survival is itself a major aim, these worries are less telling. First, ethical reflection seeks a correct structure of desires, and desires aim not at truth but at the good. As in any applied field, where results count for more than theory—Aristotle considers ethics more like carpentry than geometry in this respect (*EN* 1.7 1098a29–33)—the criteria of correctness depend on more than truth. Second, even systematic error would have to be marginal, not global. Given that we often fail to get what we need, for example, wanting more than we need may promote survival; conversely, dangerous excesses or fatal propensities do not often survive long. Finally, disputes may well be explicable if not eliminable, and the presence of some disagreement is certainly compatible with reliability.

At this point, Aristotle's method may seem a caricature of the legal presumption of innocence, with the burden of proof falling on objections and reputable views presumed true until proven otherwise. However, there would be no miscarriage of justification if our errors can be explained, and explanations are what Aristotle's "demonstrations" should provide. As he says after criticizing popular conceptions of pleasure, "one should say not only the truth but also the explanation for what is false," for the truth is confirmed "when the reason why something untrue appears true itself appears reasonable [εὔλογον]" (7.14 1154a22–25). Or as he notes when he takes up the topic of friendship, the aim is to construct an account that both "preserves the views" and resolves disagreements; that requires showing how each view is held "with good reason" (εὐλόγως), how each is true in some respects despite being false in others (*EE* 7.2 1235b13–18).

19. The phrase "soteriological epistemology" is from Barnes 1987; Barnes combines Aristotelian teleology and psychology to argue that "it is our survival which explains and justifies our claims to knowledge" (p. 63); cf. Cooper 1988: 553–55.

This in turn requires paying heed to the "testimony" of what people say (μαρτυρίοις) and the "examples" of what they do (παραδείγμασι): "We should try to seek conviction [τὴν πίστιν] through our arguments by using the appearances as testimony and examples" (1.6 1216b26–28). If this is done, even those who fail to see the truth can be "brought around" (b28–30).[20] And on the assumption that "everyone has something akin [οἰκεῖον] to the truth" (b30–31), there is some truth on all sides; if that can be isolated, it is fair to call the process "proof" (δεικνύναι, b32). Few of our views are wholly wrong, but many are so unclear that we overlook their limitations and mistake their application. Since there is truth to be recovered from our beliefs, analysis should be able to isolate it from our errors and replace our "unclear" initial insights with a newly "clarified" truth (b32–33; cf. 1217a18–20). The process is open-ended, of course, since reformulations are liable to stimulate new objections. But that is salutary and the key to further clarification. This is why it is incumbent on political theory to make "not only the fact but also its explanation apparent" (1216b37–39): by explaining more precisely where our views are true and where they are false, theory can come to the aid of practice not only by confirming conviction but also by clarifying the terms in which we think about what to do.

The key to this process is "taking the more recognized things [τὰ γνωριμώτερα] from what is usually said confusedly [συγκεχ-υμένως, literally "jumbled together"]" (b34–35). But why rely on "recognized things," especially when Aristotle insists that he means "recognized by us," not "recognized intrinsically" (EN 1.4

20. Although μεταβιβαζόμενοι does not *mean* "converted" (the verb is transitive, cf. *Top.* 101a30–34 and *Phdr.* 262a–b; the intransitive would be μεταβαίνον-τες), that is its implication here (although the verb might be in the middle voice— "getting turned around"—instead of passive). The next word (active ποιήσου-σιν) emphasizes one's own contribution to one's conversion: analysis can present a subject in a new light, but it is up to us to *see* it in that light. On this obscure passage, see Barnes 1980: 506–8, although I disagree on how to interpret the following lines. Barnes argues that the antecedent of ὧν (b31) is "phenomena" (b28) rather than "something akin" (b31); but the two have the same reference, since the singular οἰκεῖον is distributive after ἕκαστος, and its sense is objective ("akin to the subject," as in 1215a4, 1096b31, 1098a29), not subjective ("one's own," as Barnes suggests). As he concedes, it is harsh to translate μεταλαμβά-νουσι as "exchange X *for* Y" without ἀντί, but ἀντί is unnecessary if the genitive is partitive: we "take X (the truth) *from* Y (our views)," which fits my claim that we *retain* the truth in our views (Barnes's translation would have us trade them in for Aristotle's).

1095b2–4)?[21] Little would be gained if recognition signified nothing but notoriety. Fortunately, it implies much more: recognition indicates agreement, and given the general accuracy of judgment, the greater the recognition, the wider the agreement, and hence the more reliable the claim. Part of the rationale here is the fact that "each person discriminates well [κρίνει καλῶς] what he recognizes [ἃ γινώσκει]" (1.3 1094b27–28). Familiarity with a subject implies an ability to discriminate the relevant objects. That is not enough by itself to settle difficulties or explain opposing views, but it is enough to get the analysis started. The people we can recognize, for example, are those we know well enough to spot in unfamiliar surroundings, and the animals we recognize are those we can identify correctly; we may not know much about either, and we may not understand why they behave as they do, but at least we know enough to guide further inquiry. Thus, after offering a preliminary definition of virtue as "the best condition of the soul," Aristotle criticizes the formula for being "true but not clear": it does us no more good than knowing that Coriscus is the darkest man in the market (EE 2.1 1220a16–22). But rather than discard this information as unclear, Aristotle uses it to reach a more informative account: as the description of Coriscus enables us to learn more about him by allowing us first to pick him out, so the initial knowledge that virtue is the best condition makes it possible to develop a fuller account. Aristotle thus proceeds to show successively that virtues arise from doing the best activities, that they concern pleasure and pain (2.1), that they are states (2.2), that they lie in a mean-state (2.3), and so on. The result is a much clearer account of virtue, one that can also yield rules of thumb useful for action, such as "the second sailing" of steering against one's inclinations (EN 2.9 1109a30–35). In short, because recognition presupposes accurate discriminations, "recognized things" provide the first steps toward clarity.

21. Like "reputable," the term "recognized" typically describes beliefs externally: it applies to views that are *familiar* (whether well understood or not) or objects of acquaintance (such as famous people). Aristotle reserves a different term, "intelligible" (γνωστόν), for the abstract objects of intellect that are intrinsically more knowable (cf. *Met.* Z.4 1029b1–12 and *Phys.* 1.1). His method here resembles in important ways that sketched in Williams 1985: chap. 6: recognized views are roughly reputable intuitions, especially those using relatively specific or "thick" concepts—describing actions or people as courageous or dishonest rather than good or bad.

What is the content of these recognized views? As the examples illustrate, it may be either general or particular, either a claim about virtue or a fact about Coriscus. For general principles, starting from what is recognized means starting from reputable views rather than abstract principles, because even if the latter are more intelligible in the end (*EE* 1.8 1218a15–24), the former would not be reputable unless they fit some cases securely. This is why Aristotle insists that it is "enough to examine the most *obvious* views and those that are *thought* to have some reason" (*EN* 1.4 1095a28–30).[22] Indeed, "arguments *from* first principles are not the same as arguments *to* them" (a30–b1). Principles should justify and explain the subject, but it is enough if the starting points are recognized and clear: "there is no further need of the explanation if the fact is sufficiently apparent" (b6–7; cf. 1098b1–4). Most reputable views admit of exceptions, of course, but problems at the borders and borderline cases will always arise, and tinkering at the boundaries usually leaves the center intact.[23] Hard cases presuppose at least some easy cases where we say, "If anything is F, *this* is F." Everyone recognizes, for example, that killing people is typically bad, and though it is difficult to formulate general principles that define precisely what counts as murder and explain why it is bad, all too many cases are clearly wrong. By relying on the undisputed applications of a view, Aristotle has a basis for defining it more precisely and hence for settling objections and problematic cases.

Moreover, given his empiricism about the origin of ideas and the meaning of terms, there must be at least some clear cases for every term, a point implied by the capacity he calls "recognition" (γνώμη). A product of experience, this capacity depends largely on perception and develops naturally as we mature (6.11 1143b4–9). With time, we learn to "recognize" (γινώσκειν, a34) distinctions among cases and to "discriminate" (κρίνειν, a14–15, a19–24, a28–35) what is correct in the acts and pronouncements of others. But if our principles are drawn from acquaintance with

22. What "lies on the surface" (ἐπιπολαζούσας) is obvious and clear to all; see Stewart 1892 on 1095a29. Cf. *Top.* 1.1 100b27–30 (glossed as κατάδηλος) and *Rhet.* 3.10 1410b22–23 ("clear to everyone," τὰ παντὶ δῆλα), and see Irwin 1981a: 197. Such views may need further analysis, but they can be assumed to be *true*, at least in some respects, precisely because they are reputable and prevalent.
23. The image is from Anscombe 1958: 12–13. Pincoffs (1971) also cautions against attaching too much importance to "quandaries"; cf. Williams 1985: 96.

particulars (b4–5; cf. 6.8 1142a14–16 and *An. Pos.* 2.19), then experience must be authoritative, even in the absence of proofs or the presence of arguments to the contrary: "We should heed the undemonstrated assertions and views of the older and experienced, or the practically wise, no less than demonstrative arguments" (1143b11–14). It is often legitimate "to heed the appearances *more* than the conclusions of arguments" (*EE* 1.6 1217a10–13): because they cannot always diagnose the problems, let alone justify or explain their views, even the experienced may feel compelled to accept captious or irrelevant arguments they cannot refute (1216b40–17a14). The criterion here is effective action, since that is the ultimate aim.[24] Practice, not "philosophizing," makes us good (*EN* 2.4 1105b9–18), and as the proverbial contrast between word and deed suggests, actions are often a more cogent argument than words. Hesiod's maxim thus stands confirmed: lacking wisdom of our own, we do best to heed the voice of those who know more (*WD* 293–97, at 1.4 1095b8–13).

Behind this worry about misleading arguments are two factors that Aristotle mentions frequently in the methodological remarks scattered throughout his work. Both have a direct bearing on the justification of his method, and both are connected with the limits of reliability. First, just as reliability promises only general accuracy, not infallibility, so most reputable views are true only generally, not universally. Second, greater accuracy can often be obtained by being vague, and ethical judgments have limited precision. The moral of this story is twofold. As Aristotle warns at the outset, "precision [τἀκριβές] should not be sought equally in every discussion" (1.3 1094b11–14). Second, given the controversies in ethics, "we should be glad to indicate the truth roughly and in outline, and to reach conclusions that hold for the most part" (b19–22). Or as he insists again after formulating an "outline" of happiness (περιγραφή, 1.7 1098a23; cf. a20), we should seek only the precision we need for action (a26–33), and we should not demand explanations about everything, especially the principles (a33–b3).

These limits on scope and precision help clarify ethical prin-

---

24. Aristotle's remark that "the goal [of his inquiry] is not knowledge but action" (*EN* 1.3 1095a5–6) refers to the *final* goal; obviously, this implies not that knowledge is irrelevant or unnecessary (cf. a9, a14–15), but only that it has a further end, viz., its application in action. Cf. 10.9 1179a35–b4.

ciples in the two ways Aristotle names in the programmatic passage quoted earlier (1145b4–7): they help resolve disputes, and they allow some truth to be retained from each side. The key here is that both limits entail a margin of error. Conflicting claims can each be true up to a point: arguments lodged against a view may rest on unqualified generalizations that neglect crucial differences, and putative counterexamples may stem from imprecise or ambiguous descriptions of a case.[25] In short, neither kind of objection refutes competing views if they can be shown to disregard the limits on generality and precision. We can amend faulty principles by specifying further conditions, or if a case is described imprecisely, we can look for further factors to explain the difference. But even if we find no solution, we should not assume that none exists; the decisive differences may simply escape our notice. If a valid objection is only an exception, for example, then the view it rebuts cannot be entirely wrong.

A problem familiar in legal contexts illustrates the point. Because laws are general, there is always some risk in applying them. In practice, they are bound to embrace cases they should not, to miss cases they should cover, and to face "hard cases" where it is difficult to tell whether they apply. But to dispense with laws for these reasons would be absurd. Hence, "in situations where it is necessary to speak generally but impossible to do so correctly, the law takes the greater part" (5.10 1137b14–16). More to the point, occasional errors are insufficient to impugn the law itself or to disprove its application to other cases. On the contrary, it may well be that the law "is no less correct, since the mistake lies not in the law but in its maker or in the nature of the situation" (b17–18). The very existence of "equity" (the topic addressed by Aristotle's remark) shows that laws can remain sound in the face of exceptions: if it is possible "to correct the deficiency" in a law by noticing "what the lawmaker would have said if he were present" (b20–24), then his original view was sound.

25. This reflects Aristotle's distinction between an ἀπόρημα ("a dialectical argument for a contradiction," *Top.* 8.11 162a17–18) and an ἔνστασις (*An. Pr.* 2.26). Although typically particular, counterexamples are also inherently general, for they must be described in general terms. The point is not lost on Aristotle; as Irwin (1985a: 418) observes, he uses "particular" to refer both to subordinate universals (jays as opposed to birds) and to individuals (the bird in your hand as opposed to birds in general). Most reputable views in ethics are general rather than particular, e.g., "Help friends," not "Help Socrates now."

The argument applies to reputable views in ethics as well, such as the rule to help our friends (*Top.* 104a22–31).[26] This sort of generalization may be too broad to exclude exceptions (it is not always right to help friends); it may be too narrow to include relevant differences (sometimes we should benefit others instead); and it may simply be too imprecise to apply reliably (what counts as help is left altogether vague).[27] But given the limits on generality and precision, there is no need to succumb to skepticism about rules generally. On the contrary, equity in legal contexts is but one application of "practical wisdom" that illustrates the possibility of spotting what is right in a particular situation (*EN* 6.11 1143a19–35).

This is not merely a problem of extension, of capturing too many or too few *cases*. Rather, it also stems from ignoring distinguishing *features*, and that is a problem of precision. Precision, however, is not a function only of extension, for although general claims in ethics lack "precision," Aristotle considers particular claims even less precise (2.2 1104a5–7). As he observes in connection with deliberation, even with the correct generalizations, we may fail to notice relevant aspects of a situation (6.8 1142a21–23). Precision depends not on how many cases are covered, but on how many features of a case or type are distinguished. An analogy with physical magnitudes will clarify the point.[28] Different measurements are accurate for different degrees of precision. If precision is limited to inches, there is nothing inaccurate about "two-by-four" lumber, although no carpenters expect to get more than three and a half inches for their money. But increase precision by two degrees, and 3.53 inches is accurate, not 3.50. Similarly, a law against homicide is more general than a law against matricide because it covers more than one kind of murder, but a law defining first-degree murder is more precise than either because it sets more exact standards for the cases it covers. Since imprecision makes it hard to know which cases are covered, it aggravates the task of applying rules, no matter how general or

26. Cf. 5.9 1137a6–26; on equity, see Shiner 1987.
27. The third limit is shared even by universal generalizations. As Aristotle quips, "adultery" (or "seduction of free women") had no mean in Athens, where it was always wrong (2.6 1107a8–17; see Lacey 1968: 113–16), but defining the concept and applying it to cases could still be problematic.
28. In *Phileb.* 55–56, Plato uses measurement to illustrate points about precision.

specific they are. Likewise for particular cases, a description can be accurate as far as it goes but still leave out factors that distinguish similar cases. Although these problems can generate disagreement, they also provide a path to clarity and agreement: just as physical magnitudes can be measured more precisely, so ethical claims, whether general or particular, can be made more precise by attending to further factors. Precision should not be sought equally everywhere, especially in unanalyzed reputable views. But it can often be the key to preserving some truth from each of several competing views.

The underlying problem here is the irregularity (πλάνη) and variability (διαφορά) endemic to practical affairs: ethical norms can vary so much that they seem to be sheer "convention," and even things everyone considers good can be harmful to some (1.3 1094b14–19).[29] Different features may coincide irregularly and only "incidentally," and that limits the reliability of general claims. Because the descriptions used to classify a case are open-ended, two cases that are alike in most features may still differ decisively. To give in to these problems would be to give up on all principles. But that would be a mistake, for where the subject is "indefinite," we should expect the standards against which we measure it to be the same (5.10 1137b26–32). Hence, just as "time would end" before lawmakers could enumerate all the possible exceptions to their laws, so ethical principles are repeatedly tested in novel situations. And it would be as foolish to deem all laws useless as to renounce all rules of conduct (cf. *Rhet.* 1.13 1374a25–b1). The problem is not that our principles are useless but that they are of limited use. Extenuating circumstances often turn up, as Aristotle's discussion of involuntary action illustrates (esp. *EN* 3.1 1111a3–15), and extraordinary conditions may justify violating a sound principle (1110a4–26). But even though "it is *sometimes* difficult to distinguish what should be chosen at what cost, or what should be endured for what" (a29–31, cf. b7–9), some things are *never* justified, and "we should rather die suffering the worst" (a26–27).

29. These two words can have either an objective sense, referring to things themselves ("irregular and different," as in the case of the planets, πλανηταί, which owe their name to the "irregularity" of their "wandering" motions), or a subjective sense, referring to the judgments we make about them ("errant and disputed"). Irwin (1981a: 205 n21) suggests that the former sense yields a better argument here; cf. Greenwood 1909 on 1141b34.

The problem is not that all generalizations have exceptions. Aristotle thinks that adultery, theft, and murder, for example, are always bad (2.6 1107a8–21), and although it may sometimes be *better* to avoid a greater evil by doing something bad, the act itself remains *bad* (cf. 1110a4–14). Rather, since even universally valid principles still need to be applied in practice and the many differences in kind and degree make it difficult to formulate principles that are at once precise and general, questions of precision must often be left to "perception" (1109b20–23).[30] Hence, "we must always ourselves look for what fits the situation [τὰ πρὸς τὸν καιρόν] as we act" (2.2 1104a8–9). In this, ethical rules are no different from medical rules: both must be applied with attention to the variables of each situation, but neither is invalidated by the absence of formal decision procedures (a1–11; cf. 6.7 1141b14–22). So again, the difficulty of *finding* distinctions to solve problems is not proof that none *can* be found. But problems with particulars are settled by experience and "recognition."

This brings us back to the basis for Aristotle's confidence in his starting points, in reputable views. Now that we have seen the basis of his confidence in reputable views, we need to ask whether he is justified in claiming that his approach can "prove" any results. Even if we can expect some truth in his premises, and even if we can see the ways in which those premises are likely to go wrong, why should we expect his method to preserve only or mostly what is true? Why should we expect his winnowing to leave all grain and no chaff? Here it will be useful to compare his method with Socrates' favored form of argument, the elenchus. Although Aristotle's procedure, especially his use of reputable views, fits his account of dialectical argument (he argues from the reputable views to resolve problems: *Top.* 1.1 100a18–20), his reliance on refuting objections has a close affinity with the elenctic

30. Aristotle frequently underscores the variety of conditions that can make a difference in particular cases; cf. 2.3 1104b21–26, 2.6 1106b20–22, 2.9 1109b14–18, 3.1 1111a1–15, and 9.2 1164b27–30. Given the great weight some interpreters attach to perception, I would emphasize that Aristotle regularly insists that general rules are available though limited in applicability. I find much to agree with in Wiggins 1974 (esp. 232–37), but Wiggins sometimes overstates his case, as on p. 231: Aristotle claims not that nothing is subject to law but only that "not everything" is subject to law, and he recommends "the Lesbian rule" (a flexible measuring device) not for all situations but only for some (περὶ ἐνίων, 1137b27–32). Further, Aristotle thinks perception is inherently general: we perceive the *forms* of individuals by perceiving them as specimens *of types*; see *de An.* 3.8.

method displayed in Plato's Socratic dialogues.[31] To be sure, there are differences. Socrates' method is personal and adversarial, he is reluctant to expound views of his own, and he draws his premises from individual interlocutors. Aristotle's method is impersonal and constructive, drawing premises from society at large and establishing conclusions of his own. Still, the similarities are telling. First, both examine reputable views. Whereas the dialogues add nuance to the arguments by presenting vividly characterized individuals, most of the claims examined are attested in Aristotle and elsewhere.[32] More important, both confront these views with a battery of objections, and both rely heavily on refutation.

Although similar, the two procedures differ in instructive ways. Socrates typically starts with a claim (p) advanced by his interlocutor; this claim is often a reputable view. Then, after asking a series of questions that lead the other person to make further claims (q, r), he asserts that these would contradict the original claim (if q & r, then *not-p*). Sometimes he also asserts this contradictory (*not-p*). In a similar fashion, Aristotle starts with a survey of "appearances," including both reputable views (p) and objections (q, r). But even though the initial set is inconsistent (if q & r, then *not-p*), he rarely ends by denying a reputable view (*not-p*). Rather, since every proposition has a claim to truth, any or all of them are likely to be qualified in order to make them mutually consistent (leaving p^*, q^*, r^*). Typically, he thinks some of the reputable views (p) more reasonable, and he amends others to make them consistent with them (q^* & r no longer entail *not-p*). If the other propositions all pass muster, however, either he argues that the inconsistency is illusory (q & r do not entail *not-p*) or he modifies the reputable view to make it consistent with the others (q & r no longer entail *not-p**). A decisive difference, then, is that the Socratic elenchus represents only the earlier stages of Aristotle's procedure, collecting the appearances and "going through the problems" (διαπορήσαντες, 1145b4). Whereas Socrates' reliance on his interlocutors for premises

31. On Aristotle's conception of dialectic, see Irwin 1988a: esp. chaps. 1–2. My account of the Socratic elenchus is modeled on Vlastos 1983. I am interested here in justifying the method Vlastos describes, not in questions of historical accuracy (e.g., whether the method owes more to Plato than Socrates).

32. See Xenophon *Mem.* 4.6.15, cited by Vlastos 1983: 42 n39. On the difference between Socratic and Aristotelian dialectic, cf. Irwin 1988a: 488 n13.

often ends in "puzzlement" (ἀπορία), Aristotle analyzes the "puzzles" (ἀπορίαι) to remove inconsistency by formulating more precise versions and adding qualifications. Socrates may consider the initial propositions refuted and their contradictories established, but since Aristotle recognizes that few general claims in ethics are true without qualification, he tries to mark off more precisely the limits of their application by incorporating the insights behind the objections.

Both the similarities and the differences have a bearing on the justification of Aristotle's method. If the Socratic elenchus can claim to prove objective truth, then so can Aristotle's method if it is similar in the relevant respects. In fact, the differences may be to Aristotle's advantage. Gregory Vlastos has argued that on two assumptions Socrates is justified in considering his arguments *proofs*. First, if "anyone who ever has a false moral belief will always have at the same time beliefs entailing the negation of that false belief," and second, if "the set of moral beliefs held by Socrates at any given time is consistent," then it follows that "the set of moral beliefs held by Socrates at any given time is true."[33] Of course, Aristotle no more than Socrates presents this argument to justify his method. But if it accurately characterizes his approach, then it accomplishes the task for him. Accurate enough it is. Clearly, if Aristotle accomplishes his aim of resolving all disagreements on a topic, his results meet the second condition. More important, the impersonal form of his argument allows him a more plausible version of the first assumption: rather than assume that *we each* have enough true beliefs to refute our false moral beliefs, he need assume only that the *sum of reputable views* harbors enough true propositions to entail the negation of the several falsehoods it also contains.[34] Indeed, the strong assumption required by the Socratic elenchus threatens that method. Since the premises for his elenchus are drawn from his interlocutors, their status would seem to be no better than the view he aims to refute; or worse, when a refutation leads to paradoxical conclusions, it is reasonable to expect problems in some of the premises (q, r) as well as in the view under examination (p).[35] To

33. See Vlastos 1983: 52–55.

34. See the claims, discussed above, that few views are *wholly* wrong (1.8 1098b27), and that everyone has *some* truth to supply (*EE* 1216b30–32).

35. If Vlastos (1983: 34, 41, 43) is right in claiming that some of Socrates' premises must be "contra-endoxic," then those would be prime candidates for further scrutiny; but the analysis of reputable views can by itself lead to unortho-

be sure, Socrates supports many of his premises by further argument, but there too he requires the assent of his interlocutors. And since these are often reputable views, he also requires the assumption that many reputable views are true. Moreover, even if every belief he accepts as a premise has been validated by previous elenctic encounters, each depends ultimately on its consistency with the reputable views assumed before. Thus, in the course of disputing some reputable views, Socrates must assume that others—the vast collection he uses as premises—are true precisely as they stand. In this respect, Aristotle is actually less sanguine about convention, for he is ready to qualify or revise any view, provided only the process leaves some truth confirmed in most reputable views.

This points up another way in which the Socratic method is less plausible. Socrates often seems ready to discard the views he refutes even though they seem to contain some truth. Strictly, the elenchus proves only the negation of the original thesis. That is not to say that its conclusions are empty; on the contrary, far from leaving him unopinionated, the elenchus confirms Socrates in several radical views. However, although it often shocks his partners to see their views contradicted, Socrates is in fact entitled only to the contradictories, not to the contraries. In particular, the elenchus can show only that a view is flawed, not that it is wholly wrong. Refuting the view that justice is the *same* as helping one's friends, for example, does not show that helping friends is *never* just, much less that it is often *unjust*. It should not be surprising, then, that Socrates' interlocutors often respond to refutation by modifying their claim in ways that require a further elenchus, for it is rarely clear that their claim should be abandoned outright and that it cannot be modified. But in the end, his interlocutors often do forsake their views, no doubt in part because they fail to see the relevant distinctions—the very danger we have seen Aristotle at pains to avoid (cf. *EE* 1.6 1216b40–17a17). It would be unfair to charge Socrates with systematically confusing contradictories and contraries, although he does infer that doing wrong is *worse* than suffering it, when his refutation of the contrary shows only that doing wrong is *not better* than suffering it. But it

dox conclusions. Kraut (1983: 63) points out that seemingly innocuous assumptions can generate serious paradoxes. More generally, just as probabilities decrease in conjunction, so reputable views—which are true only for the most part—can be combined to support much less plausible or reliable conclusions.

does seem fair to charge that Socrates' method is ill-suited for eliciting and confirming any truth in the views it refutes, a task that Aristotle's method aims to perform. Reformulating Vlastos's argument to fit Aristotle, then, we can conclude that his method is sound if (1) there are enough true beliefs among the reputable views to entail the negation of any false beliefs presented and (2) Aristotle's set of moral beliefs is consistent. Provided the considerations I have outlined about the reliability of reputable beliefs support (1), then (3) his set of moral beliefs is true.

Aristotle's attempt to preserve something from most of the reputable views has important consequences for action. As he observes on the topic of pleasure, explaining how the reputable views go wrong "contributes to conviction [τὴν πίστιν]" (EN 7.14 1154a22–23). The point here is simply that we "have more confidence" (πιστεύειν μᾶλλον) in the truth once we see why each view seems "reasonable" (a24–25; cf. EE 7.2 1235b13–18). On the other hand, although the Socratic elenchus rids us of false beliefs, it also deprives us of any truth in the beliefs it refutes, and that can leave us with blank spots in our field of moral vision. Worse, it can undermine our confidence in any truth our views do have. When the stouthearted Laches learns that courage is not what he thought, for example, he risks being pried loose from the courage he had (Laches 194a–b). By contrast, because Aristotle's method retains our initial insights, it can sustain the "conviction" that we need in order to act. His support for the reputable views, however, does not result in blind or blinkered certitude because it also gives us a clearer, more precise grasp of where those views are true. Although "epistemic certainty" lies beyond the reach of either method, both resist the dogmatism that would abandon further inquiry. Just as Socrates never refuses to submit a view to further elenchus, so Aristotle's method depends on "the elenchus of objections" to provide "proof of the opposite views" (EE 1.3 1215a3–7). Given the indefinite nature of practical affairs, neither method can refine and confirm its views except by facing new puzzles and cases as they arise. When it comes to action, however, Aristotle's method seems better suited to sustain the "moral certainty" needed to uphold our principles even at great personal risk or cost.[36] Socrates could maintain his confidence in

36. As I use the terms, "epistemic certainty" requires that it is impossible for one's reasons for a belief to be true and the belief false, and "moral certainty" implies a willingness to act on a belief even at great personal risk or expense. It is

the face of death, but his interlocutors and later readers of the dialogues alike are often much less convinced. Although many feel compelled by his arguments to *acquiesce* to claims that contradict their present convictions, most remain unable to *act* on them. So while neither method can prove its principles beyond all doubt, the method of reputable views is better suited to fortify even unconventional claims because it aims to show precisely where those views are true as well as where they are false.

What implications does all this have for the topic of happiness? Most significant for my discussion is the importance it gives to examining traditional views in detail. Just as the propositions that survive elenctic argument are confirmed by resisting objections, so tradition—the accumulated body of collective experience handed down over time—preserves the attitudes and practices that withstand the tests of time. Or as Aristotle is reported to have said about proverbs, "they are remnants, preserved because of brevity and insight [δεξιότης], of ancient philosophy that perished in immense human destructions" (*de Phil.* fr. 13). Aristotle's method also suggests where we should seek a better understanding of his account of happiness. If happiness consists in a life of virtuous activity, we should examine the reputable and recognized views about the virtues. As Aristotle recognizes, his "outline" of happiness is still very general and imprecise: its terms need further analysis, and its application to the various ends of human pursuit needs greater detail and precision. In particular, how are the virtues related to ends not included in his formula? And what relation does rational virtue have to the major ends of human life as traditional thought conceived it? If his theory is to preserve the reputable views and explain the major disputes, as he claims it should, then he must show what should be retained and what should be amended. Hence, rather than turning immediately to the several virtues and discussing them seriatim as Aristotle's works present them, I shall start by surveying traditional conceptions of happiness and virtue. The major questions are: What ends were considered most important, and what place does virtue occupy in traditional ideals?

helpful to contrast the latter, which disregards circumstances, with the "pragmatic certainty" of being willing to act on a belief only because one does not consider it *worth* the cost of further investigation in *present* circumstances; both are compatible with "philosophical doubt," but only moral certainty is resistant to "practical doubt." This bears on the sovereignty of virtue; see II.v below.

II

THE TEST OF TRADITION

It is reasonable that neither the many voices of tradition nor the reputable views of the few are wholly mistaken, and that each is correct at least on one point or even for the most part. —EN 1.8 1098b27–29

Virtue and Prosperity

ARISTOTLE IS not alone in assigning virtue or excellence a central place in ethics and the good life. On the contrary, his account reflects a long and widespread tradition in Greek thought that considered personal excellence a major factor in happiness and held that in general the best people enjoy the best lives. But if he follows tradition in these general terms, his accounts of happiness and of virtue diverge at several crucial points. First, both the reigning popular ideals and the traditional wisdom of the poets held that happiness depends heavily on fortune.[1] Most of his predecessors equated happiness with some form of success. Some of the wise questioned the popular idols of material and social prosperity, but few of the works dominating the cultural tradition evince any doubt that happiness consists primarily in the enjoyment of good fortune. To be happy, as the title *eudaimon* implies, is to enjoy the favor of the gods; to be "blessed," as its virtual synonym *makarios* indicates, is to live a life like theirs.[2] But the splendid ease of life on Olympus presupposes immortality, and mortals can never be so secure. The paradigms of worldly success may rarely appear worried about the vulnerability of their station, but even those who deprecate wealth and power

1. Early views about fortune are a recurrent theme in Fränkel 1973, Lloyd-Jones 1983, and Nussbaum 1986.
2. See Heer 1968: esp. 4–11, 28–43, 56–58; and MacDonald 1978: esp. 10–36. For Aristotle's views about these connotations of divinity, see my discussion of *EN* 1.9 1099b11–25 in II.iii below.

claim that human life is all too likely to be wrecked by misfortune. Some may express disdain for great fortunes, but few dissent from the view that sustained prosperity is essential.

These views about the relation of fortune to the good life underlie another major difference between Aristotle's theory and traditional views. Although few denied that virtue is necessary for happiness, most valued it primarily for its consequences; personal excellence, it was thought, is simply the surest path to success.[3] Some went so far as to measure excellence by results and to equate the virtuous with the successful. After all, the most obvious test of merit is comparative performance: to be good is to do things well, and to excel is to outdo others; conversely, doing worse or failing suggests inferiority. Of course, the traits most widely acclaimed and admired were not limited to competitive excellences like strength, valor, and cunning in which the superiority of some comes at others' expense; they also included cooperative traits such as justice, moderation, and generosity, all of which benefit others too. But if happiness is equated with material and social success, this tension between personal advantage and the good of others raises a dilemma for traditional views: either moral virtues must be shown to promote worldly success, or they appear unnecessary for a good life.[4] Some sought to show that cooperation does work to the advantage of the virtuous, or at least that injustice leads eventually to misfortune; others sought to ease the tension by reducing the degree of success needed for a good life. For a few, moral virtues did not count as virtues at all; some of the cynical simply redrew the boundaries of virtue to coincide with the traits most conducive to success. But rare was the voice that doubted either that some form of vir-

3. MacIntyre (1981: 178) also offers an implicitly consequentialist account of virtue by defining it as "an acquired human quality, the possession and exercise of which *tends to enable us to achieve* those goods . . . and the lack of which *effectively prevents us from achieving* any such goods" (my italics), although he adds (p. 204) that virtues "also sustain us in the relevant kind of *quest* for the good" (i.e., even without success).

4. I use "moral" here simply to mean "other-regarding" (whether or not it involves duty and obligation, impartiality, or impersonal motives), not in the wider sense of Cooper 1975: 77 *n*104. The contrast between competition and cooperation, explored by Adkins 1960, signals a genuine tension, but it is neither as sharp as Adkins claims nor the measure of moral progress that he makes it; see Long 1970, Dover 1983, and Gagarin 1987. Moral virtue is the focus of IV.i–iv below.

tue is necessary for happiness or that virtue is valuable primarily for its consequences. People might dispute its nature and effects, but virtually everyone admired virtue itself.[5]

For those who hold these views, fortune and luck assume great importance for the good life. First, if virtue is practiced for its consequences, events beyond an individual's control are bound to affect the wages of virtue. Myth and history alike show even the most valiant unable to preserve their success and the just deprived of the high station they are supposed to deserve. Aristides "the Just" and the heroic warriors Ajax and Achilles are alike victims of fortune.[6] Conversely, success was thought often to come on its own, to the deserving and undeserving alike, as if a matter of mere chance. The story was told that even Pericles, for all his talents and influence, insisted on his deathbed that fortune had contributed at least as much to his successes as had his own exemplary qualities.[7] Similarly, the decisive Athenian victory over the Spartans off Pylos is presented, even in the often skeptical work of Thucydides, as dependent much more on a series of fortunate coincidences than on shrewd strategy or the excellence of any individuals.[8] And in the following decade, Athenians were shown on the stage how the endeavors of a vainglorious Menelaus no less than a dedicated Orestes or the pious Ion owed their happy outcome to the opportune intervention of the gods in what some have dubbed "the Fortune plays" of Euripi-

5. See *Pol.* 7.1 1323a24–b21 (discussed at the end of I.i above); cf. *EE* 1.1 1214a30–b5. For the consequentialist view of virtue among sophists, see Kerferd 1981: 111–30; Furley (1981: 81–82) argues that Antiphon condemns the virtue of justice precisely because it is liable to interfere with personal advantage. For Aristotle's objections to the consequentialist view of virtue, see II.v, IV.ii, and IV.iv below.

6. Achilles and Ajax owe their deaths to the trickery of Paris and Odysseus, respectively, and Aristides was ostracized despite his proverbial epithet (see Plut. *Aristides* 3, Aeschylus *ST* 592, and Hermann 1852 on *ST* 573). My use of literary and historical examples may seem cavalier. But all are drawn from sources that we can assume were familiar to Aristotle, and they are meant only to illustrate views that were held in *some* quarters. Since I do not claim that each view was dominant, or that it should be accepted in the *author's* name, my summary citations and neglect of context do not, I think, misrepresent the sources. Thus, some examples express views adopted only by an author's persona or a character within a dramatic context; yet even those views were in circulation at the time, and often still popular when they are reported by later authors.

7. Theophrastus fr. 21, in Plut. *Pericles* 38.

8. See 4.1–41, and Cornford 1907: 82–109; Edmonds (1975) devotes a book to the topic in Thucydides.

des.[9] We even hear how, during Aristotle's early years in Athens, one of Isocrates' most successful students, the general Timotheos, was caricatured in a painting as a pawn of Fortune.[10] Some few years later, after Timoleon liberated Sicily from Syracusan tyrants, the victor ostentatiously denied responsibility for his success by dedicating a shrine to a deified Automatia, or Chance, beside his Syracusan home.[11]

Even when the excellent do prosper, there is no guarantee that their fortune will endure. Both the mighty and the pious are repeatedly brought to ruin by unsuspected and even wildly improbable misfortunes. Priam and Heracles, and later Croesus and Nicias, are overtaken by disaster primarily because of forces beyond their control. In one of the most shocking portrayals of undeserved reversal of fortune, and a tale that Aristotle considered a model of tragic drama, Sophocles shows how Oedipus, the self-proclaimed child of fortune (*OT* 1080), for all his shrewd intelligence and service to the city, accomplishes his own misery and the destruction of his family. Although some would blame Oedipus' sufferings on his alleged pride or violence of character, or Priam's misfortunes on his neglect of Paris as a child, that seems perverse special pleading, tantamount to condemning Job for his miseries.[12] Even Heracles, the greatest hero of all, is struck by disaster simply because he so excels. Lofty mortals *must* fall, and Euripides in his *Heracles* adapts traditions about Hera's jealousy at the hero's persistent success by having her send madness personified to drive him to slaughter his own family. The misleading oracle that Herodotus cites to explain Croesus' defeat by Cyrus may reflect the actual supremacy of Persia over Lydia (1.53, 1.91), but it also illustrates the tendency to attribute great misfortune to powers beyond human control. Finally, fortune may have the last word even in Thucydides' history, which tells how Nicias, after a long and prosperous career, was chosen to head an expedition he thought misguided, became entangled with the unreliable Alcibiades, and plagued by bad luck and a

9. Although often applied to the *Helen, Ion,* and *IT,* the title "*Tyche* plays" is misleading; see Burnett 1971: 67–69.

10. See Plut. *Sulla* 6.3; cf. Aelian *VH* 13.43 and the Scholia on Demosthenes 2.14. Given Timotheos' prominence, Aristotle probably knew the allegations.

11. See Plut. *Timoleon* 36; Timoleon succeeded where Dion and members of the Academy had recently failed.

12. For a rebuttal of those who would justify Oedipus' lot, see Dodds 1966.

lunar eclipse that frightened his superstitious troops, met his end, ironically, because of his very caution in the face of a treacherous fortune.[13]

Not only is the power of fortune incidental upon our endeavors, but it also influences the very talents and attitudes we bring to those endeavors.[14] If fortune affects our character and native endowments, however, it may seem to govern the acquisition of virtue in the first place. Had Themistocles been born to lowlier station or in a small town, so the saying went, he would not have become the hero he did.[15] Conversely, had Achilles been sickly, maimed, or unsightly like Thersites, he would never have been honored as "best of the best." Legend regularly portrayed heroes as descended from the gods, and the nobles of later generations often claimed heroic lineage for themselves as well. This notion of divine favor, over which the unborn had no control, shows an extreme instance of the recognition that family fortunes can exert great influence on character and success. But similar views about fortune as a birthright appear also in secular guise. In one of the causes célèbres of Aristotle's later years in Athens, for example, Demosthenes and Aeschines pepper their mutual recriminations with insults to one another's family and early fortunes.[16]

In the traditional tales revived repeatedly on the stage, sung at public festivals and private banquets, or learned by the young as part of their education, as well as in the accounts of ancient or recent events trotted out by politicians and pamphleteers, neither personal nor social virtues are sufficient for happiness. But the greater the influence fortune seems to exert on prosperity, the less reason there seems to be for cultivating the virtues, so long as their value resides primarily in the external rewards they bring rather than in the virtues themselves. As Plato shows at length in the early books of his *Republic*, the conceptions of the good life celebrated by poets give pride of place not to virtue but to two other factors, prosperity and the absence of misfortune. He has

13. Thucydides assesses the relative weight of virtue and fortune in Nicias' life in a rare editorial comment, a virtual epitaph (7.86.5).

14. On this distinction between "incidental" and "constitutive" fortune or luck, see Nagel 1976, Williams 1976a, and Nussbaum 1986: chap. 1.

15. See Herod. 8.125 and *Rep.* 1.329e; Aristotle is said to have adapted this quip to defend his own non-Athenian origins (D. L. 5.19).

16. See Aeschines 3.157–58, which provokes Demosthenes to respond and then to compare their early fortunes (18.252–66).

Socrates censure Homer for undermining the moral fiber of the young when he portrays Odysseus praising the fairyland of Phaeacian prosperity by calling the delights of song and feasting "finest of all" (*Od.* 9.5–11, at *Rep.* 390a–b);[17] and in the following lines, Socrates goes on to criticize Odysseus for voicing the complementary view that the misfortune of hunger is "most piteous" (*Od.* 12.342). In each instance, the prince of poets stands accused of showing "the wisest man" ranking prosperity ahead of everything else and of lauding it for the pleasure it affords and the pain it dispels. But this ideal of prosperity, which equates the successful man with the happy man (ὁ ὄλβιος),[18] has dangerous implications for the moral virtues. As Socrates objects, the poets represent the unjust as happy and leave the just in misery (*Rep.* 392b). And although Athens' own Solon could in some moods claim satisfaction with a straitened wealth,[19] he too is chided by Socrates for describing the resources of the fortunate gentleman as objects worthy of love (fr. 23, at *Lys.* 212e). If excellence neither ensures the enjoyment of prosperity that traditional values identify with happiness nor offers fulfillment on its own, then its role in the good life seems tenuous at best. Much more important, it appears, is mere luck.

Fortune itself appears early as a beneficent nymph in the company of several personifications of prosperity.[20] But only in Alcman, where she is the offspring of Foresight and sister to Order and Persuasion (fr. 64), does she show a close connection with any of the virtues. As the gift of the gods, prosperity might or might not be earned by virtuous exploits, and its capricious nature seems to offer no guarantee that excellence will be rewarded.

17. Aristotle more generously recalls the lines to illustrate the part played by music in a liberal culture (*Pol.* 8.3 1338a21–30).

18. See the informal equations in Hesiod *WD* 313 (for parallels, see West 1978 on this line), Alcman fr. 1.34–39, Theognis 129–30, 933–38, 1013–16, Simonides frs. 542, 584, Pindar *Pyth.* 3.81–106, and Bacchylides 1.159–84, 5.50–55. Contrast the litanies of misfortunes in Hesiod *WD* 176–201, Semonides fr. 1, and Mimnermus fr. 2. Similar formulas occur in Euripides, e.g., *Bacchae* 72–82, 421–33, 902–11 (see Dodds 1960 on these lines).

19. See frs. 13.71–73 (cited at *Pol.* 1.8 1256b30–34), 15, 24; cf. Theognis 145–50, 1153–56.

20. See *Theog.* 360 (among the Oceanids, 346–70) and *Hymn Dem.* 2.42 (in a smaller but largely identical company); most names in each gathering suggest wealth and prosperity. Pindar exploits her propitious and nautical nature in *Ol.* 12 (see Gildersleeve 1885 on the ode). For a survey of her appearances throughout Greek literature and art, see Herzog-Hauser 1948.

Few voices pretend that the good always prosper, and the unlike-lihood that even the most virtuous will flourish without interrup-tion is an axiom of archaic song. Images of mutability and vicissi-tude abound, and freedom from suffering and loss, when human welfare is considered highly unstable and vulnerable to misfor-tune, is frequently described as something beyond our lot.[21] In Pindar's emblematic phrase, man is but "a dream of shadow" and "a creature of a day" (*Pyth.* 8.95).[22] All the legendary exem-plars of prosperity, however well they might fare for a time, met disaster before they died. Cadmus, Heracles, Peleus, and Achilles give Pindar his paradigms of the best and happiest of men, but even they end up victims of devastating misfortune. The good might endure or they might succumb; either way their suffering seemed to have little direct connection with desert.

Far from being sufficient for prosperity, excellence often ap-pears to cost more than it earns. Hearing Achilles ponder, not without some justice, whether the life of heroic virtue is worth its toils and griefs, some might well find traditional wisdom inade-quate.[23] To counter this doubt, Plato has Socrates censure Homer for showing the hero's shade lamenting the glory he won for his choice of heroism over a peaceful end (*Od.* 11.489–91, at *Rep.* 386c). But the problem is more profound, and censorship scarcely a sufficient answer. What launches Plato's critique, after all, is the worry he has his brothers express: the best reasons for being just seem to depend on whether it pays. At best, conven-tional attitudes make it an empirical question whether justice is worth its risks, its toils, and its sacrifices: we can afford to be just when the price is low and the gain secure, but reverse the stakes, or give injustice better stakes, and few are likely to follow justice before their personal gain. So, as Adeimantus protests, if Pindar was right to question the advantages of justice itself (fr. 213, at 365b), traditional wisdom has little to offer in the way of incen-tives to justice. Against these worries, some of the most authori-

21. See, e.g., Archilochus' notorious "rhythm" (fr. 128; cf. frs. 122, 130), Theognis 167–68, Simonides frs. 521, 542, 581. On Pindar's recurrent use of this theme, see Strohm 1944; Kirkwood 1975: 63–73.

22. See Fränkel 1946. Herodotus' Solon echoes the term (1.32.5), and it crops up in Aristotle's arguments against the Platonists' eternal form of the good (1.6 1096b5).

23. See *Il.* 1.161–71, 9.314–29, 9.393–416, 24.522–51; Aristotle reports what was surely the standard assessment at *Rhet.* 1.3 1358b38–59a5.

tative voices of tradition seem concerned only to reaffirm the pious platitudes of virtue's rewards. In the two passages to which Adeimantus alludes when he opens his complaint against traditional views (*Rep.* 363b), Hesiod lectures his brother Perses on the rewards of justice by celebrating the good fortunes of just communities (*WD* 213–47), and Homer has Odysseus attribute Ithaca's prosperity to the justice of its rulers (*Od.* 19.108–14).[24] Solon too exhorts his fellows to justice principally by praising the prosperity attendant upon *eunomia* or "law and order," and in Aristotle's day, Demosthenes could still declaim the same lines to Athenian audiences (fr. 4.32–39, at Demosthenes 19.255). But these promises struck many as hollow when joined with Hesiod's notoriously dark view of human fortunes (*WD* 176–201). As Adeimantus observes (*Rep.* 364c–d), even Hesiod admits that the price of these rewards is high, for he teaches that the road to excellence is long, rugged, and steep, whereas the paths of the wicked are easy and smooth (*WD* 287–92), a sentiment shared by several, and echoed even by Aristotle in his poetry.[25] So unless the labors of virtue can promise more certain returns, as Glaucon complains, few are likely to feel much concern for principles that threaten what they think they want most.

To deter mortals from the easier route, Hesiod counts finally on the watchful eye of Zeus with his roving guardians to visit vengeance on the wicked and admits that he would not follow the paths of justice were it not for the rewards (*WD* 270–72).[26] Echoing a simile found already in Homer (*Il.* 16.384–93), Solon too evokes the threat of divine vengeance in the striking image of a massive storm sent by Zeus to cleanse the land of injustice (fr. 13.7–32). But the more impiety and injustice prosper, the less plausible these proclamations seem. To make his theodicy plausible, Solon must draw out its span over several generations (fr.

24. Homer elaborates the belief that justice prospers by having Hephaestus figure Achilles' shield with a city well ordered and flourishing (*Il.* 18.490–606). Contrast the view expressed by Zeus in a speech on Olympus that mortal folly is responsible for the worst of our ills (*Od.* 1.32–43).

25. Xenophon has Socrates cite the same lines before summarizing Prodicus' parable of Heracles at the crossroads of virtue and vice (*Mem.* 2.1.20); cf. Aristotle in his ode for Hermias, ἀρετὰ πολύμοχθε (fr. 842.1), Pindar *Nem.* 6.23, Simonides frs. 579, 541, and Tyrtaeus fr. 12.43.

26. For punishment of the living, see *WD* 265–69, 282–84, 334; Hesiod invokes a demonic fraternity of "immortal guardians of Zeus" at 122–26 and 253. On Plato's various uses of this traditional authority, see Solmsen 1960.

13.25–32); yet that raises the further worry whether it is just for the sons to pay for the sins of their fathers or forefathers (31–32). Indeed, as Adeimantus observes (*Rep.* 365d–e), the myths raise grave doubts about the moral standards of the gods themselves, or at least their concern for the welfare of the virtuous among mortals. Further, the dire sermons on behalf of justice are less effective as incentives to virtue than as warnings against being caught in crime. But according to the adage Adeimantus recalls (365c–d), no great gain comes without some risk. Even the prospect of punishment may seem negligible when the opportunities for gain are great and ingenuity nourishes hope for escape. When the rewards promised for virtue are of the same currency as the gains that tempt most to injustice (366d–e), prudence dictates we choose the route with better prospects. Hence, if all that commends virtue are its supposed consequences, and if those are neither certain nor clearly worth the toll, there seems little reason to accept the sacrifices virtue demands.

Traditional lore actually makes the situation seem worse. The legendary tales of undeserved woe led some to despair entirely of happiness in this life. Solon laments that no mortal is happy ("like a god," μάκαρ, fr. 14); others even conclude that it would have been better never to have been born.[27] Aristotle acknowledges the ancient authority of this somber pessimism when he raises the same worry not only in his presumably more popular dialogue, the lost *Eudemus,* where he recounts Silenus' dark words to Midas, but also in his academic work (*EE* 1.5 1215b20–22).[28] Once born, on this view, the best remedy is to hasten to death, to be quit of this wretched world of woe. For if happiness is unattainable in this life, death may offer vindication for the virtuous in an afterlife, as some proclaimed. But in Homer's Hades,

27. Even persevering Heracles is shown drawing this conclusion, in Bacchylides 5.160–62; cf. Theognis 425–28, "Homer" in the *Certamen* (pp. 78–79 Allen), Solon and his Persian counterpart, Artabanus (Herod. 1.31.3 and 7.46), Sophocles *OT* 1186–88, *OC* 1224–28, Euripides frs. 285, 449, 908, and in the fourth century, Alexis fr. 141. Aristotle also reports that Anaxagoras was asked a related question (*EE* 1.5 1216a11–14).

28. See fr. 44 (Plut. *Cons. Ap.* 115b–e), where (as in Euripides fr. 285.1) the saying is called θρυλούμενον; cf. Cicero *TD* 1.113–15. Raising a related worry, Aristotle asks what makes life worth living, and whether in some circumstances one may not be better off dead than alive (*EE* 1.5 1215b24–30). Socrates twists the maxim to his own purpose when he asks Hippias whether one would be better off dead than alive if ignorant of τὸ καλόν (*Hip. Maj.* 304e).

the only sure vindication is the punishment of broken oaths (*Il.* 3.278–79, 19.259–60). Most, even heroes, lead a bleak existence with scant reward; the lucky few who enjoy Elysium owe their good fortune more to familial connection with the gods than to any special virtues practiced in life (*Od.* 4.561–69). When Hesiod celebrates the good fortunes won there by the heroes of an earlier age (*WD* 167–73), the dominant tone in his picture remains one of nostalgia: he wishes he too had been born in the better and more just times of the previous age (174–75, cf. 158). What struck Plato, moreover, is how the poets represent both the rewards and the punishments of the afterlife in terms patterned on earthly prosperity and misfortune: heroes frolic in an idyllic resort, and the wicked suffer penury, terrible labors, and afflictions of the flesh. Adeimantus thus criticizes the legendary wisdom of Musaeus for portraying, as Pindar did after him, the underworld's rewards for the just and punishment of the wicked in terms that emphasize comfort and freedom from toil (*Rep.* 363c–e).[29] In this life, on the other hand, such welfare is never assured.

Impressed by the mutability of fortune, some reached a forbidding conclusion: call no one happy, Solon is said to have warned, so long as they are alive. His saying became proverbial and was echoed by many, even by Plato's erstwhile student and host, the archetypal tyrant Dionysius I of Syracuse.[30] The appeal of this grave maxim is plain: it epitomizes the traditional preoccupation with fortune, first in taking prosperity as the dominant factor in

29. For absence of ills, see *Ol.* 2.56–77; for positive blessings, cf. frs. 129–31. On the traditions behind these claims, see Lloyd-Jones 1985.

30. In the earliest version to survive, Herodotus has Solon say, "One ought to examine the end of everything" (παντὸς χρήματος τὴν τελευτήν, 1.32.7, 1.32.9); cf. *CPG* I.315, Cicero *TD* 1.113, and Plut. *Cons. Ap.* 108e. Dionysius inserted the saying in his tragedy *Leda* fr. 3; cf. Plut. *Dion* 4–5. Aeschylus *Agam.* 928–29 is the earliest extant occurrence; for other instances, see Fraenkel 1950 on the line and Irwin 1985*d*: 91 *n*3 (to which add Euripides fr. 285). Regenbogen (1961) sets the story against its traditional background. Because my concern is only with Solon's status as a font of traditional wisdom, it does not matter here that there are chronological problems with Herodotus' tale; cf. the salutary remarks of Plutarch when he confesses his doubts (*Solon* 27.1). Further, since my concern is with Aristotle's perspective on Solon, I am not concerned to distinguish the character used by Herodotus (in part to introduce themes in his own work) from the man whose literary and political accomplishments are reported with varying accuracy and precision by a wide range of sources; for Aristotle associates Solon with claims found in Herodotus, who in turn presumably represents traditions about Solon current in his own day. For testimony, see Martina 1968.

happiness, and second in taking human life as extremely unstable. Indeed, to underscore the latter point and lend it an air of
mathematical proof, Herodotus has Solon calculate the vast
number of days in the normal lifetime.[31] In that span of 26,250
days, he claims, "there are many things that no one wants to see,
many too that no one wants to suffer"; and since "no day is like
any other," the likelihood of change and reversal is so great that
he sums up human life in the lapidary phrase "man is all disaster" (1.32.2–4). Fortunately, this sentiment was far from universal. But the dictum was influential enough for Aristotle to make it
a principal test of his account of happiness, and although he refutes it as it stands, he does not reject it out of hand. On the contrary, his analysis of its assumptions reveals a less paradoxical
moral and leads to a reformulation of his own account (*EN* 1.10
1101a14–21). For while Aristotle argues that traditional wisdom
overstates the importance of fortune, he also preserves two basic
truths in Solon's view: happiness must be secure, and it requires
more than virtue alone. But before turning to Aristotle's refutation, Solon's views deserve consideration, not only as essential
background to Aristotle's argument, but in their own right as
well. After all, the ideal he sketches still exerts a strong pull.

31. The calculation exaggerates slightly by intercalating too many months,
one every other year; cf. Plut. *Solon* 25. But Gomme (1954: 81–82) defends the
observational basis of this view of the human lot by pointing out the brutality of
archaic life. The point may well stem from Solon, for his poetry deploys a similar
calculus of years: see fr. 27 (a normal life has ten periods of seven years) and fr.
20 (he wishes an extra decade for himself, presumably in defiance of the traditional disparagement of old age; cf. fr. 18). Heptads were a common measure,
used even by Aristotle to organize the stages of public education (*Pol.* 7.16
1335b32–35).

The End of Tellos

"SEE THE END," Solon is supposed to have said to Croesus, the great king of Lydia, at the height of his success. Feeling secure in his ascendancy and blessed with wealth of fabled proportions, the king deems himself the happiest man on earth. But when asked to confirm his host's felicity, Solon rejects the splendors of royalty and rewards the crown of happiness to three Greeks whose names are new to Croesus, Tellos the Athenian and two brothers from Argos, Cleobis and Biton.

"How can you consider Tellos happiest?" the astounded Croesus asked sharply. "First," Solon replied, "while his city fared well, Tellos had sons who were excellent and good, and he lived to see every one of them have children, all of whom survived him. And second, not only did he fare well in his life by our standards, but his life came to a most illustrious end: in a battle between the Athenians and their neighbors in Eleusis, he saved the day, routed the enemy, and died most nobly. The Athenians erected him a tomb in a public ceremony right where he fell, and they honored him greatly." (Herod. 1.30.4–5)

When asked the traditional question of who is the happiest of men, Solon the Athenian prefers the lot of an obscure fellow citizen named Tellos, "Mr. End."[1] To be sure, Solon refuses to mea-

---

1. Cf. similar questions asked of the sage Anacharsis by Croesus (Diodorus 9.26), of the Delphic oracle by his ancestor Gyges (Pliny NH 7.45), of Anaxagoras by an anonymous wit (EE 1.4 1215b6–14), and of the Delphic oracle by Socrates' companion Chaerephon (Apol. 21a–b). Herodotus sprinkles his tale with words from the root τελ-; Tellos' name must therefore be significant, although its "meaning" remains ambiguous. It suggests dying (cf. τελευτᾶν); achievement

sure happiness by the magnitude of prosperity. But he still assigns prosperity a decisive role: the most extraordinary feature of all three lives, in his judgment, is that they experienced no serious misfortune. Solon emphasizes how exceptionally fortunate each was throughout his life and even at his death. Although his station was less than magnificent, Tellos lived to be proud of his grandchildren, and before any misfortune could befall his family or his city, he died a hero's death (1.30.4).[2] Then, echoing the view that mortals are better off dead than alive (1.31.3), Solon grants the brothers second prize in happiness, even though they met their end while still young and well before completing Solon's normal term of seventy years. Hence, Solon's point is not simply that "nothing in human affairs is secure [ἀσφαλέως ἔχον]," as Cyrus later concludes in reflecting on Croesus' fate after the fall of Lydia realized the dire prediction of the poet (1.86). Solon's pessimism derives as well from his belief that this instability infects the very foundations of a good life: if happiness is built on prosperity, then misfortune wrecks happiness as well.

Solon's attitude is not without a religious aspect. It recalls Homer's parable of the great jars of Zeus, which promises unalloyed prosperity to no mortals and continuous ill to many.[3] On this view, our fortunes and therefore our happiness or misery are all dispensations from the gods. Yet Solon calls divinity "jealous and disruptive" (1.32.1) because the gods often uproot the very people they exalt (1.32.9); and in his own voice, Herodotus attributes the ills that befall Croesus immediately after Solon's departure to "divine resentment" (ἐκ θεοῦ νέμεσις, 1.34.1).[4] The just may win favor and the wicked face retribution, but mortality rather than morality is the operative factor here: the gods simply grow resentful of human success, and they contrive disaster to

---

(cf. τελειοῦν); a goal or ideal (Aristotelian τέλος); status (Solon ranked Athenians in four property classes or τέλη); and cavalry (τέλος was an old term for a squadron of cavalry, Thucydides 2.22.2–3).

2. Solon emphasizes that he died without suffering the loss of *any* children or grandchildren.

3. Preserved first in the voice of Homer's Achilles (*Il.* 24.527–51), the parable enjoyed favor, as shown by Pindar's darker version (*Pyth.* 3.80–82) and Plato's criticism (*Rep.* 379d).

4. Although Solon treats retribution as divinely sent in fr. 13.7–28, human error evidently provokes it; cf. frs. 6, 9, 11, 12. Lang (1984: 61–62), observing that the five references in Herodotus to divine jealousy always occur in the voices of his characters, argues that he also attributes misfortunes to human error.

humble any who rise too near the invulnerable serenity of life on Olympus. The underlying belief is simply that there is "a cycle of human affairs" which ensures that human prosperity never lasts for an entire life (1.207). That cycle, not any villainous tendencies in its king, brings Lydia down. Renowned for his generosity and piety, Croesus attracted the wisest men of Greece (1.19), and once chastened by misfortune, he is revealed worthy of miraculous salvation.[5] To be sure, the fall of Croesus fulfills two Delphic oracles reported by Herodotus. One, a warning that the regicide of Gyges would be avenged in the fifth generation (1.13), makes him the victim of ancestral deeds, and the other simply increases his confidence in a planned expedition by declaring ambiguously that it would "destroy a great rule" (1.53). So, although this view of fortune as cyclical does not present the gods as indifferent to right and wrong, neither does it pretend that every calamity is in payment for sins past. Its ethical force derives more from the vulnerability of great prosperity than from a conviction that prosperity invites punishment for any arrogance it may induce.

As a positive proposal, Solon advises the lord of Lydia that people should not trust in the magnitude of their fortunes; rather, they should reduce their dependence on its gifts. Without discounting good fortune entirely, Solon insists that great prosperity is unnecessary for a good life. Content with the alternative envisaged even by Homer's Achilles as he ponders forsaking "glory imperishable" at Troy to return home, Solon's heroes of happiness lived on modest means and enjoyed the quiet if lackluster life of their private estates (Il. 9.393–400). The only advantage Solon recognizes in power and great wealth is their greater contribution to satisfying appetites and "enduring great ruin" (ἄτη), but he considers ruin a liability of the less fortunate also (Herod. 1.32.6). The resources enjoyed by his exemplary citizens while not immense (τοῦ βίου εὖ ἥκων, 1.30.4; βίος ἀρκέων, 1.31.2) were adequate. Moreover, no amount of riches can fend off death, disease, or old age (Solon fr. 24), and on those counts at least, the lord of great riches is no better off than those who have "enough for a day" (1.32.5). The latter are actually better off, if

5. Note his generous treatment of Adrastos (1.43), and when Cyrus tests his captive's piety, Croesus is saved by Apollo (1.86–87). Pindar Pyth. 1.89–98 and Bacchylides 3 (both for the tyrant Hieron) make him a paradigm of royal virtue.

only in having less to lose.[6] Solon's happiest of men lived without the vast wealth and power admired by many but also without either the larger ambitions or the great losses to which those advantages would make them prone.

This praise of moderation is nothing new, and contrasting it with the opulence of eastern potentates is a traditional device for underscoring the unimportance of wealth. Archilochus had disdained Gyges' lot, as Aristotle knew (fr. 19, at *Rhet.* 3.18 1418b31),[7] and Aristotle himself cites Sardanapallos (the Assyrian Ashurbanipal) to exemplify the costly hedonism so admired by "the many."[8] But Solon defends his modest ideal by adducing an analogy between people and their lands. Just as no single region is wholly sufficient (καταρκέει) and lacking in nothing, so too no individual is entirely self-sufficient (αὔταρκες) and supplied with everything; rather, just as the best region is one that has most good things, so the standards for human happiness should be limited correspondingly (Herod. 1.32.8; cf. ἐπαρκεῖν, Solon fr. 5). No one can have everything, and happiness belongs to any whose good fortune endures: "whoever continues in the possession of most things [not "*the* most"] and ends his life gracefully" can be called happy (Herod. 1.32.9).

Although Solon argues that happiness requires neither great prosperity nor all the good things in life, he still maintains that it requires unusually good fortune and that this must also last. Good fortune not only "fends off" the ills that afflict most of us, but it also holds multiple benefits of its own, among which Solon

6. For Solon's modest standards, see fr. 13.3–8, fr. 23; Hellman (1934: esp. 39–42) overstates what he calls the "citizen-ideal."

7. Aristotle was familiar with Archilochus' poetry; he wrote a treatise in three books entitled "Problems in Archilochus, Euripides, and Choerilus." Gyges is best known from Herodotus (esp. 1.7–15); his palace coup founded the Lydian dynasty that ends with Croesus' downfall. Plato has Glaucon exploit the proverbial tale of his ring, which made its wearer invisible, to highlight his worry that injustice often seems more desirable than justice (*Rep.* 2.359c–60d).

8. The king is named in both treatises (1.5 1095b22, *EE* 1.5 1216a16), and his way of life was apparently discussed at greater length in the *Protrepticus* (see fr. 16, which quotes an epitaph associated with him: "These things have I: everything I ate, the ways I wantoned, the delights / I found with Eros; but my great grand fortunes have all been left behind"; cf. Burnet 1900 on 1095b22). In *Pol.* 5.10 1312a1–4, Aristotle wonders whether "the storytellers" (οἱ μυθολογοῦντες) are right about Sardanapallos' assassination; cf. Theophrastus fr. 111 and Stewart 1892 on 1095b22.

lists "sound body, good health, freedom from suffering, good children, and good looks" (1.32.6).[9] This list emphasizes the personal goods of physical well-being, but it also insists on the social good of having a family, a factor that looms quite large in Solon's exemplary lives. The focus in Solon's summary of Tellos' fortunes falls on his family, both its size and its nobility, and Cleobis and Biton are the children of a priestess of Hera. To some extent these advantages are subject to the control of those who have them. Temperate living, for example, was widely considered necessary for good health. Nonetheless, by attributing them all to "good fortune" (εὐτυχίη), Solon implies that these advantages are also subject to factors beyond our control. After all, people born lame, sickly, or deformed could do little to repair their infirmities, and even the most scrupulous regimen could not prevent disease or accident. Although Solon stops short of making all these forms of good fortune necessary for happiness, the man he counts happiest of all enjoyed them all. His runners-up apparently lacked only the blessing of children. Moreover, the features listed by the poet are treated as lifelong attributes. The principal thrust of his speech to Croesus is that a few years of prosperity do not make a man "free of suffering," and his heroes are exceptional because their good fortune lasted to the ends of their lives. Tellos was survived by all of his fine family, and the brothers remained stouthearted to their dying day. But since any man requires good fortune for his natural advantages to last, Solon makes happiness depend on fortune both for the blessings essential to a good life and for their permanence. In short, rather than removing our dependence on fortune, his ideal only relocates it: if moderate prosperity avoids the vulnerability of Croesus' position, it still provides no assurance of security. Tellos' sustained good fortune, modest though it was, is for Solon the fundamental constituent of his happiness.[10]

9. Cf. Solon fr. 13.35–40 and 57–62, fr. 23, and fr. 24.9–10. Plut. *Solon* 6 preserves the tale that Thales, to show Solon why he had no family, caused Solon to grieve by tricking him into believing that his son had died. The tale seems too good to be trusted: Plutarch cites it from Hermippus, who attributes it to "Pataecus, who claimed to have Aesop's soul" (Pataecus may have been a slave, since his name is an ethnic label). Anaxagoras, by contrast, is supposed to have said, upon learning of his son's death, that he knew he'd fathered a mortal (Cicero *TD* 3.30; but D. L. 2.13 adds that some told the story about Solon).

10. Solon opens his prayer for his laws by asking for "good fortune and kudos" (fr. 31).

Where do the virtues stand in this picture? Solon does not go so far as to identify happiness with sustained prosperity. First, his paradigms of happiness exemplify the traditional virtues of devotion to family, community, and religion. Moreover, as his conclusion shows, if moderate and sustained prosperity is fundamental, it still is not enough on its own. To qualify for happiness, as Solon insists repeatedly, one must also end one's life "gracefully" (εὐχαρίστως, 1.32.9),[11] and to emphasize the importance of dying nobly, he describes his heroes' prosperity summarily and makes their deaths the climax of his tales. All go out in a blaze of glory: Tellos dies with heroic valor in the service of his city, and the final feat of the Argive brothers exemplifies their dedication to their parents, to their community, and to the gods. Thus, the prosperous, no matter how enduring their good fortune, do not thereby qualify to be called happy; they must also perform fine deeds. In particular, as Solon's exhortations to his fellow Athenians to recapture Salamis might lead us to suspect (frs. 1–3), a man must be willing to put the interests of his community before private advantage and to risk his life on behalf of his fellows.[12] In fact, to judge from his heroes, Solon seems to hold that happiness requires a glorious cause for which to die. Tellos meets "a most splendid [λαμπροτάτη] end" on behalf of his city and is memorialized by the great honor of a battlefield burial (1.30.4–5); Cleobis and Biton achieve a "best [ἀρίστη] end" by using their might in the service of Hera, and as their mother "rejoiced" and the festal crowd "blessed" (ἐμακάριζον) them, they won from the goddess "what is best for a human to get" (1.31.3–4). Only Tellos wins the warrior's meed of honor by dying in combat, but the brothers had already won renown as champions in the Pan-Hellenic games and were honored at Delphi with twin statues.[13] By contrast, the peaceful death at home envisaged by Achilles on the shores of Troy, though a fortunate end, would

11. Solon refuses to call Croesus happy "until I find out you've ended your life nobly [καλῶς]" (1.32.5); again, one must "end one's life well [εὖ] with everything noble" (πάντα καλὰ ἔχοντα, 1.32.5; cf. πρὸς τούτοισι ἔτι τελευτῆσαι τὸν βίον εὖ, 1.32.7).

12. Solon is reported to have declaimed his "Salamis" under penalty of death; see fr. 1 (esp. Plut. *Solon* 8, Demosthenes 19.252, D. L. 1.46–47).

13. Their mother prayed for what is best for them; Hera's response testifies to the view that it is better to *be* dead (perfect: τεθνάναι) than to *go on* living (present: ζῆν). The statues were unearthed at Delphi toward the end of the last century; photographs are widely reproduced.

seem by Solon's criteria to deprive an otherwise great man of his chance for happiness. Responding to Croesus' ancestor Gyges, the Delphic oracle is said to have spoken in a similar vein: Aglaos can be counted happy by reason of his modest prosperity alone, but Pedius is the happiest of all because in addition he died for his country (Pliny *NH* 7.151).

These ends as well bear the stamp of fortune, since the opportunity to die nobly was counted among the gifts of fortune, and heroes lamented the misfortune of not dying gloriously in combat.[14] Where would Tellos have stood in Solon's estimation, had he not had occasion to defend his city, or had Athens not been victorious? Likewise, had their mother not been priestess, or had it not been a holiday, the brothers would have had no chance to serve Hera and to astound their community by getting their mother to church on time. But without a glorious end, these lives could not have served Solon as models. The dictum of "seeing the end" thus has two implications. One centers on fortune: a happy life must be a completed life. If prosperity must be permanent and misfortune can at any time ruin a life, there is no way of telling whether anyone is happy until death removes them from fortune's reach. But the dictum has another point: if deeds of excellence, though insufficient, still are essential, we must also see what the fortunate do all the way to the end. Prosperity can "breed arrogance and violence," according to a famous maxim of Solon's that Aristotle cites as testimony in his *Protrepticus*;[15] and the martial virtues Solon admires are displayed only in the face of adversity. All the same, the poet's admiration appears to rest on what these virtues achieve. He focuses on the posthumous honors won by his heroes and never mentions any prior satisfaction they might have found in virtuous activity in their private lives. Yet they could find little delight in earthly rewards after death, and being denied posthumous honors would have spoiled their fortunate end. In the absence of public recognition, Solon offers no more incentive for virtue than he does to deter injustice. In the

14. Cf. Achilles and Agamemnon in *Od.* 24.28–39; Callinus fr. 1.14–21, and Simonides fr. 531 and fr. 100 Bergk.

15. The notion became a commonplace, as explained in *Protrep.* fr. 3; cf. Solon fr. 6.3–4 (at *Ath. Pol.* 12.2), and Theognis 153–54, Pindar *Ol.* 13.102, and Isocrates *Areop.* 4.

tales of his heroes at least, both pursuit and avoidance depend heavily on consequences.

Events following Solon's interview with Croesus readily inspired moralizing. To show how history upheld the sage's pessimism and his disdain for royal fortunes, Herodotus first recounts the death of the king's favorite son as the result of a decidedly oracular dream (1.34–45) and then he presents Persia's inevitable conquest of Lydia as the fulfillment of divine ordinances (1.53.3, 86.1, 91.4). Even without these further pieties, however, Solon's grim argument has force. If prosperity is decisive for happiness and human fortunes are pervaded by mutability, then happiness is precarious at best. If the value of virtue also depends heavily on fortune, few of the living have good prospects for happiness. Finally, if prosperity and virtue must both be permanent, then a good life is all but impossible for mortals. But is the argument valid, and are its premises true? In particular, is human life as vulnerable to fortune as Solon seems to think? One problem in appealing to exemplary cases is the danger of counting the exceptional as normal. In the catastrophes of legend, the loftiest lose the most, and Solon's modestly prosperous folk had less to lose than Croesus and attracted less resentment, whether human or divine. Further, although Solon limits the kinds and degree of good fortune he requires for happiness, is every feature that he retains really essential? Does a good life require the complete prosperity of a Tellos, the physical prowess of Cleobis and Biton, or the flourishing families and cities common to them all? Finally, is permanence necessary, and must prosperity continue without break from beginning to end? Even Croesus, some argued, showed such mettle in meeting his disaster and then lived out his life so nobly in the court of Cyrus, that by Solon's own criteria he deserves to be called happy again.[16] How important, then, is continual good fortune?

16. See *n*5 above.

Fortune and Prosperity

ARISTOTLE REJECTS Solon's dictum and refutes the premises on which it is based. But before we examine this refutation, it is worth exploring why Aristotle also finds much in the sage's views with which to agree. Most notably, he caps his final account of happiness by claiming that Solon's views are basically congruent with his own; for even after arguing that the finest happiness is found in a life of reflection, Aristotle cites Solon alongside Anaxagoras as agreeing on essential points.[1]

And Solon too presumably [ἴσως] described the happy well, saying they had moderate external resources and also had done very noble things (as he supposed) and lived temperately; for it is possible to do what one should when possessing moderate means. (*EN* 10.8 1179a9–13)

Nothing here implies that "one should see the end." But there is no mention of reflection either, and the passage implies that Aristotle would join Solon in calling Tellos happy. Perfect har-

---

1. F. Dirlmeier (1956: 596) notes that Aristotle appeals to Solon at critical junctures in his argument, both at the beginning and at the end of the *EN*; cf. *EE* 2.1 1219b6.–8. Aristotle shows his respect for the virtually legendary founding father of Athens in other contexts also: Solon has the honor of appearing first among the brief sketches of major lawgivers in *Pol.* 2.12, and the historical account in the *Ath. Pol.* (whether the work of Aristotle or his colleagues) not only exemplifies the general respect for Solon's achievements but shows familiarity with much of his poetry. Aristotle also recalls Solon fr. 5.1 at *Pol.* 2.12 1274a15, and he quotes fr. 13.71 at *Pol.* 1.8 1256b33 and fr. 22 at *Rhet.* 1.15 1375b34. See Rhodes 1981: 5–37, 57–63, 118–25.

mony should not be expected, since Aristotle cites neither Anaxagoras nor Solon to confirm the claim that a life of reflection is best. Rather, they are meant to corroborate only the immediately preceding argument in which the importance of prosperity is sharply restricted (1178b33–79a9). Just as the reference to Anaxagoras omits any mention of his celebrated intellectualism and notes only his rejection of the popular concern for wealth and power (1179a13–16),[2] likewise Solon is said to deny any need for more than "moderate resources" (a10), and Aristotle's gloss repeats that modest possessions are sufficient (a12–13). Moreover, although he does not claim Solon as an early proponent of reflection, neither does Aristotle endorse his views on prosperity in their entirety. First, he considers the part played by virtue only implicit in Solon's account, as he indicates by qualifying his reconstruction as what Solon "presumably" (a10) thought. Similarly, it is only his explanatory gloss that makes the standard of sufficiency depend on virtue and "doing what one should" (a13). And although Aristotle follows Solon in distinguishing a public and a private side of virtue—happiness requires noble deeds as well as a temperate way of life—he adds a parenthetical disclaimer, "as he supposed" (a11–12), to signal his reservations about Solon's counting valor "most noble."[3] Properly interpreted, "the views of the wise evidently harmonize with our ar-

2. Anaxagoras is taken as the representative of intellectualism in EE 1.4–5, where his view is characterized more fully (1215b12–14, 1216a13–14; cf. EN 6.7 1141b3–8). But neither here nor elsewhere is Solon said to have any special interest in abstract speculation; on the contrary, practical and political concerns dominate his ideal. Thus, although Herodotus names θεωρίη (1.29) and φιλοσοφέων (1.30.2) as Solon's "pretext" for travel abroad, he thinks the true explanation was political—Solon wanted to avoid being forced to tamper with his constitutional reforms (1.29). The terms of his "pretext," in fact, then had more to do with "observation" and "curiosity" than "theory" or "philosophy," and they contrast with esoteric studies as well as with political affairs; cf. Pericles' claim about most Athenians (Thucydides 2.40.1) and Hippocrates Anc. Med. 20. On early senses of "philosophy," see Burnet 1930: 25 and Burkert 1960; Aristotle apparently traced the speculative sense of "philosophy" back only to Pythagoras (Protrep. fr. 11), at least a generation after Solon.

3. For the text of 1179a11–12, I adopt the reading of the vulgate (τὰ κάλλισθ᾽ ὡς ᾤετο), rather than the manuscript preferred by Bywater (1892: 69; κάλλιστ᾽ ᾤετο); all Aristotle means to qualify by saying "he supposed" is the superlative ("doing what he supposed were the noblest deeds"), not the whole idea of noble action ("he supposed it is necessary to act very nobly"). Aristotle's use of perfect participles here (πεπραγότας and βεβιωκότας) probably reflects Solon's demand for completed lives.

guments" (a16–17), but analysis is necessary for proper interpretation.

Aristotle brings Solon's views into harmony with his own account of happiness by drawing out the poet's implicit requirement of virtue. But his summary of Solon's ideal lives still concedes a need for moderate prosperity, a need omitted in his original equation of happiness with a life of virtuous activity (1.7 1098a16–20). So if he means to endorse Solon on this point, his initial account appears to need modification. Nor is this the only problem: although Solon argues that moderate prosperity is enough for a good life (Herod. 1.32.5–9), he still exemplifies the traditional view that prosperity is the dominant factor. Unless Aristotle can accommodate these two claims or explain their error, his account fails a crucial test of tradition. As he himself insists right after mentioning Solon and Anaxagoras, if his account *fails* to stand up to "the test of the facts of life," so much the worse for his arguments (*EN* 1179a17–22).[4] If health, public honors, a good family, and material resources are worth having, his account of happiness should make room for them, and conversely, he should concede that their absence or loss destroys happiness even if virtuous activity continues. Finally, although Solon's ideal gives a place to deeds of excellence, it also reflects the tradition that values virtue primarily for its consequences, for the prosperity it yields and the honors it wins. Excellence without its due rewards, on this view, falls short of happiness, and only if virtuous activity leads to prosperity does it make for a good life. Is this the implication of Aristotle's account also? Must the virtuous meet with success and enjoy prosperity to count as happy? Or are they less dependent on fortune than traditional views allege?

Aristotle does acknowledge the necessity of some degree of prosperity by revising his initial formulation to incorporate mention of resources: we call happy "anyone who exercises complete virtue and is supplied with sufficient external resources, not for a chance period of time, but for a complete life" (1.10 1101a14–17). But the argument that leads to this conclusion is complicated and grows out of the survey of "what is said" about happiness (1.8 1098b9–12), and it is to that we should return. The first in this

4. I quote Ross's version (in Barnes 1984) of ἐπὶ τὰ ἔργα καὶ τὸν βίον φέροντας (1179a20–21); Irwin (1985a) renders it more literally, "applying it to what we do and how we live."

series of views shows that his account agrees with "the ancient view accepted by those who love wisdom" that the soul and its activities are "most sovereign and best" (b12–18). Contrasting attributes of the soul both with those of the body and with external things, this view raises immediately the basic problem of how prosperity fits into Aristotle's account. Physical well-being and material and social advantages encompass the major elements in prosperity; or in the terminology Aristotle often employs, bodily goods such as health, strength, and good looks and external goods such as wealth, honor, and power count as goods of fortune, since both our acquisition and our continued enjoyment of things in each class *depend* in many ways on fortune and events beyond our personal control.[5] To be sure, elements in each of the three classes can contribute to a good life and benefit the soul. But since the point of the trichotomy is to distinguish what *controls* our use and enjoyment of various goods, it divides them by their location rather than by their beneficiaries: goods of the soul are the least subject to fortune and circumstance because the soul controls itself, whereas bodily goods like health and strength as well as external goods like wealth and power are subject to many factors beyond our control.[6] Hence, the division offers a reason for valuing prosperity less than our souls: to put it baldly, we are more self-sufficient and have greater control over our character and mind than goods "outside" our souls.

This "ancient view" establishes Aristotle's agreement with the wise, but it also risks putting him at odds with conventional

---

5. Cf. *EE* 2.1 1218b31–35. Aristotle lists the major factors in each of the three classes in the *Rhet.* (1.5 1360b20–29); cf. Plato *Apol.* 30a. See Cooper 1985a: esp. 174–78, for passages grouping the bodily goods with external goods on the grounds that all are external to the soul; cf. the dichotomy in Democritus B37 DK. For the background to this trichotomy, see Dirlmeier 1956: 281–82 and, e.g., *Euthyd.* 279a–b, *Rep.* 618c–e, and *Laws* 726a–29a, 743e; cf. D. L. 3.78. Following Antiochus, Cicero attributes the division to Academics and Peripatetics alike (*TD* 5.85), as does Arius a short while later (Stobaeus 2.124–25), but its origins are earlier. It appeared at the beginning of the lost *Triagmoi* (or "Triads," mid-fifth century) by Ion of Chios (fr. 1), and it occurs outside Platonic circles, e.g., Isocrates *Panath.* 7–8. Aristotle would not have described the view as "ancient" if it did not predate the Academy.

6. Cf. Irwin 1985a: 307. Aristotle lists good family, wealth, and power as the three kinds of prosperity that exercise the greatest influence on character (*Rhet.* 2.15–17); he also describes physical attributes such as health (*Rhet.* 1362a2–5), size (a2–5), looks (a4–8), and aging (1361b29–31) as subject to fortune. On bodily goods, see III below; on specific external goods, see IV below.

views. Why should autonomy be more desirable than the external goods most people evidently value more? Here Aristotle recalls a point made when he first introduces happiness into the discussion: "Both the many and the cultivated believe that living well and doing well are the same as being happy" (1.4 1095a18–20, recalled at 1.8 1098b20–22; cf. 6.2 1139b3, 6.5 1140b7). His principle that happiness consists in rational activity clearly accords with this view. But so do other views as well, for behind this vague consensus lies a fundamental dichotomy: living and doing well could mean something *active* that makes happiness depend on our own actions; but they could also mean the more *passive* idea of faring well that would make it depend on external events satisfying our personal predilections.[7] Aristotle's principle fits the former sense. Yet most people evidently understood the terms in the latter sense of success and emphasized external goods like wealth, honor, and health (1095a22–25). Aristotle himself argues that something usually considered the antithesis of action, philosophical reflection, can be called "doing well" (*Pol.* 7.3 1325b14–32). So all that this test can establish is that the ultimate goal has some connection with the things people "do."

In traditional views, doing well centers on the enjoyment of success and prosperity. It is often contrasted with "misfortune" (1.10 1100a21). Moreover, in a list of views to be used in public speaking, Aristotle describes happiness in a number of ways, each of which emphasizes externals. The one most similar to his account makes happiness simply "self-sufficiency of life" (αὐτάρ-κεια ζωῆς, *Rhet.* 1.5 1360b14–15).[8] In the following lines, however, he associates this specifically with having external goods (b24). Similarly, "sufficiency" suggested to most people the several concrete benefits of good fortune listed by Solon (cf. βίος ἀρ-κέων, Herod. 1.31.2, 1.32.6–8). On a related view, happiness is "the most pleasant life with security [μετ' ἀσφαλείας]" (1360b15). This formula highlights the two major concerns of Solon, prosperity and the avoidance of misfortune (cf. Herod. 1.32.5–6), for in the following lines, Aristotle describes "security" as depen-

7. Dodds (1959) on *Gorg.* 507a4 illustrates the contrast between the active and passive senses; cf. J. McDowell 1980: 368.

8. This is the only formula in Aristotle's list reflected in the Academic "Definitions," where it appears after "a good composed of everything good" (412d); only one of its four formulas mentions ἀρετή. The term is associated with Polemo in later doxography; see Clem. Alex. *Strom.* 2.133.7.

dent on fortune (1360b29). A third view makes the dominance of external goods explicit by equating happiness with "flourishing [εὐθηνία] of possessions and bodies, with a power of retaining and achieving these things" (b15–17).[9] Finally, even "doing well with virtue" (b14) reflects the popular view that prosperity is the standard for doing well, for on a conventional conception Aristotle mentions later, virtue is "a capacity for providing and retaining good things" (1.9 1366a36–37)—the same sort of instrumental ability associated with "flourishing" in the previous formula. If all these views make well-being depend primarily on prosperity, then Aristotle needs to show either where they go wrong or how his own account satisfies the reputable views about the value of prosperity. Each formula should contain some truth but they all need analysis to remove obscurity and misconceptions.

To meet this challenge, Aristotle's next move is to distinguish the three major "desiderata" in the reputable views about happiness. Some equate happiness with virtue or some sort of intelligence; some think it also requires some pleasure; others add in "external flourishing" (*EN* 1.8 1098b24–26).[10] This list reflects views held by recent or contemporary philosophers: the Cynics held that happiness consists in virtue alone, Socrates defended practical wisdom, Anaxagoras defended wisdom, the later works of Plato combine moral and intellectual virtue with pleasure, and to these, Xenocrates added external goods.[11] But the desiderata also capture popular conceptions of happiness, for they encompass the five major ends around which Aristotle claims most people organize their lives: a life of political or theoretical virtue ranks goods of the soul first, the life of pleasure typ-

9. Cf. 1100a6. Aristotle uses εὐθηνία, along with εὐημερία and εὐετηρία (literally "good days" and "good years"), predominantly in the biological works and of animals; see the entries in Bonitz 1870 and Burnet 1900 on 1098b26. Since animals are incapable of *eudaimonia*, this usage is one reason not to translate that as "flourishing," whether specified as "human" or not. For the advantages of this suggestive proposal (from Anscombe 1958), see Cooper 1975: 89–90, although Cooper has since renounced it (1987); cf. Kraut 1979b: 169 and I.i n1 above.

10. The translation of τὰ ἐπιζητούμενα is from Burnet 1900 on 1098b22. To some extent, these three views correspond to the three classes of goods (respectively): goods of the soul, of the body (popular usage usually thought of pleasure as bodily; see 7.13 esp. 1153b34–54a1, 3.10 1117b27–18a2, and 7.4 1147b25–28), and externals.

11. For references, see Stewart 1892 on 1098b23–26; for Aristotle's view of Socrates, see Deman 1942: esp. 82–106 (on Socrates' cognitivist view of virtue).

ically values a bodily good most, and the pursuit of money or honor puts external goods first.[12] So in recalling the topic of the various "ways of life," Aristotle appeals directly to actual preferences as well as to philosophical views. Provided his account captures all these ends, as he claims it does (b22–23), it upholds the truth in popular and traditional views (b27), as well as less conventional claims (b28). But does it capture them all?

These desiderata provide good evidence about the content of happiness. As Aristotle asserts, "it is reasonable that none of them is wholly mistaken, and rather that each is correct on at least one point, or even on most" (b27–29). Thus, the aim of his discussion is not to overthrow tradition but to isolate its truths. The conflict among these views must be resolved, and their errors explained, and that involves showing how each squares with his own account. The claims of prosperity receive the lengthiest discussion, but first he summarizes the place of virtue and pleasure in his account (1098b30–99a24). Though cursory, his remarks indicate his willingness to amend and revise reputable views. First, he underscores the importance of the virtuous being *active* by criticizing Academic accounts of happiness as a "possession" (κτῆσις) or "state" (ἕξις).[13] Drawing an analogy to athletic contests, where people are crowned victors not when they are in the best physical condition but when they put their abilities to the best use, he argues briefly that the virtuous must also put their excellence to "use" if they are to attain the prize of a good life (1098b31–99a5). This reconciles one set of views with his own, but it also raises questions about the nature of virtue that are here left in abeyance (until 2.1–6). Pleasure, the second major desideratum, is also supposed to be implied by Aristotle's account. However, since the formulation cited as a reputable view is vague ("with pleasure or not without it," 1098b25), the aim of this preliminary discussion is only to claim that virtuous activity has its pleasures: while pointing out the variety of pleasures, he amends the casual association of pleasure and virtue allowed by the original formulation and claims that his account makes hap-

---

12. See 1.4 1095a20–23, 1.5, and the passages collected in I.i *n*20 above.

13. The first term is associated with Speusippus, the latter with Xenocrates; see Gauthier and Jolif 1970 on 1098b32. For analysis of what might be called the paradox of Endymion, see Dybikowski 1981: 187–91 and Nussbaum 1986: 322–27.

piness intrinsically pleasant (1099a8–21). The direction of this argument is significant, for it shows Aristotle arguing not that his account satisfies all the desires anyone may have but only that people who attain the final end he describes lead an inherently satisfying life. This route is alien to hedonism because it implies that pleasure by itself is not the final end and advances an independent standard for choosing among different pleasures.[14] It nonetheless meets a major demand of hedonism by maintaining that virtuous activity yields the "most pleasant" life (a24). Again, however, he postpones detailed argument to a later stage in the argument (until 7.11–14, 10.1–5).

Aristotle next claims that his account unites the three major ends wrongly divorced in the famous Delian inscription: happiness is at once "best, finest, and most pleasant" (1099a24–30). He has yet to say, however, how prosperity is related to happiness.[15] One of the things the epigram praises so highly, "getting [τυχεῖν] what one loves," is notoriously beyond our control, and as the phrasing of the epigram betrays, love is subject to fortune (τύχη).[16] Turning to the third desideratum, then, Aristotle offers preliminary reasons for including prosperity in happiness (a32 recalls the view ascribed to "others" at 1098b26). This claim has its adherents among philosophers, but its roots reach beyond academic debates to the traditional wisdom that Aristotle takes Solon to epitomize.

Still, happiness clearly has additional need of external goods also, as we said. For it is impossible, or not very easy, to do noble things if one is without resources, since many things are done, just as through tools, through friends and family and wealth and political power, while when deprived of some things, such as a good family, good children, and good

14. This exemplifies his starting from "the left-hand side of the equation" of living a morally good life and living a life good for oneself; see J. McDowell 1980: 368–73. On pleasure more generally, see Annas 1980.

15. The three terms of the epigram again reflect the trichotomy of goods: (1) finest is justice in the soul; (2) best is health of the body; (3) most pleasant is "getting" one's (external) object of love. Aristotle uses the epigram to open his argument in the *EE* (1.1 1214a5–6). This and similar versions of the epigram appear often in Plato and the poets; see Dirlmeier 1956: 285 and Gauthier and Jolif 1970 on 1099a27–28.

16. Solon says that Hera's gift of death to Cleobis and Biton is what it is best for mortals "to get" (τυχεῖν, Herod. 1.31.4). Bonitz (1886: 96–97), discussing a central passage from the *Euthyd.* (278–82), points out the etymological link between τύχη and τυγχάνειν that connects "fortune" with "getting" and hence success, as well as with "chance encounters" and fortuitous events.

looks, people spoil their happiness;[17] for someone very ugly in looks, or low-born, or all alone and without children is not very capable of happiness, and presumably even less capable if their children or family or friends are depraved, or though good have died. So as we said, evidently happiness has additional need also of this sort of flourishing [εὐη-μερίας]; and that is why some people rank prosperity [εὐτυχίαν] the same as happiness, although others rank virtue there.

(1.8 1099a31–b8)[18]

This epitome of traditional views about prosperity proposes a number of reasons for thinking prosperity a necessary condition for happiness. In the process it also specifies some of what prosperity involves: wealth, status, power, and good looks are each given a place, and family and friends appear especially important. All these factors also occur in a list of the "parts" of happiness that Aristotle provides after his survey of conventional views of happiness in the *Rhetoric* (1.5 1360b14–29), a list that scarcely mentions the virtues at all (b23-[24]) and is followed by a discussion only of the goods of fortune (1360b31–62a12, but note a13–14). This epitome also echoes Solon's central concerns in his conversation with Croesus. First, the prospering families of Tellos and the Argive brothers are paralleled by Aristotle's emphasis on family and children (*EN* 1099b3–6).[19] Second, although Solon

17. Ross (in Barnes 1984) translates ῥυπαίνουσι as "takes the lustre from," Irwin (1985*a*) uses "mars," and Stewart (1892) on 1099b2 and b5 calls the lost goods "ornaments." By equating the losses with tarnishing and blemishes, each suggests that happiness endures. But the verb is an uncommon word with strong connotations, and it seems to concede that some misfortunes destroy happiness (so 1101a9–11). The root (ῥύπος) means "filth" (cf. Aspasius 24.30). Aristotle uses the verb only once elsewhere, for "mudslinging" (*Rhet.* 3.2 1405a25; so the ancient lexicographers). *Ath. Pol.* 6.3 denies that Solon "filthied" (καταρρυπαίνειν) himself by corrupt political deals, on the grounds that he would not have risked ruining his reputation in exchange for slight gain (cf. Solon frs. 5 and 32–34). A related verb, ῥυπάω, is used of paupers and lost souls; see Aristophanes *Birds* 1281 (of a filthy, laconizing Socratic) and *Wealth* 266 (of a sullen and "miserable" old man). See II.v *n*18 below.

18. On this crucial passage, I follow Irwin 1985*d*: 95–97, rather than Cooper 1985*a*: 176–84, and Kraut 1989: 253–60. Here I aim only to sketch the traditional background of the passage; for further analysis, see II.v below. My periphrasis for φίλοι is cumbersome, but the word could embrace almost any people who spend much time together, whether related by blood or by choice, from fairly casual connections to the intimate relations of "best friends" and lovers. Thus, Aristotle's "utility friends" include business and political connections as well as wealthy uncles, and "pleasure friends" range from boon companions to sexual partners; see IV.iv *n*28 below.

19. Solon's εὔπαις (Herod. 1.32.6) is matched by εὐτεκνία (1099b3), and the misfortunes of being "childless" (b4) or of having one's children turn wicked or

shows little respect for opulence (b1), his paradigms of happiness were quite well off (Herod. 1.30.1, 1.32.2; cf. 1.32.8). Third, far from being "loners" (μονώτης, *EN* 1099b4), all were active and well respected in their communities (b1–4): both Tellos' leading part in the Athenian victory at Eleusis and his public burial show that he enjoyed some eminence, and the athletic victories of the brothers, together with their mother's standing as the Argive priestess of Hera, are signs of prestige and privilege.[20] Finally, Solon includes good looks among the special blessings of good fortune (Herod. 1.32.6; cf. *EN* 1099b3–4), and like splendid Achilles and in contrast with the unsightly Thersites, Cleobis and Biton were admired for their physical grace (Herod. 1.31.2). It would be going beyond the evidence to infer that Aristotle's sketch here is based on Solon or Herodotus, but it clearly reflects the values and worries they express.

If this passage epitomizes traditional views of prosperity, how much of it does Aristotle endorse? Parallels with Solon's ideals do not imply that Aristotle accepts those ideals. Rather, they indicate which elements he finds most compelling. Some of them he clearly considers less important than many people do. Like Solon, who considers greatness positively dangerous (Herod. 1.30.3, 1.32.5–6), Aristotle denies we need the great wealth and power (*EN* 1099b1–2) that loom large in conventional ideals (10.8 1179a3–16). More generally, his concession that we cannot act "*without* resources" (ἀχορήγητον ὄντα, 1099a33) is compatible not only with Solon's "moderate resources" (1179a11; cf. Herod. 1.32.8–9) but also with *few* resources. His entire sketch, in fact, deals largely in contrary extremes: if it is hard to be happy without *any* good fortune (1099b3–5), is it necessary to have *much* or *only* good fortune? Further, although Aristotle evidently agrees that happiness "has *additional* need" (προσδεῖσθαι) of prosperity, the precise nature and extent of this need have yet to be defined: what precisely is necessary and sufficient for happiness, and what criteria govern these conditions? Finally, he presents the

---

die (b5–6) contrast sharply with the good fortune of Tellos who enjoyed, as Solon emphasizes, a host of fine children and grandchildren (Herod. 1.30.4).

20. Chance has preserved the mother's name, Cydippe or "Glory of horses" (Plut. fr. 133 Sandbach), which like Cleobis ("Renown") indicates high status; see Aristophanes *Clouds* 60–67. The significance of the names is all but assured by the extraordinary "Tellos," who both achieved and met the best "end" (see II.ii n1 above).

reputable view itself in qualified terms, both initially (φαίνεται, a31) and at the end (ἔοικε, b6), and in the absence of unequivocal assertion, it remains open to revision.[21] After all, Aristotle has yet to show how, or even whether, his own account harmonizes with the "phenomena" sketched here. In short, the epitome is provisional and needs further analysis and explanation. Aristotle presumably sees some truth in the reasons here given for thinking that happiness needs external goods, but it remains to be seen precisely what the virtuous need and why.

Far from considering these views about external goods definitive, Aristotle claims that they underlie two basic confusions about happiness. First, opposite conclusions can be drawn from them: some infer that prosperity is as good as happiness; others conclude that virtue alone is sufficient (1099b7–8). Obviously, it would be inconsistent for Aristotle to accept both inferences, and he does not. The ensuing discussion of the sources of happiness opens an argument against conflating happiness with prosperity, and he has already dismissed the claim that virtue by itself is sufficient for happiness as something no one would seriously maintain (1.5 1096a1–2, 1.8 1098b31–99a7; cf. 7.13 1153b20–22). Neither extreme conclusion is justified by the evidence so far: the first exaggerates the need for prosperity, and the second exaggerates the power of virtue. Moreover, these antithetical conclusions raise another difficulty, for confusion about fortune underlies questions about the source of happiness.[22] "This is why a puzzle is also raised whether happiness is something learned, habituated, or trained in some other way, or whether it arrives by some divine lot or because of fortune" (1.9 1099b9–11).

If happiness is identical with prosperity, it is subject to fortune continually; if it is identical with virtue, then we need acquire only virtue. So before developing his solution to the problem of prosperity, Aristotle uses other reputable views about the source

21. Contrast the more emphatic assertions made about the two other desiderata: ἐστιν (1098b30), γίγνονται (1099a5–7), ἔστιν (a7), ἐστίν, εἰσίν (a13–15), εἶεν (a21). On the other hand, it would be special pleading to insist that normal usage implies the conclusion (expressed with an infinitive, b6–7) is weaker than the initial formulation (expressed with a participle, a31–32).

22. The subject of the question is happiness, not virtue, as 1099b12 shows; cf. EE 1.1 1214a14–25. Ramsauer (1878) was therefore wrong to excise the second horn of the dilemma at the close of 1.8: the sentence returns to virtue (the first desideratum) in order to introduce a new puzzle about happiness in what follows.

of happiness to prepare the way for his solution. Adapting a question familiar from the opening of Plato's *Meno* (70a), he asks how happiness is attained. But since the first three alternatives reflect a famous debate over the source of virtue and the remaining two reflect the traditional association of fortune with the gods, the question highlights the rival claims of virtue and prosperity, for they center on a more basic contrast between factors within our control (learning, habituation, and training) and factors outside our control (divine dispensation, fortune).[23] But instead of going on to analyze the part played by each factor, Aristotle directs the argument primarily against the external factors. His aim in discussing the *sources* of happiness, then, is to explore the implications of holding that it depends only on *fortune*. By drawing on other traditional assumptions, he finds independent grounds for thinking it depends very little.

First, it was widely believed that the gods have a hand in all significant human affairs: apparently fortuitous events were often attributed to the gods, the prosperous and powerful claimed their high estate as proof of divine favor, and the less fortunate blamed their fates on divine machinations. In fact, it was common practice to ascribe puzzling events to an unknown divinity or *daimon*, and *eudaimonia* was often thought a gift of the gods (cf. the proverb cited at *EN* 9.9 1169b8).[24] Even Platonist teleology contrasts the "necessary fortune" operative in material nature with the special gifts and grace of "divine fortune."[25] But this association of fortune with the gods, though common to popular and philosophical contexts alike, is obscure and imprecise. Aristotle's first move, therefore, is to distinguish an evaluative claim that happiness is "something godlike" (θεῖόν τι) from

23. Sentence structure highlights the dichotomy: πότερόν ἐστι . . . ἢ παραγίνεται; a parallel in the *EE* marks it more clearly: τούτων μὲν . . . δυοῖν δὲ (1.1 1214a21–22). Cf. *Meno* 89a (arguing against nature as the source) and 99e (an appeal to fortune and the divine). For the debate about the origins of virtue, cf. similar questions in *Protag.* 323c, *Clit.* 407b, *de Virt.* 376a, *Dissoi Logoi* 6, Isocrates *Antid.* 187–92, and *EN* 10.9 1179b21. Fortune was often attributed to divine forces, e.g., "the goodwill of the gods, which we call good fortune" (*Rhet. Alex.* 1425a21–22); cf. Thucydides 5.104–5.

24. Dodds (1951: 10–13) observes that δαίμων was typically used to refer to *unidentified* divinities, whence it became associated with "impersonal luck" (23, n65); cf. Burkert 1985: 179–81 and Gallop 1988: 273–90.

25. E.g., *Rep.* 592a; see Berry 1940: esp. chap. 5. Cf. Xenocrates fr. 81 Heinze (incl. *Top.* 2.6 112a36–38) and Heraclitus' celebrated remark that "character is a human's *daimon*" (B119 DK).

the specifically causal claim, readily conflated with it, that it is
"god-given" (θεόσδοτον, 1099b11–18). Calling something "a gift
of the gods" was a token of the highest commendation, since
their favor was thought to signal special *merit* (cf. 1.12 1101b18–
31). That is why it is "reasonable" to call happiness "god-given,"
especially when it is "best of human things" (1099b12–13). But in
fact, not all who prosper deserve their estate; if the gods actually
dispense happiness, then they, not those they favor, seem responsible for happiness. So while dismissing questions about the
causal role of the gods as extraneous to his topic (b13–14), Aristotle sees some truth on both sides: "Even if it is not *god-sent* but
comes about because of virtue and some learning or training, it is
apparently among the most *godlike* things" (b14–16). Far from sig-
nifying religious skepticism, this distinction paves the way for
arguing later that the wise *are* "most beloved of the gods" (10.8
1179a23–32). Analysis thus enables Aristotle to reconcile his account with traditional views by isolating the unexceptionable
claim that happiness is something *worthy* of the gods: "The prize
of virtue is apparently both the best end and something godlike
and blessed [μακάριον]" (1099b16–18; cf. 1.12 1101b18–27). Or as
he argues elsewhere, since the gods are the best of beings, they
would surely favor only those who deserve to be favored; it
would be "absurd" to suppose they give indiscriminately instead
of benefiting only "the best and most intelligent" (*EE* 8.2
1247a28–29).

Aristotle draws another conclusion from the "godlike" nature
of happiness: if happiness rests primarily on virtue, then "it must
be shared by many [πολύκοινον], for it can be attained by all who
are not thoroughly maimed with regard to virtue [τοῖς μὴ πε-
πηρωμένοις πρὸς ἀρετήν]," provided they receive due care and
learn how to live (*EN* 1.9 1099b18–20).[26] By contrast, if happiness
depends only or primarily on fortune or the gods, then most
would have "little hope" of achieving it (*EE* 1.3 1215a11–15). But

26. Although this claim mentions neither gods nor fortune, it relates to both,
as the parallel discussion in the *EE* shows (1.3 1215a8–19; note κοινότερον, a16,
17). Aristotle's claim is worth emphasizing: if virtue is the basis for happiness, it
is possible for *all* normally endowed people to be happy (although it is not necessarily *easy*; cf. 2.9 1109a24–30). Nussbaum (1986: 320–22) emphasizes that this
is an appeal to reputable views (but I fail to see the refutation of determinism she
detects in it; cf. Cooper 1988: 555–56).

on Aristotle's account, even "the many" who can trace no divine heritage and who lack the exceptional talents traditionally viewed as gifts of the gods need not despair, for virtue is something we can achieve for ourselves. In addition to making happiness "shared by more" (a15–18), this account also makes it "more godlike" by making it depend on the character of people's lives and actions (a18–19). The power to influence events and do largely as one wishes was widely considered distinctive of the divine; so virtue has a better claim to dominate happiness if virtue is also something godlike. The life of the gods, then, confirms the primacy of virtue, for they enjoy happiness "not because of any external goods, but because of themselves and by being the way they are in their nature [τῷ ποιός τις εἶναι τὴν φύσιν]" (*Pol.* 7.1 1323b23–26). Provided human happiness is analogous, it must also depend on the way we live and behave, not on fortune or the gods, and popular usage, which expresses the supreme value of happiness by calling it *eudaimonia*, is vindicated on Aristotle's account.

A related reputable view can also be confirmed on this account: the world will be better off if virtue is the basis for happiness. If it is "better" for happiness to result from our own efforts than from fortune, then it is only "reasonable" that it does (*EN* 1.9 1099b20–21). This is more than casual optimism about human capacities, for Aristotle bases his claim also on two general teleological principles: first, most natural causes tend toward order, and second, human art and reason generally supplement the natural order (b21–23). If the regular order of nature is enhanced by arts, which are productive skills whose ends are products beyond the activity of each skill, it should be enhanced even more regularly by "the best cause" (b22–23), nonproductive reason, whose ends are internal to the exercise of reason. So natural teleology is preserved if happiness consists in rational activity, as Aristotle holds. By contrast, when it is "the greatest and finest thing" that anyone can attain, it would be simply "too discordant" to leave it solely up to fortune (b24–25). Rather, it deserves to be ascribed to the better and more regular causes of nature and reason. Indeed, if happiness follows from its causes as regularly as Aristotle's account implies, then it could not depend on fortune, which by definition applies only to *irregular* events.[27] The irregularity of fortune, in fact, explains the popular view that prosperity is "unstable" (ἀβέβαιον): anything irregular is unstable, and since "prosperity" (εὐτυχία) is simply "good fortune" (ἀγαθὴ τύχη) of some magnitude or importance, it cannot be expected to last (*Phys.* 2.5 197a25–32).

None of these considerations is conclusive. Proof, however, is not their aim. Rather, they are part of the test of tradition that shows how Aristotle's account squares with reputable views. Although he says little to substantiate those beliefs and many of them remain in need of analysis and revision, his survey does help confirm his account. Not only does it show how his account preserves and explains some truth in traditional beliefs about fortune, but it also shows how the claim that prosperity is the dominant factor in happiness conflicts with widely accepted beliefs about the gods and the natural world. The precise relation between happiness and prosperity is still to be explained, and the fundamental problem of the stability of happiness also has to be examined. But before we turn to those topics and Aristotle's refutation of Solon's views about prosperity, his analysis of fortune itself deserves a look, for it reveals why fortune seems so important to so many.

The epitome of traditional views ended on the horns of a dilemma: some equate prosperity and happiness; others equate virtue and happiness. Aristotle denies both claims. The second he dismisses as merely a debater's thesis (*EN* 1.5 1096a2). The first, however, is a very popular opinion, and the frequency with which he addresses this conflation of *eudaimonia* and *eutuchia* shows how seriously he takes it. In a summary sketch in the *Politics*, for example, he cites the life of the gods to confirm that "prosperity is necessarily different from happiness" since the gods enjoy a blessed existence by virtue of their excellent nature rather than fortune (*Pol.* 7.1 1323b23–29). Again, while analyzing the role of pleasure in a good life, he explains the conflation as an inference from the view that happiness has "additional need" for fortune (*EN* 7.13 1153b21–23). Although this shows that *some*

27. See *Phys.* 2.5 196b10–17; cf. an application to happiness at *EE* 8.2 1247a31–39, b9–15, and for conventional notions, see *Rhet.* 1.10 1369a32–b16. On the relation between chance, necessity, and purpose in Aristotle's theory of nature, see Sorabji 1980: 143–81, esp. 178–80.

prosperity is necessary for happiness, he denies that they are identical on the grounds that excessive prosperity actually hinders happiness (b23–25). Aristotle attributes this popular misconception to that handy scapegoat, "the many" (*EE* 1.1 1214a24–25, *MM* 2.8 1206b31).[28] Impressed by tales from myth and history of the eminent and happy made miserable by misfortune, many people naturally singled out the contribution of good fortune and prosperity. But as the argument about pleasure indicates, this exaggerates the need for prosperity and neglects the importance of other factors. Even if the virtuous cannot be happy without *some* favor from fortune, it does not follow that they need *much* favor or that anyone could be happy by its favor *alone*. In short, the necessity of prosperity entails neither its primacy nor its sufficiency. Yet as Aristotle observes at the close of his epitome, this is precisely the mistake that many make: "Happiness evidently has additional need of this sort of flourishing; *and that is why* some people rank prosperity the same as happiness" (*EN* 1.8 1099b6–8; cf. 7.13 1153b21–22 and *EE* 8.2 1246b37–47a2).[29]

Aristotle suggests a deeper explanation for this misconception when he analyzes the concept of fortune. There he cites the view that prosperity is "the same or nearly the same" as happiness to support a distinction he draws between fortune (τύχη) and chance (τὸ αὐτόματον). First, a word about context. Aristotle presents his analysis to answer doubts about the very existence of fortune (*Phys.* 2.4). His solution, which is to mark its domain more precisely, rests on three contrasts. The first concerns regularity: whereas some effects follow their antecedent causes always and "out of necessity," and others follow their causes "usually," what occurs "by fortune" is unusual (2.5 196b10–17). Here the point is not that fortunate events are infrequent, either as types or tokens; rather, however frequently they occur, events can be ascribed to fortune only if the link between cause and effect is "not usual." In short, nothing that occurs by fortune has a

---

28. Aristotle reports but does not endorse: "some think" (but "it is not in fact," *EN*), "many say" (*EE*), and "the many suppose" (*MM*).

29. In the last passage (the text is corrupt, as Dirlmeier 1962 notes; Woods 1982 misreports the mss.), Aristotle argues that "not only does *wisdom* produce doing well and virtue, but we say that the prosperous also do well, on the grounds that *prosperity* too produces doing well." This means only that prosperity contributes to a good life, not that it is sufficient; Aristotle denies the sufficiency of any single factor without denying that more than one is necessary.

regular cause. However, this is a necessary condition for fortune, not a sufficient condition, since some unusual events result "from nature" or "from thought" (b19–21). So a second contrast is needed to isolate what happens by fortune. Aristotle invokes teleology: nature and thought embrace causes that are directed in some way at their effects, but fortune is invoked when the cause is not directed at its effect. Or in Aristotle's terms, the causes of what happens from nature or thought operate "for the sake of" those effects, whereas what happens by fortune occurs "by coincidence" (b17–24).[30] That is not to say that events ascribed to fortune have no causes at all; on the contrary, they must have some causes since no events are wholly uncaused. Aristotle's point is simply that the causes of fortuitous events are directed at *other* ends: to ascribe an event to fortune is to deny that its cause or causes operate "for *its* sake" or with *it* as an end. Infrequent or "unusual" events are ascribed to nature or thought if they result from natural or mental processes directed at them as ends. Conversely, even a frequent occurrence can be ascribed to fortune if its causes are directed not at it but at other ends.

The third contrast brings us back to the problem of prosperity. Aristotle cites the conflation with happiness to distinguish fortune from chance, which turns out to be its genus; or as he puts it, chance "covers more" (2.6 197a36).

Everything from fortune is from chance, but not vice versa. For fortune and what is from fortune are found where prospering [εὐτυχῆσαι] and action [πρᾶξις] in general might be found. Therefore, it is also necessary that fortune involve things done [τὰ πρακτά]. A sign of this is the belief that prosperity [εὐτυχία] is the same or nearly the same as happiness, whereas happiness is a kind of action since it is doing well [εὐπραξία]. So any who cannot act cannot do anything from fortune either.

(a36–b6)[31]

30. Ascribing an event to fortune, in short, denies that it has a final cause; see Balme 1939: 135–38 and idem 1987. That does not imply that *no* final causes were at work, but only that all operative final causes had *other* ends. Fortuitous events can have any number of causes, even regular causes, provided their intersection or conjunction is irregular. Further, since this intersection is itself an actual event, many modern accounts would count fortune as a genuine cause, not simply an explanation; cf. Charles 1984: 47.

31. Since Aristotle cites the conflation of prosperity and happiness to support his distinction between fortune and chance, he may seem to endorse it. In fact, all his argument requires is that prosperity be found only among those who *could* be happy—not that all or only those who prosper *are* happy—for it rests on three premises: only those who act *can* be happy (197b5), only those who can be happy *can* prosper (b4), and only those who can prosper *can* experience fortune (b1–2).

Everything said so far about fortune applies equally to chance: chance events are neither usual nor the ends for which their causes operated. Like fortune, chance does not imply the absence of causes, even of final causes. On the contrary, chance events presuppose the operation of some final causes, although none that have those results as their end. Or as Aristotle puts it, chance is found "among things that occur unconditionally for the sake of *something*, whenever things that have an external cause occur *not for the sake of what results*" (b18–20). As the term suggests, what happens by chance (αὐτόματος) is "pointless" (μάτην) in that it is not the end for which its causes operated (b22–31).[32] It is caused, although only as a coincidental byproduct of causal chains directed at other ends. When a stool falls upright ready for sitting, Aristotle observes, "we say" that it fell that way "by chance" because it did not fall *in order* to be sat upon, although its falling into that position did have *some* cause (b16–18). What marks off fortune as a special form of chance, then, is not whether or not an event is caused; neither implies causal indeterminacy. Rather, since fortune is restricted to chance events in the sphere of human action and "things done" (b1–6), fortune implies a distinctive kind of cause and a distinctive kind of result. Or as Aristotle puts it in his definition, fortune is "an explanation by coincidence of things for the sake of something that accord with deliberate choice [ἐν τοῖς κατὰ προαίρεσιν τῶν ἕνεκά του]" (2.5 197a5–6).[33] The formulation is obscure, but the connection with deliberate action is not. And as a later comment shows, it implies two things: first, events are ascribed to fortune only when they occur to people who act from choice; second, the outcome must involve things in which they have some interest

32. See I.i n33 above.

33. For the sense of "explanation by coincidence" (αἰτία κατὰ συμβεβηκός), see Sorabji 1980: chap. 1. Aristotle's notion is parasitic on his notion of coincidental attributes: when a builder is "coincidentally" a musician, we can give a "coincidental" explanation of his building a house by saying a musician built it, although the strict ("by itself") explanation would refer to him as a builder (196b24–29). Since a coincidence is not itself caused, it can be explained only as the "coincidental" outcome of caused events. Suppose a man is killed "coincidentally" by bandits at a well (i.e., they did not go there *in order* to kill him); we can explain both why the bandits went there and why their victim did, but we call his death a "coincidence" because it results from the conjunction of two independent causal chains. My account conflicts verbally with Sorabji's conclusion that coincidences have no cause, but the difference (which stems from Aristotle's preference for specifying the "by itself" cause, something coincidences lack) is immaterial, since Sorabji allows that they are necessitated.

(b20–22; cf. b7–13).[34] If a stool falls and lands upright beside someone who wants to sit down, then this chance event is at the same time a case of fortune, provided the result is something the person wants and might have chosen to do. In short, fortune occurs only to people and only when something they would choose to do or avoid results. Unearthing someone's horde in a garden, to take a famous case, is a case of fortune only if the horde is deemed valuable.[35]

Aristotle's own example clarifies his account. A man goes to market, unexpectedly meets someone who owes him money, and gets repaid (2.4 196a3–5). His trip certainly has a cause— namely, his wanting to go to market (a4–5)—but provided he goes not because he intends to find his debtor, but for some other reason ("the possibilities are limitless: to find someone else, to go to court, or to see a play," 2.5 197a15–18), then their meeting happens both by chance and "from fortune." This is a case of fortune for two reasons: the man acts deliberately; and he "values" the end he happens to achieve, recovering the debt (196a4). Although his getting repaid is not itself a deliberate action, it results from deliberate action because he was acting for other reasons. Or in Aristotle's terms, getting repaid "coincides" with his intended action (b35). Hence, the encounter results from thought and choice (197a1–3, 6–8), although not from any thought about the encounter or from any attempt to recover the debt (a3–5). Moreover, the result is something the man would have deliberately pursued if he had expected to find his debtor. Since he "would have gone if he had known" (196b33–34), the encounter is also something he wanted; he did not *go* to meet his debtor, but he did *want* to meet him. Getting repaid is a chance event, but it is also a fortunate one, because it is coincident upon the man's deliberate actions and achieves an end he wanted.

To generalize, fortune occurs whenever the chance results of

34. The phrase is obscure, but I take it to mean that the outcome must occur to "people who exercise decision" (τοῖς ἔχουσιν προαίρεσιν), and it must be "something they would decide" to seek or avoid (τῶν προαιρετῶν), although their actions at the given time do not result from any such decision.

35. Recall the etymology of τύχη from n16 above. In an age when a hole in the ground was often the safest depository, this example flourished: see *EN* 3.3 1112a27, *Rhet.* 1.5 1362a8–9, *Met.* Δ.30 1025a16–19, and Aristophanes *Birds* 599– 602; cf. Davies 1981: 39 n3, noting that we know of seven comedies entitled *Thesaurus.* See the illumination in a 15th-century ms. of Boethius, reproduced as the frontispiece to Sorabji 1980.

our action fulfill or frustrate our desires. In fact, this is what determines whether fortune (τύχη) is good or bad, as well as whether it qualifies as prosperity or misfortune. If the chance result of an action is good, we call it "good fortune" (ἀγαθὴ τύχη); if it is bad, we call it "bad fortune" (197a25–26). When the result is an important or "great" good, we call it "prosperity" (εὐτυχία); when a great ill, "misfortune" (δυστυχία) (a26–30). But if fortune involves what we do and want, and if prosperity is the fulfillment of valued ends whereas misfortune is their denial, then all are extremely important for ethics and happiness. Hence, the intimate connection fortune has with action and desire provides a deeper explanation for popular confusions about happiness and prosperity. Although Aristotle considers the conflation a mistake, his analysis of fortune shows that it stems from a genuine and serious worry. If the major ends of human life are heavily subject to fortune, then a good life also depends heavily on fortune; if our major ends result only "coincidentally" from our actions, then deliberate action itself seems pointless from the perspective of happiness. Fortune, in short, is important for human life. The question is how important. Are the most important ends subject to fortune, or can they be regularly attained and reliably retained by deliberate virtuous activity? In particular, what ends do the virtuous value most, and what effect does fortune have on their pursuit of those ends?

A Complete Life

TRADITIONAL views, by exaggerating both the value of prosperity and the dangers of misfortune, subject the good life to the play of fortune. It is hardly surprising, then, that views about fortune dominate the survey of reputable views Aristotle uses to test and refine his own account. Indeed, after sketching some of the reasons behind those views, he raises the problem of fortune in an especially acute form: if the great heroes of legend can end in misery, what chance of happiness can the less fortunate have? This worry, which pervades archaic poetry, leads Aristotle to an extended discussion of Solon's dictum about seeing the end. Although he refutes the saying as it stands, his analysis shows that it holds some truth. After all, epic and tragedy are not the only places where great men fall from the height of prosperity; faced with the tales of catastrophe in Greek history itself, one might well conclude that human life is prey to such ills that the living can never be secure enough to warrant being called happy.

For many reversals and all sorts of fortunes occur in life, and it is possible for the most flourishing person to fall upon great disasters late in life, as the tales in the Trojan cycle tell of Priam. No one calls happy anyone who has undergone fortunes of that sort and come to a miserable end. So should no other human beings at all be considered happy so long as they are alive, and ought one to see the end, as Solon says?

(*EN* 1.9 1100a5–11)[1]

1. Aristotle's response to Solon is also discussed in Irwin 1985d. Irwin's analysis is acute and especially helpful on the relation between virtue and happiness. But more needs to be said about the elenctic nature of Aristotle's response and about his notion of "complete virtue."

The example of the legendary lord of Troy has no point here unless his previous life was happy. No vain Eastern potentate like Croesus, Priam is a paradigm of undeserved misfortune. His stature and station had seemed to make his life as secure as any, and certainly as prosperous. Yet after presiding over his city through ten long years of devastating war, after watching the slow and inexorable ruin of his family, he was impiously butchered on an altar as his home was sacked and the few surviving members of his family were slaughtered or enslaved.[2] However, the rare, perhaps unique severity of his misfortune is not enough to support a general claim about all human lives, and in the absence of further reasons, it would be a mistake to infer that "no one else" (a10) can be happy before his or her end. Hence, one problem with Solon's view, as Aristotle suggests, is that it gives too much weight to extreme cases: few are ever exposed to such great loss because few have so much to lose.[3] Still, there is a genuine worry here. If misfortune has as much sway over human life as Solon's remark implies, if it can wreck even Priam's life, then *a fortiori* it can affect the less powerful too. And if it is only by escaping the influence of fortune entirely that anyone can be secure enough to be happy, Solon may be right to conclude that only the dead should be counted as happy, for only they are beyond the reach of fortune.

As Aristotle points out, this conclusion can be taken in more than one way. Does Solon mean that we can be happy only after we die? But what removes the dead from the reach of fortune? So Aristotle uses the fortunes of the dead to show how absurd it would be to think total invulnerability a prerequisite for happiness.

And if indeed we should accept this claim, is one happy after he dies? But this is utterly absurd, especially for those of us who say happiness is a kind of activity. If we don't say a dead man is happy—and Solon didn't mean this, but that someone might securely consider a person su-

2. The extant Homer has nothing to say of Priam's end, but his misery is vividly portrayed in his efforts in *Il.* 24 to bury his dearest son, Hector. The story was quite familiar, a subject of epic and drama as well as a favorite motif in painting. For the literary evidence, see Austin 1964 on Vergil's celebrated account (esp. *Aen.* 2.506–58), and for the pictorial evidence, see Wiencke 1954. The surviving evidence presents Priam predominantly as a good king, pious and just, whose fall was precipitated by forces beyond his control; it resists facile moralizing about his failure to raise Paris well, for example, and does not see his downfall as retribution for past sins.

3. Rare exceptions can leave a general rule intact; cf. I.ii *n*23 above.

premely happy at that time, since he is by then beyond suffering and misfortune—still there is a real problem here, since it is thought that there is both some good and some bad for the dead, provided those things can occur also to the living when they are unaware: honors and dishonors, for example, and both successes [εὐπραξίαι] and misfortunes of their children and other descendants.   (1.10 1100a11–21)

First, Solon did not mean that only the dead are happy. After all, they can hardly lead a good life when they lead no life at all, as Aristotle's account explains: happiness consists in virtuous activity, and even if the dead survive in some Hades, they are no longer active in the requisite ways (a13–14).[4] Moreover, if the dead simply migrate to Hades, as legend commonly had it, then they are still subject to fortune. For if they can still learn about the world above, then death secures only their own safety but leaves them vulnerable both in the posthumous fate of their deeds and reputation and in the impact of fortune on others they hold dear (a20–21). The wraiths of Achilles and Agamemnon, for example, can rejoice to hear of the exploits of their sons (*Od.* 11 and 24), but others can only grieve over their posterity. When Hector gives his life to save his family and city, it must matter to him in Hades whether Troy falls and whether he wins his meed of glory. The problem stems not only from the epic hero's worry about dying in obscurity—a worry felt by others too—but also from the belief that fortune can affect the lives of the living even without their being aware of it (*EN* 1100a18–21). Had Priam left Troy before the Achaean attack, it is not at all clear that he could have remained happy simply by remaining ignorant of his city's fate. And if ignorance of serious misfortune is not enough to keep the living happy, it is not clear why it should protect the dead from fortune either. So even if the dead are unaware of anything after they die, as Aristotle is inclined to believe, they will still be subject to fortune.[5] Hence, the question is not whether fortune affects us before or after our death, but whether it ever affects us enough to make a difference in happiness.

Aristotle insists that "it appears too unkind [ἄφιλον] and contrary to people's views to say that the fortunes of our descendants

4. This consequence is quite strong, for it conflicts not only with ancient hopes for an afterlife in the Elysian fields or on the Isles of the Blessed but quite generally with most beliefs in a happy afterlife, be it heaven, nirvana, or most anything else.

5. See Furley 1986: esp. 85–91.

and friends contribute nothing at all" (1.11 1101a22–24; cf. 1100a29–30). But he also argues that their influence on us after death is "slight and small" (1101b2–3) and that fortune never makes the dead happy or deprives them of any happiness they had while alive (b1–9). He bases this conclusion on his argument that fortune rarely makes a difference either way for happiness (a28–34, referring back to the argument of 1.10), so it would be circular to invoke his views about the happiness of the dead first. But he does use the case of the dead to show that Solon's dictum undermines his assumption that happiness is sometimes possible: if the happiness of the dead could be affected by the fortunes of the living, then the changing fortunes of successive generations would leave the dead swinging in and out of happiness time and again (1100a21–27). Happiness would never be stable, and Solon could never call anyone happy (a27–29). To avoid this absurdity, however, Solon need only concede that the fate of the things people care about is not always decisive for their happiness, either before or after they die. Fortune may have some influence on the dead as well as the living, but Solon's own claims about Tellos and the Argive brothers imply that some people overcome fortune and that external events do not always affect happiness either for the dead or for the living. But then why wait until people die before calling them happy?

This raises the possibility that Solon's worry rests on epistemological problems. If he agrees that only the living can be happy, his refusal to call anyone happy before they die suggests a demand for certainty. The living, Solon may have thought, remain subject to disaster; if disaster is enough to wreck happiness, then it may be wise to suspend judgment until they die.[6] But this caution has its problems.

If indeed we must see the end and only then call people happy, not because they are at the time, but because they were before, then isn't it absurd if (1) when they *are* happy, what does belong to them will not be said truly of them, simply because (5) we do not want to call the living happy because of (2) the reversals they undergo, and because we believe that (3) happiness is something lasting and not at all liable to change, whereas (2) the same people's fortunes turn round many times [ἀνακυ-

6. Aristotle's formulation emphasizes the observer and speaks not of people "*being* happy," but of anyone "*considering*" them so (εὐδαιμονιστέον, a10, b1; μακαρίσειεν, a16, a33). His reference to judging "securely" (ἀσφαλῶς, a16) has the same focus.

κλεῖσθαι]?[7] For it is clear that if (4) we follow a man's fortunes exactly, we will call the same man first happy, then miserable, again and again.

(1.10 1100a32–b6)

Solon thought "secure" claims about the happiness of the living impossible. In response, Aristotle argues that they are possible on the grounds that reliable judgments do not have to be certain. We can call the living happy, in short, because certainty is not necessary for knowledge. Even if happiness must be permanent, we do not have to "see the end" because the claim that someone is happy can be true even when it remains subject to future contingencies. True predictions are made about other things; Solon himself commends human expertise in a number of areas subject to contingency (fr. 13.49–62). The burden therefore lies on Solon to show how happiness is different and why calling people happy should require certainty. As it stands, his view rests on a fallacy, which schematic formulation makes apparent.

2. The living are subject to misfortune (*EN* 1100b1).
5. So the living cannot be called happy (a33).

But (5) does not follow from (2) without a further assumption:

4. People subject to misfortune cannot be called happy (cf. b4–6).

Solon claims that human vulnerability and the likelihood of misfortune make *certainty* about happiness impossible. But he assumes that the possibility of false claims about happiness makes *secure judgment* about the living impossible. To bolster this assumption, Solon could claim that reversals are inevitable. Error then would also be inevitable because every ascription of happiness would turn out false in the end. But that is implausible. Solon is rightly skeptical of some people's claims to happiness. But reversal, however likely, is not inevitable. Solon himself allows that Tellos and the Argive brothers can be called happy at the end of their lives. If they are no longer subject to fortune then, why not push the threshold back earlier? Why should the mere possibility of reversal rule out "secure" judgment?

Solon's worry about happiness trades on the uncertainty in

7. A similar allusion to the wheel of fortune occurs in Herodotus' Lydian narrative: to deter Cyrus from repeating his own mistake of crossing a river to expand his empire, Croesus cites "the cycle of human affairs" (1.207.2); cf. 1.5.4, 7.49.3, 7.50.2.

predicting continued prosperity to infer that we cannot know about present happiness. To be sure, it is often hard to tell whether people are happy, let alone whether their happiness will last. Croesus thought he was secure, but time would show that he was not. Or as Solon's maxim had it, "Rule shows the man"; people who flourish in a private station often collapse when raised to positions of power. But the difficulty of knowing about others' lives is not the root of his worry. On the contrary, his view assumes that we generally can know enough about their affairs to call some people happy when their lives are over. So his worry seems to be that no matter how secure anyone's life may seem, it is all but sure to change in decisive ways. To this Aristotle rejoins that someone whose life does not change decisively could have been called happy earlier (1100a34–35). More precisely, if we call people happy on the basis of how they live, then we can call them happy during their lives as well. Predicting the weather can be as hazardous as predicting continued prosperity. But if it is true to say at the end of the day that the weather *was* fine, then it is also true during the day to say that it *is* fine. Clouds on the horizon counsel caution but invalidate our predictions only if they precipitate significant change. A single swallow, Aristotle warns, does not show winter is over (1.7 1098a18–19). The moral, however, is not to discount the proverbial harbinger of spring or to wait for all the swallows to return. Error is always possible, but it is caution enough to be wary of hasty or premature judgment. Likewise, little is gained by waiting to "see the end" before venturing to call people happy. Only death eliminates all chance of reversal. But if certainty is unnecessary, it is enough to recognize that a period of prosperity is not a sure sign of happiness. When good fortune persists and virtues prove secure, then even Solon should be willing to call people happy before their end.

Solon's skepticism about happiness stems in part from problems in statements about the future. Aristotle does not explore these puzzles in connection with Solon, but it is clear from his discussion of "tomorrow's sea battle" (*de Int.* 9) that he was aware of the potential for confusion on this topic. One worry he addresses is that all events would be necessary if singular statements about the future are true.[8] If Plato is pale now, for example,

8. The passage is one of the most controversial in Aristotle's corpus, in part because it briefly discusses determinism. But the details of interpretation are not

then it was true to say earlier that he would be pale (18b9–11). But if it was always true to say he would be pale, then his pallor risks being necessary, on the principle that eternal truths are necessary (b11–16). In the course of defusing this contention, Aristotle insists that the truth of statements depends on the way the world is—the "situation," as he calls it (18b36–39, 19a33)—not vice versa. In particular, although it is logically necessary that Plato is pale if it is true to call him pale, his pallor is not causally necessary because our calling him pale does not make him pale. More generally, the logical necessity of consequence does not by itself entail any necessity for the consequent, in this or any other case. A sea battle tomorrow, for example, entails that today's predictions of the battle turn out true. But true predictions do not make any battle inevitable. Battles are rather what make predictions of them true.

Few if any events on earth happen "from unconditional necessity," and "things about to happen" (τὰ μέλλοντα, 18a33) do not always transpire (19a7–22).[9] That is one reason why we cannot be *certain* about what will happen in the near or distant future. But the presence of contingency does not make *true* predictions impossible, since truth depends on what happens, not on when we speak. Events tomorrow determine the truth of today's predictions, but no statements determine those events. In the same way, past events govern the truth of today's talk about the past, not vice versa. The situation is the same for happiness: people's lives determine the truth of talk about their happiness, be it past, present, or future. If it is now or ever true that someone *was* happy, then it was also true earlier and we could have said so then. If Solon can call people happy after their death, it is not because only then do they attain any happiness; that would be "absurd" (1100a13–15, a33). Rather, what underwrites the truth in obituaries is the way we live. Since we can be called happy after death only if we were so before (a34), earlier claims about our happiness can be true as well.[10]

---

important for my purposes. For a thorough discussion and recent bibliography, see D. Frede 1985.

9. On the peculiar modality of "what is about to happen," see the discussion of hypothetical necessity in sublunary events in *Gen. Cor.* 2.11 337b3–9, and the meteorological examples in *de Div.* 463b22–29.

10. This confirms a suggestion of Irwin's (1985d: 104 n22).

In his view of happiness, Solon seems to have succumbed to a belief that pervades early Greek thought, the belief that knowledge requires certainty.[11] In part this rests on a failure to distinguish the true and undisputed principle that knowledge implies truth from the highly questionable thesis that only necessary truths can be known. But in the context of archaic pessimism, the demand for epistemic certainty acquires added force. On the other hand, few if any people abide by this demand for proof in their ethical reflections, much less in their daily lives. Even Solon, who thinks misfortune is virtually certain to strike us all, adopts weaker standards for knowledge about happiness. In refuting his dictum, then, Aristotle upholds the more reputable and reasonable view: although we cannot be certain how people will conduct themselves or how their fortunes will fare, we can still make reliable judgments about many. To be sure, our claims are sometimes defeated, and events sometimes prove us wrong. But events can equally prove us right and our evidence sound, and in that case, we may reasonably claim to know. In this respect, then, Solon's reliance on exceptional cases proves misguided. The vulnerability he ascribes to Croesus is extraordinary and supports only his doubts about *Croesus* (Herod. 1.32.5). It does not license his generalization that we can never know whether *anyone living* is happy, since few are so vulnerable to fortune.

This analysis does not resolve Solon's worry, but it does pinpoint its source. The problem behind the epistemological confusion, as Aristotle goes on to show, centers on the role of fortune in human life. If (2) human fortunes are as unstable as Solon implies (*EN* 1.10 1100b1, b3–4) and (3) happiness is extremely stable (b2–3), then (5) it would be wise to wait and see whether prosperity endures before calling someone happy (a33). Even if we got away with calling some people happy before their end, the extreme mutability of human affairs would ensure that most of our claims would end up false. However, Aristotle refutes Solon's conclusion by eliciting the two assumptions behind it—(2) and (3)—and then showing that it does not follow without a further premise—(4). Solon's assumptions entail that mutability rules out happiness *only if* fortune has a decisive effect on happiness.

11. For the influence of this "Eleatic" view of knowledge, see Barnes 1982: 136–51; cf. Vlastos 1985: esp. 17–18.

But since Solon's conclusion is so implausible, Aristotle argues, we have good reason to reject the missing assumption. Hence, given the expressed premises (2) and (3), it follows that happiness is *less dependent* on fortune than Solon supposed. In short, the paradox involved in "seeing the end" yields an argument for modifying its basis, Solon's view of happiness. In the end, his claims help confirm that virtuous activity controls happiness.

It is clear that if (4) we follow a man's fortunes exactly, we will call the same man first happy, then miserable, again and again—representing the happy man as a sort of "chameleon and based on shoddy foundations." Or is following fortunes closely not at all correct? For living well or badly does not depend on them; rather, as we said, human life has additional need of them, whereas the activities of virtue are sovereign over happiness and the contrary activities sovereign over the contrary condition. (1.10 1100b4–11).

As Aristotle reconstructs Solon's argument, it centers on three premises, the explicit claims (2) and (3), together with a missing assumption (4) that misfortune is sure to ruin happiness. His refutation simply invokes the further premise (1), implied by Solon's assessment of Tellos and sustained by the preceding analysis (a13–17, a33–34), that some people attain happiness.[12] The argument can be filled out as follows.

1. Some of the living lead happy lives (a34).
2. But all of the living are subject to fortune (b1, b3–4).
3. And happiness is not liable to change (b2–3).
4. And anything subject to fortune is liable to change (b4–7).
5. So the living cannot be happy (a33).[13]

In addition to being paradoxical, Solon's conclusion is inconsistent with his view that some people have happy lives: his infer-

---

12. Herodotus has Solon report that the Argives "blessed" (ἐμακάριζον, 1.31.3) the brothers for their strength. When he says that "no mortal is blessed [μάκαρ]" (fr. 14), his point is probably that no humans attain a life like that of the gods; see II.i n2 above.

13. On the elenctic form of this argument (proving the negation of a thesis), see I.ii above. It could be schematized differently to draw out the related assumption that vulnerability to misfortune is incompatible with happiness.

1.* Some who are alive are happy.
2.* But everyone alive is vulnerable to misfortune.
3.* No one vulnerable to losing happiness is happy.
4.* Everyone vulnerable to misfortune is vulnerable to losing happiness.
5.* So anyone who is alive is not happy.

ence (5) from premises (2) and (3) contradicts his own hypothesis (1). But his premises do not by themselves yield a valid argument, since his conclusion follows only on the additional assumption (4), itself rather dubious. If the conclusion is unacceptable but his expressed premises are true, then the implicit premise can be rejected. Rather, it must be modified: things can be subject to fortune without being liable to change. In particular, happiness can be stable even if subject to fortune, though less stable perhaps than Solon thought.

Although Aristotle refutes Solon's dictum, his analysis explains its attraction by isolating two plausible premises behind it. But by isolating the further premise needed to establish Solon's view, he also shows that it rests on two related confusions: one mistakes possibility for probability; the other conflates happiness with prosperity. First, Solon is wrong to equate being susceptible to misfortune with being prone to misfortune. Only the latter implies instability, and life can be secure without being invulnerable. Even a fragile vase can endure for ages. Despite the image evoked by Solon when he says that "god shows many people some happiness only to overturn them from the roots" (Herod. 1.32.9; cf. 7.10.5 and Solon frs. 9 and 13.11–28), lofty trees are more exposed to storms, but some also have the strength to withstand great force. If the roots of human happiness run deep like those of an oak, then it can be sturdy and stable, and we can live a good life even while exposed to fortune—even though we can never be invulnerable or immune to loss. Second, the missing premise also trades on confusion about what is subject to change, prosperity or happiness. Solon implicitly relies on the instability of the former to infer instability for the latter: he thinks happiness is liable to change because he thinks it depends on fortune and that is liable to change. But if happiness depends primarily on character and virtue, then it is as secure as virtuous character; if that is secure against most fortune, then happiness is so too. The virtuous will still encounter misfortune, but their happiness will often be able to endure. The decisive error behind Solon's paradox thus stems from his equating happiness with sustained prosperity, and the implausibility of his dictum helps refute that misconception.

Solon's view of happiness contradicts his own view that some people attain it. But this inconsistency leads Aristotle to modify, not to reject Solon's account, for properly interpreted, his reputable views capture some truth. To start with premise (2), Solon simply overstates the dangers of human life: although little in human life is *invulnerable* to fortune, few people are *vulnerable* to it. Everyone is *susceptible* to misfortune, and most suffer *some* undeserved or unfortunate loss, but few are *prone* to major loss, much less to *devastating* loss. The exceptional case of Priam shows that great disaster ruins *some* lives, but not that it is *likely* to ruin our lives or that it does ruin *all or most*. Likewise for premise (3). Solon demands too much of happiness: few would deny that happiness is *enduring*, but it need not be *permanent* to avoid being ephemeral. Aristotle maintains "our intuition that happiness is something *hard* to take away" (δυσαφαίρετον, *EN* 1.5 1095b26), but not the demand that it "*cannot* be taken away" (ἀναφαίρετον). He considers it enough to show why happiness is "lasting" (μόνιμον, 1100b2, b14–15) and "stable" (βέβαιον, b13), instead of "easily reversed" (εὐμετάβολον, b3, 1101a9). In short, he locates it *between* the extremes of vulnerability and invulnerability, though much nearer the latter.

Solon's view gets its force by overstating some common and reasonable beliefs. But once those beliefs are clarified and made more precise, it no longer follows that happiness is as fickle as fortune. In particular, the danger of misfortune ruining a life is greatly reduced if the concerns that are most important for happiness turn out to be least subject to fortune. If Aristotle can show how "virtuous activities are sovereign over happiness" (1100b9–10) and that they are the most stable thing in human life (b12–16), as Solon also held (fr. 15, cf. fr. 4), then he can revise the missing assumption (4) and claim instead that happiness is stable even without being invulnerable to misfortune.[14] Although Solon's assumptions capture some truth and the virtuous do have some need of good fortune, his paradoxical conclusion should be rejected because the virtuous can experience misfortune without losing their happiness. Although they are susceptible to the loss

14. More should be said about how virtue makes for stability, and why some states of character are more secure than others; see Irwin 1985d: 110–24. I rely on his account, with one minor proviso: whereas he has Aristotle conclude that "though happiness itself is unstable, its dominant component [the Aristotelian virtues] is stable" (p. 123; cf. 106), I take 1.10 to show that happiness itself is stable, precisely because its dominant or essential component is the most stable thing in human life (1100b12–16). See II.v and IV.iv below.

of external goods and prosperity, what they value most is extremely stable and secure against many misfortunes. But before we ask how Aristotle's analysis accommodates the need for external goods and how fortune is related to virtuous activity, we must settle one other problem raised by Solon's dictum. Aristotle incorporates what seems to be a similar demand in his own account: after defining happiness as virtuous activity, he adds that it must be "in a complete life" (ἐν βίῳ τελείῳ, 1.7 1098a18); even after refuting Solon's claim, he adds that virtuous activity must last "not for a chance time but a complete life" (1.10 1101a16). Does this imply that happiness is predicated only of *completed* lives and that it must last throughout life after all?

Given Solon's talk about seeing the end (τέλος), it is easy to assume that a life must have ended to be complete (τέλειος). But these terms have other meanings as well, and Aristotle's interest is not only or primarily in duration. Indeed, the reasons he gives for adding this rider to his formula say nothing about a long life, let alone permanence. On the contrary, all he requires is more than a brief time. He supports the initial claim by arguing that "*one* swallow does not make it spring, nor does *one* day; likewise, one day does not make anyone blessed and happy, nor does a *brief* time" (1098a18–20). When he reiterates the point, he requires not that the virtuous live happily ever after but only that they "both have and *will* have" what they require to be happy (1101a20).[15] Happiness cannot come and go, but it need not be

15. After reformulating his account of happiness (1101a14–16), Aristotle wonders, "Or should we add that (a) they *will* live this way and (b) *will die* accordingly, since (c) the future is unclear to us, and (d) we consider happiness an end and entirely complete in every way" (a16–19). (I have adjusted Bywater's punctuation, which creates asyndeton: ἐπειδή in a17 introduces [c] and [d] as reasons for adding [a] and [b], so the question ends in a19.) If his answer is affirmative, then he reverts to Solon's position, which is inconsistent with a7–13 (quoted above), as Rassow (1874: 116–19) showed long ago; cf. Irwin 1985d: 106 n24. But there is no need to excise the lines and the passage can be read to give a negative answer: after conceding "if this is so" (a19; οὕτω refers only to the reasons [c] and [d], not the inference [b] they were alleged to support), he says only that (e) the happy "will have" (a20) the conditions for happiness, which affirms only (a)— that they will act virtuously *some* time into the future—not (b)—that they live happily *forever* after. In short, Aristotle's conclusion affirms two reasons for Solon's view but weakens his claim. Cf. EE 2.1 1219b5–8, where Aristotle cites Solon's dictum with approval but evidently interprets it to suit his own account: he glosses it by saying that one must "reach one's *end*," which he has just defined as virtuous activity (a39), and he explains it by adding that "nothing incomplete is happy, since it is not whole," which refers back to "complete and whole virtue"

permanent. In fact, after conceding that happiness can be lost, Aristotle adds that it can also be regained. His explanation shows what makes duration important.

Happy people would never become miserable, but they won't be happy like a god [μακάριος] if they fall upon fortunes like Priam's. Yet neither are they shifting and liable to change, for they will not be moved out of happiness easily, and not by chance failures but by many great ones; and afterward, they would not become happy again in a brief time, but if at all, in much and complete time, by achieving great and noble things in that time.   (1.10 1101a6–13)

The reason happiness is impossible in "a brief time" is that *virtuous activity* takes time to be complete. But if happiness can be acquired and lost, then that activity can be complete in less than an entire lifetime; if happiness can be regained, then it can be complete more than once in a lifetime. In short, "a complete life" need not last an entire lifetime. Indeed, happiness can never last from beginning to end, since no one is eligible during childhood (1.9 1100a2–5). Moreover, a life need not be long to be complete. Solon himself counted Cleobis and Biton happy, even though they died before their natural time, and not for A. E. Housman's reason, that they were spared a fall from grace by dying young, but because they had already accomplished great things. For Solon too, what makes a life complete is its activity. But what makes that complete, and why does that take time? Before he raises the problem of Priam and the possibility of disaster striking adults (a5–9), Aristotle gives part of his answer when he explains why neither animals nor children can be happy.

So with good reason we do not call cattle or horses or any other animals happy, since none of them is able to share in this kind of [rational] activity. This explains why children are not happy either: because of their age they are not yet capable of doing noble things; and children who are so called are called happy because of an expectation. For as we said, happiness requires both complete virtue and a complete life.

(1.9 1099b32–1100a5)

The problem with animals and children is that their way of life is qualitatively deficient, not that their lives are too short. Al-

---

and "complete life" (a36–39). These, in turn, involve the development of human rationality (cf. a25–28, b20–24, and the subsequent function-argument, esp. 1220a13–14).

though Aristotle goes on to raise worries about permanence and vulnerability, he first emphasizes the quality or way of life, not its length or chronological end. Animals *never* attain what is necessary, since they are by nature incapable of rational activity (cf. 1.7 1097b33–98a4, a12–15). Hence, their fate confirms Aristotle's account because it explains the convention of not calling any animals happy, even when they lead flourishing and contented lives.[16] Similarly, although custom sanctions calling children happy, it still confirms his account because children can *develop* the necessary capacities whereas animals cannot: we call children happy only "because of an expectation" (1.9 1100a3). As Aristotle adds, what we expect is that they will develop their rational capacities ("complete virtue," a4) and exercise them in the necessary ways ("a complete life," a5). Not all promising children mature or perform. To call someone happy, then, we must see more than the preliminary stages of rational virtue, and we must see their virtue expressed in more than a few activities. Both maturation and performance require time and favor from fortune. But since the virtues themselves are primary, time is needed for maturity, not for security. In short, it is premature to call children happy because they have to mature—or in Aristotle's terms, because they are "incomplete."[17]

Aristotle denies that children (παῖδες) can be happy. He also thinks that youths (νεοί) are too young, and his discussion of their deficiencies sheds more light on why time is important here. In a survey of the traits peculiar to early, middle, and later life, he allows that the young tend to value what is noble more than their personal advantage (*Rhet.* 2.12 1389a32–35), that they are fond of friends (a35–b2) and generous in their judgments of

16. The version of this "hapless horse" argument given by *EE* 1.7 1217a24–29 specifies the missing element as "something divine," i.e., rational capacities (so *EN* 10.8 1178b24–31, and frequently; cf. the collocation of "god" and "mind" at 1.6 1096a24–25, 10.7 1177b27–31 and *EE* 1.8 1217b30–31, 8.2 1248a23–29).

17. Aristotle calls children ἀτελείς (*Pol.* 1.13 1260a10–20, a31–33; cf. *EE* 1219b5–8, discussed above in n15). A further sign that Aristotle's primary interest is in the kind or quality of life, not its length, is that he always refers to a way or form of life (βίος, ζωή) and never uses the word that refers unambiguously to a lifetime (αἰών). I agree with Cooper (1987: 213–15 n14), who argues, against Keyt 1983, that βίος refers to a way of life or life-style (e.g., the Spartan way of life) rather than an isolated aspect of it (e.g., someone's social life; contrast ζωή, used of nutritive as opposed to perceptual functions, e.g., 1098a1). In any case, Cooper and Keyt agree that βίος is qualitative.

others (b8–10), and that they are "optimistic, trusting, and sincere" (a16–18).[18] But since it takes time for these traits to take root and become habitual, their idealism and romanticism do not qualify them for virtue or happiness. Their interests are fickle (a6), they are overly passionate (a7–8, b3), highly irascible (a9–11), too competitive (a12–13), and in brief, "they do everything to excess" (b2–8). Instead of doing what is right by reasoned choice, they abide by the laws out of a sense of shame, since "they do not yet know of other noble things" (a28–29). The character of the young is unstable not only for want of time, but also because of the inexperience this entails. Their goodwill and optimism stem not from conviction but largely from their not having encountered hardship, meanness, or dishonesty (a14–25, a30–31), and their "innocence" (ἀκακία) leads them to show sympathy even toward people who deserve none (b8–10). Worst of all, they are prone to commit wrongs: they are "uncontrolled" (a3–5) and given to violence (b5–8), not least because "they are stubborn and think they know everything" (b5–7). Thus, however content and fortunate the young may be, their lives remain "incomplete" as long as they are incapable of the sustained rational activity that is sovereign over happiness.

It takes time to remove these deficiencies in youthful character—to learn about the range of human needs and ends and how to coordinate their pursuit, and to learn about the ways other people act and think and how to interact with them. But nothing here requires a long time, much less a long life, and a life does not become complete merely with the passage of time. The longer we live, the more experiences we have. However, the kind of experience that Aristotle considers necessary for happiness consists not in the number of events experienced, but in the insight they can yield, and that can be acquired before old age, though not necessarily even then. The young are unfit to profit from ethical theory, he claims, not only because they are inexperienced, but also because they "follow their feelings; and it makes no difference whether one is young in age or in character, since the deficiency is not from time but because they live by feelings and pursue each inclination" (*EN* 1.3 1095a2–8).[19] The problem is not that

18. See Nussbaum 1986: 337–39, although she overstates the positive side of these observations about youthful exuberance and goodwill; cf. Dover 1974: 103–5.

19. Cf. 4.9 1128b16–18, 8.3 1156a31–34, 3.12 1119b5–7, and *EE* 2.8 1224a26–30; see Burnyeat 1980: esp. 82–88.

the young know nothing but that their knowledge is not "practical" (πρακτική) in two crucial ways: they need practice in applying general principles in their deliberations, and they need to acquire the habit of acting on their decisions.[20] Even if few are corrupt and most have quite a few correct beliefs, inexperience leaves their beliefs so imprecise and disorganized that they have trouble both deciding how and when to do what and then doing what they decide. Theory can help those who deliberate about their actions and then act on their decisions, but until and unless the young learn to govern their desires and actions by reasons and plans, no general knowledge of what to do can do them much good. That is why most resemble the "uncontrolled" (a8–11).[21] The best most can do is exercise "natural virtue": they can do what they should, but they lack the correct reasons and convictions needed to make their virtue complete.

We should examine virtue once again, since it too has a relation analogous to the relation practical wisdom has to cleverness, which is not the same but similar: this is how natural virtue is related to sovereign [κυρ-ίαν] virtue.[22] For everyone thinks that each trait of character occurs somehow naturally; for we are just, inclined to temperance, courageous, and the rest, straight from birth. But still we seek something else as the sovereign good, and we seek to have these traits in another way; for the natural traits [αἱ φυσικαὶ ἕξεις] occur in children and animals, but they are clearly harmful in the absence of reason.   (6.13 1144b1–9)

Aristotle defines "cleverness" (δεινότης) as a capacity that "enables one to do the things that are conducive to a set goal and to obtain that goal" (6.12 1144a23–26). But this executive talent is praiseworthy only if used to seek the right ends; in the service of bad ends, it is the vice of "ruthlessness" (πανουργία, literally "do-anything-ness," a26–28). Practical wisdom (φρόνησις), by contrast, includes a clear grasp of the right ends as well as insight

20. In calling wisdom πρακτική, Aristotle means not only that conduct is its subject matter but also that it regularly leads to action (unlike the nonpractical knowledge possessed by the incontinent: contrast 7.2 1146a5–9 with a31–b2 and 1147a14–24); see 6.5 1140b5, b21, and cf. 6.4 1140a10–16, 6.13 1145a2–6.

21. See Winch 1972: 84–86, reflecting on Collingwood's memories of reading Kant's ethics at the age of eight; cf. 6.8 1142a10–20 and Greenwood 1909: 206–7.

22. For this translation of κυρία, see II.v n19 below. Here the point is that "sovereign" virtue is virtue in the full and primary sense of the word, the sense on which other senses depend. This seems to be a case of "focal meaning": see 8.4 1157a30–31 and EE 1236a16–22 (cf. κύρια ὀνόματα in Rhet. 1404b5–8 and Poetics 22); see also Owen 1957: 109 n40, and 1960: esp. 165–69. On "natural virtue," cf. EN 3.8 1117a4–9, EE 3.7 1234a24–29, and MM 1.34 1197b36–98a21.

into how to achieve those ends; so it requires being virtuous as well (a28–34).[23] Aristotle claims that there is a parallel relation between the two forms of virtue: just as wisdom completes cleverness by supplying insight into the right ends, so sovereign virtue completes the right habits of feeling and action found in natural virtue by adding the insight and guidance of wisdom (b14–17). The difference often shows itself in practice: people who have a general sense of what they should do ("what the laws ordain," a15) and have been raised to act and feel correctly are still liable to go wrong, and like people who do not know how to use their strength, they "take strong falls" until they acquire a better grasp of the right principles and ends to guide them (b10–13). But behind this, there is also a difference in motive. Those who have natural virtue often do what is right and like doing so—which is just what it means to have natural virtue—but because they lack the right reasons, they choose their acts "because of something other than the acts themselves" (a13–17). They do things that are noble, such as acting bravely or giving generously, but only to earn approval or avoid disapproval—or, as Aristotle would put it, only out of "shame."[24] Those who have sovereign virtue, on the other hand, act and respond rightly "because of a decision and for the sake of the very things done" (a18–20). Thus, as Aristotle says in amending a view he attributes to Socrates, the conduct of those who have sovereign virtue is not only "in accord with [κατά] the right reason" but also done "*with* [μετά] the right reason" (b21–30).[25]

23. Aristotle's claim is not that virtue *supplies* the end, but only that the end cannot be *seen* "without virtue" (1144a29–30). Hence, it distorts his position to think that cleverness added to virtue yields wisdom; wisdom presupposes both (note "not without" each), but it also supplies something of its own, a view of the overall good, i.e., a conception of the human good and happiness. When he claims that virtue "*makes* [ποιεῖ] the goal correct" (a8), he means not that it *reveals* it to the virtuous, but that it ensures that they *act* on it; or to paraphrase, since virtue is the habit of enacting the right decision, it "makes" the end we decide upon the end of what we actually do. Cf. Sorabji 1974: 212–13.

24. Aristotle defines αἰδώς as "a kind of fear of disapproval" (4.9 1128b11–12) and thinks it suited especially but only for youth (b15–21); cf. *Rhet.* 2.12 1389a25–b2. As Burnyeat (1980: 78) puts it, "shame is the semivirtue of the learner"; although the young often enjoy doing what virtue requires, they do not act virtuously because they do not enjoy it "properly"—for the right reasons.

25. On the behavioral and motivational shortcomings of natural virtue, see Irwin 1988b: 69–72 and Kraut 1989: 247–51. Seeing the right reason is one factor that makes sovereign virtue so stable; the inclinations of natural virtue may be capricious and unreliable (as Kant worried), but wisdom secures and maintains

This difference in motive implies a further difference, one that explains why sovereign virtue is complete. Having the right reasons in turn requires three things: first, one must see one's action as a correct pursuit of some specific ends of human life; second, one must have a true conception of the overall human good; and third, one must also see how one's specific ends fit together in the overall good. In short, one must have a conception of happiness that clarifies the relations among its several parts.[26] But since virtue implies not only *having* the right reasons but also *acting* on them, sovereign virtue also implies actively pursuing the several ends of human life as we should. Finally, since each of the several particular virtues is concerned with one or more of those ends, sovereign virtue is also complete or "whole" because it embraces all the particular virtues. In fact, although it is possible to have some virtues in their natural form without having others, sovereign virtue entails having all the virtues (b30–36) because it im-

those feelings by supplying insight. Virtuous motives are not pure of all feeling; on the contrary, the right reasons shape and confirm the right feelings.

26. For happiness as a comprehensive end, see I.i above; for wisdom as implying a conception of this end, see esp. 6.5 1140a25–28 and the evidence discussed in Sorabji 1974: 205–9. The third requirement involves some theoretical insight. But I see no sign that Aristotle thinks complete virtue presupposes the philosophical acumen to articulate a detailed theory of happiness, let alone to defend one's views against the objections and doubts of others. Rather, one meets the third condition if one sees how one's ends are connected to happiness. In short, a thorough understanding of ethical theory is not a precondition for having the right reasons. After all, unless Aristotle means to invent sovereign virtue, he must think that people can have it without having learned his theory. If "complete virtue" does not *presuppose* theoretical wisdom (σοφία), it can hardly be the *same* as it. Thus, Aristotle speaks of justice as "complete [τελεία] virtue" (5.1 1129b14–30a13) and of "dignity" as "total [παντελής] virtue" (4.3 1124a4–8, a25–29; see IV.iii below); both of these are practical and moral rather than theoretical virtues. Kraut (1989: 241–47) distinguishes these from "the best and most perfect [τελειοτάτη] virtue" mentioned at 1.7 1098a18, which he would identify with theoretical wisdom on the basis of 10.7–8. I agree that Aristotle considers the happiness found in reflection better and "perfect" and the happiness of ethical action "secondary." But he nowhere exploits a parallel distinction between theoretical wisdom as "*most* perfect" and ethical virtue as only "perfect." Kraut thus seems mistaken in using 10.7–8 to gloss 1.7; rather, virtue is perfect or complete if it is *rational* (based on *practical* wisdom), whereas happiness is perfect or complete if it includes the best *exercise* of reason (reflection) on the best *objects* (immutable truths of science and philosophy). More generally, the best and "most perfect" activity of any perceptual or intellectual capacity occurs when it is in its best condition and directed at the best objects (10.4 1174b14–31); the practical exercise of reason can still be complete by attaining its best condition (complete practical virtue) and being directed at good objects and the pursuit of good ends.

plies practical wisdom, and anyone who is wise has them all (1145a1–2).[27] Those who are naturally temperate, for example, are not always courageous, and vice versa, but sovereign temperance requires practical wisdom. Since that implies having the other virtues, anyone who has one virtue in its sovereign form has them all. First, to be wise, one must *know* the value, for example, of physical pleasure—the focus of temperance; that is impossible without knowing its relation to the other ends of human life and hence knowing the value of those ends as well. Second, since the wise also *act* in ways that express what they know, their actions give every end its due, which is nothing other than acting in accordance with all the virtues.

It is time to recapitulate the argument. Aristotle argues that children, most youths, and even many adults do not lead a complete life for the simple reason that they have yet to acquire practical wisdom. This means essentially two things: they do not have a clear view of the human good as a whole, and so they do not see how the diverse ends of human life fit together as a whole.[28] But their lack of wisdom has three other distinct but closely related consequences. First and most important, they cannot see the full point of what they do. Although they may do what they should, even with great regularity, they act only by inclination; until they recognize why their actions are right, the reasons for which they act are incomplete. Second, their natural virtue is inherently unstable. Without a clear view of the good life as a whole to guide them, they have difficulty coordinating its parts. They may see what to do in most ordinary situations, but without sovereign virtue their conduct and even their virtue depends largely on fortune, since they are prone to go wrong if their circumstances go bad or they are obliged to make difficult choices. Finally, unless they advance beyond natural virtue, they

27. Cf. 1144a1–6, 10.8 1178a16–20, and *EE* 8.3 1248b8–16 (discussed in IV.ii below); cf. *EN* 5.1 1130a8–10 (with 1129b14–25), and *EE* 2.1 1219a36–39, b21, 1220a2–4, a13–14. On the unity of sovereign virtue, see Irwin 1988b: 67–72; for the idea that each virtue governs a special sphere of life (which I develop in III and IV below), see Kraut 1988a: 80–82.

28. Irwin (1988b: 71) emphasizes the "organic structure" of the human good: "we cannot *understand* the full value of each element in it without understanding its relation to other elements" (my italics). This implies not that happiness has no "partial goods that can be independently *appreciated* at their true worth" (my italics), but only that without a conception of the overall good, our appreciation of any parts rests at best on true beliefs, rather than understanding.

also fall short of happiness. That does not mean that they do nothing good or enjoyable. With luck, their shortcomings may not be put to the test, and if their inclinations develop into habits of action and feeling, they can enjoy doing what is right regularly and throughout their lives.[29] But it does mean that they do not enjoy their conduct in the right way and that they have much less control over their lives than they might. In addition to depending on fortune to spare them difficult choices and not to confound their good intentions, they miss the distinctive pleasure of virtuous activity that comes from seeing that one's actions are good in themselves and part of a good life.

In the end, the requirement of living a complete life comes down to two things, each implied by Aristotle's analysis: first, one must live long enough to develop the rational virtues, and second, one must live long enough to exercise them in the pursuit of good ends. Neither requires a long life, for it is enough to realize or complete one's nature, and there is no need to exhaust it. Rather, the time needed to attain happiness depends on what ends one seeks and what actions one undertakes in their pursuit. Had Socrates lived longer, his life would have been no more complete; had he died thirty years earlier, it would have been no less complete. He might have been less admired and less masterful in argument, but he would have been virtuous, wise, and happy all the same. In fact, the more the value of what we do depends on the exercise of virtue and other states of our own souls, the less it depends on external results and the less time it needs. Naturally, success in virtuous endeavors is more desirable and better than failure. But since failure detracts from the value of our efforts only to the extent that we are responsible for failure, virtuous actions

29. There is a problem here: Can the activity of natural virtue yield happiness? If natural virtue is not a misnomer, then Aristotle seems obliged to make room for "natural happiness," a prosperous life spent following the right inclinations; cf. the model of obedience to the wise quoted from Hesiod (1.4 1095b11), which could fit most people in most cities. But Aristotle never refers to happiness in this way. If he did, moreover, it would undermine the crucial role he assigns to deliberately choosing right actions for their own sake. The explanation may be that he considers natural virtue so unstable that no one could long continue having only inclinations to do the right thing, unless they eventually advanced to complete virtue by coming to see why their inclinations are right. After all, the "naturally virtuous" lack two of the three conditions for virtue: they know what to do, but they do not choose virtuous conduct for its own sake or reliably; see 2.4 1105a22-b5, cf. *EE* 8.2 1247a3-21, 1248a30-34.

thwarted by external forces and fortune are no less valuable in themselves.[30] It would have been better had Socrates won the case that cost him his life, but his defeat and conviction do nothing to detract from either the goodness or the correctness of his efforts.

Solon's pessimism is unjustified because he overestimates the degree of influence fortune has on happiness. He is right, of course, to observe that fortune does in fact influence many lives greatly, but he is wrong to think that its influence is inevitable and irremediable. In some ways, then, Aristotle is an optimist about human nature: he thinks that most of us are born able "to receive" the virtues (*EN* 2.1 1103a25), that many develop "natural virtues," and that we can in principle develop complete virtue. But his optimism is by no means naive or rosy. He recognizes that the seeds of virtue must be "completed [τελειουμένοις] by habit" (a25–26), and although he thinks happiness is *accessible* to all who are not "maimed" for virtue, he insists that it takes "learning and practice" to *attain* it (1.9.1099b18–20). The prospects for a good life are much improved if he is right that it depends primarily on virtuous activity. But both that activity and the acquisition of virtue still seem to depend on fortune. Or as Aristotle concedes, the virtuous have "additional need" for external resources and prosperity. How serious is this need, and how is it related to virtuous activity? What in particular do the virtuous need, and can virtue make their life secure, even if they encounter serious misfortune?

30. The division of responsibility here is hard to see in practice, for an agent as well as observers. But difficulty in finding the line does not imply that there is none to be found; see the discussion of precision in I.ii above. Irwin (1985d: 105 *n*23) cites *Poetics* 8 and observes that "quantitative addition" does not necessarily affect "qualitative completeness"; cf. 1450b22–25, 1451a9–15.

Sovereign Virtue

IN REFUTING Solon's conception of human happiness, Aristotle does not deny that prosperity contributes to a good life or that some good fortune is necessary. On the contrary, he tries to show more precisely how fortune can influence the lives of the virtuous. Thus, after rejecting Solon's conclusion, he goes on to sketch how virtuous activity makes human life secure, even in the face of adversity. The result preserves Solon's insight that happiness depends more on our actions than our acquisitions, but it weakens both his demand for permanence and his worry about misfortune. The key to the argument is the contrast Aristotle draws between fortune and virtuous activity: "Living well or badly does not depend on one's fortunes; rather, human life has an additional need [προσδεῖται] for these things, as we said, but virtuous activities are sovereign [κύριαι] over happiness, and contrary activities are sovereign over the contrary state" (EN 1.10 1100b8–10).

What Aristotle means by calling virtuous activity sovereign is best settled by first clarifying what he means by an "additional need." He uses the same term to describe the relation between happiness and prosperity in his preliminary sketch of traditional views about fortune (1.8 1099a31, b6).[1] There already he assigns

1. See Gauthier and Jolif 1970 on 1099a15, and Cooper 1985a: 173 n2. When Aristotle initially names this third desideratum, he treats prosperity not as the sole constituent of happiness but only as something that some people "include alongside" virtue (on this verb, see Stewart 1892 on 1098b26; "also" (καί, 1099a31, b7) is pleonastic after "additional need" unless virtue is also present.

the primary role to virtuous activity, and his initial explanation for this need appeals to prosperity's contribution to virtuous activity: "It is impossible or not easy to do fine things without resources" (a32–33). In short, his point is not that prosperity is on a par with virtue but only that happiness is impossible without it. But why is this so? Do the virtuous need external goods only in order to exercise their virtue in the first place? Or do they need something more from fortune? If the former, then the worry is only that *being* virtuous is not sufficient for happiness, and that concession is consistent with Aristotle's account. But if the latter, then the worry is that virtuous *activity* is not enough to make us happy, and that seems inconsistent. So what precisely does this "additional need" for prosperity entail?

In his initial account of how the two other major desiderata are related to his account of happiness, Aristotle argues that both virtue and pleasure are integrally related to a good life. Although virtue is obviously the basis for virtuous activity, it is wrong to think that *being* virtuous is sufficient for happiness. If life is inherently active, living well depends on *exercising* virtue (1098b31–99a3); just as Olympic crowns go only to those who compete and win, so the prize of happiness goes only to those who are active and "achieve the fine and good things in life" (a3–7). Likewise, the "additional need" that happiness has for pleasure is not for anything extraneous to virtuous activity, not "for something fastened on" (περιάπτου τινός, a15–16);[2] rather, since virtuous activity is "pleasant by itself" (καθ' αὑτὸν ἡδύς, a7; cf. a14–15) and the virtuous *enjoy* doing what is virtuous (a17–20), happiness is intrinsically pleasant, and living virtuously "has its pleasure in itself" (ἔχει τὴν ἡδονὴν ἐν ἑαυτῷ, a16). So if the additional need for prosperity parallels the need for virtue and pleasure, it is directly related to the activity of virtue. But then, far from being inconsistent with his account, this need is explained by his ac-

---

2. Parallel to this preliminary argument is the question raised early in the *EE* whether we should "attach" (προσάπτειν) bodily pleasures to the good life: even before analysis, Aristotle suggests that "it is necessary to share in *these* pleasures in some other way" (i.e., they should not be extraneous) and that the happy find pleasures of *another* kind as well (1.5 1216a30–36). The need implied by his terms is illustrated by a claim Plato makes about the guardians: since they have golden souls, they "have no additional need for human gold" and should not "fasten it on themselves" (*Rep.* 3.416e–17a; cf. the mere ornaments called περίαπτα, 4.426b).

count because it depends on the essential constituent of happiness, virtuous activity. In short, "additional need" has a precise and technical sense: such needs are supplementary conditions that depend on or derive from what is primary and essential. In particular, the virtuous have additional need of prosperity and external goods only because their activity requires them. But if this is Aristotle's claim, does his analysis sustain it? Do the virtuous view any external goods as *ends* of their activity that they must achieve to be happy?

Aristotle distinguishes three reasons behind traditional views about prosperity. The first is the instrumental need previously mentioned: the virtuous need resources to pursue many of their goals (a32–33). He then adds that "people spoil their happiness" in the absence of certain advantages (b2), and in his explanation he raises two different worries: one about constitutive luck (how fortune can influence whether people ever become virtuous), and one about incidental luck (how events can affect the lives of those who are already virtuous).[3] But before looking at these worries, it will be helpful to clarify Aristotle's first reason. To explain his claim, he adds that "many things are done, just as through tools [καθάπερ δι' ὀργάνων], through friends and wealth and political power" (a33–b2; cf. 1.9 1099b27–28). Although wealth and power number among the major ends of conventional ideals, the only value Aristotle acknowledges here is instrumental; and he has more to say about friends in the second reason, although they too can be used like tools. Thus, Solon needed all three to accomplish his program of social reform; and in a celebrated case of the day, Dion could never have attempted, much less succeeded, in liberating Syracuse from tyranny had he lacked resources and powerful connections.[4] But if the need for external goods depends only on the ends they can be used to achieve, their necessity is contingent on those activities; and if resources are necessary for happiness only because they are in-

3. Cooper (1985a: 178–84) argues that both reasons reduce to one, but see Irwin 1985d: 96 and Kraut 1989: 253–60. My reasons for distinguishing two factors in the second explanation will emerge below.

4. Aspasius offers tyrannicide and Solon's legislation as examples of the virtuous use of friends and power (24.10, 24.20–23). Dion's exploits, detailed in Plato's letters, exemplify the former, as Aristotle recognizes when he discusses tyranny (*Pol.* 5.10 1312a33–39); cf. his report of Dion's betrayal by Callippus (*Rhet.* 1.12 1373a18–21; cf. Plut. *Dion* 54–58).

strumentally necessary for virtuous actions, they rank not as essential parts but only as preconditions.

Aristotle's position here is an application of his general account of instrumental relations. Clearly, in crafts and other human endeavors, where tools are designed specifically to suit the determinate aims of the craft or ends they serve, tools are defined in terms of those activities: a saw, for example, should be defined as "a kind of dividing," for to determine that a saw must have teeth of a certain sort and that those must be made of iron, a carpenter must first specify the kind of cutting he wants to do (*Phys.* 2.9 200b5–7). Aristotle extends the same principle to natural beings: the "organs" (or "instrumental" parts) of living creatures are what they are by being part of a living *whole*; for if a hand is severed from its owner, or the owner dies, the hand is only "homonymously" a hand, because then it can no longer perform the functions that make it a hand.[5] So in nature as in crafts, not only the need for tools but their very makeup depend upon and derive from the ends they serve. But this makes them subject only to "hypothetical necessity," since it is for the sake of the user that tools are necessary and need to be the way they are, not vice versa. In short, the end to be served is what determines which tools to use and whether to use any at all.[6] Hence, to the extent that external goods are valuable as tools, the additional need is consistent with Aristotle's analysis; and unless external goods have some further and independent value, his concession that resources are necessary is not a revision of his initial account but simply an explication of its implications.

Furthermore, since the need for tools depends wholly on the ends of virtuous activity, Aristotle registers reservations about its extent, for in denying that happiness is possible "with *no* resources" (*EN* 1099a33), all he rules out as incompatible are the extremes of indigence or isolation. Similarly, he does not concede that the virtuous could do *nothing* fine without resources, but only that *some* actions would be impossible and that *others* would only be "not easy" (a32). Yet, fine things are proverbially hard: ill fortune may close some avenues for virtuous action, but it rarely

5. See, e.g., *de An.* 2.4 416a5; on the relation between "spurious homonyms" and Aristotle's other ideas about homonymy, see Irwin 1981b: esp. 527–29.

6. Cf. *EE* 7.10 1242a13–16 and *Part. An.* 1.5 645b14–20, 2.7 652b7–15; see Cooper 1985b: 151–54.

closes all, and the very struggle against adversity is what calls for virtues like courage and endurance. Conversely, good fortune brings difficulties of its own: Solon is said to have used the proverb in reference not to misfortune but to external goods and the conduct of two of the "Seven Sages," to Periander's failure to use his power and prosperity well and to Pittacus' reluctance to risk the test.[7] Thus, as Aristotle argues before invoking Solon himself, many people exaggerate the need for resources: wealth and power *can* contribute to a good life, but neither is *required*, and it is possible to do with much less.

We certainly should not suppose that someone who is going to be happy will need *many great* things simply because it is not possible to be happy *without* external goods. For self-sufficiency does not depend on excess, nor does action, and it is possible to do fine things even without ruling land and sea. In fact, one could act virtuously even from moderate means, and this can be seen quite clearly, for ordinary people [οἱ ἰδιῶται] are thought to do the right things no less than those in power do, but rather even more. It is enough to have moderate resources, for the happy life will belong to the person who exercises virtue.   (10.8 1179a1–9)

The contrasts are rhetorical, addressed presumably to proponents of power politics and empire, but the argument is clear. If virtuous activity is the essential component of happiness, then all it requires are the resources needed in the pursuit of noble ends; the kind and quantity of resources needed depend on what activities and ends the virtuous pursue. Moreover, as Aristotle indicates when he restricts external goods to the role of prerequisites or sine qua nons (a2), having the necessary resources is not enough by itself, since a good life depends first on using them well.[8] In short, wealth and power contribute to happiness if, but only if, they are used "to do fine things." Not only is there no need for abundant resources, but in terms that recall Solon's model lives, Aristotle adds that happiness is found less among the high and mighty precisely because ordinary citizens like Tel-

7. The saying was a favorite of Plato's: Socrates' closing words in *Hip. Maj.* 304e; his opening words in *Crat.* 384a; in *Rep.* 4.435c, 6.497d; parodied by Adeimantus at 2.365c. According to *Protag.* 339a–47a, Pittacus' own version provoked Simonides' celebrated ode to the Scopadae (fr. 542). Solon was widely credited with the maxim, as we learn from the scholia on these passages (cf. *CPG* 1.172, 2.89–90); and although Aristotle attributes a similar maxim to Bias (5.1 1129b33–30a2, with a8; cf. Sophocles *Antig.* 175–77, D. L. 1.77), he too cites it in reference to the dangers associated with prosperity (cf. *Pol.* 5.8 1308b13–15 and *CPG* 1.212).
8. Cf. *EE* 1.2 1214b11–27, discussed further in III.i below.

los whose needs are moderate are more likely to lead virtuous lives (a6–8). The clear implication is that external goods can interfere with "doing what is right"; power in the wrong hands, for example, does even the powerful more bad than good. As Aristotle emphasizes, "self-sufficiency and action do not depend on excess" (a3). On the contrary, far from ensuring a good life, prosperity "can interfere with happiness when it is excessive, and then it presumably is not right to call it prosperity, since the limit [ὅϱος] for prosperity is relative to happiness" (7.13 1153b21–25). Finally, the value of resources depends on their use, so the more resourceful we are, the less we need; or as Aristotle concludes after analyzing the needs of a good society, "living nobly needs some resources also, but less for those who are in better condition, and more for those who are in worse condition" (*Pol.* 7.13 1331b41–32a2).

The basis for this account is Aristotle's denial that the virtues are valuable solely or primarily for their results. To be sure, the instrumental conception of virtue looms large in conventional views, and many considered virtue "a capacity for providing and preserving good things" (*Rhet.* 1.9 1366a36–37). But whereas others valued virtue for the resources it enabled them to obtain, Aristotle turns this view on its head and argues that the external goods valued most by many contribute to happiness only when they serve the pursuit of virtuous ends.[9] First, most people want these goods not simply to *have* them, but to *use* them and *do* something with them; people envy the riches and power of Sardanapallos because of the sensual delights they procured him (cf.

9. On the instrumental conception of virtue, see also II.iii above and IV.ii below. It is tempting to assume that Aristotle accepts this view. Cooper (1975: 125), for example, suggests "that Aristotle regards as moral virtues those states of character which one ought to acquire if one is to be in the best position (so far as this is determined by oneself) to secure the basic, first-order goods, including prominently the goods distributed by fortune." After citing *Rhet.* 1.9 1366a36–38, he continues, "On the view I am suggesting, to flourish is not actually to possess a full portion of all the basic good things, but rather to be living in accordance with principles which are rationally calculated to secure them. The correct ultimate end to pursue is not the collection of first-order goods themselves but the maintenance of the pattern of control designed to bring about their attainment." Cf. Cooper 1985a: 194–96 and the "Aristotelian" consequentialism in Rawls 1971: e.g., 65. The mistake is to stop at acquiring and securing external goods, for the principal concern of the virtuous is to *use* them for noble ends; cf. Irwin 1985d: 96 n12. Engberg-Pedersen (1983: 80) diagnoses the mistake, but turns Aristotle into a sort of Kantian utilitarian instead (see esp. p. 47).

1095b21–22). But as Solon lectures Croesus, his treasures enable him to sate greater appetites but the virtue of temperance would reduce his appetites from the start. Further, if *misuse* can transform good fortune to bad and bring ruin on the fortunate themselves, then many people are better off doing without. Finally, to do anything with their resources, the prosperous must have *other* ends to pursue, or they will be caught in the paradox of Midas, who could do nothing with all that he had. So although a good life needs some resources, the end is not simply to own or acquire them but to put them to use in valued activities that offer their own rewards. But what ends do these activities seek, and are those subject to fortune? In particular, do the virtuous have ends that they can attain only with luck?

One end is virtue itself, and after summarizing the additional need for resources, Aristotle suggests a deeper worry: we are "not very capable of happiness" in the absence of some gifts of fortune (1099b2–6). As his examples show, he has in mind both constitutive fortune and incidental misfortune. Our physical endowment and family circumstances affect our chances for developing virtue in the first place (b3–4), and virtuous activity cannot eliminate all chance of having wicked children or losing loved ones (b5–6).[10] Aristotle's account of happiness is secure, of course, against the objection that constitutive bad luck can spoil a life by preventing the development of virtue in the first place. But that would be a sorry response to the worry that accidents of birth might determine our lot in life, for it fails to explain either when native gifts are influential or how they affect the development of character. In fact, the case Aristotle outlines in support of the traditional view runs to extremes, and few start out with either the severe disadvantages or the great advantages that he describes. Further, his concession that some accidents of birth make people "not very capable of happiness" (b3–4) falls short of claiming that bad looks or a bad upbringing make happiness impossible or that good looks and a good family are necessary.[11] Clearly, this undercuts any prejudice that virtue and happiness

10. On the contrast between constitutive and incidental fortune, see II.i, *n*14 above; clearly, coming from a good or bad family (εὐγένεια, δυσγενής, b3–4) is not incidental luck, and losing loved ones is not constitutive.

11. Aristotle's term, εὐδαιμονικός, denotes capability or likelihood, not the actual state. Anaxarchus, for example, was known as "the happiness man" (εὐδαιμονικός), not "the happy man" (εὐδαίμων); see D. L. 9.60.

are exclusively an aristocratic birthright based on good breeding and inherited excellence, for in addition to making happiness accessible even to those whose hereditary gifts are modest, it does not guarantee a good life for all whom heredity favors. Yet by implication, Aristotle also makes it harder to excuse bad conduct by appealing to heredity or a deprived childhood; for the less influence family and society have, the weaker the plea that birth and circumstance are enough to make people go wrong. The question remains, How much importance does he assign constitutive luck, and why?

Aristotle's rejection of traditional views about the importance of constitutive luck is connected with the account of "responsibility for character" he presents to cap his discussion of voluntary action.[12] After developing criteria for voluntary action and analyzing the nature of decision and deliberation, he argues that virtue and vice are "up to us" and voluntary because the actions that express those traits of character are deliberate and voluntary (3.5 1113b3–17). But as he observes, this move remains open to objection if people have no control over their own character. To meet this objection—which involves the worry about constitutive luck, that the character each of us acquires is determined by external forces—Aristotle advances a series of three counter-arguments. First, he cites the universal reliance on incentives to influence action: in private and public affairs alike, people try to discourage or deter some actions by reproach or a threat of punishment and to encourage other actions by praise or honors (b21–26). To be sure, incentives do not always work. But if they ever do change our minds—either as we are growing up and forming our character, or after we have grown up and our character is more settled—then not all our actions are determined by character. Unlike such bodily reactions as getting hot or being hungry, what we do is subject at least in part to what we think; and depending on whether or not we are "persuaded" by incentives, we can decide to act one way rather than another (b26–30).[13] But what if

12. Aristotle's aims and arguments here have provoked extensive discussion. In the main, I follow Sorabji (1980: chaps. 14–16), who also assesses others' accounts.

13. The argument remains open to the objection that *character* determines who responds when to what incentives. But Aristotle's third argument faces that worry: his target is not the thesis that *all* conduct is determined, but only the thesis that all *bad* conduct is, as in the Socratic claim that no one errs willingly. If

some people are beyond change? Against this second worry, Aristotle argues that character is still voluntary because it is formed by the way we live (1114a3–10); if people who were healthy initially can be blamed for ruining their health by the way they live, then by analogy, even people mired in bad habits can be blamed for having made themselves bad, provided they could have lived differently at the start (a14–21). So it is no objection to point out that wishing to improve does not always change our ways; for if we knew that our earlier conduct was bad, then our resultant habits and character are voluntary (a11–14). In short, bad traits are voluntary if they could have been avoided.

Aristotle sees only one way that character could be set from the start, and that is if it is given at birth. This third worry goes to the heart of the problem: just as congenital physical defects deserve sympathy rather than reproach, so it is unfair to hold people responsible for inborn character traits (a21–31). If birth does determine some people's character, then it may also determine their chances for happiness. However, Aristotle makes this seem an implausible plea by showing how much it assumes. For someone's character to be determined at birth, both their *view* of the good (the "apparent good," a31–b1, b13–15) and the *actions* in which they pursue it (b15–16, b18–21) must be *totally* determined at birth. But anyone who is "responsible in a way" for their character will also be "responsible in a way" for their view of the end (b1–3). Yet Aristotle has already argued that how we fare after birth influences our actions and hence our habits, so our initial endowment does not determine our character entirely. In short, each of us makes some contribution to our own moral development. Second, even if people are born with a view of the good, it could determine their character only if three further conditions hold: each person's vision of the good is "not chosen" and cannot change (b6), it is like a power of sight for discriminating and choosing both means and ends (b7–8), and it cannot be learned or acquired from others (b9–10). Certainly, anyone born with so thorough a vision of the good would enjoy "the complete and genuine good nature [εὐφυία]" (b11–12). But so complete a vision

it is agreed that *good* conduct is voluntary (as his opponents maintain), then conduct can be voluntary even if character determines it; hence, his opponents must either stop praising the virtuous or start blaming some bad conduct. Cf. Sorabji 1980: 230–31, 245–48.

is implausible, and the previous arguments show that it would be neither necessary nor sufficient, for people do change their views about what is good and they do learn from others. Finally, Aristotle appeals to a principle of parity to argue that if an innate vision of the good did determine character, then people would deserve no more credit for virtue than blame for being bad (b12–15; cf. 1113b6–14). Heredity is bound to have some effect, but even the best natural endowments and the best constitutive fortune must still develop and be realized in action: people contribute "something" to their view of the end, and actually *doing* what is virtuous involves "referring the rest to this end" (1114b15–19). So virtue, Aristotle concludes, is voluntary for two reasons: "We are ourselves *jointly* responsible in a way for our traits, and we set our specific ends by being the sort of people we are" (b22–24).[14] In short, character is not determined at birth, and although heredity and environment shape our lives, there usually remains room for change.

Aristotle's argument that bad character is voluntary may suit the prejudices of the well-born, but his insistence that heredity and upbringing are not enough for virtue does the opposite. Moreover, although his position narrows the room for excuses based on early disadvantages, his response to the problem of constitutive luck is essentially egalitarian. On the one hand, he admits that a good natural endowment makes one "truly fortunate" (10.9 1179b21–23).[15] But far from leaving virtue and happiness in the hands of fortune, he argues that not even the best luck is sufficient for either, and that habit and learning are not only necessary but far more important. In particular, to make happiness more widely attainable, he recommends state supervision of education, and to promote the continued practice of good habits, he recommends a broad system of laws.

14. See Sorabji 1980: 231–33, 266–67.

15. "True good fortune" is essentially "natural virtue"; see *EE* 8.2 1247b15–28 and II.iv above. On Aristotle's proposals to minimize the effects of fortune here, see the discussion of his theory of distributive justice in Nussbaum 1988: esp. 160–71. Constitutive luck raises the problem of developing what she calls our "B-capabilities" (the capacities built into human nature: first potentialities) into "I-capabilities" (developed capacities to exercise those: second potentialities or first actualities); the problem of resources centers on arranging for "E-capabilities" (the latter plus requisite circumstances).

But it is hard for the young to get a correct upbringing for virtue unless they are raised under good laws; for temperate and hardy living is not pleasant to the many, especially to the young. Therefore, their upbringing and practices should be organized by laws, since those will not be painful once they become habitual. But presumably it is not enough for them to get a correct upbringing and supervision when they are young; rather, since they should practice and get accustomed to the same things also after becoming adults, we need laws for these things too, and so for all of life as a whole.   (10.9 1179b31–1180a4)

The rule of law is inherently impersonal, and Aristotle is careful to leave some control over education in private hands. Although he thinks it best for a society to arrange for "a common supervision" that works through laws (1180a29–35), and that to do otherwise is to "live like the cyclops" (a27–29), he also sees the need for parental discretion, because affection and familiarity can be more effective than general rules (b5–19). To minimize the effects of chance, he recommends that parents "should try to become lawmakers" by looking for general principles to guide their practice even in the home (b20–28). Hence, although he concedes that some start off ahead in the pursuit of virtue and happiness and others start off very far behind, he argues that most accidents of birth can be neutralized by public education and laws. In practice, of course, family circumstances were important, because few societies provided the remedies Aristotle proposes. But since it is possible to manage upbringing well—if not by just laws, then at least by good parents—constitutive luck can in principle be drastically reduced.

People have additional need for good fortune, then, both to develop a virtuous character and to have the resources to exercise virtue in pursuit of the ends they value. In neither case is the need inherently hard to fulfill; nor is either need inconsistent with Aristotle's account, since each is a *precondition* for virtuous activity. But the third kind of additional need does not seem consistent, nor do the prospects for meeting it seem so hopeful. Even in the best of societies, everyone is likely to suffer some serious misfortune, be it personal loss or the ills of the society as a whole. If such events can ruin happiness without ruining virtuous activity, then his account seems inadequate; and if they are all but inevitable, then the third need seems to make happiness virtually unattainable. After all, some external goods seem valuable by themselves, regardless of any other ends they may help us pursue; and quite apart from any need for resources or a good start in life, the virtuous need worthy ends to pursue. For if accidents of birth can make people "not very capable of happiness," as Aristotle says in his epitome of traditional views, "people are presumably even less capable if their children or friends are depraved, or if they are good but have died" (1099b5–6). Or as he argues later:

Many things occur by fortune, and they vary in importance. Clearly, minor cases of good fortune do not change one's life, and likewise for minor cases of bad fortune. But if many important things go well, they will make one's life more happy, since (1) they naturally enhance life, and (2) making use of them is noble and virtuous; but if many important things go badly, they stifle and damage one's happiness, since (1) they bring about suffering and (2) impede many activities.   (1.10 1100b22–30)

Even the best people can be affected by fortune, and for better or worse. Events can make them *feel* better or worse (the first reason in each case above), and events can increase or decrease opportunities for *action* (the second reason in each case). In the latter case, the connection with Aristotle's account of happiness is clear: good fortune simply expands the opportunity for exercising virtue, and bad fortune contracts it. But the relation between this and the former effects is puzzling. Is life enhanced *because* more activities are possible, or vice versa? And does suffering *result* from reduced activity, or vice versa? Unless the improvement or damage depends on virtuous activity, the effect seems inconsistent with Aristotle's account; for although his account allows some lives to be happier than others,[16] the possibility that either joy or suffering alone could affect happiness—while virtuous activity continues unchanged—seems to contradict his account directly. To be sure, he concedes that misfortune can ruin happiness even for the virtuous (b28; cf. 1101a6–11), but it is not yet clear whether it does so only by reducing their activity. Does he,

16. I doubt that Aristotle intends to mark degrees of happiness by using different terms, as if it were better to be μακάριος than εὐδαίμων; see Irwin 1985d: 100 n16 and Nussbaum 1986: 329–33. But he does think that some people are happier than others, and he uses both terms in comparative and superlative degrees, as here (1100b26, 1117b10, 1178a8, 1179a31). The distinction works two ways: we may fare better in our virtuous pursuits (as he suggests here), and we may have better goals (as he thinks philosophers do). See IV.iii below and White 1990.

in short, show that suffering is linked to virtuous activity? Or does his honesty here undermine his theory?

At least as early as Theophrastus, Aristotle's position here was subject to serious debate: some found his concession to fortune "too soft," for even if deprived of friends and family, "one could be active in principal things, and if active, then necessarily one is happy."[17] But against this virtually Stoic demand, Aristotle sides with Solon and concedes that great misfortune *can* overthrow happiness. After all, virtuous activity is no proof against the constant and inevitable risk of serious personal loss, especially in an age of frequent war. On the other hand, he is far from Solon and near the Stoics when he denies that misfortune *inevitably* ruins a good life and when he goes on to describe how the virtuous respond to great loss: "Even in these situations, nobility shines forth when someone bears many great misfortunes with equanimity, not because of insensitivity but because of integrity and dignity" (1.10 1100b30–33).

The emphasis here is on how the virtuous *respond* to events, and Aristotle draws an analogy with good generals and craftsmen who do the best they can with whatever they have available (1101a1–6). As he suggests in his epitome of the traditional view, it is not fortune by itself that can "spoil" our lives for us; rather, depending on how we respond, we may "spoil" our own lives (1099b2).[18] If Socrates, for example, remained happy through decades of war and turmoil, even when wrongly condemned, then it was because of the way he responded to his fortune. Of course, not everyone can face misfortune with fortitude and dignity or do what virtue demands. But for all who do, Aristotle's account seems to imply, happiness is secure. Still, why should this response count as happiness? Is the very fact of activity enough, or does happiness depend on attitudes and feelings as well? Similarly, when he argues that even those who lose happi-

---

17. Aspasius 24.24–27; cf. Cicero *Fin.* 5.12 and *TD* 4.38. The translation of ἐν προηγουμένοις is problematic; see Huby 1983: 125–29. I take the point to be that "principal" activities are involved in achieving something correctly considered good by itself, as opposed to achieving some means or avoiding something bad. Thus, the principal exercise of liberality is giving, not acquiring, and happiness consists in the virtuous pursuit of ends valued by themselves, not just resistance to ills. See below on 1153b9–19.

18. The verb (ῥυπαίνουσι) is active, and its subject is not the losses or things lost, but the people who lose them; cf. II.iii *n*17 above.

ness may eventually regain it "if they attain many great things" (1101a11–13), is this solely because of what they do, or also because of how they feel? In short, when the virtuous do remain happy, how do they do so? If external loss can ruin happiness but need not, what makes the difference? The key is the sovereignty of virtue: "Living well or badly does not depend on one's fortunes; rather, human life has an additional need for these things, as we said, but virtuous activities are sovereign over happiness, and contrary activities are sovereign over the contrary state" (1.10 1100b8–10).

To describe the dominant role of virtuous activity, Aristotle borrows a term used in political contexts: just as the body (individual or corporate) that holds the supreme and final authority in a community is its sovereign, so virtuous activity is sovereign over happiness.[19] The first thing to notice is that this is a factual claim; the question is not what should have sovereignty, as in disputes between royalists and democrats or between hedonists and patrons of virtue, but simply what does hold control and make final decisions, whether on questions of legislation and expenditure or on happiness and its contrary. But further, as that suggests, the claim is not that virtuous activity by itself is sufficient for happiness. If a sovereign has questions to decide, there must be alternatives. If virtuous activity is decisive for happiness, it decides only whether a life is good or not; it does not guarantee a good life. To call virtuous activity sovereign, then, does not mean that any and all who exercise virtue are happy; rather, it asserts that any who are happy find their happiness in their virtuous activities.

In effect, this restates the earlier thesis that equates happiness not with virtuous activity alone, but with that activity "in a complete life" (1098a16–18): although not itself sufficient, virtuous activity is decisive because it determines or controls whether

19. For κύριος in political contexts, see, e.g., *Pol.* 3.6 1278b8–15, 3.7 1279a25–28; see Barker 1946: lxvii and Gauthier and Jolif 1970 on 1.2 1094a26 (a suggestive passage; cf. I.i *n*7 above). Aristotle argues that happiness is the end of the most sovereign pursuit, which he equates with "politics." But politics aims to promote happiness by instilling virtue in the citizenry and providing the conditions for its exercise; hence, its pursuit of happiness depends on its pursuit of virtue. On κύριος, cf. Nussbaum 1986: 494 *n*8, 489 *n*56; on its use in semantic contexts, see II.iv *n*22 above. In Murdoch 1970, "the sovereignty of good" has a very different sense, connected with Platonist views about the metaphysical and epistemological primacy of the good.

happiness is attained. This involves three claims: first, that happiness depends primarily on virtuous activity; second, that it has other needs as well; and third, that each need is in turn dependent on that activity. Hence, the way in which happiness depends on virtuous activity differs crucially from the way in which it depends on anything else: all other needs are "additional" because they are necessary either for virtuous activity in the first place or for that activity to suffice for happiness. More precisely, virtuous activity is sufficient for happiness *if it meets certain further conditions*; but since those conditions derive from the nature of virtuous activity, that activity is sovereign and has decisive control.[20] But how does this work, and what are these further conditions? Later in the argument, Aristotle suggests an answer.

> If one's activities are sovereign over one's life [τῆς ζωῆς], as we said, no one who is happy would become miserable, since they will never do hateful and base things. For we think that truly good and thoughtful people bear all their fortunes gracefully and always do the finest [τὰ κάλλιστα πράττειν] out of what is available. (1.10 1100b33–1101a3)

Again, the point cannot be that virtuous activities guarantee a good life, since Aristotle goes on to concede that happiness can be lost (1101a7–8). Rather, just as virtuous activity decides whether people are happy, so it decides what the virtuous do in any situation they face. But that implies that virtuous activity is sovereign in another way: it is what the virtuous value more than anything else. For "doing the finest" is virtuous activity, and that implies deliberate choice. If they choose to exercise virtue and avoid "doing hateful and base things" at any price—even when their options are severely limited and their convictions severely tested—then acting virtuously must be what they themselves value over every alternative. Being unwilling to forsake one's principles does not guarantee that one will never act unwillingly;

20. My translation of κύριος echoes Vlastos 1984. Vlastos entitles the basic thesis of Socrates' eudaimonism "the sovereignty of virtue": "Whenever we must choose between exclusive and exhaustive alternatives which we have come to perceive as, respectively, just and unjust or, more generally, as virtuous (καλά) and vicious (αἰσχρά), that very perception of them should decide our choice" (p. 187). Aristotle, I argue, accepts this thesis but denies Vlastos' further claim, that virtue and happiness are "inter-entailing" (i.e., virtue is sufficient for happiness). In Aristotle, "sovereignty" describes a different relation: X is sovereign over Y if and only if X is decisive (though not sufficient) for Y. How exactly it is "decisive" remains to be seen.

people can and do forsake what they value more than anything else.[21] But so long as the virtuous do act on behalf of what they want most, virtuous activity remains sovereign over their lives, since they consider it sovereign over all their other pursuits. Further, if this sovereignty involves psychological as well as ethical priority, it is easier to see how virtuous activities are sovereign over happiness: they are also sovereign from the perspective of the virtuous themselves. In some situations, the exercise of virtue may not be enough for happiness; that is why it is sovereign rather than sufficient. But in other situations, even in what may seem dire or miserable straits, adherence to virtuous principles can be enough for happiness if the virtuous do something they consider most valuable. If they consider this enough, then their activity makes them happy. If not, they fall short. But in either case, their activity provides the criterion for whether they are happy.

Aristotle's claim that virtuous activity is sovereign over a good life is based on his argument that rational virtue is generically the best condition we can attain, and that its exercise is—other things being equal—the best activity we can perform. Of course, other things are not always equal: we can be more or less virtuous ourselves, and the circumstances we face can be better or worse (*Pol.* 7.13 1331b39–32a3). Still, in any given situation, we do better, he argues, if we respond with virtue. However, he also claims that the virtuous know what is best, which implies that they know that virtuous activity is better than any other form of activity. Hence, not only is virtuous activity in fact the best form of human life, but it also seems best to the virtuous themselves. When faced with misfortune, therefore, the virtuous consider it better to abide by virtuous principles than to follow any alternative, even if they could escape misfortune at the cost of violating their principles. On the other hand, they would prefer to exercise their virtue under better external conditions. This is why their activity is sovereign but not sufficient for happiness; for their happiness depends finally on their view of their activity. Thus,

21. Aristotle considers complete or sovereign virtue the most stable condition humans can attain; see esp. 1100b9–17 and II.iv *nn*14, 23 above. That does not mean it cannot be lost, and I know of no text where he makes so strong a claim. But virtue is more stable than happiness. Nussbaum (1986: 336–40) exaggerates when she claims that Aristotle considers virtuous adults "vulnerable" to losing virtue; such radical incontinence is possible, but only under extraordinary pressures.

virtuous activity is sovereign in two ways, one objective or external, and one subjective or internal: first, it does control happiness, and second, because the virtuous know that, it controls how they live and what they want to do.[22] After all, objective sovereignty gives us excellent reason to cultivate and practice complete virtue, and to make virtuous activity subjectively sovereign; for if we value virtuous activity most, we thereby attain a necessary and by far the greatest part of the supreme end of life and of all we do.

An example will help. Socrates led a virtuous and happy life: he did what virtue required, and he enjoyed doing so. As one of his more striking paradoxes illustrates, he considered virtue sovereign over all his other interests, for he maintained that he would rather suffer injustice than commit it—that he would suffer anything rather than do any wrong. Since he considered virtuous principles more important than anything else, abiding by them was doing what he himself wanted most to do. Hence, his actions achieved what he valued most, and that made him happy. He might have enjoyed more fortunate circumstances or more external success in his endeavors: Athens might have shown him more respect, or he might have convinced more of his interlocutors. But even if he would have welcomed such luck, his manner and bearing in the dialogues show how much he enjoyed his life as it was. Then again, he might not have found his activities rewarding enough: the friends he lost to civil strife and to war, the dangers he faced under the tyranny of the Thirty, and his final condemnation in the courts might have ruined his life. But they did not: rather than suffering the fate of Priam (1101a7–8), he remained happy to the end by continuing to act on behalf of what he valued most (a17, a20). His activity was sovereign over his happiness both because he continued to do what in fact was best, and because he continued to do what he thought was best—because he considered virtue sovereign over the rest of his life and over his other ends.

The sovereignty of virtue implies neither that nothing else is

22. My terms are vague but they highlight a real difference. If Aristotle is right, it is an "objective" fact that virtuous activity is sovereign over happiness; but the conviction that virtuous activity is more valuable than anything incompatible with it is "subjective" or "internal." (I say "anything incompatible" rather than "anything else" because, e.g., the virtuous value virtuous activity more than any *other* activity, but not more than happiness, which necessarily *includes* it; see White 1990: 124–27.)

good or that the virtuous value nothing else as ends. On the contrary, they know the true value of other pursuits, some of which Aristotle considers "good by themselves" and hence final ends.[23] Indeed, many other things are good even in the absence of virtue; or as Aristotle puts it, health, pleasure, honor, and the virtues themselves are each *intrinsically good* because they are worth having even when they serve no further good. Of course, they are not *unconditionally final* because they are not worth seeking or having *in all conditions*; on some occasions it is better not to choose them. But they are conditionally final because they are generally worth seeking and valuable "by themselves." So although no one can ever lead a good life, no matter how successful in these other pursuits, unless they also exercise virtue, other things are good and remain correct ends of pursuit for nearly everyone.

This puts Aristotle at odds both with Socrates, who argues that nothing else is good except in conjunction with virtue, and with the Stoics, who argue that nothing is good except virtue, the virtuous, and their actions.[24] Everything else people call good, they observed, can be harmful and used even by the bad. So they reserved the term "good" exclusively for virtue, on the grounds that only what is always and only beneficial is really good. But rather than concede that health, for example, is not good at all, or that it is good only for the virtuous, Aristotle maintains that it too is intrinsically good, and not only for the virtuous. Not only is it something we *naturally have* as the realization of human nature, but also—except in special conditions—everyone *wants* to be

23. See, e.g., 3.4 1113a25–33. On the relation between goodness and finality, see I.i above. If virtuous activity were strictly identical with happiness, it would be sufficient by itself. By adding that virtue be exercised "in a complete life," Aristotle implies that it is not identical or sufficient; rather, by calling virtue "sovereign," he implies that happiness has other constituents as well. This leaves happiness less "inclusive" than Irwin (1986: 206–7; cf. 1985a: 303–4) does in claiming that happiness includes "all the goods that a rational person is justified in pursuing." Everyone is bound to lack some things that they are justified in wanting: we rightly want our friends and good people generally to survive and do well, but it does not ruin a good life when some of them do not. Hence, virtuous activity does not require the best imaginable internal and external conditions in order to be complete and pleasant; all it requires is enough to make the virtuous rightly consider their lives satisfying.

24. For Socrates, see Vlastos 1984: 191: "In isolation from virtue, [all other goods] would be worthless." On the relation between Socrates' claims and the Stoic thesis, see Long 1988: esp. 165–71; Long argues that Socrates agrees with the Stoics that other so-called goods are not good at all (rather than good only in conjunction with virtue, as Vlastos argues). Cf. I.ii *n*5 above.

healthy, and anyone, whether virtuous or not, *is better off* healthy than ill. On occasion, of course, even the virtuous have reason to prefer being ill—to avoid serving a wicked tyrant, for example, as some Stoics argued.[25] But in Aristotle's terms, this means only that intrinsic goods can sometimes be bad—they are *conditionally* bad. More generally, then, virtuous activity is sovereign over happiness, but it is not the only good; and that activity is the sovereign end in the lives of the virtuous, but it is not their only end. Nothing else is *as good*, and they value nothing else *as much*; but other things are still good, and happiness includes other ends as well.

A major source of confusion here is the way other ends are related to virtuous activity. If it were the only good or the only end valued by the virtuous, then nothing else would be good except to the extent that it contributed to that activity. This would suit Aristotle's account of the two additional needs for external goods as instrumental resources and as conducive to the development of virtuous character, but it would leave the very exercise of virtue without any point. Saving others' lives, for example, would not be a good thing to do unless human life has some value on its own, whether or not the people saved are virtuous or have much chance of becoming virtuous. Or if rationality were the only valuable end in human life, it would not matter what we did so long as we advanced the cause of rationality; unless other things have independent value of their own, rational activity would outweigh every other claim, and it would be justifiable even to eliminate anything or anyone who interfered with rational life. But Aristotle's claim is not that the exercise of rational virtue is the only end in a good human life. Rather, he holds that other things are good and are ends for virtuous activity, although none should be sought at the cost of violating any virtues. There are virtuous ways to seek health, pleasure, and honor and to interact with others, and each of these external goods is itself good. Although none can be part of happiness except in conjunction with virtuous activity, it is generally better to have them rather than their contraries, even in the absence of virtue. But then, since other things are good not only instrumentally or as occasions for exercising virtue but intrinsically, virtues are not the

25. See Sextus *AM* 11.65 and *PH* 3.192. For more on health, see III.ii–iii below.

only things that are good "by themselves," and the virtuous have other ends beside virtue.[26] If the virtuous have any reason to choose one thing over another, some other things must have some value on their own. Otherwise, no one way to seek or use them would be more or less rational than any other. Similarly, to know what are the virtuous and rational ways to seek anything else, we must know what value those things have. To choose some of them over others, we must know which are more valuable. But things that have some value of their own are worth pursuing as ends.

The fact that the virtuous seek other ends that are intrinsically good helps explain why virtuous activity is sovereign. First, it is not sufficient because happiness is a composite end consisting of an organized range of ends, not only virtuous activity but also the exercise of virtue on behalf of at least some other valuable ends. Although the virtuous consider virtuous activity more important than any other single end, they also consider other ends necessary for happiness. In short, virtuous activity by itself is not enough for happiness, but it is enough when conjoined with other intrinsic goods.[27] Second, sovereignty implies that the exercise of virtue outweighs any conflicting pursuit. The virtuous consider other ends good by themselves, but they seek them only in ways consistent with virtue. Quite often, of course, the pursuit of other ends coincides with the exercise of virtue, or at least it does not violate virtue. In providing good food for friends, hosts act for their own pleasure and health, for the pleasure and health of their friends, and for the conversation and amusement of all. But these actions also fall within the sphere of generosity, temperance, and justice, and the virtuous choose these actions also because of virtue.[28] Whenever the pursuit of other ends would

26. Cooper (1985a: 179–84) argues that external goods are important because they provide options or opportunities for virtuous actions. But having children, for example, is good not only because they provide a "central context for the exercise of the virtues" (p. 183) but primarily because reproduction and family life are natural parts of human life. To invert Cooper's claim, the reason why having children is a *central* context (whereas having pets or fine pottery is not) is that children are major goods in the first place. Indeed, if Aristotle had held that ethical virtues are good utterly by themselves (rather than because they deal in the right way with various intrinsically good human concerns), then he would not have denied that the gods, who do only what is best, have these virtues (10.8 1178b8–18).

27. Cf. Irwin 1985d: 98–102 and White 1990: 118–20.

28. Cf. the example sketched by Vlastos (1984: 185): a typical exercise of temperance has virtue, pleasure, health, honor, and happiness among its ends.

require violating some virtue, however, the virtuous forgo those ends. If maintaining their health, for example, requires stealing food, they let their health suffer. But they do this quite willingly, for although they would prefer to exercise both health and justice, they value the latter by itself far more than the former by itself. Hence, subjective sovereignty blocks the worry that there might be occasions when the virtuous would *want* to forsake their virtuous activity; even when virtuous activity fails to yield happiness, they *know* that nothing else is as valuable, no matter how desirable it might be in other circumstances. In short, they recognize the objective sovereignty of virtuous activity: although they know that other things are *good* even in the absence of virtue, they also know that no amount of success in the pursuit of those goods can ever make them *happy* unless they exercise virtue.

Objective sovereignty implies that virtuous activity is the single most important part of a good life—so important that even by itself it is better than any combination of other goods that lacks it. And subjective sovereignty implies that the virtuous want to act and generally do act accordingly. In some situations, the claims of competing goods are "silenced" and lose all attraction for the virtuous, even if they would want them otherwise.[29] Socrates, for example, could gladly accept gifts from Crito, but he has no interest at all in Crito's offer to suborn the prison guards. In other cases, however, the virtuous may still feel the attraction of an option they reject as contrary to what they know they should do. Since they know that other ends are intrinsically good—by themselves and even without virtue—they recognize the attraction of those ends even in some situations where pursuing them conflicts with virtue. Moreover, if they did not, they would be less able to balance competing claims and make difficult choices correctly, which is a major way in which complete virtue is superior to natural virtue. When Socrates refuses to evade execution because he thinks it would be unjust, he can still see the attractions of what he must sacrifice (cf. 3.9 1117b7–13). Indeed, his very devotion to his way of life and his friends underlies the way he meets his unjust and unfortunate fate in the *Phaedo*. In

29. For the idea that some reasons "silence" other claims, see J. McDowell 1980: 369–70; cf. Irwin 1985d: 100–102 and Winch 1972: 203–7. Vlastos (1984: 186–89) speaks only of other reasons as having no "countervailing" weight against virtue; that seems to allow other reasons still to exercise some pull. The example from the *Crito* that follows in the text is part of the evidence for Vlastos's account (p. 187).

valuing the exercise of their virtue more than anything else, then, the virtuous neither disregard everything else nor count all conflicting claims null and void.

An abiding respect for other ends, even when outweighed by the claims of virtue, is what enables the virtuous to find a mean. It is not always possible to give each end its due, but there are always better and worse ways to respond to the circumstances. Antigone and Creon both claim to uphold justice and piety, but they each err precisely in "silencing" the other's claims.[30] Complete virtue, by contrast, knows the true value behind each claim. At least one claim must yield in some way, but even then there is no reason to violate virtue. Thus, after showing why it can sometimes be right to do "something shameful" to prevent greater evils (3.1 1110a4–22), Aristotle warns that sometimes the alternative is so bad that it should never be done at any cost (a26–29). The case he cites, from a lost tragedy by Euripides, is instructive. After killing his mother for having sold his father into certain death, Alcmaeon tries to justify his action by saying that he had sworn, under pain of his dying father's curse, to avenge his father's death. Although justice demands her punishment and Alcmaeon's oath and his father's curse give him strong reasons to act, nothing justifies murder; Alcmaeon "should rather die suffering the most terrible things" (a27). Here there are claims on justice from several sides; although Alcmaeon's choice upholds some of those claims, it violates the most important, and that makes his act wrong. Indeed, his choice would be all the more reprehensible if, as his excuses suggest, he "silenced" the claims of his mother's life. Had he shown anguish or regret, he might at least have deserved sympathy instead of ridicule (a28).[31] "Sometimes it is difficult," Aristotle concludes, "to distinguish what should be chosen or endured in exchange for what" (a29–30). But if the choice is right, and if the agent abides by it (a30–33), then not only is the action voluntary, but it is also admirable. Further, if the agents are virtuous and know their action is right, they too admire their own action as noble. But although this eliminates

30. See Nussbaum 1986: 51–82; she calls the failure "simplification."

31. In his account of voluntary action, Aristotle argues that observers should not always adhere to strict liability, but his remarks about Alcmaeon and about regret (3.1 1110b18–23) suggest that he thinks agents should adhere more closely to those standards. Even when it is right for others to condone or pity someone for doing something bad, it can be a sign of moral failure if the agent readily condones his own conduct.

regret at having chosen as they did *in that situation*, they may still regret the circumstances that obliged them to make such a choice. Although they would always be wrong to wish that they had chosen differently, they would often be right to wish that fortune had offered them better options.

As the possibility of conflict shows, the sovereignty of virtue does not guarantee an untroubled life. Like anyone else, the virtuous encounter unfortunate situations that leave them no choice but to accept less than they would like. So long as they retain their convictions and act accordingly, they see no reason to have acted otherwise. That is why the virtuous are secure against the extreme of unhappiness: so long as they act on their principles, they cannot end up "miserable [ἄθλιος], since they will never do hateful and base things" (1100b34–35).[32] If they are convinced that nothing can ever give them reason to act contrary to virtue, then they always have something to admire in their lives so long as they uphold their principles. But they are not secure against the middle ground of losing happiness because they may have sound reasons to wish that their options had been better. This is why virtuous activity is only sovereign over happiness rather than sufficient for it. If most of their effort is directed at avoiding ills, they do little that they consider good by itself; but without intrinsic goods to pursue, the ends of their actions are not final and their lives are incomplete. Or as Aristotle puts it in connection with his analysis of pleasure, fortune can "impede" their activity and prevent it from being "complete."

Presumably, whether happiness is the unimpeded activity of all states or of some one of them, some kind of pleasure must be most choiceworthy—if the activity is unimpeded, and that is pleasure. Hence, the best must be pleasure of some kind, even though many kinds are bad intrinsically. And this is why everyone thinks the happy life is pleasant, and why they weave pleasure in with happiness—reasonably so, since no activity is complete [τέλειος] when impeded, and happiness is something complete. Therefore the happy person has additional need for bodily goods and external goods and fortune, in order not to be impeded in these ways.   (7.13 1153b9–19)

The virtuous have "additional need" for good fortune because even their activity is not sufficient for happiness if it is impeded.

32. In standard Greek usage, "misery" is the contrary of happiness, not only its contradictory. Aristotle concedes that not all the virtuous are always happy, but he maintains that none are ever miserable. See IV.iv *n*30 below.

But since impeded activity can still be virtuous, Aristotle's point cannot be only that the virtuous need good fortune before they can exercise virtue. Rather, his point seems to be that some activities are better than others *because of their ends*; that is why only some are sufficient for happiness. If impediments were only a question of resources and instrumental needs, any activity would be as good as any other. If some are better, however, then it is because they are directed at or achieve better ends. Wealth and influential connections, for example, extend the range of ends we can pursue and make many other ends easier to pursue (cf. 1099a31–b2). But greater opportunities for action would make no difference for happiness unless acting for some of those ends is necessary for happiness, and greater ease would not matter unless it is better for activity to be easy—unless success or enjoyment make a difference for happiness. Impeded activity is not sufficient for happiness, then, because the pursuit of some ends is not sufficient, even when successful. Or as Aristotle puts it, impeded activity is not "complete," and happiness is something complete (1153b16–17).

Whereas many actions are choice-worthy not by themselves but only because of some further end they serve, activities that are complete are desirable "by themselves" and "because of themselves" (1.7 1097a25–34). But if impeded activity is not desirable by itself, then it is not sufficient for happiness, which is always desirable by itself, since it is "unconditionally final" (a33–b6). The virtues, of course, are valuable both because of themselves and because of happiness (b2–5).[33] But when fortune leaves the virtuous few opportunities to act for the sake of ends that are good by themselves, it removes one of the necessary conditions for happiness. The virtuous, like everyone else, are willing to act for the sake of some ends even despite impediments. But unless they can exercise their virtues in pursuit of ends they consider intrinsically good, they fall short of happiness because they have nothing else to choose "because of itself." It is a great and admirable achievement for anyone to face adversity with vir-

33. See I.i above on the "formal condition" of "finality." Given 1153b10–12 and 16–17, I think it right to connect Aristotle's analysis of pleasure here with his account of "final ends" in 1.7. But how and whether this coheres with his discussion in 10.4–5 are questions beyond my present scope. On the relation between his two accounts of pleasure, see Gosling and Taylor 1982: chap. 11.

tue and fortitude. But as the virtuous recognize perhaps best, it is better and more desirable to make good use of prosperity. Sharing deserved good fortune with friends, for example, is more desirable than rescuing ourselves and others from injustice and oppression. What determines whether the virtuous are happy, then, is the ends they seek in their actions. If their lives are dominated by actions aimed at avoiding impending ills, then they fall short of happiness, but if they also can act to achieve something good by itself, then their action is sufficient for happiness.

Aristotle clarifies the crucial distinction when he outlines the conditions necessary for happiness in a community. To be complete, he says, the exercise of virtue must be "nonconditional" rather than "hypothetical"; or as he explains, it must be more than compulsory or "necessary" (*Pol.* 7.13 1332a9–11). Because it is just to bring criminals to trial, for example, it is also noble, but "that has its nobility necessarily, since it is more desirable not to need to do that sort of thing" (a12–15). The just exercise of political office, by contrast, or the just use of property is "intrinsically noble"; whereas punishment only removes something bad,[34] these actions "construct and generate good things" (a15–18). More generally, he continues, the virtuous are best equipped to handle "poverty, sickness, and other bad fortunes nobly, but happiness depends on the contraries" (a19–21). Indeed, as he argues elsewhere, if the virtuous ever choose something bad such as poverty or sickness, they choose it "hypothetically" and "for the sake of something intrinsically good" (*EE* 7.2 1238b5–9). The point, once again, is that a good life requires more than fending off ills and responding to bad situations; to be happy, the virtuous must be able to pursue ends they rightly consider intrinsically good. Virtuous action compelled by circumstances is no less noble or admirable than the virtuous pursuit of good ends; but it is less good and less desirable. Like everyone else, the virtuous would prefer to enjoy what is good, and unless they exercise their virtue in pursuit of at least some ends that are good by themselves, their activity is not complete.

This account adds precision to the analysis of happiness by making explicit further conditions that virtuous activity must

---

34. The manuscripts speak of "choosing" (αἴρεσις) something bad, but some editors emend this to "removing" (ἀναίρεσις). Either way, my point stands; see Newman 1887–1902 on 1332a16.

meet before it is sufficient for happiness. Moreover, by connect-
ing this activity with pleasure, Aristotle also upholds one of the
major reputable views from which he starts, that a happy life is at
once the best, the noblest, and the most pleasant life (1.8
1099a21–30). Admitting that some pleasure is necessary is a major concession to fortune; for whether the problem is a shortage
of resources, the absence of valued ends, or simply lack of external success, the implication is that virtuous activity is not always
sufficiently enjoyable. This concession stops well short of hedonism, of course, because rather than asking from the start how we
can lead the most pleasant life, Aristotle first identifies happiness
with certain kinds of activity and only then argues that this also
makes life most pleasant.[35] But it does uphold a truth hedonism
overstates, that happiness is inherently satisfying. It would be
foolish, Aristotle insists, to think that physical torture or grievous
disaster leaves anyone happy (1153b19–21); good people may respond bravely and face their trials virtuously, but happiness requires more. To find sufficient enjoyment in their lives, even the
virtuous have additional need for good fortune. The need is not
great, and prosperity itself is excessive if it interferes with doing
what they value most (b22–25).[36] But a good life is impossible
when the most important activities are seriously impeded and
incomplete. The virtuous can be happy with less than the best,
and they do not need to exercise their virtues always and only in
the best ways and in the successful pursuit of the best ends. But
they do need to exercise virtue in pursuit of other final ends and
to have other interests they value as intrinsically good.

Aristotle's account provides no algorithm for measuring happiness, but it does specify the criteria for settling the question:
the sovereign factor is virtuous activity, but the virtuous have
some additional need for prosperity. On the other hand, since
different people seek different particular ends, the final standard

35. See Annas 1980: esp. 288–90; cf. J. McDowell 1980: 368–72. In McDowell's
terms, I claim that Aristotle's demand that happiness be pleasant starts "from the
left-hand side of the equation" (that a happy life is a pleasant life): happiness is
complete virtuous activity, complete activity is unimpeded, unimpeded activity
is pleasant; so happiness is pleasant. This part of Aristotle's account meets one
of the major objections to translating *eudaimonia* as happiness; cf. Kraut 1979*b*.

36. Aristotle uses ἐμπόδια to describe anything—good (as in 1153b23,
1119a17, 1175b1–16) as well as bad (as in b16–18)—that interferes with activity;
cf. 10.8 1178b3–5.

for happiness rests with the virtuous themselves: only they can say whether their activities are impeded and incomplete, and only they can say whether they are happy. In short, by making completeness and choice decisive, Aristotle makes the choosers decisive. Just as "the limit for prosperity" depends on their virtuous activity, so the measure of what is good, noble, and pleasant depends on what the virtuous enjoy; or as Aristotle puts it, they are "like a standard and measure [κανὼν καὶ μέτρον] of these things" (3.4 1113a25–33).[37]

Still, the relation between prosperity and happiness can be made more precise by asking what kinds of activity and what ends are essential for virtue, and how the pleasures of virtuous activities can constitute a good life. Two questions are central: What ends do the virtuous consider intrinsically good, and what exercise of virtue do they value most? First, in reaching his "outline" account of happiness, Aristotle argues that human virtue is essentially rational. How is specifically rational activity related to the several other ends that dominate traditional conceptions of a good life? And how is reason related to physical, material, and social well-being? Second, is there any place for specifically *moral* virtue in this account? Does rational virtue entail any standards for acting toward others? To be sure, Aristotle considers friendship and love important concerns for others. But can he explain justice toward people to whom we are not personally attracted or attached? In particular, does his account make room for duties or obligations, and acting for the good of others even when it seems detrimental to our own interests? Or is Glaucon's worry realized in Aristotle's theory? Does he fail to provide reasons for sacrificing one's own well-being for the sake of others, even in the absence of any personal ties of family or friendship?

The best place to start is the first aspect of human life that Aristotle mentions in the argument leading to his outline account. After proposing to present a "more illuminating" account of happiness by identifying the human function or activity, he eliminates "the nourishing and growing part of living" on the grounds that this is not "distinctive" of human life (1.7 1097b23–98a1). But this is not only a necessary part of life but also the source of the pleasures that many people equate with a good life.

37. Cf. 9.9 1170a18–22, *Pol.* 7.13 1332a21–23, and *EE* 8.3 1248b26–30 (analyzed in IV.ii below).

This part of life also raises another problem for his account, since no life, let alone a good life, is possible unless our basic biological needs are satisfied. People perish for want of external sustenance and shelter, and the entire species would perish if it failed to reproduce. But food and sexual partners are external and subject to fortune. Do they therefore count as another "additional need" for external goods? How does Aristotle fit these needs into his account? And how are these goods related to the virtuous activities that he considers sovereign over happiness and human life?

III

THE RATIONAL ANIMAL

He said the soul should be treated by certain incantations, and that these in-cantations are noble discourses. From these discourses temperance is engen-dered in the soul, and once it has been engendered and is present, it is easy to furnish health both to the head and to the rest of the body. So when he taught me both the potion and the incantations, he said, "Make sure no one per-suades you to treat his head unless he has first allowed his soul to be treated by you. For this is precisely the problem with people these days: some try to be doctors of temperance and of health separately." —Plato, *Charmides* 157a–b

Vital Needs and
the Human Function

BEFORE HE will offer the young Charmides a cure for his hang-over, Socrates insists on the importance of treating what ani-mates the body as well as the body itself. One of his aims is to illustrate the importance of taking care of our souls, but since part of the value of temperance resides in its contribution to health, his point implies that physical well-being is worth caring for too. But just how valuable is it? What place does physical well-being have in Aristotle's account of the good life and what is its relation to the virtuous activity that is sovereign over happiness? All hu-man pursuits presuppose a modicum of physical well-being, and it was widely agreed that a good life is impossible without a sound body as well as a clear mind. In most of what we do, we must be sensitive to our surroundings and able to move about more or less as we will. There were disputes about degree, of course, and opinions varied over how much or how little the body might need. Most popular and traditional ideals demanded a good deal more than the minimum. Solon, for example, took as his paradigms a war hero and two champion athletes in excellent physical condition, and physical traits account for three of the five items on his list of the elements of happiness (Herod. 1.32.6). But even ascetics gave physical fitness a major place in their ideals, and the crippled or sickly were universally considered poor candidates for happiness. Much-enduring Odysseus might survive for days adrift on Calypso's raft, but even he would need sustenance and would hardly be happy if he continued long in such desperate straits.

One effect of these views is to guarantee some external goods some place in the good life. The most austere way of life still requires provisions, and even if physical condition is good only for what else it enables us to do, it remains instrumentally necessary. In short, since fortune can deprive anyone of food and drink or clothing and shelter, happiness is subject to some physical need. Despite the contention of some, Aristotle insists that happiness can be wrecked by physical pain (*EN* 7.13 1153b19–21). Theorists may quarrel over the limits, but at some point pain makes a good life impossible. Moreover, if tradition is right that happiness must be pleasant, as Aristotle thinks it is, then the mere absence of pain is not sufficient either.[1] Human life consists in the pursuit of valuable goods, not merely the cautious avoidance of ills. Some carried the banner of self-sufficiency to paradoxical extremes, but total independence of the external world lies beyond human capacity. Gods can disdain mortal sustenance entirely, but people must meet certain animal needs just to stay alive. Cynics and others might boast of doing without society, but even they need external provisions to stay alive. In short, our physical nature demands sustenance before we can do anything, let alone pursue virtuous goals. "Anyone who is human will have need [δεήσει] also of external flourishing, for human nature is not self-sufficient for reflection; rather, the body must [δεῖ] be healthy, and food and other provisions must be available" (10.8 1178b33–35).[2]

Self-sufficiency comes in degrees, and even the most self-sufficient mortals still have some needs. Aristotle's discussion of physical needs thus implies a negative response to the controversial question of whether virtue by itself secures happiness. Although he argues that reflection is more "self-sufficient" than political activity, he contends only that philosophers have *fewer* external needs, not that they have *none at all*. Reflection is possible without many resources, but the activities of the mind still presuppose some basic goods; even philosophers need to eat.

1. Some of Aristotle's contemporaries reduced happiness to "living painlessly" (ἀλύπως ζῆν). But the wholesale condemnation of pleasure is one of the few views that Aristotle cites as controverting universal consensus; see his rebuttal of Speusippus, esp. 10.2 1172b35–3 1174a12, and cf. 2.3 1104b24–26.

2. The phrase τὴν λοιπὴν θεραπείαν seems to refer to what is necessary for normal life: given human susceptibility to heat and cold, even philosophers need shelter and clothing; cf. *Pol.* 1.8 1256b19–20 and Xenophon *Mem.* 4.5.9.

The self-sufficiency being discussed would be found especially in reflective activity; for although a philosopher [σοφός] and a just man and the rest have need of what is necessary for life itself [τῶν πρὸς τὸ ζῆν ἀναγκαίων δέονται], once they are adequately supplied [ἱκανῶς κεχορηγημένων] with those things, the just man needs people for whom and with whom he will do just things—and similarly for the temperate and the courageous and each of the others—but the philosopher can reflect even by himself, and the more so the wiser he is. Presumably he could reflect better if he had associates, but still he is most self-sufficient.

(10.7 1177a27–b1)[3]

A life centered on reflection comes as close to self-sufficiency as human life can, but even it is still subject to fortune for the satisfaction of some basic needs. More important than quibbles over degrees of self-sufficiency, however, is the question of how these needs are related to the good life. Aristotle regularly assigns them a special status: the needs he singles out here are the food, drink, and shelter required to maintain the vital functions of life itself.[4] Unlike immortals, who sustain their activity without external support, the human animal has bodily needs that must be met before it can act at all. But if material sustenance is necessary for human happiness, it is because it is a precondition for any kind of life, for happiness and its contrary alike. Similarly, these biological needs are basic not only because satisfying them does not make life satisfying as a whole but also because not satisfying them is harmful to the organism. Unless they are met, they threaten survival as well as happiness. Finally, basic needs have less connection with a good life than additional needs do. Whereas the latter are necessary specifically for doing something good and pursuing our ends, vital needs are necessary for doing anything at all, whether good or not.

Since basic needs are prerequisites for any activity at all, whether virtuous or not, they are compatible with Aristotle's outline of happiness, and there is no reason to add an amendment detailing these needs. On the contrary, his account helps explain their insignificance. A definition tells "what something is," which includes only what is essential to it. A definition of happiness, then, should mention only its essential factor and not make

3. Cf. 1177b6–15, 10.8 1178a22–b7.
4. It is noteworthy that Aristotle consistently refers to these physiological requirements as "necessities" (ἀναγκαῖα, 1177a29, 1178a25) or "needs" (δεῖσθαι and δεῖν, 1177a29, a30, 1178a24, a29, b2, b6, b33, b34, 1179a1), without once mentioning "additional need" (προσδεῖσθαι). See II.v above and further below.

explicit everything presupposed or implied by its essence.[5] Or in Aristotle's terms, which distinguish what modern usage often conflates, not everything necessary is essential. In particular, although preconditions are necessary (ἀναγκαῖα), they do not appear in a formula of essence because their very necessity depends on that essence. If "rational animal," for example, adequately defines the human essence, a great number of human attributes are omitted; but provided this formula explains the place of those other attributes, there is no need to list everything necessary for human life, let alone every human trait. Likewise, anything presupposed equally by a happy or an unhappy life, such as the "necessities" of food and shelter, does not count as a component of happiness or a part of its essence, nor does it belong in a definition of happiness. What we seek in our pursuit of the good life, after all, is not merely to live like plants or other animals, growing and reproducing, but to live in specifically human ways. Essential to the good life are the ends we value for their own sake, not the innumerable things that are needed to pursue anything at all.

In the *Nicomachean Ethics*, which approaches happiness by way of the hierarchy of ends, Aristotle neglects to make explicit this distinction between the essence of happiness and its prerequisites. But in the *Eudemian Ethics*, he explains the distinction and underscores its importance at the outset. After a brief preamble citing the Delian epigram, he sets two questions for his inquiry: "On what [ἐν τίνι] does living well depend?" And "How is it acquired?" (1.1 1214a14–15)[6] Then, turning to the first question after a brief survey of the reputable views on each question, he emphasizes the importance of distinguishing the components or "parts" of happiness from what is only necessary for happiness,

5. Devereux (1981) highlights some of the connections between Aristotle's account of happiness and his essentialism.

6. The key phrase in the first question, "is in" (here with an ellipsis of ἐστι), has more than one sense. Woods (1982: 53–54) understands it as referring to constituent parts (as "consist in"), given the references in the following lines to the thing itself (b15, 16) and "what it is" (b25–27). But the sense of "depend on" better fits the contrast between two kinds of causes, provided "X depends on Y" is understood in the strong sense of "Y is the dominant constituent of X." Similar usages abound: happiness is sure to depend on one of three major goods (εἴη ἂν ἐν, a31), but it "consists of" one or more of them (εἶναι ἐκ, b2–5); the question "What is happiness?" (τί εἶναι) depends on character (ἐν τῷ ποιόν τινα εἶναι, 1.4 1215a21–23); hedonists say happiness depends on enjoyment (ἐν τῷ χαίρειν, 1.5 1216a18); and happiness depends not on fortune, but on the "sovereign" activities of virtue (ἐστι understood, EN 1.10 1100b8–11).

its prerequisites. The tendency to confuse the essence of happiness with its necessary means, he charges, is "responsible for the dispute" over what happiness is. Many people mistake its prerequisites (ὧν ἄνευ οὐχ οἷόν τε) for its parts (μέρη)—"through what it comes to be" for "what it is" (1.2 1214b24–27).[7] Hence, it is crucial "to distinguish, neither rashly nor carelessly, (1) *on what* [ἐν τίνι] of ours living well depends, and (2) *without what* [τίνων ἄνευ] it is not possible for people to live well" (b11–14).

To illustrate his point, Aristotle draws an analogy with the more familiar case of health. Health is essentially a certain physical condition, but that condition cannot be attained or maintained without a number of prerequisites, ranging from air to exercise (b14–24). A second distinction, within the class of prerequisites, neutralizes the potential objection that some "necessities" are not necessary for each and all. Both common or general needs shared by all (κοινά, such as "breathing, being awake, or being able to move," b19–20) and more specific needs peculiar to some but not others (ἴδια, such as "eating meat or walking after dinner," b23–24) count as prerequisites, even though only the former are necessary for everyone. The needs "common" to every form of life are hardly sufficient for health by themselves; the sick breathe and move as surely as the healthy, though not as well. But neither are the specific forms of diet and regimen sufficient for health, let alone part of its essence. Meat and exercise are conducive to health, at least for some, but it is what the body can do as a result of these, not the dining and walking themselves, that constitutes health. Even if these factors together specify a set of conditions sufficient for health, they still fail to characterize the resulting condition, the physical condition that explains why each belongs to the set of things that are healthy. To explain which feature of Callias is his health, for example, it is not enough to pick out the several things that "make" him healthy, such as his having the necessary food. Rather, we must specify the condition produced by these preconditions, the condition that shows why that food is necessary and how it suits his needs.

7. Aristotle exploits a similar distinction between constituent parts and "necessities" or prerequisites in his discussion of the ideal city: those who defend the city and deliberate about its good are "parts" of the city because they perform functions distinctive of city life, whereas those who provide food, materials, and other basic services are only "necessary" (*Pol.* 7.8–9). On Plato's analogy between city and soul, the parallel would be exact.

To do that, we first need to identify his condition as healthy, which depends on the nature or essence of human health. In short, the very necessity of these preconditions derives from the nature of health. If we were different, if we were gods, for example, then our health would not depend on these conditions, and the "necessities" would not be necessary. The point is not that no set of prerequisites can yield sufficient conditions, but (to deal in paradox) that their necessity is contingent on the nature of their end, the essence of health. Prerequisites help explain how someone is healthy, but the essence has a more fundamental role because it explains why they are needed in the first place.

Aristotle acknowledges the connection between necessity and essence, but he tries to isolate the latter from prerequisites by distinguishing different kinds of necessity. In principle, he argues, we can distinguish necessary conditions from the unconditional necessity of what is essential (*Met.* Δ.5). The latter, which he characterizes as "what cannot be otherwise" (1015a34), covers the attributes that yield the "primary" premises for demonstrations (b7–9). With this he contrasts "that without which it is not possible [οὗ ἄνευ οὐκ ἐνδέχεται] to be alive as a joint-cause [ὡς συναιτίου], as breathing and food are necessary for an animal since it cannot exist without them" (a20–22).[8] Since these "joint-causes" assist in the achievement of a previously established goal, their necessity derives from the nature of that goal. But they are only prerequisites for attaining the goal, since they make its realization possible but are not part of its essential character. They are thus necessary "in accord with" (a35) or "on account of" (b11) the simple necessity of essences. Since the necessity of prerequisites follows from the determinate goal that requires them, Aristotle calls this necessity "hypothetical": *if* the goal is to be achieved, *then* they are necessary.[9] The point is

---

8. On the status of "joint-causes," see *de An.* 2.4 416a9–18 (fire is only a συναίτιον of digestion and growth; soul is the αἴτιον), *Phys.* 1.9 192a13 (material substrate is συναίτιον to *logos*), and *Sens.* 4 441a27–29 and b15–20 (heat is not αἴτιον, but συναίτιον of flavors). The *locus classicus* for distinguishing mere prerequisites from causes and explanations is *Phdo.* 99a–b (αἴτια are mind and good; bodily parts are ἄνευ τοῦ . . . οὐκ ἂν οἷός τ' ἦ); cf. *Tim.* 46c–e (an αἰτία stands to a συναίτιον as explanation by the good stands to mechanical or material explanations), 68e–69a (same contrast between θεῖον and ἀναγκαῖον). Cf. Sorabji 1980: 143–74; M. Frede 1980: 237–41.

9. For this conception of conditional necessity, see *Gen. Cor.* 2.11 and Cooper 1985b; cf. the discussion of instrumental needs in II.v above. In the *EN*, Aristotle claims that αἰδώς is "good hypothetically," since it would be right to feel shame

clearer when the prerequisites serve a good end, when they are "things without which something *good* cannot be or come into being, or one cannot be rid of or remove something *bad*, as drinking the potion is necessary in order not to be ill" (a22–25). Since the healthy do not take medicine, medicine can scarcely be part of health; rather, it is necessary only with a view to restoring health, on the "hypothesis" of that end to be achieved. Whereas the necessity of prerequisites is explained by health, health itself is explained by reference to the form of life and the characteristic activities of the individual and its species.[10]

The "common" prerequisites for health are necessary because without them "nothing either good or bad would be present in us" (*EE* 1214b20–21). If the physiological functions of respiration and digestion fail, life stops, taking with it everything good and bad equally. But unless life is to be maintained, neither these functions nor the materials necessary to sustain them are necessary. Indeed, unless there is some point in remaining alive, unless there is something to be done by the living being, then presumably there is no need for any of the prerequisites. Similarly, health presupposes the adequate functioning of these and other physical processes, but since health is a kind of physical condition—the fitness to perform the physical activities of life well—none of its prerequisites are necessary unless there are other activities to perform. In fact, it is the nature of those activities that determines what condition is "adequate" in the first place, and the standards of health depend on the characteristic activities of the individual or species. In the standard fourth-century model of health as "a blending and symmetry of hot and cold" (*Phys.* 7.3 246b4–6),[11] the physiological processes of breathing and eating that provide for cooling and heating, and also the air and food processed by them, count only as preconditions for health, not as components of its essence. Moreover, which symmetry is healthy depends on the activities to be performed. Health for people differs from health for fish (*EN* 6.7 1141a22–23), because different species lead different sorts of lives, differing not only in

---

if one did something bad, although it would obviously be better not to do anything bad in the first place (4.9 1128b29–31).

10. For the notion of a "form of life" in Aristotle, see Clark 1975: 16–17.

11. This conception of health dates back at least to Alcmeon (fr. 4), and Aristotle cites it as a reputable view suitable for dialectic (*Top.* 6.6 145b8–11; cf. 10.3 1173a24–28).

the media they inhabit and hence the prerequisites they consume but also in the activities they perform. The crucial point, then, is that what an organism needs to achieve and to maintain good physical condition is determined by what it does. In an analysis of health offered to illustrate the nature of dispositions, Aristotle makes the same point: health itself and hence its prerequisites differ according to the form of life the organism leads. First, health belongs to the class of dispositions (ἕξεις), because it consists in "having some condition relative to something [πρός τι πὼς ἔχειν]" (Phys. 7.3 246b3–8).[12] In particular, it is the "perfection" (τελείωσις) of the body (a10–16). Many, in fact, considered it a "virtue" or "excellence" of the body because it enables people "to avoid illness when they use their bodies" (Rhet. 1.5 1361b3–4). It is, however, relative to the ends people use their bodies to perform; as Aristotle puts it, health "conditions [διατίθησι] its possessor well toward its own experiences [περὶ τὰ οἰκεῖα πάθη], and those are the experiences by which it is naturally generated or destroyed" (Phys. 246b9–10). Health, then, is a disposition of an organism's "internal parts not only toward themselves but also toward its surroundings" (b6). The criteria for health in an animal can therefore be specified only by reference to the ways it interacts with its environment and the activities it normally performs, not merely by what suffices to keep it alive in a quasi-vegetative state. To be a specimen of its kind, it has any number of needs to maintain its "common" functions such as respiration and digestion. But the distinctive kind of life sustained by those processes is what determines how much of what it needs for a healthy life. In fact, there is even variation within the same species, depending on the individual's constitution and interests. Milo the wrestler needs much more fodder to sustain his mighty bulk (EN 2.6 1106b1–5), but he needs to maintain his dimensions only if he wants to continue his wrestling. The prerequisites for health are necessary but only hypothetically, since their very necessity depends on the kind of life one leads.

This analysis of health has important implications for the argument by which Aristotle tries to establish, at a very general

---

12. More precisely, Aristotle counts health only as a "condition" (διάθεσις), rather than a "disposition," because it is not stable enough or resistant to change; cf. Cat. 8 8b25–9a13.

level, that happiness consists essentially in excellent rational activity. That conclusion follows, he thinks, from the distinctive form of human life, what he calls the human function or activity (ἔργον): if rational activity is the human function or form of life, then "the human good" (which has been equated with happiness) is simply the *good* performance of this function, or "virtuous activity" (ἐνέργεια κατ' ἀρετήν, 1.7 1098a3–17). This argument has occasioned immense discussion, to which I cannot do justice here.[13] But four points are important for what follows. First, the generality of this conclusion deserves emphasis. Far from settling the place of reason in ethics, the conclusion leaves wide open the question of what activities are both rational and virtuous. In particular, by introducing the term "virtue," the argument opens the door for Aristotle's subsequent analysis of moral virtues, but it does not limit the discussion to moral qualities. The term applies equally to qualities of mind (as in *EN* 6) and to physical qualities like health (as we have seen above). In fact, inasmuch as the term could well be translated as "excellence," Aristotle's conclusion is virtually tautological: for *anything* defined by its activity, being a good specimen of its kind is doing its activity well; or as he puts it, "generally, the good of anything that has a function and action is thought to depend on its function [ἐν τῷ ἔργῳ εἶναι]" (1.7 1097b26–27).[14] Thus, in the course of analyzing virtue, he recalls that any virtue not only "perfects" (ἀποτελεῖ) what has it but also makes the thing perform its activities well (2.6 1106a15–17). Since the function of eyes, for example, is seeing, the virtue of an eye makes the "virtuous eye" a good eye, and that means it sees well (a17–19; cf. *de An.* 2.1 412b18–20). By analogy, just as good eyes see well and good musicians play well, so good humans do well what humans do. If the human function is rational activity, then the human good is good rational activity. The implications of this for ethics remain to be seen, and only further analysis can settle whether human virtue is moral virtue. In short, the function argument is not meant to show that moral conduct is rational. That can be done

13. Hutchinson 1986: 39–72 contains a detailed reconstruction; brief and especially helpful are Whiting 1988, Clark 1975: 14–27, and Nagel 1972. Nagel characterizes a thing's *ergon* as "what it does that makes it what it is" (p. 8).
14. For the translation "depends on," see *n*6 above. Cf. 1098a8–12, a15, and *EE* 2.1 1218b37–19a8 (which ascribes "virtues" to cloaks, boats, and houses).

only by examining the moral virtues one by one and showing how they provide the rational way to live a human life.[15]

The second point is closely related: the function argument does not show, and is not meant to show, that a good life is good *for us*, if that means it must be conducive to survival or satisfaction.[16] Arguments about human nature may *justify* giving rational activities priority—they may show that it is *good* to live rationally—but none can ensure that living by those priorities is good, let alone best, for either our survival or our pleasure. The argument shows that leading a human life is living rationally; hence, any way of life that is good *for us as humans* must be a rational one. But that shows only that enjoying other activities is not enough for a good *human* life and not that no other activities make life pleasant or that rational activity does. Aristotle, of course, goes on to argue that the exercise of rational excellence is "most pleasant," on the grounds that rational activity has pleasures of its own (*EN* 1.8 1099a7–31). But many people consider physical pleasure the primary factor in a good life; the function argument simply does not address hedonism or egoism, and only further argument can show that each is wrong. Thus, to know whether rational activity is "good for us" and makes life satisfying, we need to know more about the nature and variety of rational activity. If Aristotle can show that rational life is conducive to survival and enjoyment, then he can meet the demands of hedonists and egoists. But the function argument is silent about pleasure, whether of food and sex, of art and play, or of friendship and philosophy, because pleasure is not its focus, any more than morality is.

A third point is connected with the worry that people are not the kind of things that have a function. Since this possibility would undermine Aristotle's argument, he supports his thesis by

15. The function argument aims to show only that the "good man" does well what humans do, not that he is "*morally* good" or finds his life *satisfying*. Similarly, the claim is only that "the human good" (or "the good for man") consists in good human functioning, and it remains to be argued that this is also "good *for others*" (or moral) and "good *for oneself*" (or satisfying). As J. McDowell (1980: 366–67) puts it, the function argument is "neutral" between competing candidates for happiness; cf. Hutchinson 1986: 46. Aristotle himself signals the need for further analysis to make the formula more precise: *EN* 1.13 1102a5–7 gives the motive for Books 2–6; cf. *EE* 2.1 1220a13–22.

16. Cf. Wilkes 1978, which contrasts "the good man" and "the good for man"; only the latter raises the question of satisfying our interests.

drawing analogies with bodily parts or organs, with animals, with artifacts, and with professions that make and use those artifacts.[17] The point of an analogy can be elusive, and critics have not failed to observe that these examples present some damaging disanalogies. First, organs and artifacts have merely instrumental functions and serve the ends of those who use them: the function of a hand or flute depends on what we want to do with each. On this analogy, the human function would have to serve some larger purpose, but Aristotle does not liken us to hands for the world or to flutes playing the tune of higher beings. Similarly, the fact that artifacts are endowed with a function only by the design of their makers suggests that humans receive their function from a creator, yet Aristotle denies the existence of any cosmic creation.[18] However, if the analogy is restricted to the forms of activity designated by a function, and if questions about what or whose larger ends those activities may serve are beside the point, then all Aristotle requires is that the standards for evaluating things that do perform some characteristic activity depend on those activities. His point, in short, is not that eyes are good because they serve the good of those who see, but that they are good at doing what eyes do; good eyes "work well," and since seeing is their defining activity, they see well, whether or not they are also attractive.[19] Likewise, a good sculptor is one who sculpts well and makes good sculpture. If rational activity is what makes us human, then a good human is one who exercises reason well.

This brings me to my fourth and final point, that the human function is the essence of human life. This explains both why Aristotle restricts it to a *single* form of activity and why he restricts it

17. Different versions of the argument use different examples: the *EN* cites *individuals* and the bodily parts that perform functions; only the *EE* mentions the (potentially misleading) *products* of crafts.

18. See Annas 1988a: 154–57. Aristotle notoriously distinguishes two senses in which one thing can be "for" (or "for the sake of") another: eyes are *for their owners* in that they benefit them; but they do that because they are *for seeing* (see *EE* 8.3 1249b14–16, *Phys.* 2.3 194a35, *de An.* 2.4 415b20–21, and *Met.* Λ.7 1072b2); see Whiting 1988: 35. My claim is simply that Aristotle relies primarily on the second sense in discussing functions.

19. Aristotle forestalls another disanalogy by distinguishing two kinds of *erga*: some are products over and above any activity, but others reside in the activity itself (e.g., 1.1 1094a3–5, *EE* 2.1 1219a13–18); his argument is not that happiness is a "product" of virtuous activity, but that it resides in it.

to our *distinctive* activity. First, his own argument suggests that many if not all people have more than one function. Sculptors, for example, appear to have two: both sculpting and the rational life they share with every other member of the species. But the suggestion is mistaken, since sculpting is itself a form of rational activity. Sculpture is a craft or skill (τέχνη), and every skill involves some exercise of reason (6.4 1140a6–10). More generally, Aristotle does not limit the human function to a single activity; rather, he limits it to one *general kind* of activity, a genus that embraces a host of *specific types*. In the same way, his essentialism implies that sculptors are primarily or essentially humans and only secondarily or accidentally artisans. But defining us as rational animals no more makes us pure thinkers than limiting our function to one generic activity excludes its specific forms. If Aristotle is right, then, all the multifarious activities that reputable views associate with a good life involve using our capacity to reason.[20]

There is no need to list the many species of rational activity because they are embraced by that genus. But why does Aristotle limit our function to a single genus of activity? At the most general level, the human activity is living, and we share nutritive capacities with all creatures and perceptual capacities with all animals (1.7 1097b33–98a3). So why is he unwilling to equate our function with life quite generally? Why not assign us a complex function that includes our vital capacities? The explicit answer is that everything but rational activity is "common" (κοινόν), and a function is "distinctive" (τὸ ἴδιον, 1097b33–34).[21] But again one

20. In the initial formulation of his conclusion (1098a4–5), Aristotle himself distinguishes two kinds of reasoning, each of which takes diverse forms. Further, laughter (cf. *Part. An.* 3.10 673a4–10), the use of tools (as in τέχναι), social life (cf. *Pol.* 1.2 1253a1–18), and even perversity (1253a31–37) are distinctively human, and all depend on some use of reason. Clark (1975: 17–22) argues, moreover, that all the various forms of human life are expressions of our capacity for rational choice. Hence, the charge that Aristotle wrongly restricts our function to one activity rests on misunderstanding; cf. Annas 1988a: 157–60. Aristotle finds similar variety in other animals as well: he describes the function of horses as threefold—running, carrying, and facing danger (*EN* 2.6 1106a19–21); despite its anthropocentric perspective, this set is meant to pick out the species of generic animal-movement characteristic of horses.

21. Cf. 1.13 1102a32 (esp. the contrast of "common" and "human," b3; cf. a14–16), 6.12 1144a6–11, *EE* 1.8 1218a31–37, and *Pol.* 7.13 1332b3–5. I agree with Whiting (1988: 37–39) that "distinctive" here refers to attributes that are "essential" rather than merely "necessary but non-essential"; cf. n23 below. The point

wants to ask why. One reason is that it is a reputable view, if any-thing is, that humans differ decisively from other species, and primarily in our capacity for thought. Despite the way some people behave, despite what totemist myths imply, and despite the extensive similarities that biology reveals, nearly all agree, from ascetics to sensualists, that human life differs radically from animal life.[22] Cattle may have little else to do than ruminate and propagate, but humans are capable of more, do more, and want more. Make us as lithe, fecund, and perceptive as possible, but take away all trace of thought, and none would call us happy.

Consensus is not all Aristotle has to offer. He also outlines a psychological theory to clarify his thesis (1.13; cf. *EE* 2.1 1219b26–20a4), and he elsewhere defends that theory and the essentialism underlying it.[23] A full and precise explanation would be "more work" than necessary here, as he says (1102a25), but one point of analogy can clarify the problem. Isolating a thing's distinctive function is parallel to defining its kind: just as a definition differ-entiates humans from other species in our genus, so the human function specifies our distinctive form of life; and just as a full list of the congeries of attributes a species has is unnecessary be-cause the differentia implies or explains the other attributes, so there is no need to list more than the distinctive form of life even if it embraces other activities. The point is not that all activity of our vital capacities is excluded from human life. On the contrary, if the human species is defined as "rational animal," the differen-

is crucial, for it meets the charge that our function must include all activities that are uniquely human, such as wearing clothes, cooking, and playing flutes, to name but a few: if only essential attributes are distinctive, then non-necessary activities are excluded, and only what we must do to be human is included. In short, what is distinctive need not be peculiar or unique; cf. *n*20.

22. Cf. *Rhet.* 1.1 1355b1 and (e.g.) Isocrates *Antid.* 253–54; see also III.ii below.

23. For analysis of how Aristotle's metaphysics and psychology underpin his account, see Irwin 1980, 1981a, and esp. 1988A. Irwin also argues that these theo-ries play the major part in his argument. I agree that Aristotle has the materials to provide a deeper defense and explanation of his account, but I think he re-stricts himself largely to reputable views in his ethical works; see I.ii *n*17 and *n*18 above, and cf. Annas 1988a: 159 *n*24, and Roche 1988: esp. 55. Thus, Aristotle uses conventional terms and not the more precise technical apparatus found in his discussions of metaphysics; "common" and "distinctive," for example, stand in for genus and differentia, and neither substance nor essence is mentioned. This need hardly reflect an early stage in his thought; more likely, he means to make his discussion accessible to the wider audience interested in ethics. Essen-tialism can back up the account, and Aristotle argues for essentialism elsewhere, but here it remains below the surface.

tia refers explicitly only to our distinctive activity, but all the generic activities of animal life—from nutrition and reproduction to motion and sensation—are implied by our genus.[24] Likewise, the human function is rational activity, but we also perform other activities rationally. On Aristotle's theory of definition, however, genus and differentia are intimately connected. A human being is not two homunculi, a reasoner and an animal, with two unrelated sets of needs and attributes, but a single uniform creature, an animal that lives by reason.[25] Similarly, the human function is not a disembodied activity performed in isolation from every other activity; rather, it includes any exercise of reason and caters to bodily needs as well as to abstract thought. In short, because we are animals, rational activity embraces physical activities, but because we are rational, many of those activities have a distinctive character. The basic question, then, is not why our function has to be distinctive, but how it is related to the great variety of things we do.

The "common" activities are necessary for any life, so they must have some place in a good life. Clearly, their primary role is instrumental: they make rational activity possible. But Aristotle characterizes our function in a way that suggests a larger role and a closer connection to rational activity. After defining our function as "a practical way of life belonging to what has reason," he distinguishes two ways in which we are rational, both by "obeying reason" and by "having it and thinking" (1.7 1098a3–5).[26] As he makes clear later in the argument, the former centers on desire: "The appetitive and generally desiring factor in the soul shares in reason by listening to it and obeying" (1.13 1102b30–31). Hence, the practical activities of forming rational desires, of deciding which to act on, and of acting to satisfy them are part of our function to the extent that they are based on reasons—on beliefs and reasoning.[27] So the human function embraces two

24. I skate over a host of puzzles and refinements; but see de An. 2.3, esp. 414b28–15a11 and 415b8–14 (to live [ζῆν] is what it is for an animal [ζῷον] to be).

25. On the unity of definitions, see Met. Z.10–12 (esp. 1038a18–33) and H.6.

26. A "practical" (πρακτική) life is distinctively human, since Aristotle denies that animals have any share in "action" (πρᾶξις); see 6.2 1139a17–20, cf. Phys. 2.6 197b1–8. Since he also denies that the gods perform actions (10.8 1178b8–22), practical activity is *uniquely* human.

27. See Hutchinson 1986: 50–52, 57–59; Hutchinson calls this "rationalism" because our function is "doing things with reasons" or "conduct rather than an-

general forms of rational activity: the practical thinking involved in rational desire and action, and the theoretical thinking involved in observation and reflection. Since our "common" capacities generate and influence many of our desires, they too are closely connected with our function. The nutritive capacities we share even with plants give rise to appetites for food and sex, and perception and motion prompt a vast variety of desires.[28] Although none of these vital but generic capacities is itself a part of our function, rational activity concerned with them is. Digestion, for example, is not a form of rational activity, but using reason to guide or shape our appetites is.

In limiting the human function to rational activity, Aristotle makes it exclusive in one sense but inclusive in another. Although he denies that our function is a mere conjunction of all we do, he does not consider it entirely homogeneous. More precisely, a function is neither an unordered set of activities nor a single specific activity. Rather, it is a general type of activity, and as such, it embraces the many varieties of rational activity, some of which utilize other capacities together with reason. In short, our function also has traffic with our vital capacities. The nutritive capacity, for example, is not part of our function because reason has no direct control over the physiological processes of digestion and growth. Eating is still included in our function, however, to the extent that it is a practical activity in which we engage on the basis of reasons and desires. Similarly, bodily sensations are not part of our function to the extent that they occur all by themselves, but any sensing that engages our thought is rational and so part of our function.[29] The point here is not simply that capacities are arranged in a hierarchy—that rationality presupposes the other capacities, or that the others only serve it. On the contrary, the gods are rational but have no digestion,

---

imal movement; rationality is the mark which distinguishes conduct from mere behavior" (59).

28. In *de An.* 2.2 413b21–24, 2.3 414b1–14, Aristotle argues that having the capacity for perception entails having the capacity for desire.

29. Cf. *EN* 9.9 1170a14–b14: to help explain why the virtuous need friends, Aristotle says that human life is defined (ὁρίζονται) by "a capacity for perception or thought," and that for us, living is "in the sovereign sense" (κυρίως) perceiving or thinking (a16–19); in arguing that it is good to *perceive* our friends being good (b7–14), he implies that our perception is distinctively rational and informed by reason.

and reason serves other needs as well as its own.[30] Rather, the crucial idea is that our function is a way of life that integrates a wide range of pursuits by guiding and shaping other activities as well as by pursuing ends of its own. After all, rational activity has many species. Some like the "pure" reasoning of mathematics and metaphysics have ends all their own, but others like tasting cuisine, viewing art, and listening to music or language utilize perceptual capacities, as well as deliberation about how and where to move and what desires to pursue. In short, we exercise reason on objects of sense and appetite as well as on mathematical objects, and though different in species, these activities are all of a kind. The former are accompanied by the exercise of other capacities. Nonetheless, all are species of rational activity, and they differ from the "common" activities in the way that listening to significant sound differs from hearing noise, and decisions to eat differ from hunger pangs.

Digestion and our other vital capacities are not part of the human function or of the human essence. But the rational supervision of digestion and the vital capacities is. *Excellent* supervision of those capacities is part of happiness, because happiness consists in excellent rational activity, and rational supervision is part of our rational activity. Indeed, if the exercise of rational virtue is the essence of happiness and if there are virtuous ways of attending to our vital needs, then exercising virtue in attending to our common capacities is part of the essence of happiness. In fact, excellent supervision of our vital capacities is a necessary part of

30. Hierarchy takes many forms: superiority may depend on greater generality (as on a Porphyrean tree), greater breadth (genera have larger populations than their species), greater value (some species may be better than others), greater control (as in bureaucracies), and so on. Aristotle thinks that rational activity is superior in all but the first way: reason is no less determinate than sensation, but it includes other activities, is better than them, and controls them. Nagel (1972: esp. 10–11) invokes hierarchy to explain how our function is "that around which all other human functions are organized." This avoids equating our *ergon* with "a collection of sub-erga without orderings of priority and support" (p. 13), but Nagel worries that it makes theoretical reason despotic (seeking only its own good) and reduces practical reason to "essentially a care-taker" (p. 12). Practical reason, however, also has its own theory: it *knows* what is good, e.g., that giving a gift to this person now is better than saving for oneself (or vice versa); even in catering to bodily needs, it utilizes *knowledge* of what is valuable. Thus, as Nagel suggests in parting, our function "is not just intellectual but involves both theoretical and practical concerns" (p. 13). In fact, we cannot learn what is good without perceptual experience or become good without practical experience.

a good life, since those capacities are necessary for any life. Still, it remains to be seen what kind of supervision is rational and what makes it excellent. Part of the aim must be to supply our animal needs; or as Tom Nagel has put it, one task of reason is to be "janitor or pimp of the passions."[31] But if that were its only task, it would only make us more efficient beasts, and happiness could be attained by Apis, the sacred bull pampered by the Egyptians (*EE* 1.5 1215b30–16a2). One higher aim, of course, is to make room for exercising reason on ends of its own, on learning and reflection, for example. But again, if that were reason's only aim, it would be right for reason to ignore our vital needs as much as possible. In fact, reason has a wider aim: in catering to our needs and in seeking ends of its own, it aims to do justice to all of human nature and to do rationally whatever we as humans need to do.

Everyone who acts on the basis of reasons engages in rational activity, and in the broadest sense, this embraces most of what people do. But of course, the excellent exercise of reason is much narrower, and rational activity in any sphere can be better or worse in two important respects. First, our beliefs may be true or false, and our inferences correct or mistaken; that is one reason why the human good is *excellent* rational activity—in other words, the exercise of rational *virtue*.[32] Second, even those who exercise reason correctly may exercise it on better or worse objects, on the heavens or on their bellies; this is part of why Aristotle thinks reflection makes life better than practical activity alone can.[33] Hence, any activity that engages one's reason counts as the performance of our function, but only its excellent exercise constitutes happiness. All humans act rationally, but some act more rationally than others, and only those who act for good reasons and exercise reason on good objects engage in the excellent rational activity on which happiness depends. In limiting our

31. Nagel 1972: 11; cf. Clark 1975: 21.

32. This distinction between beliefs and inferences reflects the one Aristotle draws between having the correct principle (ἀρχή) or target (σκοπός) and reasoning correctly about how to act on it; see 6.12 1144a7–9, a20–36; cf. *EE* 2.11 and the discussion of "complete virtue" in II.iv above.

33. See 10.4 1174b14–31, where Aristotle distinguishes two ways in which an activity can be better or worse and more or less pleasant: our faculties may be in better or worse condition, and the objects on which we exercise them may be better or worse.

function to rational activity, then, Aristotle does not eliminate all other activities from happiness; any activities we perform rationally can be part of a good life. That is not to say that any specific activity is necessary for happiness: dining well is not necessary either for a good life or for survival. But it does imply that anyone who is happy engages in a range of rational activities. If dining well exercises rational capacities of taste on worthy food, or if it occasions and stimulates discourse and conviviality, or even if it is done simply on the basis of good reasons—to facilitate rather than impede other rational activities, or simply because it is naturally better to enjoy our food—then the rational activity involved in it can make it part of happiness, though only a subordinate part. In the absence of special reasons to the contrary, it is rational neither to deny our animal needs nor to refrain from enjoying their satisfaction. Reason enables us to refine these physical pleasures in ways that can enhance a good life. Few of these refinements are necessary, of course, but they may still be intrinsically good and—other things being equal—worthy of choice by themselves.

Rational activity is not simply something humans should pursue but something we do pursue. Every conception of the good life gives reason some part; the dispute is over whether it should have the leading part. This involves more than the question whether it is best to devote one's life to theory and reflection or to engage in practical affairs instead or as well. It also involves disputes about sensualism and the relation between reason and our animal nature. And it raises questions about how reason should oversee our practical ends. What place in happiness does Aristotle assign to practical activities that only rational animals can perform? Does the value of reason here depend primarily on its ability to attain external ends, or does the exercise of practical rationality have some value of its own? Before turning to these questions, I should clarify the place of physical needs and pleasures in Aristotle's conception of the good life. Not only is it necessary to satisfy these basic needs, but their satisfaction can also enhance life by making it more enjoyable, and Aristotle refuses to banish physical pleasure entirely: "The bad man pursues an excess of physical pleasures, not simply the necessary ones, since everyone enjoys cuisine and wine and sex, but not everyone enjoys them as one should [ὡς δεῖ]" (EN 7.14 1154a16–18).

How then should one pursue these pleasures, and how are they related to reason and virtuous activity? In particular, what is the rational way to satisfy physical needs and appetites, and what attitude does Aristotle think the virtuous should have toward food, sex, and physical well-being?

The Pleasures of Temperance

THE MOST POPULAR conception of happiness had it that the pleasures of food, drink, and sex are the most important part of a good life. Sardanapallos exemplified the ideal, and many people considered a "life of gratification" the most attractive one (*EN* 1.5 1095b16–22).[1] After all, not only do food and sex satisfy our vital needs, but in the process they afford pleasures that many seek for their own sake. To judge from actual practice, the pleasures of the flesh are intrinsically good. Moreover, when Aristotle argues that the human function is the exercise of rational excellence, the enlightened voluptuary could respond that physical pleasure sets the standard for rationality. The aim, one might argue, is to maximize enjoyment, and by devising ways to avoid pain and to gratify our appetites, reason is adept in helping us achieve that aim. Hedonists, it seems, can embrace the function argument as well as the pleasure principle.

One problem with a life of gratification, Aristotle argues, is that it is usually self-defeating. The sybarites' pursuit of pleasure threatens both their own goal of physical well-being and the material resources they need to gratify their appetites: people "are harmed more than helped by these pleasures, as they disregard their bodies and property" (10.6 1176b9–11). If hedonists themselves have good reason to refrain from gratifying some desires, the question is not whether to pursue pleasure, but rather which

1. The translation of ἀπολαυστικός, which refers specifically to physical pleasures (ἡδονή is the general term), is Irwin's (1985*a*); cf. *EE* 1.4 1215b4–5.

pleasures to pursue, and how much and when. Another problem involves fortune: some pleasures are easily found, but if the aim is to maximize gratification and if Sardanapallos is the ideal, then not many people will have the means to indulge themselves, and the good life will rarely be attained. Although some physical pleasure is sought "by itself," and many people seek it even at the cost of great harm (b6–9), the life of gratification is not "self-sufficient," since it leaves hedonists still "in need" of other factors to make their life worth living (b4–6). Again, nearly everyone recognizes things they would never be willing to do, no matter how great the physical pleasure they afford (10.3 1174a3–4). One person's horror is another's delight, but in every case, anyone who is repelled implicitly acknowledges there are some things more valuable than gratification alone.

To back up these internalist worries, Aristotle connects the function argument with a number of reputable views. First, as he observes in his analysis of pleasure, each species has its "own" (οἰκεία) pleasure, just as it has its own way of life, since pleasures are distinguished by the activities they accompany (10.5 1176a3–6; cf. 7.13 1153b29–31). Alluding to Heraclitus' observation that asses prefer garbage to gold, he draws the general moral that the distinctively human pleasures are not found in the enjoyment of food (1176a6–8 = B9 DK). By contrast, to live for the pleasures of food and sex is in effect to treat oneself as a beast (*EE* 1.5 1215b31–36). Worse, living to gratify nothing more than the needs of digestion and reproduction is tantamount to treating oneself as a vegetable, for these processes we share even with plants (1216a2–6). By giving priority to the needs of our nutritive capacities, which are most active during sleep, sensualism implies that we might as well spend our lives like Endymion in everlasting sleep (cf. *EN* 1.13 1102b3–11, 10.8 1178b18–20). As for any who do value physical pleasure above all else, Aristotle thinks we should no more trust their judgment of what is best than we would that of children: neither have enough experience to make sound judgments (10.6 1176b19–26). No one, or at least no one "in his right mind" (εὖ φρονῶν), is willing to revert to the life of a child and forsake the exercise of mature reason, even with the sorrows to which it exposes us, in favor of the mindless pleasures of infancy (10.3 1174a1–4; cf. *EE* 1.5 1215b22–24, 1216a6–9). Reversing the priorities of sensualism, therefore, Aristotle contends that happiness and sustained satisfaction are attained not by gratifying any and all of our animal appetites, but by rationally regulating the number and kind of appetites we have. Although sensualism is inadequate as an account of happiness, the question still remains, How important are the physical pleasures associated with external goods? Does Aristotle think fine food and wine or the pleasures of sex are of marginal value? Or does he consider them ends and good by themselves? In particular, what role does he assign health, "the virtue of the body," in the virtuous activity of happiness?[2]

The best approach to these questions is through Aristotle's account of the virtue of temperance (σωφροσύνη). In the first place, he explicitly restricts this virtue to the domain of bodily pleasures, and specifically to the pleasures of food, drink, and sex that loom largest in conventional hedonism. Although temperance also tends to physical comfort in general, Aristotle thinks its primary task is to govern the appetites for eating and intercourse.[3] Thus, since the temperate enjoy these vital functions correctly, his analysis should reveal how important he considers these external goods for happiness. For Aristotle, moreover, the preservation of physical well-being is a distinctive concern of temperance, and health is one of the standards against which the virtuous measure their pursuit of physical pleasures. Although temperance cannot guarantee good health, temperate conduct is at least conducive to physical well-being. And other things being equal, the temperate are the least susceptible to having their physical appetites frustrated by external influences and fortune.

2. Cf. *Rhet.* 1.5 1361b3, 1.6 1362b14–15. The belief that health is a virtue is not a popular error. Rather, it fits Aristotle's own account of excellence: the best condition of something is its "virtue," and health is the best condition of the body (*EE* 2.1 1218b37–19a5, 1220a18–19).

3. This restriction makes the traditional translation of σωφροσύνη as "temperance," despite its overtones of self-denial, more apt for Aristotle than for many authors, including Plato, who often uses the word in extended senses; see North 1966: esp. chaps. 4–5; cf. Young 1988: 521 *n*1. Because Aristotle restricts this virtue to physical pleasures, "moderation" is too general (it applies to any class of actions or objects); "moderation" also risks conflation with "the mean" (cf. Urmson 1973: 160–62). More misleading would be "self-control" or "self-restraint"; although temperance was often equated with ἐγκράτεια (e.g., Xenophon *Mem.* 4.5; cf. *Rep.* 430e and Dodds 1959 on *Gorg.* 491d11), Aristotle distinguishes them sharply. "Good sense" would capture some nuances of the term and reflect its etymology, but it is too general and would suggest that ἀναισθησία is its major contrary.

The virtuous thus appear to have as much control as anyone can over the physical aspects of happiness, because they regulate their appetites and behavior within the limits of what is suited to preserve their health. Moreover, by keeping their appetites limited in accord with their overall conception of happiness, they are also the least likely to have difficulty either in satisfying their appetites or in enduring situations of need. Finally, the major vice opposed to temperance consists in pursuing physical pleasure for its own sake, without regard to health or other ends. Whereas the temperate subordinate the enjoyment of physical pleasures to their physical well-being and other pursuits, the unrestrained (οἱ ἀκόλαστοι) tend to pursue physical pleasure at almost any cost.[4] The reason they give too large a place to these pleasures in their lives is that they misunderstand the human good.

Aristotle's standard procedure for determining the essential characteristics of each virtue is to circumscribe a specific range or area of human behavior that it governs.[5] To establish what temperance is, therefore, he begins by demarcating its scope, or as he puts it, "what it is concerned with" (*EN* 3.10 1117b24–28). Basing his discussion on ordinary usage and what people say about temperance and unrestraint,[6] he simply adopts from the start the conventional view that both traits concern some kind of pleasure.[7] Although he recognizes that unrestraint does have some connection with pain (b26), he attributes that pain directly to being deprived of certain pleasures (3.11 1118b28–33, 1119a3–5). However, since his analysis treats all character traits as disposi-

4. A number of considerations commend this translation of ἀκολασία, despite the solecism: Aristotle himself appeals to its etymology as "unpunished" or "unrestrained" (1119a33–b7; cf. *EE* 3.2 1230a38–b8); he assigns temperance two contraries, but "intemperance" would misleadingly suggest that it is the only vice; ἀκολασία is not cognate with σωφροσύνη, whereas "intemperance" would be cognate with "temperance." Although traditional usage tended to equate ἀκολασία and ἀκρασία (e.g., Xenophon *Mem.* 4.5), Aristotle distinguishes them sharply; cf. *n*3 above.

5. Virtues of character are dispositions to feel and act in certain ways (2.6 1106b16–24, cf. 2.5 1105b25–28), and Aristotle assigns different virtues to different kinds of feelings and actions, as outlined in 2.7 (cf. *EE* 2.3, esp. 1221a13–15); see Urmson 1973: 163–64.

6. Aristotle appeals to τὰ λεγόμενα at 1117b32, 1118a1, a5, a8, a11.

7. Cf. 2.7 1107b4–8, 3.10 1117b24–25. Although Plato regularly starts from the connection between temperance and physical pleasure, he expands the domain of temperance: see *Gorg.* 507a–b (following a discussion of pleasure, before arguing for the unity of virtues), *Rep.* 3.389d–90d, 4.430e, and *Symp.* 196c (in Agathon's speech, which is replete with conventional wisdom).

tions to feel pleasure and pain of some sort (2.3), Aristotle tries to specify which kinds of pleasure temperance governs. First, he adduces the evidence of ordinary usage to show that temperance is concerned not with "psychic" (ψυχικαί) and "mental" (τῆς διανοίας) pleasures but with "bodily" or physical pleasure (3.10 1117b28–18a1). All pleasure is something felt, something of which we are aware (10.5 1175b34–35). In that respect, all pleasures are "psychic" (1.8 1099a8) or "in the soul" (EE 2.1 1218b31–35).[8] Some pleasures, however, depend on the body itself being affected (πάσχοντος τοῦ σώματος, EN 3.10 1117b30–31), and it is among these that the pleasures associated with temperance are found.

Conventional usage also shows that the pleasures associated with the senses of sight, hearing, and even smell generally fall outside the range of this virtue (3.10 1118a3–9).[9] After conceding that people aroused by the smell of perfume or food are sometimes called unrestrained, Aristotle argues that this confirms his restriction: their unrestraint is only "coincidental" (a9), since their pleasure, though prompted by the sense of smell, depends on their recollection or anticipation of the physical pleasure to be gotten from what emits the smells. Hence, their appetite is not specifically for smells, but for the sex or food they associate "coincidentally" with those smells (a9–13).[10] Similarly, any pleasure animals find in sight or hearing is "coincidental" (a17), since it derives originally from the appetite for food or sex aroused by those senses (a16–23). In short, the only pleasures that fall within the domain of temperance appear to be those connected with taste and touch (a23–26). Even in the case of taste, however, Aristotle argues that we fault people for unrestraint not when their aim is to distinguish flavors but only when their goal is the "gratification" found in eating.[11] Sauciers and sommeliers cater to un-

8. See Bostock 1988: 254–55, 269–71.

9. As Bostock (1988: 271) observes, "Aristotle automatically classifies bodily pleasures by the kind of perception [i.e., the sense] involved, which is exactly what one would expect him to do if he thinks that all bodily pleasures *are* perceptions."

10. Aristotle describes the operation of association in the pleasures of memory and expectation in *Rhet.* 1.11 1370a27–b29; cf. *Phys.* 7.3 247a6–14.

11. In this light, Aristotle's remark that most people "haven't even any idea of noble things and the truly pleasant, since they have no *taste* of it [ἄγευστοι ὄντες]" (10.9 1179b15–16; cf. 10.6 1176b19) is pointedly ironical. Incidentally, Athenians used the title "temperators" (σωφρονίσται) for the men assigned specifically to oversee the *diet* of the ephebes (*Ath. Pol.* 42).

restraint in others, but they also put their refined sense of taste to its primary and natural use as a tool for "discriminating" among phenomena (κρίσις, a26–29).

On the other hand, since sheer gratification requires nothing more than contact with the objects desired, it depends very little on the cognitive powers of the senses. That fact, together with Aristotle's contention that the sense of taste is ultimately a form of touch (*de An.* 2.10 422a8–11), confirms again that temperance is concerned primarily with the appetites and pleasures stimulated by food and sex (*EN* 3.10 1118a26–b1). The few other pleasures and pains that sometimes appear in connection with these traits (such as feeling hot or cold, 7.4 1148a8; cf. Xenophon *Agesilaus* 5) are also directly connected to the sense of touch, since they are associated with physical comfort. Strictly, however, Aristotle attributes these feelings not to unrestraint but to "softness" (μαλακία, *EN* 7.7 1150a23–27, a32–b5), on the grounds that they involve unwanted feelings of pain and discomfort rather than a susceptibility to the attractions of pleasure. Unlike incontinence or "weakness" (ἀκρασία), which has the same scope as unrestraint,[12] "softness" has *physical pain* as its distinctive domain. Hence, the strict limit on the scope of temperance once again coincides with the sensual pleasures of food and sex. Conventional usage suggests one more qualification on the primacy of touch: no one is considered unrestrained for enjoying the "liberal" pleasures experienced "in physical training" (or "at the gym") because those are related not to the pleasures of food and sex but to exercise and hence implicitly to the natural good of health (3.10 1118b4–8).

Aristotle's demarcation of the scope of temperance has two closely related consequences. First, since the pleasures associated with the sense of touch are principally those derived from food, drink, and sex, temperance turns out to be the virtue that governs our care for the vital functions of the nutritive soul: nutrition and reproduction. The domain of temperance is specifically the "necessities" (ἀναγκαῖα) required for the operation of these two basic physiological processes (7.4 1147b25–28). Both functions are necessary, and practiced correctly, both are good for us and often pleasant. But given the wider range of human functions, both deserve to occupy a limited place in our lives, and that

---

12. Cf. 7.3 1146b19–24, 7.4 1148a13–17, b9–14, 7.5 1149a18–20, 7.7 1150a9–15.

is what temperance oversees. Second, the pleasures associated with these external goods are precisely what stimulate our "appetites" (αἱ ἐπιθυμίαι), or what Plato calls the appetitive part of the soul.[13] As many have observed, Aristotle's analysis restricts temperance to the domain of what were widely known as "irrational" appetites. But if our appetites are irrational in the sense that they can arise without any promptings from reason (hunger, thirst, and sexual arousal spring up on their own and often despite our better judgment), they are nonetheless rational in the sense that they are subject to the influence of reason. Not only can we choose to satisfy or deny our appetites in the light of a conception of some good, but the specific objects of our appetites usually depend on acquired tastes and habits. So, developing the very general account of our rational nature "outlined" in the *ergon* argument, Aristotle's account of temperance examines in more detail the relation between reason on the one hand and the physiological processes and consequent appetites on the other. To be sure, he denies there is any "human" virtue of the nutritive soul by itself (1.13 1102b1–12; cf. 6.12 1144a9–11). However, the needs of this part of the soul give rise to appetites. Since reason can and should govern all desires of the soul, some human virtue should regulate the desires arising from the operation of the nutritive soul. That is the role of temperance. Aristotle's account of temperance thus characterizes what he considers to be the reasonable way to satisfy the appetites and the virtuous way to seek physical pleasure.[14]

The connection between temperance and the appetites has the further consequence that this virtue embodies the proper relation between the distinctively human capacity of reason and the

13. Throughout his discussion of temperance, Aristotle refers only to the appetites (nineteen times) and never to rational desire; cf. 2.1 1103b17–19, 3.10 1117b23–24 (courage and temperance "are thought to be the virtues of the irrational parts of the soul"; cf. 3.2 1111b12–13). As Grant (1885) and Stewart (1892) suggest in commenting on 3.10, *EN* 3.6–9 and 10–12 (on courage and temperance; cf. *EE* 3.1, 3.2) reflect Platonic influence in their focus on θυμός and ἐπιθυμία respectively; cf. Fortenbaugh 1975: 83–87.

14. Hursthouse (1981: 62) objects that the unity of temperance is spurious, on the grounds that it governs three distinct kinds of desire (for food, drink, and sex). But since Aristotle considers each a form of appetite and hence connected with the nutritive soul, temperance does have a genuine unity. As for those who indulge too much (or too little) in only one of these areas (gluttons, drunks, or libertines), Aristotle's position mirrors the conventional view that no one who indulges too much in *any* of these areas deserves to be called "temperate."

animal side of human nature. Aristotle claims at several turns that the appetites involve the functions we share with animals.[15] It is precisely from the appetites that we derive the pleasures "the rest of the animals share in common [κοινωνεῖ]" (3.10 1118a23–25). In fact, all the pleasures felt by other animals, Aristotle evidently holds, depend on their sense of touch (a16–23). Since that is the one sense possessed by all animals, "unrestraint occurs in connection with the most common [κοινοτάτη] of the senses" (b1).[16] Unrestraint therefore "would justly be thought reprehensible because it occurs not insofar as we are human, but insofar as we are animals" (b2–3). That is why the unrestrained are called "brutish" (θηριώδεις, a25, b4): those who devote their lives primarily to the gratification of these desires instead of developing or exercising their distinctively human faculties give precedence to what we have in common with other animals. Thus, Aristotle's preliminary rejection of hedonism, when he likens the life of gratification to "a life of grazing animals" and calls it "servile" (1.5 1095b19–20; cf. 1118a25, b21), is based on more than reputable views or prejudice; it also has a theoretical basis in his analysis of human soul.

Aristotle's objections to the gratification of our animal appetites should not be exaggerated. Excessive indulgence is what he criticizes, not indulgence per se. Indeed, since the appetites governed by temperance are for the external goods necessary for the operation of the vital functions, they have natural and necessary functions: sustaining the individual and perpetuating the species. Aristotle thus distinguishes two forms of appetite: "common" or general (κοιναί, 3.11 1118b8) appetites for food in general that are shared by all, and "distinctive and acquired" appetites (ἴδιοι καὶ ἐπίθετοι, b9) for specific types of food that vary from person to person. Food and drink per se are objects of "common" appetites, since everyone seeks nourishment. When we

15. Aristotle draws parallels with animal behavior throughout the discussion in which he restricts temperance to the pleasures of touch: 3.10 1118a17 (animals), a18 (dogs), a20 (a lion), a22 (an Homeric lion, *Il.* 3.23–26), a25 (animals), a33 (a crane); cf. *EE* 1.5 1215b35–16a2 (the bull-god Apis), 3.2 1230b36–38, 1231a12–18. At the level of the nutritive soul, rather than the appetitive soul, temperance is concerned with what we have in common with plants; 1.13 1102a32–b5, *EE* 1.5 1216a2–6, *de An.* 2.4. See Young 1988: 526–28, 539–40.

16. Aristotle recognizes the existence of species without any other sense, but he thinks no species lacks the sense of touch; see *de An.* 2.2 414a2–3, 2.3 414b3, 415a3–6, and III.i above.

seek specific kinds of food and develop preferences and tastes, our appetites become "distinctive."[17] To the extent that our appetites spring from natural needs, they too are natural, since they aim at filling those needs and restoring or maintaining the proper functioning of the nutritive soul necessary for life. "The appetite for food is natural, since everyone in need [ἐνδεής] has an appetite for dry or moist food [i.e., food or drink]" (b9–10), and "replenishing [ἀναπλήρωσις] this need is [the goal of] a natural appetite" (b18–19).[18]

The appetites, however, are intimately connected with pleasure and pain. According to the prevailing analysis of pleasure, pain was equated with "the need for what is according to nature" and pleasure with the replenishment of that need (10.3 1173b7–8).[19] Although Aristotle denies that pleasure and pain are identical with these processes, he agrees that physical pleasure and pain both depend on the appetites. This reveals another natural and beneficial role for the appetites. Since unsatisfied appetites are painful (3.11 1119a4; cf. 7.12 1153a32), both they and the pleasures resulting from satisfying them perform the salutary function of stimulating us to fill our natural needs and thus to attend to our preservation. Within limits, then, satisfying our appetites is natural and necessary, and the pleasures of supplying the prerequisites of our animal nature have a legitimate place in a good life.

One objection Aristotle has to identifying pleasure with replenishment and pain with depletion is simply that it gets the facts wrong: not every pleasure involves need or replenishment (10.3 1173b15–20). Moreover, this account removes a criterion for

17. Cf. the contrast between "common" and "distinctive" conditions for health (*EE* 1.2 1214b14–24, discussed in III.i above). Gauthier and Jolif (1970) mistake the point in their note on this passage: they connect the common appetites with "everyone's" preference for Burgundy over *vin ordinaire*, and distinctive appetites with an individual's preference for Burgundy over Bordeaux. The difference is rather Plato's distinction between "thirst itself" for "drink itself" and thirst for wine or any other type of drink; cf. *Rep.* 4.437d–39b.

18. I follow Irwin's (1985a) interpretation of this obscure sentence, which seems to require the bracketed phrase for sense; the point would be the same if ἀναπλήρωσις were emended to the genitive: "the natural appetite is *for replenishment* of this need."

19. For the earlier background, see Dodds 1959 on *Gorg.* 493d–95b, Hardie 1980: 300–302, and Gosling and Taylor 1982: 16–25, 37, 80, 115–21. Plato seems to have associated this view with the medical tradition: he makes the pedantic doctor Eryximachus cite the theory (*Symp.* 186c).

determining which pleasures are worthy of pursuit; if all replenishment were good because it removes a need, every pleasure would be good. By contrast, Aristotle's account of the relation between pleasure and replenishment provides a basis for determining limits for the temperate pursuit of physical pleasure. On his analysis, pleasure arises from some activity of the soul, and the question is whether this activity is worthy of pursuit. Consider the case of food and drink, which the conventional theory fits best and which Aristotle claims inspired it (b8–20). Equating pleasure with replenishment confuses the physical conditions for pleasure with the activity of soul that constitutes the pleasure. The pleasure of eating or drinking is not identical with those processes, although it often occurs concurrently (b11–12). What is pleasant in these processes, according to Aristotle, is not the process of "getting full," much less the food and drink themselves, but the activity of the underlying natural capacities of the soul exercised in consuming them (7.12 1152b33–53a12; cf. 7.14 1154b15–20).[20] Contrary to the prevailing theory, then, replenishment itself—the mere transition from need to satiety—is pleasant only "coincidentally" (1152b34). Indeed, too much or too little food, and eating too much or too little, is painful precisely because the nutritive soul is then unable to function as it should. Similarly, the pain of hunger is not identical with the need for sustenance; rather, just as our pleasure in eating consists in tasting the food and feeling the operation of our nutritive soul, so need gives rise to the pain of hunger when we perceive our nutritive soul being impeded by lack of nutriment.[21] Further, since both the process of digestion and the appetites for nourishment are natural and necessary, Aristotle considers the pleasures found in these processes likewise natural, at least within limits. Those limits are established by "what is natural" (τὸ κατὰ φύσιν), namely, the "replenishment of need" (3.11 1118b17–19). Only be-

20. I take it that "the remaining state or nature" (1152b35–36) and "the remaining healthy thing" (1154b18–19) refer to the soul as a whole, including its nutritive, sensory, and rational capacities. Bostock (1988: 265–69) argues that it should be equated with our perceptual capacity, but although he is right that perception occurs when we feel pleasure, we feel pain rather than pleasure to the extent that our digestive capacity does not also function well.

21. The necessary connection between pleasure and perception here is shown by cases of depletion or replenishment during sleep or sedation: we may *be empty or full* while asleep, but unless we *are aware* of those states, we feel no pleasure or pain.

yond that point does excess begin; only when the pleasure accompanying a natural process excites an appetite for further indulgence does appetite exceed the natural limits, and only then is its satisfaction no longer natural. But the common appetites are simply for what will fill a natural need; hunger itself is for food itself, in Plato's terms. Given this vital function, the common appetites are natural.

For the common appetites, the only error is excess, something Aristotle considers uncommon (3.11 1118b15–18). His point presumably is that gluttony like Pantagruel's or Erysichthon's, eating whatever is at hand (τὰ τυχόντα, b17; cf. b15), is fairly rare; only the bulimic or "belly-mad" (γαστρίμαργοι, b19; cf. EE 2.3 1221b2) have insatiable appetites, since a full stomach normally calls a halt. Most overeating occurs rather in connection with distinctive appetites, when our natural appetite for food in general develops into various "tastes" for specific foods and flavors, and these likes and dislikes stimulate pursuit and avoidance quite independently of any needs we have.[22] Of course, the pleasure we find in specific flavors is natural and beneficial, at least to the extent that it motivates us to satisfy the needs of the nutritive soul and to avoid harmful kinds of food. As Aristotle recognizes, not everyone finds the same foods attractive (EN 3.11 1118b12–15), and this has a natural basis in our diverse constitutions. So, despite their diversity, the "distinctive" appetites acquired by different people "still have something natural" (b13). But these appetites also involve the operation of the senses of taste and touch, each of which provides its own additional pleasures. Although this capacity to discriminate flavors is the natural function of the sense of taste, the appetites connected with these pleasures, focused as they are on specific foods rather than replenishment, readily lead to excess.

The problem is that we develop appetites for the physical pleasures found in satisfying our needs even when we do not have those needs, and hence even when the pursuit of those pleasures interferes with more important ends. In contrast with common appetites, moreover, distinctive appetites may err in kind as well as degree. Some people develop a taste for the wrong foods from

22. The analogue for sexual appetites is the difference between the common appetite for intercourse (but few are indiscriminately profligate) and a "distinctive" attraction for sex with certain people (or at least for certain types of people).

the start, and others acquire and indulge "hateful" tastes (b22–25).[23] The replenishment of necessities establishes the principal quantitative limit for the common appetites and their gratification, but what determines which distinctive appetites are acceptable? Do circumstances affect which are correct? Although Aristotle sees nothing inherently wrong in the pleasures found in replenishment, what considerations determine when and how the virtuous should pursue these pleasures? Are there ever reasons for the temperate to forgo even the natural physical pleasures?

23. In his discussion of incontinence, Aristotle reports some outlandish examples of "distinctive" appetites gone astray in both degree and kind (7.5 1148b17–31).

Health and Happiness

AT THE ROOT of Aristotle's analysis of the virtues of character lies his thesis that each consists in a "mean-state" (μεσότης) of feeling and action, a settled habit of feeling and doing "the mean" (τὸ μέσον) in one of the several fields of human activity.[1] Temperance, for example, is the "mean-state" of having the right feelings and doing the right actions in matters of physical pleasure, and what is right is determined by "the mean." At this general level, the standard that the virtuous use to determine when and how to satisfy their appetites is simply the mean. But this scarcely settles where the mean lies, or what appetites are right in what circumstances. Some equate the mean with the moderate—"nothing too much," as the proverb has it. But Aristotle disagrees. Although he thinks moderation is often commendable, his theory does not counsel moderation in everything. In some cases, anything at all is too much: some kinds of appetites are ruled out entirely, not just in immoderate amounts or frequency. In others, the mean may be ample or often: moderate care for some things is wrong, and sometimes immoderate concern is acceptable or even commendable.[2] Since the mean is "relative to

1. The theory Aristotle develops in EN 2 (and EE 2.1–5) underlies his definition of virtue as "a habit of choosing, consisting in the mean relative to us that is determined [ὡρισμένῃ] by reason and as the man of practical wisdom would determine it" (2.6 1106b36–7a2). For background, see Wehrli 1951; a thorough account of Aristotle's theory is still wanting, but see Urmson 1973 and the cautionary remarks in Young 1988: 521 n1.

2. Aristotle thinks adultery is always wrong (2.6 1107a8–27), not just with the wrong people or too often; and moderate effort or expenditure on behalf of a

us," moderation for some is sure to be excess or deficiency for others (*EN* 2.6 1106a26–b6). Where then does the mean in physical pleasure lie?

Aristotle takes it as uncontroversial that the virtues of character accord with "correct reason" (2.2 1103b31–34), and reason is the standard by which the proper mean for each of them is determined.[3] His account of temperance is no exception: the temperate enjoy physical pleasure as correct reason determines (ὡς ὁ ὀρθὸς λόγος, 1119a20), and even their appetites "agree with" their reason (b11–18). Conversely, the unrestrained are like children and practically "mindless" (ἀνοήτῳ, b3–10), and their "insatiable" (ἄπληστος) and indiscriminate (πανταχόθεν) appetites for pleasant things often "knock out" their reasoned deliberations (b7–10). The function of reason is thus to set limits for these appetites, both by determining in general what is good for the appetites and by calculating when and how the appetites should be satisfied in particular situations. But if reason settles what to do, on what are its decisions based? In particular, if reason discovers the correct limits for the appetites, where does it acquire its knowledge, and on what grounds are its commands based?

Ascetics would keep physical pleasure to a minimum. If the human function were limited exclusively to the activities of reason, then physical pleasure would be acceptable only as an unavoidable concomitant of maintaining the life of reason. But Aristotle's account of the human function is not exclusive in this way, nor does it require the virtuous to maximize theoretical reasoning single-mindedly. In particular, his account does assign temperance the role of limiting the pursuit of physical pleasure, but he does not restrict temperance to a wholly negative role. Rather, since the appetites involve nutrition and reproduction, reason bases its calculations on a grasp of the part these activities play in a good life and what they need to function well. Thus, whereas traditional views of temperance tend to characterize it wholly in negative terms, because it involves forgoing a number of plea-

---

great cause would be faulted, as appears from his accounts of the "great" virtues of dignity and magnificence (esp. 4.3 1124b6–9, 4.2 1122a22–28). In the case of temperance, modest portions would be wrong for the mighty Milo, and it would be "insensitive" not to recognize Helen's beauty or to feel no passion for one's mate (see below on the vice of insensibility).

3. See the references in Irwin 1985a: 423, esp. 6.1 1138b20–25.

sures that most people want,[4] Aristotle assigns it the positive function of arranging for physical well-being, so far as this is compatible with the pursuit of other, more important goals. Although this entails some limits on physical pleasure, it does not entail abstinence, except under extraordinary circumstances. On the contrary, it enjoins the temperate to enjoy the physical functions necessary to maintain physical well-being. Thus, after summarizing the negative account of the temperate as those who neither enjoy nor desire what they should not (EN 3.11 1119a11–15), Aristotle proceeds to connect those limits with the positive good of health.

As for everything pleasant related to health and fitness, the temperate will want these in a measured way [μετρίως] and as they should [ὡς δεῖ]; and they will want the other pleasant things if these do not impede health and fitness [μὴ ἐμποδίων τούτοις ὄντων] and are neither contrary to what is noble [παρὰ τὸ καλόν] nor beyond their means [ὑπὲρ τὴν οὐσίαν]. (3.11 1119a16–18)[5]

The temperate measure both their needs and their appetites for necessary external goods against the standard of health. The preservation of health thus provides the primary limit for their enjoyment of physical pleasure: they follow a diet and regimen that maintains health (a16–17), and they keep their pursuit of related pleasures within the same bounds (a17–18). Just as health calls for measured amounts of food and exercise, so temperance consists in having measured appetites for the pleasures connected with those necessities. Consequently, the temperate have as much control over their own health as people could in Aristotle's day, before the discovery of microbes and when proper regimen might seem practically a guarantee of health. In the words of Zalmoxis, which Socrates reports to Charmides, the best way to care for the body is to care first for the soul (Charm.

4. Young (1988: 533) observes that EE gives only this negative account; cf. Engberg-Pedersen 1983: 68–69. For the popular background, see Dover 1974: 68. The closing summary in EN (3.12 1119b16–17) discards the negative formulation.

5. Cooper (1975: 108–9) emphasizes the denial of asceticism implicit here, saying that the virtuous seek physical pleasures "just [because] they are pleasant," but Aristotle rests his claim that there is nothing inherently wrong with enjoying physical pleasure on his account of the human function. Hursthouse (1981: 63–66) also notes the connection between health and temperance, but her worry that Aristotle fails to set any moral constraints on seeking health is answered by the last clause here (1119a18).

157a–b)—that is, to foster temperance, both the beliefs and the appetites appropriate for giving physical pleasure and well-being their due place in human life. In short, temperance represents a sort of mental health that supervises physical health.[6]

In order to maintain their appetites within healthy limits, the temperate must in turn have an accurate conception of health. They have no need, of course, for any precise or comprehensive medical knowledge: "Although we value [βουλόμενοι] being healthy, we nonetheless do not learn medicine" (*EN* 6.12 1143b30–33). After all, since our primary aim here, as in all practical affairs, is not only knowing what to do but also doing it, all that the temperate need is the knowledge sufficient to develop the right habits, not medical science. In the dictum of Hesiod, which Aristotle cites approvingly, "Noble too is he who credits one who has spoken well" (1.4 1095b11 = *WD* 295). Someone who knows that fowl is wholesome, for example, is more likely to eat the right food than is one whose general knowledge leaves him unable to recognize what to eat (*EN* 6.7 1141b14–21); unless we act on our knowledge, merely knowing what food is beneficial is of no use (7.3 1147a5–7). The first condition for temperance, then, is having the right habits, and that requires the right upbringing: laws should promote temperance in the young by prescribing good diet and exercise for them (10.9 1179b29–35). Still, even if most can maintain the right habits without medical expertise, good legislation requires some to have "correct reason" in the form of knowledge about human health. More important than medical expertise, however, is a correct conception of the place of health in the human good. Experts can tell us how to achieve and maintain health, but it is a task for practical wisdom—which deliberates not only about what serves particular ends such as health but also about what is conducive to "living well as a whole"—to decide when to follow medical advice and

6. Later Peripatetics make this connection more explicit, describing temperance as the healthy condition of the soul analogous to the body's health; see Stobaeus 2.124.2–5, 125.2–4. In addition to reducing all virtues to one, Zeno's erstwhile colleague Ariston of Chios called that unity "health" (*SVF* 1.375). A little later, the Stoic Hecaton espoused the similar view that health "accompanies" (or perhaps "is entailed by," ἀκολουθεῖ) temperance (D. L. 7.90); see North 1966: 227 *n*92. Plato's picture is somewhat different: although he makes health the limit for temperance (*Rep.* 8.558d–59d), he connects the health of the soul with justice (4.444c–d).

when to neglect it in order to seek other, more valuable ends (6.5 1140a25–30).

The connection between health and temperance does not of course imply that unrestraint inevitably leads to illness, nor does Aristotle claim that it does. Although he often draws an analogy between the healthy and the virtuous on the one hand and the ill and non-virtuous on the other, he avoids the facile conclusion that unrestraint is always bad for health.[7] Many of the unrestrained after all are likely to act prudently enough to avoid the physical distress of illness they dread. But if health is an objective for both the unrestrained and the temperate, they view that objective in very different ways. Whereas the former may be reluctant to indulge their appetites when they expect indulgence to cause them pain, the temperate have no appetite in the first place for unhealthy pleasures. In fact, the pains peculiar to unrestraint, on Aristotle's account, result not from illness but from the nature of unrestrained appetites themselves. In addition to the painful sense of deprivation the unrestrained feel when their appetites are denied, their very pleasures seem to cause them pain (3.11 1118b30–32). Since appetite itself is "accompanied by pain" (μετὰ λύπης), they suffer not only when denied their customary gratification but also when in the state of desire (1119a3–4). Like Tantalus, they are in the paradoxical position (ἄτοπον) of "feeling pain on account of their pleasure," since they seek pleasures which are painful for them to desire (a4–5). And since they let their appetites for replenishment grow beyond control, they end up like the Danaids with appetites for "filling" (ἀναπλήρωσις) that "cannot be filled" (ἄπληστα).

Aristotle's argument to this point accords with traditional views about the desirability of health. Three of the five advantages of prosperity listed by Herodotus' Solon involve health and physical well-being ("not crippled, not ill, in good shape," 1.32.6). In the Delian epigram, which Aristotle twice invokes, health is called "most valuable" (λῷστον), it is "golden" in Pin-

7. Nothing more than analogy is found at 3.4 1113a23–b2, 7.8 1150b32–35, 2.2 1104a14–25, and EE 8.3 1248b22–23; cf. EN 3.5 1114a20–28, where Aristotle suggests that souses may drink themselves blind. By contrast, Plato's pedantic Eryximachus generalizes the connection of unrestraint and illness (Symp. 187e). To support his claim that Aristotle thought sexual activity harmful, Foucault (1985: 118) cites only Probs. 4.8, a work with dubious ties to Aristotle; see EN 7.14 1154a15–18 and Pol. 7.16 1335b35–38; contrast the judicious discussion of 7.5 1148b15–49a20 in Dover 1978: 168–70.

dar's ode to the ailing Hieron (*Pyth.* 3.73), and it is "best" (ἄϱιστον) in a line Aristotle quotes from Epicharmus (*Rhet.* 2.21 1394b13).[8] Songs praising health appeared in a spate with the expansion of the cult of Asclepius in Aristotle's own day: often personified, Health is invoked as "loftiest mother" and "Queen of our yearning" in Licymnius' hymn to her (*PMG* 769), and in a popular paean, she is "illustrious" among her retinue of healers (*PMG* 934). In Ariphron's celebrated hymn (*PMG* 813), a hymn that Aristotle himself seems to have imitated in the ode he addressed to virtue,[9] Health is "most reverend of the blessed gods," because all other human joys depend on her and none can be happy without her. But does Aristotle mean only to sanitize hedonism and to replace sensualism with a brand of "sanitarianism"? Does his account of temperance defend simply an enlightened form of self-interest, what Plato called "slavish" and "popular" virtue (*Phdo.* 68e–69c, 82a–b), the prudential calculus of physical pleasures designed to maintain health and hence physical comfort? Or does he see a higher standard?

When Aristotle cites the authority of Epicharmus, it is not without an important proviso: "so at least it appears to most people" (*Rhet.* 2.21 1394b14). His discussion of the Delian epigram similarly rebukes it for separating what are in fact connected, and he reunites health with what is noblest and most just (*EN* 1.8 1099a24–29). And if Ariphron sings that only the healthy can enjoy life's other blessings, Aristotle offers even higher praise to virtue: no mere necessity, virtue is worth giving up all other blessings for, even life itself. And in an elegiac encomium of Plato, he corrects Ariphron with the even stronger claim that "a man becomes both virtuous and happy at once" (fr. 673). Only the ill would make health their greatest priority, and if they equate health with happiness (*EN* 1.4 1095a23–25), their judgment is notoriously aberrant. Once well, they too turn to other ends, showing that even they see the error of that preference.[10]

8. On the Delian epigram, see II.iii above; cf. Sophocles fr. 356, Euripides fr. 714, Simonides fr. 604 (quoted together with Licymnius and Ariphron by Sextus the doctor in his lengthy discussion of disputes about the value of health, *AM* 11.47–67).

9. Bowra (1938: 182–85) argues that Aristotle modeled his ode to virtue (*PMG* 842) on Ariphron's ode; cf. Renehan 1982.

10. Errors of the ill mentioned by Aristotle involve pleasures of taste (10.3 1173b20–25, 10.5 1176a12–15) and curative pleasures (7.12 1152b29–33, 7.14 1154a27–31).

Finally, although supreme happiness includes good health, virtuous activity can continue even in illness (*Pol.* 7.13 1332a19–21), and ill health deserves blame or fear only when people make themselves ill (*EN* 3.5 1114a21–28, 3.6 1115a17–18). But if health is subordinate to virtue, does Aristotle grant health an important place in a good life?

Although he rejects the belief that health is best, Aristotle tries to explain the mistake by identifying the truth behind it. Physical well-being, he affirms, is definitely worthy of concern. But people err when they go on to infer that health is the most valuable part of life merely because it is "responsible for two of the things most people consider most valuable [τιμιωτάτων]," pleasure and life itself (*Rhet.* 1.6 1362b15–18). Everybody has a natural desire to be alive: life, like pleasure, is something choiceworthy "by itself" (b26–27; cf. *EN* 10.4 1175a10–12, a15–17). And it may be a matter of dispute whether we live for pleasure or want pleasure because of life, but there is no dispute that the two are "yoked together and admit of no separation" (1175a18–20). However, since life consists in activity of various sorts and our pleasures correspond to those activities (a12–16), our enjoyment of health derives from its role in the performance of those activities. After all, the pleasure of being healthy comes from the unimpeded performance of other desired activities, not from bodily sensations of health. If health makes for a pleasant life, it does so only in the context of our favored activities; by itself and inactive, it would be a source of little pleasure. The healthy tend rather to feel distress if prevented from exercising their abilities. Fitness is being fit *for* something, and what makes health choice-worthy are the activities the healthy are fit to perform. Even the Cynics, who sought to rid themselves of everything but the minimum necessary for health, valued their condition not for itself but for the autonomy and tranquillity they found in their simplified way of life. Just as the temperate consider physical pleasure subordinate to their health, so in turn they consider their health subordinate to the activities it enables them to pursue.

Health is sought not for its own sake but rather for its uses. Indeed, Aristotle ascribes its value to its use: it produces many results (ποιητικὰ πολλῶν, *Rhet.* 1.6 1362b15). But since the best things are sought for their own sake (*EN* 1.7 1097a25–b6), health deserves a subordinate position among the good things in life. To the cult of the body and health fanatics, then, Aristotle's response is clear: health is desirable primarily for what else we can do when healthy, and exalting physical fitness over all else flies in the face of both theory and reputable views. Against the infamous doctor Herodicus, whose regimen combined harsh exercise with almost total abstinence from physical pleasure, he claims that "no one would consider his patients happy for that kind of health, because they refrain from almost everything human" (*Rhet*. 1.5 1361b4–6). Such extreme asceticism, caricatured already by Plato (*Rep*. 3.406a–e),[11] actually masks a paradoxical kind of hedonism that rates the well-being of the body so highly that it treats the body brutally. But this "sanitarianism" is insane, since health is not desirable at any price. Just as it would be absurd to acquire money by betraying our friends, so it would be absurd to pursue health if it required a wretched diet (*EN* 10.3 1173b27–28).[12] Happily, and not by chance, human nature is such that the health worth striving for is compatible with physical pleasure as well as other ends.

If health is not the supreme goal of the temperate, what determines how far it deserves to be pursued? What other standards are superior to it? When Aristotle introduces health into his discussion of temperance, he adds two further constraints on the temperate pursuit of physical pleasure. One is primarily a prudential limit: the temperate should avoid indulging in pleasures that would strain their material resources (3.11 1119a18). Addressing what may have been an early instance of high medical costs, he observes that "some healthy things are bad for finances" (7.12 1153a18). Worse, the "wasteful" (ἄσωτοι) tend to be found among those who cannot control their appetite for pleasure (4.1 1119b31–33, 1121b7–10); as etymology suggests, the wasteful are "unsafe" and destroy their "substance" because they indulge their immediate appetites at the expense of their future security (1120a1–4). Their pursuit of gratification can even cause them trouble with the law, since the cost of their consumption drives the unrestrained to support their habits in any way they can (1121a30–b1, 1122a6–13). On the other hand, although the temperate do not avoid physical pleasure at all costs, neither

11. In his note on *Rhet*. 1.5.11, Cope (1887) cites Macauley's amusing reaction to this passage; in Plato's defense, cf. Phillips 1973: 191. Plato disparages this early guru of health elsewhere (*Phdr*. 227e, *Prot*. 316e), but the good man evidently was a teacher of Hippocrates and may have influenced the important tract *On Regimen*.

12. The same two extreme cases occur together in *Pol*. 7.1 1323a30–32.

do they pursue it beyond their means. For their own good, the temperate pursue pleasures only within the limits of health, and they also keep the preservation of health within the limits of their resources. The temperate recognize the primary value of wealth, which Aristotle contends is not lavish consumption for its own sake but the works of liberality, such as gifts, celebrations, and sacrifices for the gods.[13] Though not averse to feasts and banquets that pose no threat to their health or other more important concerns, the temperate are quite willing to forgo such pleasures whenever the expense interferes with more important matters. But what does Aristotle consider more important?

The other constraint Aristotle mentions introduces a moral dimension into the discussion.[14] As implied by the proviso that the temperate do not even have any appetite for pleasures "contrary to the noble" (3.11 1119a18), the temperate maintain their desire for health within the limits set by the principles of virtue. A rational concern for physical well-being subordinates it, when the situation requires, to other forms of rational activity. So the temperate have only "measured" (μετρίας) appetites (a17, 3.12 1119b11–15), since their natural and "common" appetites are shaped into "distinctive" appetites that they measure against health and their other tastes and interests.[15] Although hunger and the appetite for food, for example, are unavoidable, they are still subject to rational control. When no higher concerns impinge, the temperate dine as they need and indulge their distinctive and acquired tastes within the limits compatible with health; when other ends do conflict, they refuse what they would otherwise find attractive. Sometimes their appetites are "silenced"; even if the pangs of hunger grow insistent, they may resist satisfying them, at least to some extent, because of a greater good. This involves no temptation, because their reason effectively overrides their appetite and they themselves prefer not to satisfy hunger at the expense of their other ends.[16] Rather, the appetite

13. Cf. 4.2 1122b19–23, 1122b35–23a10; on liberality, see IV.i below, esp. n6.

14. Engberg-Pedersen (1983: 69–70) observes the moral connection here, but he exaggerates the role of altruism in Aristotle's idea of morality; see II.v n9 above.

15. On these two kinds of appetites, see III.ii above, esp. n17.

16. Aristotle allows that the temperate *exercise* "self-control" on occasion, but he sharply distinguishes them from those who *are* "self-controlled" in that they regularly experience excessive appetites (7.10 1151b32–34); cf. II.v n29 above.

of the temperate is "measured" because they use reason to govern and shape it in the light of other ends. Likewise, whereas the unrestrained suffer if their appetites are denied, the temperate have only "measured" pain if their needs are denied (3.11 1119a14; cf. 1118b30–34), partly because they have only moderate needs, but also because they find other ends more attractive. In particular, the temperate have no appetite for any pleasures that involve wrong to others. Since the unrestrained, on the other hand, enjoy bodily pleasures "more than they are worth" (1119a19–20), they "have appetites for everything pleasant, or what is most pleasant, and are led by appetite to choose these things over other things" (a2–3),[17] even in violation of the law and the interests of others (esp. in adultery, 2.6 1107a9–17, 5.2 1130a22–30, 7.6 1149b13–26).

Temperance rests on what the virtuous themselves prefer: it expresses their own priorities and the desire for what is noble that is their sovereign concern. This is why self-restraint is not the primary manifestation of temperance. The fundamental difference between the virtuous and the unrestrained consists not merely in their response to the appetites of the nutritive soul but in the specific appetites they have in the first place. Aristotle's point, then, is not that we all have the same appetites, which the temperate gratify as they should and the unrestrained overindulge. That would represent only the contrast between continence or "self-control" (ἐγκράτεια) and incontinence or "uncontrol" (ἀκρασία).[18] Rather, he claims that the temperate maintain the right appetites from the start. Although the appetites concerned with our physical needs are "unrational," in that they often arise independently of any rational decision (*Rhet.* 1.11 1370a18–25), they can be "rationalized" if reason finds the limits of these needs and controls when and how these needs are filled.

17. This claim helps explain the puzzling major premise in the practical syllogism for the incontinent, "I should taste everything sweet" (7.3 1147a29): although the incontinent "think" the same major as the temperate, they also have the same appetite as the unrestrained (a31–34), and this is reflected in their having a second major, namely, the appetite expressed by the unconditional and "unrestrained" belief that all sweets should be tasted.

18. See, e.g., *EE* 2.11. The scope of self-control and weakness (or continence and incontinence) in the strict sense (ἁπλῶς) corresponds exactly to the scope of temperance and unrestraint (*EN* 7.4). Thus, Aristotle dubs susceptibility to pleasures other than those of food and sex weakness "by similarity" (1149a3), "by transference" (κατὰ μεταφοράν, a23), "partially" (1148a4), or "by addition" (a10).

Accordingly, the temperate are habituated to want only what they need and what is healthy, and their appetite extends only to the pleasures attendant on satisfying those needs. Moreover, their habits are based on a correct conception of the relation between rational activity and physical satisfaction. Whereas the unrestrained fully believe that physical pleasure is their most important end, the temperate simply have no interest in seeking pleasures that would interfere with their more important concerns. Hence, unlike the continent, they rarely have any appetites to restrain; their conception of the good governs their appetites from the start and spares them any internal conflict. Although the continent recognize the right limits, they still desire more than they should, and they are "self-controlled" rather than temperate because they still must resist the impulses of their own appetites. The temperate, by contrast, want precisely what their reason decides, without any dissent from their appetites (EN 3.12 1119b15–18). In fact, they can "hold back from physical pleasures and enjoy [χαίρων] doing this" (2.3 1104b5–6).[19] Unlike the self-controlled, their beliefs about the value of physical pleasure determine their appetites as well as their action; and unlike the unrestrained, they think there are better ends than physical pleasure to pursue.

For the virtuous, since all ends fit into a comprehensive and correct conception of the human good, the rational pursuit of health and physical pleasure has that end as its ultimate aim. As Aristotle insists at the close of his account of temperance, the correct appetites of the temperate are rational not simply because they aim at health but because they have something noble in view: their appetitive part "says the same thing as their reason [συμφωνεῖν τῷ λόγῳ]," since "the noble is the target [σκοπός] of both" (3.12 1119b15–17).[20] The point here is not simply that appe-

19. Aristotle may mean that the virtuous enjoy abstinence for its own sake, but I think his point is rather that the virtuous abstain from physical pleasure because they have other ends in view, which they enjoy in its stead. This seems to be borne out by the claim in the next lines that the courageous "enjoy, *or at least do not suffer*," in fearful situations (1104b7–8): just as the courageous do not enjoy enduring fear, so they do not enjoy abstinence itself, and in each case, what sustains their virtuous activity is some other end they value more.

20. The association of συμφωνία and temperance has Platonic echoes, but seems to have become part of conventional psychology by Aristotle's day. Thus, it occurs in the sketch of "exoteric" psychology in EN 1.13 1102b13–28 (ὁμοφωνεῖ, b28); cf. Top. 4.3 123a33–37, Plato Symp. 187b, Rep. 4.430e, 432a, 9.591c–d (con-

tite and reason independently fasten on the same object, which happens to be something noble; that would neglect the role reason has in giving "distinctive" shape to temperate appetites from the start. Nor is it that the appetites of the temperate, though not themselves for anything noble, simply stay within the bounds of the noble. Rather, some objects of the appetites are "choiceworthy by nature" (7.4 1148a22–26), including health and procreation.[21] Hence, when the appetites are "measured," both they and reason have a noble end—not only the exercise of physical well-being as a part of happiness but also the fulfillment of part of human nature. In regulating the pursuit of physical pleasure, reason makes the lower faculties of the soul rational by making them perform their part of the human function. No mere handmaiden for the appetites and physical pleasure or even for health, temperance is a virtue with a noble end because it achieves part of our supreme end, namely, the form of practical activity that consists in reason controlling our appetites. In short, Aristotle's account of the relation between the physical and rational parts of human nature culminates in his account of temperance.[22]

If health is not desirable solely for its own sake, neither is it by itself noble. The healthy may be noble, and health is necessary for most noble activities, but like external goods, its value depends ultimately on its use, since it may also serve harmful or base ends.[23] Single-minded cultivation of the body is bound to interfere with more important pursuits, and all that happiness requires in Aristotle's account is health enough for unimpeded virtuous activity (7.13 1153b9–12; note the mention of bodily goods, b17–19). Although life is more pleasant for the healthy and those who can enjoy the pleasures of food and sex, happiness is still possible without much of these external goods, and

---

nected with health), and *Phileb.* 25d–e (with the example of health); for Pythagoreans, see D. L. 8.33.

21. Aristotle considers it noble to participate in eternity, which mortals do by propagating their species into eternity; see *de An.* 2.4 415a23–b7, *Gen. An.* 2.1 731b18–32a12, *Gen. Cor.* 2.11 338b1–19, Lennox 1985, and Young 1988: 538–39.

22. See 1.7 1198a3–6, 1.13 1102b30–32; cf. 6.12 1144a1–11, where Aristotle argues that virtues of character are "choice-worthy because of themselves" (and hence necessary parts of a good life) because they are excellences of rational parts of the soul, whereas health is not, because it is the excellence only of the nutritive soul, which does not participate directly in rational activity.

23. E.g., *Rhet.* 1.1 1355b4–7, *EE* 8.3 1248b27–34 (discussed in IV.ii below).

enjoying them is not a necessary part of the good life. The pleasures essential for happiness are found rather in virtuous activities themselves (cf. b12–15). In fact, the principal pleasure of
health derives from its role in our activities, namely, its facilitating other pursuits. Further, just as the pleasures of health differ
for different activities, so the degree of health we need depends
on our ends. Not everyone needs to be in the excellent physical
condition of an athlete, let alone a pentathlete, and Aristotle reserves the term "good shape" (εὐεξία) for exceptional fitness.[24]
In the same way, the standards for physical beauty differ according to age, as Aristotle illustrates when he reports the conventional wisdom that the young are handsome when they are athletic and attractive, whereas an adequate digestion and freedom
from pain are sufficient for the aged (*Rhet.* 1.5 1361b7–14). By extension, the minimum physical well-being necessary for a good
life in any circumstances depends on virtue, since the limit is set
by what the virtuous need in order to engage in the activities that
are sovereign over their happiness.

Are such austere needs all the virtuous want? To rest content
with a bare minimum of physical pleasure when more is available
smacks of the asceticism that Aristotle rejects when he dismisses
Herodican hygiene. More to the point, although he considers the
excesses of unrestraint the principal contrary of temperance, he
also insists upon the existence of a vice of deficiency at the opposite extreme. Total disdain for physical pleasure, which for want
of an accepted name he calls "insensibility" (ἀναισθησία, *EN* 2.7
1107b6–8), is contrary to our nature because it implies disregard
for the perceptual faculties with which we are endowed. All animals "discriminate" their food and enjoy some foods but not others, and since sensory perception is an essential part of our life,
insensibility would not be "human" (3.11 1119a6–8). Different
fare is good for different people, and although the pleasure we
find in our fare can mislead us, it is a primary test of whether the
food is good for us. So any who fail to form any preferences for
what their senses distinguish "would be far from being a human"
(a9–10). We are unique in being rational animals, but we are ani-

24. See 10.3 1173a24–28; cf. the different definitions of "healthy" as well as of
"good" for people and fish (6.7 1141a22–24). In the *Categories*, Aristotle tries to
explain how quality-attributes such as health, without themselves admitting of
degrees, may be possessed by individuals in various degrees (8 10b26–11a5).

mals nonetheless, and the function of reason is not to eliminate any part of human nature but to shape and guide all our activities. Since both the appetites and the pleasures of satisfying them are necessary for life, the temperate aim not to deny their appetites but to satisfy them in ways that enhance other rational activities. This is why acting on appetite qualifies for praise and blame: even though our appetites are irrational (ἄλογα πάθη) in that they arise from physical needs no matter what we may think, they are nonetheless subject to rational control and direction, and we are responsible for what we can control by reason (3.1 1111a29–b2). Indeed, there are some things, Aristotle holds, "for which we should have appetites" (δεῖ ἐπιθυμεῖν), and health is one of them (a30–31; cf. 3.11 1118b26). But what deserves praise is correct, and if done for the right reasons, it is virtuous as well. So if it is right to gratify some appetites, it is fine to enjoy their gratification as well. Those who refuse to enjoy doing what we should deserve blame, not praise.

Aristotle concedes that the vice of insensibility is extremely rare (3.11 1119a6, a10–11). That is to be expected when it concerns life's "necessary pleasures, since everybody finds some pleasure in cuisine and wine and sex" (7.14 1154a15–18). The problem is not that some people feel no physical pleasure at all, which is patently impossible. It is rather that some people attach too little importance to the pleasures found in activities necessary for self-preservation. And the absence of a recognized name for this vice reflects not its impossibility, but most people's failure to distinguish the temperate interest in pleasure from the excessive restraint widely mistaken for temperance.[25] By rejecting the asceticism of the Cynics and their ilk, Aristotle answers the hedonist's objection that people who avoid all pleasure are scarcely human and insensitive "like a stone" (*EE* 2.3 1221a21–23; cf. *Gorg.* 494a). Physical pleasures deserve blame only when harmful, but "whenever harmless, they are blameless" (*EN* 7.14 1154b4–5).[26]

25. The absence of a familiar term (now as then!) for this vice of deficiency is a prime example of the way in which reputable views are "spoken confusedly" and need further analysis (see I.ii above); cf. Aristotle's objection to those who would define virtues simply as "kinds of unfeeling" (2.3 1104b24–26). Young (1988: 525 *n*11) wrongly denies that Aristotle thinks anyone has this vice: οὐ πάνυ γίνονται (1107b7, 1119a6, a11) means only that it occurs "not very much," rather than not at all; cf. 1099b3, followed by "still less" in b5. Cf. North 1966: 132–35.

26. Similarly, Socrates does not dissent when Glaucon lists "harmless pleasures" in the class of things good in themselves, and health among things good

In short, it is wrong to deprive our nature of its natural pleasures, so long as they do not interfere with the higher concerns of health, resources, and virtue. Nor is there any good in celibacy or a diet of Spartan black gruel, unless it serves some higher goal. Sometimes physical pleasure is to be avoided, but at other times it is not. The task for the temperate, then, is not to abstain from physical pleasure as much as possible but to recognize when to enjoy it. Their task, in short, is to find and observe the mean.

The virtuous, on this account, need not lead a cramped and abstemious life. On the contrary, temperate living by itself is not sufficient for a good life, partly because, as Aristotle observes in objection to Plato's austere standards in the *Laws* (737d), temperance is compatible with severe toil and hardship (*Pol.* 2.6 1265a28–38). After all, Aristotle requires of the temperate not that they minimize the physical pleasure in their lives, nor that they seek only noble pleasures, but only that they avoid physical pleasure when it is "contrary to something noble" (*EN* 3.11 1119a18). That leaves them free to enjoy pleasures that are not noble. There is nothing noble in abstinence for its own sake, on this account, but only when it serves some other end. Rather, the good life has a place for the pursuit of physical pleasure, and any pleasure the virtuous may find in abstinence derives from their preference for other activities, not from self-denial for its own sake. The error in unrestraint lies not in the pursuit of physical pleasure per se, but in pursuing it excessively in the belief that it is better than it is. Likewise, the error in insensibility lies in excessive avoidance of these pleasures in the belief that they are worse than they are. Between these two errors lies the virtue of temperance, the rational enjoyment of physical pleasure. Unlike the insensible, the virtuous enjoy physical pleasure, but unlike the unrestrained, they enjoy it only as they should. Because they recognize its basis in human nature and its function in human life, the temperate do not disregard it, but because they consider it less valuable than most of their other goals, they enjoy it only when it is compatible with those other goals.

Because temperance aims at the personal goods of health and physical pleasure, it is a prudential virtue that serves each per-

---

both in themselves and for their results (*Rep.* 2.357b); cf. *Phileb.* 63e (health and temperance).

son's own good. But it also has wider aims. First, temperance helps preserve health, and that facilitates the pursuit of other goals, not least other virtuous activities. Further, it connects with other virtues in that having temperate appetites removes a major source of motives for vicious actions, especially injustice. Thus, in accordance with the folk etymology invoked by Plato as well as by Aristotle, temperance frees the virtuous for the pursuit of more valuable ends by "preserving their wisdom" (*EN* 6.5 1140b12; cf. *Crat.* 411e). And as Solon shows in his tales of the happiest of men, temperance also contributes to happiness by enabling the virtuous to live with "moderate" resources (*EN* 10.8 1179a9–13). But this virtue is not purely instrumental since it contributes directly to virtuous activity as well. As Aristotle suggests when he counts health among the "parts" of happiness, the principal exercise of health is found not in any regimens that we follow to promote our fitness but in the vigorous performance of activities that we value because of other ends (*Rhet.* 1.5 1361b3–6). So first, by limiting the virtuous to healthy physical pleasures, temperance facilitates their performance of all activities, and that can provide pleasure that helps "complete" virtuous activity. Second, because their appetites are measured, the temperate avoid being distracted by appetites and so enjoy their favored activities more. Temperance thus contributes to happiness by enhancing both the physical pleasure and the other pleasures of a good life.

Not only is the healthy performance of virtuous activities conducive to pleasure on a physical level, but temperance also contributes to the distinctive pleasures of rational activity. After all, the needs of the nutritive soul bring people together in situations that promote some of the most important parts of human life. Dining together and sleeping together satisfy not only our physical and animal nature but our rational and social nature as well. In line with the sentiments expressed at Agathon's celebrated symposium, the temperate hold that at the best parties conversation flows more freely than the wine.[27] And although Aristotle is

27. See *Symp.* 176–77; cf. Theophrastus fr. 138. As Young (1988) emphasizes, Plato has his Alcibiades credit Socrates with the greatest enjoyment of physical pleasure (*Symp.* 219e–20a), and Socrates alone still has a clear head when the party ends (223c–d); Epicurus later made similar claims for his brand of "sober" hedonism (D. L. 10.130).

remarkably discreet about sexual relations, he backs up his claim that the "common" appetites are natural with an allusion to Thetis' consoling advice to her son Achilles that he assuage his grief at the death of Patroclus by turning to the pleasures of the board and the bed (*EN* 3.11 1118b11, *Il.* 24.128–32; cf. Achilles to Priam, 24.601–20).[28] Rather than defend temperance on purely prudential and instrumental grounds as a reliable road to health and a tool for what Epicurus was to dub "sober hedonism," Aristotle connects it with his account of our rational nature and indicates how it makes room for a rational enjoyment of physical pleasure.

More generally, physical pleasure is intrinsically good, or worth seeking for its own sake, other things being equal. Hence, it is rational to give it independent weight in our deliberations and to choose pleasant means over unpleasant ones when we can. It can therefore be a part of happiness, when it is chosen within reasonable limits and in the recognition that it is a natural and good part of human life. Enjoying a good meal, for example, is itself a form of rational activity; if it is done for good reasons—in the recognition that physical pleasure has its place in human life—then it is also a virtuous exercise of practical rationality. Physical pleasure sometimes interferes with the pursuit of more valuable ends, but it can also be a desirable part of many of those pursuits and thus integral to some of the virtuous activities that are sovereign over happiness. In short, temperance can contribute directly to happiness by rendering us rationally active animals.[29] But just as Aristotle denies that gods would ever need this

28. In a thoughtful discussion of Aristotle's views on erotic love, Price (1989: 236–49) shows that Aristotle was no prude. However, since his remarks about sex are few and far between, I have focused on food and drink, about which he has more to say.

29. How does this account bear on intellectual pursuits? Even when Aristotle claims that we should "do everything for living by what is most powerful in us" (i.e., reason, *EN* 10.7 1177b33–34), or that the "best and finest" pursuit of physical and material goods is what "most produces [ποιήσει μάλιστα] thought about god" (*EE* 8.3 1249b16–19), he leaves it an open question how much care we *have to* give to our merely mortal nature, and he never suggests that we should not *enjoy* that care. Indeed, even in these contexts, he criticizes paying *too little* attention to our mortal and animal needs as well as paying too much (1249b19–21). Although he says it is best "to be least aware of the other part of the soul," he adds the rider "as such" (ᾗ τοιοῦτον), which leaves room for being aware of the irrational soul *as ruled* by correct reason (b21–23). I infer, then, that his account of temperance addresses a question left open by intellectualism, since he argues not only that the virtuous have to give some place to physical needs but that they

virtue (*EN* 10.8 1178b15–16), so the best things in human life are of a different order. Although there are some things that, because we are animals rather than gods, we humans need, there are other activities that, because we are rational, we alone among the animals can enjoy. The next step is to look at these distinctively human concerns.

---

should find some place for physical pleasure, albeit a place subordinate to other concerns.

IV

VIRTUES IN ACTION

This kind of justice is complete virtue, not absolutely but [strictly] toward others. For this reason justice is often thought to be supreme among virtues. "Neither evening star nor morning star is so marvelous"; and we assert the proverb "In justice resides all virtue together." It especially is complete virtue: it is complete in that one who has it is able to exercise virtue also toward others and not only by himself; for many are able to exercise virtue in their own affairs but unable in affairs involving others. This is why Bias' saying, that "Rule will show a man," is thought to be right, since a ruler acts toward others and is thereby in a community. For this very reason, justice alone of the virtues is also thought to be another's good, because it is shown toward others; it does what is advantageous to another, whether a ruler or a member of the community. —EN 5.1 1129b25–30a5

The Economics of Liberality

BESIDE THE opulence of Croesus, the fortunes of Tellos and the Argive brothers appear negligible. Solon nominates them for the crown of happiness because of their lasting good luck and honorable ends, not for riches, power, or prestige. But although the emphasis falls on their exceptional freedom from misfortune, Solon insists that all were well off by local standards (Herod. 1.30.4, 1.31.2), and though well beneath the station of kings, they flourished among their peers. In short, Solon's models, like Solon himself, belonged to the upper, not the middle, class of their communities. Is this the ideal Aristotle upholds when he endorses the "moderate resources" of Solon's ideal (*EN* 10.8 1179a9–13)? Both deny any need for great wealth or power, but do they demand a gentleman's estate and make happiness the preserve of the landed and affluent who can live free from toil? The question is important, for although its theoretical solution is clear, its implications are large. In theory, the sovereignty of virtue entails that the contribution of wealth and power to happiness depends on the pursuits of the virtuous. If they need great resources to achieve their ends, then the human good will be an aristocratic privilege; if their needs are few, then the path to happiness will be more democratic. In practice, however, what ends do the virtuous pursue? Does their happiness depend on pursuing ends attained only through wealth, power, or prestige?

Part of the question here concerns Aristotle's attitude toward the values of his time. Is he a conservative whose account enshrines, albeit systematically, the values of a contemporary elite? Is it true, as Sir David Ross suggests, that Aristotle's analysis of the several virtues "presents a lively and often amusing account of the qualities admired or disliked by cultivated Greeks of Aristotle's time"? And is his paradigm what Alasdair MacIntyre calls "the Athenian gentleman"? Or is he a social critic, reproving the dominant ideologies of the day and concerned to show his cultivated audience how they go wrong? Was Marx true to his cause in calling him "the greatest thinker of antiquity"? And is G. E. M. de Ste. Croix on the mark when he says that Aristotle "certainly does come closer to Marx than any other ancient thinker I know"?[1] The question is of more than historical interest; it is not merely an issue of whether Aristotle was a proto-Marxist or an apologist for the ruling classes. Behind the worry about his alleged elitism lurks a deeper problem about moral psychology and the motivation behind the specifically moral virtues. What place does Aristotle give to concern for the good of others, not just when we consider it part of our own good as we do with our friends, but when our actions affect strangers or even enemies and when preserving justice for others seems inimical to our own good? Is there any room in his account for *obligations* toward others? Or is his account vulnerable to Glaucon's worry, that we have no good reason to uphold what is just when it competes or conflicts with our own ends? In short, Aristotle needs to show how *moral* virtue relates to *rational* virtue, and how the duties associated with justice contribute to happiness. We need to ask why it is not simply misleading to translate his formula for happiness as "virtuous activity" rather than "excellent activity."

What makes these problems acute is the status of external goods. In a word, they are "fought over" (περιμάχητα): there are rarely enough to go around, yet people want them so badly they fight to get them.[2] But scarcity is not the only problem here, for

1. Ross 1923: 202; MacIntyre 1981: 170; cf. Burnet 1900: 163: Aristotle's "principles must be shown to explain what the average Athenian understood by καλο-κἀγαθία, or they stand condemned" (although "the importance of [*EN* 4] is entirely missed if we imagine that Aristotle is setting before us types of character for our admiration and imitation," for "his aim is not edification"). For Marx, see De Ste. Croix 1981: 70; see also p. 78 for De Ste. Croix's claim that Aristotle gives him a precedent for applying an analysis of economic class to ancient history.

2. See *EN* 9.8 1168b16–19 (property, honor, physical pleasure), 1169a20–32 (property, honor, and rule: the goods that give self-love its bad name), *EE* 8.3 1248b25–30 (honor, wealth, physique, prosperity, power), and *Rhet.* 1.6 1363a7–9. Xenophon's Socrates jokes that poverty is "least fought over" (*Symp.* 3.9).

even where there is abundance, allocation remains a problem. The pursuit of external goods is both competitive and comparative, and the two most popular possessions seem inherently exclusive: people measure wealth relatively and expect the wealthy to have *more* than others; if power is control *over* others, then it always requires subjects. Moreover, the domain of justice corresponds closely to that of prosperity, and justice is connected with "the equal" and injustice with "the unequal" (*EN* 5.1 1129a32–b1). Indeed, the predominant motive for injustice is "having more" (πλεονεξία)—not more virtue or health, but more external goods.

Since the unjust person wants more [πλεονέκτης], he will be concerned with good things—not all, but any that involve prosperity and misfortune. These things are always *intrinsically* good, but not always good *for somebody*. People pray for these things, and they pursue them. But they should not; they should rather pray that everything that is intrinsically good be good for them too, but they should choose what is good for them. (5.1 1129b1–6)

The sovereignty of virtue makes external goods subordinate to virtuous pursuits, and Aristotle argues that only rational virtues enable people to benefit regularly from the use of other goods. But this argument from enlightened self-interest looks less cogent in the face of scarcity and competitive ends, and Aristotle acknowledges that "justice alone among the virtues is thought to be another's good, because it is shown toward others," and that makes it "a difficult task" (1130a3–8). Further, what if external goods are necessary for virtuous ends? Can those ends justify "fighting over" instrumental goods? In principle, Aristotle's answer is yes—provided the fight is consistent with rational virtue. But what sets the standard here? What uses of wealth and power are rational? In particular, are conventional ideas about property and rule correct, and are they inherently exclusive and scarce? Or is wealth a function of use, and power pointless without noble ends to serve? Finally, are they ever necessary for a good life, and if so, why? What contribution can they make to a good and virtuous life?

Aristotle never sets a price on happiness, but his analysis of wealth (πλοῦτος) and its uses does provide a framework for settling these questions. Widely considered one of the three "greatest" forms of prosperity (*Rhet.* 2.17 1391a30–32) and counted a "part" of happiness by most (1.5 1360b20), wealth figures prominently in the hedonistic ideal exemplified by Sardanapallos that is one of the leading candidates for a good life (*EN* 1.5 1095b21–22). Some even identify it with happiness (1.4 1095a20–23). So much was it admired that it even gained the title of "a virtue of property" (ἀρετὴ κτήσεως, *Rhet.* 1.6 1362b18, *Pol.* 1.13 1259b20). Aristotle, however, is ready without argument to deny that a life devoted to its pursuit, no matter how successful, deserves to be called "happy conduct" (*EE* 1.4 1215a32); calling the life of businessmen "forced," he considers wealth, like tools and instruments, "useful and for something else" (*EN* 1.5 1096a5–9, 1.7 1097a26–28).

Part of the basis for these claims, with their air of elitism, lies in current attitudes: the contemporary economy was relatively "embedded," with economic activity intimately tied to social and political status.[3] The welter of controls and constraints, social as well as legal, to which commercial and financial markets were subject limited the possibilities and hence the incentives for accumulating material wealth, and in keeping with aristocratic traditions, the best life was widely thought to consist in leisure rather than the busy pursuit of profit. Thus, the crucial economic division was not between wealth and poverty, but between work and leisure: the poor *needed* to work for their livelihood, but the wealthy did not, whether they *chose* to or not. At one extreme were the "well off" (εὔποροι), whose estates made them liable to liturgical service (*Pol.* 4.4 1291a33–34), the public works required annually of the wealthiest by many cities, such as financing a naval ship or producing plays for a festival. At the other extreme were beggars and slaves, the only people who owned no property at all. In between were not only the "poor" (πένητες), who held livestock and homes of their own but still had to work for their living, but also many of the "wealthy" (πλούσιοι), whether farmers or merchants or craftsmen, whose property at least *afforded* them time free from work, whether or not they took it.[4]

3. The term comes from Polanyi 1957: 68–78, which provides an idyllic sketch. See also Humphreys 1969 and Finley 1970, 1973.

4. On the liturgical class, see Davies 1971: xx–xxiv (adapting Aristotle's criterion for being "well-off") and 1981: 10–16, where Davies sets three talents as the threshold for liability to these public services. For an idea of how much expense liturgies could involve, see Morrison and Williams 1968: 254–63: trierarchs had to maintain a ship and its crew of up to 200 for a year. Aristotle regularly uses the term for dramatic liturgies (χορηγία) to refer to resources quite generally (e.g.,

Wealth, in short, belonged not only to an aristocratic elite, but also to many who worked, even to most who were "free" (ἐλεύθεροι).

The embedded state of the ancient economy is not the only explanation for Aristotle's attitude toward wealth. Whether or not "the organization of the material conditions of life" was *in fact* integrated with other interests, he thinks it *should* be integrated and tied even more closely to the rest of life than it then remained.[5] He holds this position not out of allegiance to any reigning ideology, but on the basis of analysis and argument. In brief, to engage in economic pursuits in isolation from other ends, he argues, is to confuse means with ends, for the object of economic activity is simply to provide the "material conditions" for life, not sufficient conditions for a good life. Indeed, economic activity provides materials not only for survival but for social and ethical ends as well, something most who seek wealth for its own sake lose sight of. So by studying economics and the wealth that is its end in the context of life as a whole, Aristotle is not part of a rearguard action against encroaching progressivism. On the contrary, his analysis shows why property has no value by itself, and he disparages any who would lay claim to virtue or happiness purely on the basis of wealth. The value of property is instrumental, not only because its primary function is to preserve life, but also because it "liberates" us for other pursuits, be it pleasure, politics, or study. True wealth serves other ends, and the ideal is to be "free" (ἐλεύθερος) from labor and engage in "liberal" (ἐλευθέριαι) pursuits.[6] But before asking what kinds of action are liberal, we need to look further at Aristotle's views on economics.

1101a15), but he also allows that "most manufacturers are wealthy" (*Pol.* 3.5 1278a24–25). The word for "poor" (πένης) is connected with "labor" (πόνος), and it retained the force of "worker" rather than "indigent"; see esp. Aristophanes *Wealth* 552–54: "It's a beggar's life you describe, to live having nothing, but a poor man's life is to live frugally and attending to his work, getting nothing extra, but not coming up short either"; see Markle 1985: 267–71 for passages in which Aristotle speaks of the "poor" having property.

5. The quoted phrase is used by Polanyi (1957: 71) to describe the economy.

6. The central idea in ἐλευθεριότης is freedom (ἐλευθερία), both negative (freedom from the control of others) and positive (freedom to do what one chooses); those who have this virtue display the character and conduct befitting a free citizen. Aristotle's analysis, reflecting the widespread belief that freedom presupposes economic independence, counts generosity (giving "freely") its major expression. But since that is only one of its forms, "liberality" seems a better translation.

The home is the elementary unit of political community (*Pol.* 1.1 1252a17–31, 1.2 1252b15–18, 1.3 1253b1–4), and Aristotle opens his political theory with an analysis of the home, its parts, and its principal activities. This approach has a polemical side, since the contrast between city and home serves to refute those who assimilate rule over cities to rule over subjects, over a home, and over slaves (*Pol.* 1.1; cf. 1.12). But it is also integral to both his political and his ethical theory. The individuals who make up a political community are at the same time heads of homes, and their union is for the purpose of achieving complete "self-sufficiency": cities "originate for the sake of living but are for the sake of living well" (1.2 1252b27–30).[7] However, the home is not a purely political cell; it is also the primary and original locus of individual sovereignty, for it is the center for survival, for personal relations, and for private property. The home may not be a castle, but its head governs his wife, raises his children, and supervises their resources and means to survival. In a word, the father is "king" or aristocrat in the home (b20–21; cf. b9–27, 1.12). So if a city is a union of autonomous homes, then political theory must examine the nature of the home and its ways of life (οἰκία); or as Aristotle puts it, politics (πολιτική) starts with "economics" (οἰκονομική).[8]

In its primary sense, "economics" denotes the management of a home quite generally. But because the home was the primary locus of ownership, the term acquired the economic emphasis that persists today. Some of Aristotle's contemporaries identified it with "business" (χρηματιστική); others thought business its greatest part (*Pol.* 1.3 1253b12–13).[9] Against this trend, Aristotle

7. The *Politics* opens with the thesis that political life aims at the supreme end of human life (i.e., happiness), and Aristotle sees ethics as a part of politics; see I.i above. For the Platonic background that is a target of the opening polemic, see Newman 1887–1902 on *Pol.* 1.1.

8. The nature of ancient economies, where most economic activity remained private, makes translation problematic here; see Finley 1973: 17–34. "Economics" has some misleading connotations, but it reflects Aristotle's focus better than "home management" does; cf. our archaisms of "Home" versus "Foreign" Office, and "domestic" versus international economy.

9. Aristotle's terminology is precise but obscure; since he neglects to define his terms explicitly, they must be explicated contextually. I rely on the following equations: acquisition = κτητική (cf. *EN* 4.1 1120a8–9); business = χρηματιστική; trade (usually without the intervention of money, i.e., barter) = ἀλλαγή; exchange (generically, with or without money) = μεταβλητική; retail (involving money) = καπηλική; money = νόμισμα; profit or gain = κέρδος. Within this

bases his analysis on the family—not as factors in production and exchange, but as the people for whom those activities are performed. Formed primarily for the twin ends of survival and reproduction (1.2 1252a26–34), the home consists of people and only derivatively of economic factors, for although economic activity is necessary, its aim is to secure the survival of the people who make up the home. Thus, the three "parts" into which he analyzes this community are not economic elements such as produce and means of production, but social relations, namely, the three that unite its members in marriage, parenting, and labor (1.3 1253b3–12, 1.12 1259a37–40).[10] Wealth is one goal of economics, but it has "more concern" (πλείων σπουδή) for people than for property. In particular, it has more concern for human virtue than for "the virtue of property we call wealth" (1.13 1259b18–21). To be sure, with wealth as one of its goals, economics oversees the factors of money, land, livestock, slaves, and movable property that count as its "parts" (*Rhet.* 1.5 1361a12–15). Aristotle insists, however, that wealth consists primarily in using these goods, not in merely owning them (a23–24). The first use of wealth is to meet the daily needs of the home (*Pol.* 1.2 1252b12–16). But since the home is part of a larger community, this is not its only use, and though one of "the most honored" pursuits, economics is subordinate to politics (*EN* 1.2 1094b2–6). Two implications of this hierarchy, which is cited as a recognized fact, are that the good of the home is subordinate to that of society and that private property should also serve public ends. But before looking at the public uses of wealth, I shall examine Aristotle's account of economics in the home.

Although Aristotle's analysis of ownership and property is dominated by the topics of acquisition and exchange, his aim throughout is to clarify the *use* of property for the people in the

---

scheme, Aristotle uses "business" to refer to two different practices of exchange: one provides materials for the home; the other aims only at profit and making money. The former is part of economics; the latter involves retail and is not a part. Thus, Aristotle thinks it wrong to identify business either with economics (which it should serve) or with retail (which it may utilize). See *EE* 3.4 1231b38–32a4; cf. Polanyi 1957: 91–93 and Finley 1970: 15 *n*33.

10. Cf. Polanyi 1957: 81: "The economy—as the root of the word shows, a matter of the domestic household or *oikos*—concerns directly the relationship of persons who make up the natural institution of the household. Not possessions, but parents, offspring and slaves constitute it." Cf. Humphreys 1969: 63.

home. As he observes at the outset, acquisition (ἡ κτητική) is a part of economics because property (ἡ κτῆσις) is a part of the home (*Pol.* 1.4 1253b23–24). But to explain this truism, he appeals to human need: economics includes acquisition because "it is impossible to be alive or to live well without the necessities" (b24–25). The discussion of slavery likewise arises as an inquiry into this "necessary use" (τὴν ἀναγκαίαν χρείαν): as the major factor in production, slaves were needed to meet the material needs of life (1.3 1253b14–16).[11] Further, an item of property (κτῆμα) can be defined as "a tool for living" (ὄργανον πρὸς ζωήν, 1.4 1253b31), or "a separate tool for action" (ὄργανον πρακτικὸν καὶ χωριστόν, 1254a16–17). More generally, property is simply "an abundance of tools" (1253b31–32). In this respect, economics is like other disciplines and crafts, in that each requires "its own tools" (τὰ οἰκεῖα ὄργανα) in order to accomplish its work (b25–27). Thus, since the primary function of property in the home is instrumental, serving to meet the "necessary needs" of the people in the home, Aristotle can conclude that, contrary to popular belief, business and the accumulation of wealth are not the same as economics but only "subordinate" to it (1.8 1256a3–13). Although both business and economics are concerned with property, they differ in their goals: the job of business is only "providing" property; the head of the home is concerned more generally with "using" it (a10–13).

Since the importance of business depends on the ends sought by economics, the next step is to ask what needs economics has. In addition to providing for the basic needs of subsistence, eco-

11. The relevant concept of "need" (χρεία, "need for use," or "use-need," if solecism be permitted) here derives from its semantic connections with "use" (χρῆσις, χράομαι) and "usables, possessions" (χρήματα); cf. Finley 1970: 15. Thus, "things *needed for use* [ὧν χρεία] can be *used* well or poorly" (*EN* 4.1 1120a4–9). Throughout his discussion, Aristotle uses this term consistently to refer to an instrumental need (for things to *use*) that depends on a projected end. In the phrase quoted above, only the adjective "necessary" restricts the term to basic needs. This counts against the anachronistic equation of χρεία with "demand" or consumers' desire, which often have little or nothing to do with need or use; cf. Finley 1970: 9 n13 and Meikle 1979: 60 n8.

The topic of slavery is largely tangential here, but three points deserve note: Aristotle emphasizes the "services" slaves perform for the home, not their status as property; in defining them as "tools that act," he argues that, though subordinate to their masters, they differ from tools for "production" by participating in the "action" of life (1254a1–8); finally, many slaves in antiquity led better (and more autonomous) lives than many free peasants did; see Finley 1973: 62–122 and De Ste. Croix 1981: 133–204. See also Price 1989: 173–78 and n38 below.

nomics also supplies the resources needed for a good life in the home and city. But what standard does Aristotle offer for these additional needs? Following the logic of his subject, he discusses business in two stages, first the production of materials (*Pol.* 1.8) and then their exchange (1.9). In production, the standard for need is clear: first, the basic needs of food and shelter must be met (1256a18–19, b19–20); second comes the broader goal of self-sufficiency and a good life (b4, b31–32).

> One kind of acquisition is a natural [κατὰ φύσιν] part of economics, namely what either needs [δεῖ] to be available or what economics needs to provide, so there will be available the storable possessions [χρημάτων] (1) necessary for living and (2) useful [χρησίμων] in the community of a city or home; and true wealth evidently consists of these things, for self-sufficiency of this kind of property is not unlimited relative to good living.   (1.8 1256b26–32)[12]

Just as acquisition has a natural function, so it has natural limits, determined primarily by survival but also by family and civil life. Together, these limits allow for more than sheer subsistence: Aristotle recognizes a natural place for differences of taste (a27–28) and for "living pleasantly [ἡδέως] by mixing various modes of life and filling out the most basic needs of life [τὸν ἐνδεέστατον βίον] where it happens to fall short of being self-sufficient" (b2–8). He finds nothing wrong with improving the standard of living to some extent, but he thinks this has its limits. Farming, herding, hunting, fishing, even raiding, can all be acceptable ways of improving life (a30–b2). But what makes them acceptable is, in the first instance, that they are "natural" and "given to all by their very nature" (b7–10); for just as human nature provides "enough" sustenance for the newborn ("the nature called milk," b10–15), so the environment provides abundant sources of food and shelter for the grown (b15–22).[13] The implication is that any

12. The text here is problematic, but its central thesis, that economics is limited by the needs of a good life, is not in doubt; see Jowett's (1885) brief and lucid note on *Pol.* 1.8.13. Newman (1887–1902), on 1256b26, lays out the problems fully, though inconclusively. Three points need defense: (1) because the first aim here is to specify what kind of acquisition is a part of economics, the antecedent of the relative (ὅ in a27, not the emendation ὅτι) is production, understood concretely in terms of its produce, and it is the subject of ὑπάρχειν, but the object of πορίζειν; (2) the subject of the *latter* infinitive is αὐτήν, with οἰκονομικῆς as antecedent; (3) the purpose-clause explains *both* infinitives by giving two reasons why provisions must be available (cf. the structure of 1258a19–25).

13. This notorious bit of teleology may not have cosmic significance: the nature mentioned is not a universal *spiritus mundi* but the internal principle peculiar

scarcity here springs from some human interference with the natural order, be it people's own excessive desires or depredations or hoarding by others, each attributable to the first motive. Hence, the first limit on economics is "as the need to *use* [χρεία] compels" (b6–7), and any scarcity comes from excessive demand.

The distinctive features of human life, however, generate another standard over and above subsistence, since property also serves life in a family and city (1.8 1256b29–30). The difference here lies not in *what* is needed, but only in its *use*. Food is consumed socially whether in the family or in common dining halls and at public festivals, and clothing has social and ceremonial, as well as protective, uses.[14] Still, these uses are not unlimited either, and "true wealth" is limited to what serves "good living" (b31–32). Thus, Aristotle seconds Solon, who in dismay at the rapacity of his peers lamented that "there lies no boundary for wealth obvious to men" (fr. 13.71, at 1256b33–34). The problem is not that there *are* no natural limits, but rather, as Solon frequently proclaimed, that so many people fail to *observe* the limits and instead seek property without end.[15] Although Aristotle says nothing precise about these limits, he draws an analogy with other skills to argue that the need for wealth is finite since no art uses

to the members of each natural kind, and the formula "for the sake of"(b16, b17, b19, b22) here refers not to an originating purpose but to the beneficiaries—not to a goal but to a secondary result accompanying the goal; see Kullman 1985. Hence, I translate b22 as "the nature [of each species] has made all creatures *of benefit* to humans." Newman (1887–1902), on 1256b21, suspects an argument against vegetarianism in the background. Aristotle tries to justify "raiding," which he counts as a form of hunting (b23–24), by appeal to our political nature: war is "naturally just" when used to subdue "people who are not willing to be ruled" (b24–26), i.e., humans who reject *political* life; cf. 1253a3–7 ("city-less" people "have an appetite for war"; cf. *Il.* 9.63) and a31–37 (humans "separated from law and justice" are the "harshest" and "most savage" animal).

14. For the social, political, and moral significance of clothing in Classical Athens, see Geddes 1987.

15. Confusion over the scope of ὥσπερ has led many to detect criticism of Solon here, but Aristotle cites the poet to confirm not that wealth *has* no limit but that its limit is "nothing *obvious*" (οὐθὲν πεφασμένον). Solon's preceding couplets (fr. 13.65–70) deny any hope of foreknowledge; note the following lines (13.72–73), and cf. fr. 16 on the difficulty of *knowing* the ἀφανὲς μέτρον. Similarly, a law attributed to Solon (in Lysias 10.19) uses πεφασμένως for "in broad daylight." Moreover, Aristotle says Solon limited private ownership of land (*Pol.* 2.7 1266b15–18), and similar tirades by Solon against his peers' exploitation of debtors can be found in frs. 4, 5, 36, 37 (all from *Ath. Pol.*; cf. 5.3).

"unlimited tools" and wealth is simply "an abundance of tools for the arts of economics and politics" (b34–37). In short, just as other arts choose or design their tools to serve definite ends, so economics should seek only the kinds and the amounts of wealth that it can use to serve the ends of life in the family and city.[16] "Therefore," Aristotle concludes, since the acquisition of wealth is *natural* when it serves to meet the needs of social life (b37–38), it is also *limited* by those needs. "Since it is in some ways for the economist and the ruler to look after health too, but in some ways it is not but rather for the doctor, so too it is in some ways for the economist to look after property, but in other ways it is not, but rather for something subordinate" (1.10 1258a32–34). Although people must be healthy and have property to pursue their other ends, moderate health or wealth serves for most ends; exceptional fitness or wealth is rarely necessary. Hence, the major concern of economics is to distribute resources where they can be used. In this respect, the head of a home is just like the weaver who has others provide the wool and attends rather to its use (a21–27; cf. 1.8 1256a5–10).

Life in a political community makes another form of acquisition possible, the exchange between homes that is called "business" (1.9 1256b40–41). Like production, business provides goods for the family, but though similar in aim, they differ significantly in method. Production (including hunting and fishing as well as farming) acquires goods by labor or effort, but business uses the same goods to acquire other goods by exchange. Although in principle both supply products to be used by the home, business also puts products to a further use. One result is to weaken the link with need and the primary use of goods. In business, property has "a double use" (διττὴ ἡ χρῆσις): shoes, for example, can be worn, which is "their own [οἰκεία] use," or traded for something else, which is "their exchange [μετα-βλητική] use" (1257a6–13).[17] The aim should be to provide for the

16. Newman (1887–1902), on 1256b35, cites a pun used by Aristippus to show a *disanalogy* between wealth and other tools: shoes "get in the way" (ἐμπο-δίζει) when they are too large (fr. 75 Giannantoni). But Aristippus too implies that wealth is only instrumental when he claims that extra wealth is valuable for its *use* in emergencies (χρῆσθαι κατὰ καιρόν).

17. Aristotle often wears his economic ethics on his sleeve: his homely examples reflect the scope of what he thinks basic. Earlier, elitists reproached Socrates for peppering his talk with mundane examples, a habit they found undignified.

first use; business simply takes advantage of the other use to do so. Because the link between exchange and need is indirect, however, the second use can obscure the first. That is why "it is thought that there is no limit for wealth and property" (1256b41).

This leads to a further problem, one that links business and economics inescapably to justice and morality. Whereas production acquires *unowned* goods, business uses exchange to obtain *owned* goods, and this difference in source involves property in relations *with other people*. In theory no problems need arise, but since in practice exchange between homes involves competing claims to ownership—claims that do not exist within the home—distribution becomes problematic when the primary uses of goods are ignored. In short, by freeing property from the needs it should serve, the practice of exchange lends itself to the acquisition of wealth for its own sake, purely for "profit." In principle, since both business and production serve the needs of life in the home and city, the standard of value remains the same, namely, the limits of natural wealth. But because they use goods in different *ways*, they are thought to have different *ends*, and beside natural and legitimate uses of exchange in economics, there arises "through experience and art" a form of business that is "not natural," the unlimited pursuit of gain Aristotle labels "retail" (κα-πηλική).[18]

Aristotle's analysis of business comes dressed in historical garb, as a sketch of the development of exchange to its current state. But there is no sign of historical research, and the entire reconstruction clearly derives from logical analysis.[19] Objections to the historicity of his account miss the mark, for he distinguishes successive stages on the basis of logical priority and uses a developmental model to clarify the relations between economics and exchange. In short, his primary aim is to indicate the purpose of exchange and its role in society. Starting from the observation that property has two uses, he tries to show that exchange has a basis in natural needs but should be limited to attaining self-sufficiency: because not everyone can grow wine, those who produce more than they need can exchange the surplus to meet their other needs.

18. The term has Platonic background, although it may have enjoyed wider usage: both *Rep*. 371d and *Soph*. 223d introduce it as used; see Kurke 1989 on the archaic background and Finley 1970: 14, 16, esp. *n*34.
19. Cf. Weil 1965: 179–80.

There is an exchange use of everything, starting first from what is natural, because people have more than enough of some things but not enough of other things. From this it is also clear that retail is not naturally a part of business, for people were compelled to trade to get enough for themselves. So it is clear that retail has no function [ἔργον] in the first community [κοινωνία]—i.e., a home—but only when the community is larger; for families shared [ἐκοινώνουν] everything, and people living separately shared many other things that they were compelled to give back and forth according to their needs [κατὰ τὰς δεήσεις], just as many foreign nations still do, by trade. They trade useful things for useful things, and nothing more—giving wine, for example, and getting grain, and so on with other things of that kind. Therefore this sort of exchange is neither contrary to nature nor a kind of business, since it arose to fulfill natural self-sufficiency. (*Pol.* 1.9 1257a14–30)

Claiming that exchange serves natural needs, Aristotle emphasizes repeatedly that its purpose is to provide us "enough" of what we need. At its most basic level, this is accomplished by exchanging gifts (μεταδόσεις, a24): like the sharing that occurs within each family, reciprocal giving between families can fill the needs of both (a20–25).[20] Inspired by need, this process may pose no threat to either property or justice. If each party gives to get what it needs (a10–12), neither has any motive to take more than it needs or to give when it has no need, and the process is complete when natural self-sufficiency is achieved. Still, the situation is not entirely idyllic. Problems can arise when a home that has no needs has something others need; then the motive for exchange is absent on one side. To minimize this possibility and to secure social solidarity, many cities tried to encourage reciprocity by erecting shrines to the Graces or Charities (Χάριτες) under whose auspices cities "stay together by giving back and forth (μεταδόσει)" (*EN* 5.5 1133a2–5). Unfortunately, since private ownership within the home tends to reduce kindness or "charity" (χάρις) toward others outside it, giving is usually replaced by barter (ἀλλαγή), which occurs not spontaneously but by agreement and with an expectation of return. Instead of giving his work to farmers, the cobbler negotiates with them to get wine in

20. Polanyi (1957: 93) emphasizes the significance of this term. The motive for "gifts" is χάρις, which requires not aiming to get anything in return and also presupposes some need on the part of the recipient. Aristotle defines it as "help for one in *need* [δεομένῳ] that is not *for* anything in return" (*Rhet.* 2.7 1385a17–19). In his analysis of liberality, he insists that "giving" predominates over "taking" (*EN* 4.1 1120a8–16); and in his analysis of friendships based on utility, he calls those who *give* help "character" friends, but those who *trade* goods "legal" friends (8.13 1162b21–63a8).

return (*Pol*. 1.9 1257a27–28). Nonetheless, here too the motive for exchange and the limit on its practice typically remains need and utility.

From these humble beginnings, in which exchange is tied directly to needs, business develops and the natural limits of self-sufficiency grow obscure. Communities that are "in need" (ἐν-δεεῖς) of materials from afar or have a surplus to export use foreign trade to obtain the "natural necessities"; because transport makes direct exchange impractical or impossible, money is used "of necessity" (1257a31–35). Introduced to meet these needs, money here is not only "useful" but fills a natural need (a35–37). But by minimizing the obstacles to exchange, money also introduces new possibilities for accumulation, and it is here that Aristotle locates the origin of retail, which had in his day appropriated the title "business" (b1–10).[21] Although unnatural when pursued for profit and without regard to need or use (a4–5, b3–5), this form of business is still a "rational" development of exchange (a31) and not in itself unjust at all. On the contrary, Aristotle concludes that business practiced for the economic needs of a home is not only "natural" but "necessary and praised" (1.10 1258a37–40; cf. a14–18).

One advantage that business has over barter is that it solves the problem of the unwilling trader. Money makes it easier to accumulate wealth, and while that makes it easier to exceed natural limits, it also encourages trading even in homes that have no needs. Moreover, business also has a function in achieving justice in exchange. Although money opens new room for injustice, it also makes it easier to find just rates for exchange; without these no society of any size can long survive. Thus, exchange is necessary to achieve natural self-sufficiency, just exchange is necessary for social stability, and money helps determine when ex-

21. If Aristotle is right that the word for business had coalesced with the word for specifically commercial exchange, then many of his contemporaries equated economics with money-based markets, not mere barter and haggling (note δοκεῖ, 1257b5; τιθέασι, b8). This should count as a datum in the debate over whether Aristotle and his contemporaries "had the concept of economy"; see Finley 1970: 22–23, 1973: chap. 1. Granted, Aristotle offers little in the way of "laws" of economic exchange (he finds the principle of monopoly in Thales; 1259a5–33) and he refuses to address market mechanics (a2–3), but he does recommend further study (a3–6, a33–36) much as he does for politics (*EN* 10.9 1181a12–b22), and his account argues that economics should not be isolated but studied "ethically" because it is an instrumental *part* of a larger organic whole.

change is just, as Aristotle argues in his analysis of justice. There he presents an analysis of money in connection, ironically, with the retaliatory principle of "the justice of Rhadamanthus" (*EN* 5.5 1132b25–27). Whereas certain Pythagoreans "defined the just without qualification as what reciprocates with another" (τὸ ἀν-τιπεπονθὸς ἄλλῳ, b21–23),[22] Aristotle argues that reciprocity fits neither distributive nor corrective justice exactly (b23–31). However, for the specific task of measuring justice in voluntary transactions (cf. 1131a1–9), he does consider the principle sound, and he adopts the Pythagoreans' term to characterize what "holds together [συνέχει] the sort of justice involved in communities where there is exchange" (5.5 1132b31–33).[23]

Since society "stays together by people reciprocating [τῷ ἀντι-ποιεῖν] proportionally" (1132b33–34), this form of justice is fundamental to the preservation of social life. If the parties to an exchange do not get a proportional return, Aristotle observes, they count themselves slaves; or if they cannot get something they want or need, they do not exchange what they have (1132b34–33a2). So without some assurance of fair exchange, the community would be in danger of dissolving because of its inability to meet even basic needs, let alone social needs. The problem here is acute, for unless there is some basis for establishing reciprocity between diverse products and needs, there can be no exchange and hence no lasting association (1133a21–25). Since people exchange different, not identical, items (a16–18), the reciprocity they seek cannot be exact equality (κατ' ἰσότητα) but only "proportional" (κατ' ἀναλογίαν). A cobbler, to use one of Aristotle's examples, needs to exchange his work not with other cobblers but with farmers and other artisans (a7–10, a32–33). But since shoes and food are not equal in any obvious way, there must be some way of treating them at least as commensurable (σύμμε-τρα), if reciprocity is to be achieved. Hence, the very existence

22. The idea of reciprocity had a long history, but the mathematical proportions on which it is based remain obscure; see Harvey 1965.

23. The obscure phrase ἐν ταῖς κοινωνίαις ταῖς ἀλλακτικαῖς has puzzled commentators. Contrary to the standard interpretation, derived from Will 1954: 215 n1 ("les relations d'échange qui ont pour cadre la communauté"), my translation retains the adjectival force of ἀλλακτικαῖς and connects the phrase specifically with the stage of communal life in which people meet their needs by exchanging goods instead of giving gifts. The difference is significant, since Will's phrase emphasizes the exchange itself, whereas Aristotle's highlights the association and hence the *people* who exchange.

and continuation of society presuppose some method of equalizing property, "for neither would there be a community if there were no exchange, nor would there be an exchange if there were no equality, nor again any equality if there were no commensurability [συμμετρία]" (b17–18). In short, the task is to find an acceptable basis for treating diverse items as commensurate.

At one level, this is the function of money, which serves as "a sort of medium [μέσον], since it measures [μετρεῖ] everything" (a18–21). Anything can be exchanged, provided it has a price. But what determines the price? Money is only a measure; what does it measure? Here again Aristotle invokes a standard of use: "Everything needs to be measured by some one thing, as was said before. In truth, it is the need to use [ἡ χρεία] that holds everything together; for if people are in no need [δέοιντο], or not as much in need, either there will be no exchange, or it will not be the same" (a25–28).[24] Money provides only the *unit* of measure; *what* it measures is the factor of need and utility. Or as Aristotle puts it, money is only "like a substitute for the *need to use*" (ὑπάλλαγμα τῆς χρείας, a28–29). To confirm the point, he adds that people simply do not exchange their goods "whenever they have no *need to use* them (μὴ ἐν χρείᾳ ὦσι)" (b6–10). To be sure, few goods are exactly "commensurable," but "in relation to the *need to use*," even very different items can be made commensurate "enough" (b18–20). Not only the motive for exchange, then, but also the standard for price depends on the needs of the parties to the exchange. Money measures the value of things exchanged, but it does not create or constitute that value. Its function is only to facilitate the comparative evaluation of items to be exchanged, and it arises only "by convention" (νόμῳ), as its very name (νό-μισμα) indicates (a29–31; cf. *Pol.* 1.9 1257b10–13). Indeed, since prices and monetary values themselves can fluctuate, as Aristotle realizes (*EN* 5.5 1133b13–14),[25] there must be something else

24. Aristotle refers to need (δεῖται) three more times (once in 1133b9 and twice in b11). The claim made elsewhere that χρήματα are "the things whose worth is measured by money" (4.1 1119b26–27) does not contradict the present argument, since worth is prior to monetary valuation.
25. The point of Aristotle's remark that "all must be valued" (δεῖ πάντα τε-τιμῆσθαι, 1133b14–15) is that money itself can change in value. "All" refers not to all goods but only to money (τοῦτο, b13), and his claim is that currency must be *accepted* (cf. our "honored"), not, as Polanyi (1957: 88–89) assumes, that "prices have been set," or, as Finley (1970: 11 n22) suggests, "that everything is

to cause changes in this measure. Here again it is need, for even when there is no present need for certain goods, money serves "as a guarantor" for getting them "when there is need" (b10–12). In short, the just value of the goods exchanged depends on people's need to use them.

When exchange is necessary to meet natural needs, money is not only useful but an instrument of justice. An exchange is just when goods of equivalent value are exchanged (5.5 1134a1–7); so by measuring the value of the goods exchanged, money helps avoid the disputes that can disrupt social life. But exchange can also be unjust if some get more than they give and profit at others' expense (a5–6); like most tools, money can also be misused and promote injustice. In fact, by facilitating exchange and making it easier to hoard, money gives rise to the business of "retail." In itself a useful method for the exchange of necessities (τῆς ἀναγ-καίας ἀλλαγῆς, *Pol.* 1.9 1257b1–3), retail centers on money and tends to treat money as its end (b3–10). Retailers themselves are only middlemen, serving like money as a "medium" for exchange. The process of retail, however, reverses the relation between ends and means in exchange, for whereas economics uses money only to obtain what it needs, retail makes money its end, and when it exploits others' needs rather than satisfying retailers' own, retail pursues money beyond natural limits. Business transactions governed by economics (in Aristotle's sense of the word) begin and end with usable property, and money serves only as a medium of exchange. A farmer sells his crop to buy what he needs in a process that can be represented schematically as G-M-G ("goods-money-goods").[26] But inverting this relation, retailers treat goods as instruments for exchange and make money their goal (b20–22); or as Aristotle puts it, "money is both an element and a limit [στοιχεῖον καὶ πέρας] for retail exchange" (b22–23). Beginning and ending with money, retailers buy goods

---

expressed in money." As the argument shows, goods must be valued on their own and prior to exchange before anyone will buy them, let alone at "just prices." Thus, when Aristotle later adds that people use different weights and measures depending on whether they are buying or selling (5.7 1134b35–35a3), he implies that prices and exchange rates are not set. See Humphreys 1969: 50–53.

26. This helpful scheme comes from Meikle 1979: 61–63, although to follow Aristotle in making *use* primary, I write "G" in place of Meikle's "C" (for "commodity," which would reduce goods to articles for commercial exchange).

only to sell at higher prices (M-G-M). In short, retail differs from other exchange not only in method, but also in its end: going beyond "replenishment of natural self-sufficiency" (a30–31) to seek more than needed for use in the home, retail exchanges goods for profit (κέρδος, b4–5).

> There is no limit to the goal of this form of business; its goal is this [monetary] form of wealth and acquiring possessions. But for business in economics there is a limit, since this [i.e., money-making] is not the function [ἔργον] of economics. This is why there appears to be a necessary limit of all wealth in economics, although in practice we see the opposite happening, since all who do business [οἱ χρηματιζόμενοι] increase their money without limit.   (Pol. 1.9 1257b28–34)[27]

Aristotle objects to retail, it should be noticed, not for dealing with money, but for the way it is typically practiced (b32–33). In principle, economics takes its limit from natural self-sufficiency (a30), and its aim is "natural wealth" (b19–20). Retail can serve this end by making available at a fair cost what different homes need, just as direct exchange can violate these limits even when no retailers intervene as middlemen. In short, retailers could earn a fair return, determined by their efforts and the natural needs of their own homes. But in practice, they and businessmen make their business their life: experience and skill show them "where and how they will make most profit in exchange" (b3–5), and taking the means of their exchange as their end, they end up without any limit on their wealth (b23–24). Quite apart from questions of justice, this lands them in the paradox of Midas, whose enormous wealth in gold could not save him from hunger because he could not use it to meet even his basic needs (b10–17). Or more theoretically, business must serve some end other than wealth because it lacks any finite end of its own: "There is no limit to the goal of this form of business; its goal is [nothing but] monetary wealth and acquiring possessions" (b28–30). Other disciplines pursue their ends "without limit" but use their materials and means only within the limits set by those ends. Medicine, for example, aims to produce health everywhere it can, but it uses only the treatment it needs to achieve that goal (b25–28). By contrast, if the end of business were only the "abundance of money"

27. Text and interpretation are again problematic; the crux is in 1257b30, where I adopt the easy emendation of αὖ for οὐ (Jowett's proposal would require μή).

that is often confused with wealth (b8–10), its means would be entirely "endless" (b22–24). As Aristotle concludes, although business is often a necessary and natural part of economics (1258a14–18), its role in acquisition should be governed by the larger aims of family and home: provisions "need to be available," but the goal of business should be to acquire and distribute only what is needed (a21–27).

Although the nature of retail makes misuse possible, misuse would not occur if retailers did not seek profit. The root of the evil here, in short, is not retail or money but the values and motives of retailers. Their error is understandable. "The explanation is the proximity of the two forms of business, for the *use* in each overlaps, since each use in business is *of* the same thing [τοῦ αὐτοῦ]; for the use is *of* the same property [in economics and retail], but not *for* the same reason [οὐ κατὰ ταὐτόν], since economics has a further goal, but the goal of [retail] business is increase" (*Pol.* 1.9 1257b35–38).[28] Economics and retail both use property for exchange, so their use is "of the same thing" (b36–37). But they differ in their goals (b37): whereas the head of the home has its needs as his end, the retailer trades with a view to profit. The misuse of exchange is an easy mistake since the primary and exchange uses "overlap" so closely (b35–36), but it is nonetheless a mistake. For just as medicine has health as its end, not the wealth its practice may earn, so economics has meeting the needs of social life as its end, not the surplus it can acquire by exchange (1258a8–14). And just as the head of a home can look out for its health without himself being a doctor, so he should look after its wealth without being a businessman devoted to wealth (a28–34). Thus, although business makes it easy to take profit as one's end, Aristotle sees a psychological explanation behind this technical explanation. The motives for the unlimited pursuit of wealth are two, each of which simply exaggerates otherwise reasonable concerns: "Some people do not use their wealth; others misuse [παραχρῶνται] it."[29]

28. The text is difficult, but the thought clear; I find the antecedent for αὐτῶν (b35) in the two forms of business distinguished in b28 and b30, I punctuate b36 as in Newman 1887–1902, and I adopt Göttling's easy emendation in b37 (reported in Newman 1887–1902 on 1257b35).

29. This aphorism from Plutarch has been attributed to a dialogue "On Wealth" (fr. 1 Ross = fr. 56 Rose); but the thought is present in *Pol.* 1.9, *EN* 4.1, and *EE* 3.4.

Some think that increase is the function of economics, and they keep on [increasing their wealth] in the belief that they should either preserve or increase their monetary estate without limit. The explanation for this condition is their concern [τὸ σπουδάζειν] for living instead of for living well. Thus, because their appetite for life is unlimited, they also have an appetite for an unlimited amount of products for life. But those who also apply themselves to living well seek things for physical gratification. Hence, since this too appears to depend on property, their whole effort goes into business. This is why the other kind of business [i.e., retail] has arisen: since gratification depends on a surplus, they seek what produces a surplus for gratification.   (*Pol.* 1.9 1257b38–58a8)

Each of these two contrary tendencies exaggerates a natural concern. Worriers who hoard against an uncertain future seek more security than human life warrants (recall Solon's conflation of stability with invulnerability), and sensualists who need wealth to pay for their pleasures mistake life's priorities (recall the function of temperance). These are errors, moreover, from the perspective of the agents themselves: quite apart from any harm or injustice either group does to others, satisfaction in the endless pursuit of money is inherently unstable, and their continual need for resources makes their lives essentially "pointless."[30] In short, each confuses the *use* of property: hoarders use too little because, like Midas, they mistake *having* the necessary means for life with enjoying their use in life's pursuits; and sensualists use too much because, while they try to enjoy life, their expensive tastes compel them to spend too much time *acquiring* goods.

These two motives to which Aristotle attributes the misuse of business correspond closely to the pair of vices contrary to the virtue of liberality (ἐλευθερία).[31] First, the defining mark of "illiberality" (ἀνελευθερία) is "being concerned about wealth more than one should" (*EN* 4.1 1119b28–30). This devotion to property can have either or both of two effects (1121b16–21): some it makes niggardly and reluctant either to give or to spend what they have (b21–31); some it makes acquisitive and willing to profit from anything (1121b31–22a13); and some are both. The first set worries about losing what they have (1121b12–16). Security is their

30. Both ways of life exemplify the "empty and pointless desire" that Aristotle associates with an "endless" series or regress of goals (*EN* 1.2 1094a20–21).

31. The *EE* links the two vices to the distinction between proper and exchange uses: both vices involve a "coincidental" use of goods (3.4 1232a1–9).

paramount concern: they refrain from taking advantage of others but only from fear of disgrace (b23–26) or reprisal (b28–31).[32] The others tend to do much worse. Some are willing to do anything for gain (1121b31–32, 1122a8–13), from pimping and usury (1121b33–34), to cheating, robbery, and raiding (1122a7–8). The end of each group is only to *have*, not to use, and that is to mistake the value of wealth.

At the opposite extreme are the "wasteful" (ἄσωτοι) who care so little for their future security that they exhaust their resources, usually on the treadmill of appetite (1119b30–20a4). Without denying them their pleasure, Aristotle simply argues that extravagance endangers their livelihood. As their name suggests, great expenditure "wastes" their livelihood. In particular, destruction of one's resources is tantamount to "self-destruction" since resources are necessary for life and action (1120a1–3). Wastefulness, however, although usually motivated by other misconceptions, especially intemperance (1119b30–34, 1121b7–10), is much closer to liberality than illiberality is, because the wasteful at least recognize that wealth is to be used, and they give and spend, although not as they should (a19–30). Excessive giving benefits others but hoarding benefits none (a27–29), and for most "private citizens," excess cures itself by leaving them with nothing left to give (a20–25, b11–12). In short, both vices mistake natural priorities: the illiberal value life's necessities over a good life, and the wasteful value those necessities too little for their own good.

Unfortunately, these misconceptions about the use of property affect not only the lives of the illiberal and wasteful but also the lives of others. First, their exaggerated sense of the value of external goods stimulates their desire for wealth, which leads to excess in acquisition, and in many circumstances, that involves injustice toward others. At a venial level, retailers exploit others' natural needs for the goods they sell. One effect is personal: the exploited resent their loss (*EN* 5.5 1132b34–33a1), and the exploiters earn ill will. Thus, profiting *"from* one another," as Aristotle puts it, is "justly reproached," and usury "is hated" (*Pol.* 1.10 1258b1–2).[33] The illiberal seek to gain even *"from* their friends"

32. This represents the justice of the weak mocked by Thrasymachus (*Rep.* 1). With Aristotle's "marks" of miserly illiberality (1121b21–31), cf. Theophrastus *Char.* 22.

33. The phrase "from another" is glossed as *"at the expense of others"* by Finley (1970: 17; his italics). This distaste for usury should not be taken as a sign of

(*EN* 4.1 1122a10–11). In contrast with "living *from* others," doing things *for* others inspires respect, goodwill, and friendship (*Rhet.* 2.4 1381a19–25), and liberal acts are "liked most of all virtuous acts since they are beneficial" (*EN* 4.1 1120a21–23). But since valuing wealth as an end implies at least a willingness, if not always a readiness, to commit injustice in its pursuit, there are also larger consequences. The wasteful have "many vices," including unrestraint and incontinence (1119b30–33); out of greed, the illiberal are especially liable to crime (1122a7–10); and by violating justice in exchange, exploitation interferes with distributive justice and threatens the social fabric (5.5 1133a2–5, 5.6 1134a23–34). Still worse, although private greed leads only to illiberal conduct, people with the same values who attain the power to act as they wish can become "tyrants pillaging cities and plundering temples" (4.1 1122a3–6). No longer merely "illiberal," acts so heinous are injustice and impiety of the worst order (a6–7).

Aristotle considers it worse to be illiberal than wasteful (a13–16), not only because our various incapacities and needs make it more natural (1121b14), but by implication also because it is better to give too much than not to give at all. Thus, the principal mark of liberality is *giving* from one's own property to others; for "giving and spending is thought to be *using* property, whereas taking and maintaining is rather acquiring" (1120a8–23).[34] Moreover, the liberal give not for their own sake or to receive some benefit in return but "for something noble" (a23–29; cf. 1121b1–10). Motives are of primary importance here, for they are what cause and constitute liberal conduct, and they are what make liberality a moral virtue. First, the liberal don't constantly "look out for themselves" (1120b6), and they won't "take property from where they should not" because they "honor" it not for itself but only for giving (a31–33, b15–17). Indeed, although liberality has

---

Aristotle's conservatism and leisure-class ideology; he reports it as a common attitude, and "hatred" for bankers remains common, especially among the poor, where inequities in wealth are the starkest and usury most exploitative. Moreover, though outlawed in Athens by Solon (*Ath. Pol.* 6.1, 9.1), the use of "personal security"—a chilling euphemism for taking a person's life and liberty as collateral—did not disappear from Greece.

34. Aristotle emphasizes giving over spending throughout (59 references to giving in 4.1, thirteen to spending, eight of which involve the vices), because liberal spending is indirect giving: X pays Y for goods or services to be *given* to Z. Thus, spending is a species of giving: "We put spending in giving" (1121a12).

its prudential side (a34–b4), it is not inconsistent with using up one's estate; although "fortune is criticized because those most deserving are least wealthy," the cause is not fate but virtue, since "they can't have property if they don't care how to get it" (b17–20). Further, liberal acts vary with the resources of the giver. Having few resources does not stifle virtuous giving, since liberality is measured not by quantity but by character: it "depends not on the amount given but on the character of the giver, which gives by his estate," and some who give less are actually more liberal because "they give *from* less" (b7–11). Finally, with this attitude toward property, the liberal *enjoy* giving for good causes (a26–27) and are pained—though "moderately and as they should be"— if they *fail* to spend where they should or spend where they should not (1121a1–7).

Aristotle's account of the virtuous use of wealth as exemplified by liberality has major ethical consequences. First, in keeping with his argument for economics, the liberal want and take wealth only for its uses. That means they are guided by self-sufficiency, which they achieve more readily than do people with expensive tastes. It also implies that they enjoy what they have, rather than longing for more. But liberality also has specifically moral implications. The liberal are reliable in any relations involving property, and far from *doing wrong* to others, they are actually liable to *be wronged* (1121a4–7). Since they exercise justice in exchange, whether in giving or in business, their acquisition is no threat to social solidarity or distributive justice. On the contrary, although Aristotle thinks some characters *should* be "poor" (i.e., work; he names toadies, b5–7),[35] liberal giving is "beneficial." It often goes where there is need, and that is bound to redress some inequities (4.2 1122a26–29). In particular, the liberal use of great wealth, according to Aristotle's reforming account of "magnificence" (μεγαλοπρέπεια), serves the public good above all.

After restricting this "great" virtue to *spending* wealth (4.2 1122a20–22; large *gifts* would presumably suit only selfish recipients), Aristotle insists that magnificent spending must be for great causes if it is to be "fitting" (πρέπουσα), as its name implies it is (a22–25). In general, greatness is in the act and its object, not

35. Cf. *n*4 above.

in the cost or the agent's wealth (a25–28, b2–6). But greatness is also *relative* to the agent and object (a24–25). Although some great causes are great in expense (civic liturgies and public buildings, a24–25, b19–23), smaller expenditures can still be great in "effect" (ἐν τῷ ἔργῳ, 1123a10–18). Thus, a fine ball or flask "has magnificence as a gift for a child, although each is small and illiberal in price" (a14–16). Like liberality, this virtue is measured not by property alone but by the context and motive of its acts. The crucial factor is again that one act "for something noble," rather than for gain or personal advantage, and not only willingly but gladly (1122b6–10). Magnificence, then, is not reserved only for the very rich. Few can afford the great liturgies but many can perform less costly service. Although its greatest expression is in public works, especially for public festivals and monuments (b19–23, 1123a1–10), it can also be shown in private acts (1122b35). There too its ends are essentially social: weddings fete the family and celebrate its extension, and gifts to foreign guests or hosts are "not for oneself but for common ends" (1123a1–5). By contrast, the vices of excess and deficiency aim at display and conspicuous consumption on unworthy ends and for personal prestige (a19–27), or they conserve private wealth to the detriment of others' ends (a27–31).

Some of Aristotle's criticism of business and illiberality smacks of elitism and the disdain some aristocrats felt toward the nouveaux riches. But his objections, backed up by argument, are not to business itself or to wealth but only to the pursuit of wealth for its own sake, and that applies to old wealth as well as to new. At bottom, his critique is based on character, not on status, and is directed at ethical types, not at economic classes.[36] His views may echo conservative prejudices, but his rationale is liberal and inclusive rather than elitist and exclusive. First, he dissects the behavior of the wealthy with a satirist's blade. They tend to be "violent [ὑβρισταί], insolent, self-indulgent, ostentatious," and vain; they think they have everything good, that anything can be bought, that everyone admires them, and that they deserve to rule; and they are prone to crimes of assault and seduction (*Rhet*.

36. Himself economically and politically marginalized as a resident foreigner who could own no land in Athens, Aristotle is unlikely to condemn universally the foreigners who transacted the bulk of business in his day; see Whitehead 1975, and Finley 1973: 150–76.

2.16). Even when claiming that inherited wealth tends more to liberality than new wealth does, he cites observation and adds the explanation that the latter have experience of need and "like parents and poets" feel concern for the product of their work (*EN* 4.1 1120b11–14). For although work performed for gain is typically illiberal, the same work is at least necessary when it fills genuine needs, and it can be valuable in the service of noble aims, as Solon proclaims in his hymn to the Muses (fr. 13.43–62). On the other hand, the total disdain for property urged by some radicals would undermine moral concern. There would be little point in generosity or liberality and little wrong with theft or the inequities that leave many poor or even destitute, if the material needs of human life had no ethical importance. Further, as Aristotle recognizes, inequities in wealth are a major source of political instability and conflict, and he commends Solon's economic reforms (*Pol.* 2.7 1266b14–18).[37]

The object of Aristotle's criticism, in short, is not wealth itself or those who were compelled to earn a living from business or crafts, but any who would rest content with wealth and prestige or who demanded power simply on the basis of their means. Against such complacency and presumption, he argues that only the virtuous merit these goods, because only they know how to use them well. Tellos merits praise, and Socrates the stonemason is a model no less than Plato the aristocrat, not least because each preferred virtuous pursuits to business for gain. Thus, some resources are necessary, but not the great success idolized by many. The happy, on this account, have property, but they need not be of the elite. On the contrary, success and prosperity by themselves are not enough for a good life, and to be happy, the wealthy must put their fortune to work for more valuable ends.

The conservative aspects of Aristotle's economics are rooted not in a rejection of egalitarian principles but in moral psychology. His principal aim is to establish that property is valuable for its use, and that both strikes at the *motives* for gain or "having more" and provides a rationale for institutional reform. His theory of "economics" is thus an integral part of his theory of justice, for it argues that excess—the desire for which is a major

37. Economic factors are crucial in Aristotle's lengthy analysis of political conflict in *Pol.* 5–6; cf. his introduction to the views of the ancient communist Phaleas (2.7 1266a36–39). See De Ste. Croix 1981: 72–80.

source of injustice—has no value. Further, his antipathy to business, although a cause of complaint from modern students of
economics, stems from his ethical focus. There is no need, then,
to invoke the excuse that Aristotle's disapproval of business reflects the limits of his age, an excuse that is worse than feeble for
other parts of his theory of economics. His defense of slavery, for
example, or of the inferior status of women is not to be excused.
Much of his conservatism, however, can be explained.

First, there is tension in Aristotle's theory between his recognition that many of the finer things in life require leisure and his
refusal to call a home or city happy unless most of its members
fare well (*Pol.* 1.13 1260b13–20, 2.9 1269b12–19). He is reluctant to
make political offices accessible to hired laborers, merchants, or
those who work the fields, much less to women and slaves (7.8–
9), but his reason is that effective public service is time-
consuming and incompatible with the pursuit of private gain (7.9
1328b39–29a2). Further, he thinks everyone has access to happiness in the exercise of private virtues, since even slaves, as well
as women, children, and workers, can exercise all but deliberative excellence (1.13, esp. 1260a12–21; cf. *Po.* 15 1454a19–22).
Courage, temperance, and justice are not entirely the same for
all, he argues, and Socrates was wrong to reject Gorgias' distinctions (1260a21–31; cf. *Meno* 71–73). Not everyone can acquire
practical wisdom or "complete virtue" (1260a17), but the virtues
of character can and should be exercised by all: all need to "have
their souls in good condition" and "do what is right" (a26). Those
who do acquire good habits of conduct thereby gain the basis for
happiness. Finally, he insists that heads of homes, like officials in
cities, should deserve their authority not only by having superior
virtue and reason but also by striving to make the lives of everyone under them as good as circumstances allow. Slaves are "partners in life" (a40), and masters "should be responsible for virtue
in their slaves" (b3–4) and direct them by "advice" (νουθετητέον),
not just "by orders" (b5–7), much less by force.[38] True sovereigns,
whether at home and in politics, *care* for their people and rule

38. Aristotle here rebukes those who deny slaves are rational, and he assigns
slaves the capacity for "following" reason and "being persuaded" that distinguishes one part of the rational soul (cf. *EN* 1.13 1102b30–34). In his analysis of
friendship, he argues that slave and master should be friends because both are
human and that there should be justice between them since both "can share in
law and contract" (*EN* 8.11 1161a32–b8, esp. b5–8).

justly because of their ability to contrive welfare for all (*EN* 8.10 1160a35–b8, b22–61a2).

These explanations amount to little more than benevolent despotism, and in granting autonomy only to educated males with leisure, Aristotle draws a distinctly inegalitarian conclusion. But here again, the flaw in his argument stems not from his principles but from his empirical approach. Accepting the evidence of virtually universal practice, he fails to ask how much the observed inferiorities of slaves, women, and laborers were the effect of oppression rather than an expression of "natural" tendencies. Thus, although he toys with the idea that slavery would be unnecessary if only people had tools that could work "automatically" (αὐτόματοι) like the legendary machines of Daedalus or Hephaestus (*Pol.* 1.4 1253b32–54a1), Aristotle shows no inkling of the possibility that improved economic conditions might also eliminate many disparities and, by making leisure and education more widely available, liberate slaves and women from the deficiencies that putatively justified their inferior status. This neglect of the possibilities of ameliorism shows the limits of Aristotle's power to rise above the status quo but does not impugn his analysis. After all, he makes a strong case for educating children, who are similarly deficient but will become citizens: just as they must be educated for freedom by training in virtue, so could the rest of the populace.[39] In short, his own arguments provide the premises for justifying reform: if rulers *should* be superior to the ruled in both the degree and the kind of virtue they have (1.13 1259b34–38), but the education afforded by economic improvements can *remove* those disparities, then all should have access to rule. However, when few could imagine that the material standard of living would ever rise very far, it is understandable that greater wealth was seen as a threat to social justice rather than a means to it. The worry was that the fruits of economic progress would be enjoyed only by the few, leaving most people no better off. Given subsequent history, in fact, it seems presumptuous to assume that this worry was groundless.

39. Aristotle emphasizes the importance of education in *EN* 10.9, and after arguing that parents make a decisive contribution (1180b3–20), he contends that parents should learn general rules, which would in effect make them lawmakers (b21–28); see also *Pol.* 8, and the analysis in Lord 1982. On the ancient neglect of economic progress, see Finley 1970.

The virtuous use of wealth, whether magnificent or only lib-eral, puts private property to work for others. Although liberality also serves one's own good by seeking to obtain property, its aim is to use what it acquires to benefit city, family, and friends. Both virtues, then, are inherently social and moral. Further, neither requires any great wealth. Even if happiness requires the activity of *all* the virtues, it is not a privilege attained only by affluence; the poor can *have* magnificence, and even they can exercise it in some contexts. Finally, liberal economics is like temperance in function and effect. Each governs a natural good (health and wealth) that is valuable not for itself but as useful in the pursuit of other ends, especially in distinctively human pursuits.[40] Since neither requires special expertise, both leave the virtuous free to pursue more valuable ends. As illustrated by the tale of Thales' monopolizing the olive presses—a tale "beneficial for those who value business" (*Pol.* 1.11 1259a5–6)—people who seek more val-uable ends have no interest in exploiting others for gain. Thales meant "to demonstrate that it is easy for philosophers to be wealthy if they want, but that this is not the object of their con-cern [περὶ ὃ σπουδάζουσιν]" (a16–18). What then are their con-cerns? One of the most common, and one that carries the title of Aristotle's entire subject, is public life and political power, to which I turn next.

40. Although never explored in the discussion of economics, these pursuits lurk in the background throughout: see *Pol.* 1.5 1254b29–32, 1.7 1255b34–37, 1.8 1256b36–39, 1.11 1259a16–19, a33–37.

Sparta and the Perils of Power

THE HOME is the primary human community, and people are "by nature inclined more to couple in marriage than to form cities" (*EN* 8.12 1162a16–18). But the home is also the elementary unit of political community, and just as people form homes not only to meet basic needs and to propagate but also to share in life and love (a18–25), so they unite to form cities not only for living but also for living well—not only for survival but for social activity and a good life (*Pol.* 1.2 1252b27–31; cf. 3.9). Life in isolated homes, "each setting rules over children and wives," as Homer knows, is fit for the Cyclops but not for humanity (b22–24, citing *Od.* 9.114–15). This is why Aristotle calls us "political animals," why he makes happiness the central topic for ethics, and why he presents his ethical theory as a part of political theory. If happiness depends on virtuous activity, it follows that "the true politician has labored most on virtue, for he wants to make his fellow citizens good and law-abiding" (*EN* 1.13 1102a5–10). Aristotle is aware, of course, that many cities and politicians do not take virtue, law, and the common happiness as their aim. Nonetheless, "the lawmakers of the Cretans and Lacedaimonians," two peoples widely admired for both the aims and the achievements of their social and political systems, provide the "paradigm" (a10–12; cf. 10.9 1180a24–29).

Sparta especially was held up as a model. In the judgment of many, its way of life exemplified nobility and virtue (*Pol.* 7.14

1333b5–7).[1] Endowed with a constitution that gave rare attention to the training of its citizens, home to men celebrated for their deeds rather than their private station, and graced by a long history of success on the field, Sparta held a leading position among the states of Greece that was acknowledged, if not appreciated, by all. A judicious blend of disparate elements, monarchic, aristocratic, and democratic, made its constitution a model of *eunomia*—of "law and order"—that was attractive to partisans across the political spectrum,[2] and it won accolades from the learned as well as respect from the many who faced its troops in war. Individually the citizens were a byword for the free or "liberal" way of life; hence the proverb "more liberal than Sparta" (*CPG* 1.246). Dining in common *phiditia* from the products of helots or serfs, hindered from acquiring money by the use of iron bars for currency, and denied the pleasures of luxury by sumptuary laws, the Spartans were supposedly freed from the worries of business and domestic economics and trained for common tasks. United, powerful, and celebrated for manly virtue, Sparta was thought to have attained the pinnacle of prosperity, and the wisdom of their "lawmaker" to have established a society flourishing, stable, and happy.[3]

A large body of literature extolling the successes and virtues of Spartan institutions circulated widely in the fourth century, in a tradition that still survives. One admiring pamphlet bears the name of Xenophon, Plato's *Republic* and *Laws* prefer Sparta to other existing societies, his uncle Critias praises it in poem and prose, and its own Thibron and Pausanias join a chorus of historians and orators in proclaiming the marvels of their culture.[4] Ar-

1. Aristotle uses "Laconian" to specify the Spartan elite (the *homoioi*, or "equals") who ruled the region, but "Lacedaimonian" when he includes the helots they ruled; I use "Sparta" because my subject is the ruling system and its members.

2. Aristotle calls the constitution "mixed" (*Pol.* 2.6 1265b31–41, 4.9 1294b13–41; cf. 2.9 1270b14–25). *Eunomia*, which was also the title of Tyrtaeus' famous military elegies (*Pol.* 5.7 1307a1), was a Spartan byword; Aristotle says the popular sense was "law-*abiding*," not "*good* laws" (1294a1–9, discussed below); cf. Andrewes 1938.

3. Although Aristotle seems to have rejected the tradition that Lycurgus gave Sparta all its institutions, he regularly speaks of "*the* lawmaker"; cf. *Pol.* 5.11 1313a25–30, and see Boer 1954: 200.

4. The *Const. Lac.* attributed to Xenophon dates from the earlier fourth century, as does Xenophon's *Agesilaus*. Plato names Sparta to exemplify timocracy, the second best to a just society (*Rep.* 8.544c, 545a), and a Spartan is one of three

istotle too, in addition to citing its attention to training, gives it pride of place in his review of existing societies (*Pol.* 2.9–12): he discusses it first, at greatest length, and directly after a critique of the utopian proposals of his predecessors (2.1–8). But Sparta had fallen on hard times by the middle of the fourth century: after championing freedom in the wars against Persia and Athens, it yielded preeminence first to Thebes and then to Macedonia. Accordingly, the eulogies did not lack somber tones. The Xenophonic account closes with harsh thoughts on Sparta's fall from grace (*Const. Lac.* 14), Plato makes it a foil for his own more elaborate visions, Critias died in disgrace as a leading member of the Thirty in the "laconizing" regime Sparta imposed on Athens, Thibron was judged a reckless bandit and a famous flop in his service to his state, and the exiled Pausanias wrote bitterly for reform. But if the image was tarnished, this very fascination with Sparta's flaws in the fourth century proves the high esteem accorded its constitution and earlier success. Still widely considered the finest society in existence, its failures, like those of laconizers who took it as a model, were usually attributed not to its institutions but to the individuals who controlled them, and to many it seemed only to need new blood or minor reforms.

Aristotle, however, argues that the conventional ideals underlying Spartan culture are seriously flawed. Given the city's high reputation and its patent success in achieving those ideals, his critique of Spartan character and fortune amounts to a more general critique of conventional values. His principal objections rest on his account of the relation between virtue and prosperity. At the root of Sparta's ills, he argues, lies the belief that power and wealth, not virtuous activity, are the dominant components in a good life. In his analysis, the city's eventual demise refutes this assumption and reveals the perils of valuing prosperity over excellence. Counting virtues not as ends but as valuable only for

---

speakers in the *Laws*; see Morrow 1960: esp. 40–73, and cf. *Protag.* 342–43. For Critias, see B6–9 and 32–37 DK; on Athens' Thirty (the number of members in the Spartan council), see Whitehead 1982–83. For Thibron and Pausanias, as well as many others who wrote on Sparta, including Aristotle's colleague Dicaearchus, see *FGrH* 580–98; cf. Ephorus (*FGrH* 70), esp. frs. 148–49. Aristotle would have been familiar with most of these works, given the Lyceum's research on the Lacedaimonian constitution (frs. 532–45 Rose), and he names Thibron among "the other writers" on Sparta (*Pol.* 7.14 1333b11–20). Ancient opinions about Sparta are surveyed in Ollier 1933.

their utility in acquiring external goods, the Spartans proved incapable of enjoying the success their ancestors had fought so hard to win. And since the system epitomizes traditional aristocratic ideals of political supremacy, the fall that followed its success testifies not only to failures in leadership and execution but to a basic misconception at the core of these ideals. If his diagnosis is correct—and for my purpose, which is to examine the ethical basis for Aristotle's critique rather than to assess its historical accuracy, his aims are more significant than any factual mistakes—then the fault lay not only with its stars, human or divine, but with the principles on which the society was founded. In short, his analysis of Spartan society is an exercise in showing "why the empirical study of political systems might reasonably be intended to support his ethical principles."[5]

While recognizing Sparta's strengths, Aristotle is not sparing in his criticism, and he dissects its institutions one by one. Following his usual practice, he starts with the basic elements of society in their private and economic relations. First comes the infamous use of helots (*Pol.* 2.9 1269a34–b12), then relations between men and women (1269b12–70a15) and the distribution of property (a15–b6). Turning next to political institutions, he analyzes the *ephorate*, or supervisors (b6–35), the *gerousia*, or council of elders (1270b35–71a18), the dual kingship (a18–26), and finally the *sussity*, or common mess, and the navy (a26–41).[6] Throughout he focuses on the ways in which Spartan institutions fall short of the ideal society, either because they neglect the good life or because they foster discord. But while criticizing the aims of the system as enunciated in its laws or implicit in the conduct of its citizens, he also measures how well the Spartans realize their aims. Two questions, he insists at the outset, need to be asked in social criticism: "first, whether something has been legislated well [καλῶς] or poorly relative to the *best* system, and second, whether something has been legislated contrary to the principle

5. The remark, though not its application, is from Irwin 1985c: 151–52. Modern accounts of Sparta rely heavily on Aristotle, not always for want of other sources, e.g., Forrest 1968: 106–42, a succinct account of the demise of Spartan supremacy that echoes much of Aristotle's ethical critique.

6. See Braun 1956. The order of treatment in *Pol.* 2.9 reflects the order of the *Politics* as a whole: first economics (slaves, women, children, as in *Pol.* 1), then politics (the democratic ephors first, followed by the oligarchic *gerousia*, then the monarchy; cf. 2.6 1265b31–66a1, 2.9 1270b23–26). Aristotle often follows this sequence, in whole or in part: *Pol.* 3.8–18, 4.1–10, 5.5–12, 6.1–8.

and character of the established constitution" (1269a29–34). In short, not only the ideal but also the actual aims of a society count toward success or failure. An imperfect constitution that achieves its goals to its own satisfaction is one form of political success, for social harmony is a goal shared by all societies deserving the name. A bad constitution that leads to widespread discontent fails doubly since concord is a necessary though insufficient condition for political success.

Sparta fails on both counts. Near the end of his critique, Aristotle recalls this principle to introduce three final objections that summarize his objections (*Pol.* 2.9 1271a41–b1). More general and basic than the preceding analysis, these appeal to the Spartans' own aim (a41) to show that they too have reason to prefer being governed by different priorities. In short, Aristotle appeals to the course of Spartan history to show the basic errors in the Spartans' aims. Since their aims epitomize conventional ideals, his argument also shows that those ideals are inherently flawed. He begins with the notorious militarism of Spartan life and its principal goal, the external good of power. Aristotle recognizes three reasons for military training (or national defense, as we would say): "first, so as not themselves to be slaves to others; then, to seek to govern for the benefit of the ruled, though not for mastery over all; and third, to rule as masters over those who are worthy of being slaves" (*Pol.* 7.14 1333b40–34a2).[7] Originally instituted for the first reason, the Spartan regimen enabled the city to achieve "mastery over all" but left them unable to "benefit the ruled"; and as for the third, their opponents were usually free Greek states.

Their entire system of laws is directed at a part of virtue, military excellence, since this is useful for winning supremacy [τὸ κρατεῖν]. Therefore, they remained safe while at war, but once they acquired rule, they perished because they did not know how to use free time [σχολάζειν] and they were trained in no other discipline more sovereign [ἄσκησιν κυριωτέραν] than military excellence. (*Pol.* 2.9 1271b2–6)

7. See Defourny 1932: 487–89. The first reason, defense, is still widely recognized, and the interventionism of the second is widely practiced, although usually criticized, as here, for ulterior motives. Only the third, which would justify imperialism provided it is beneficent (note 1334a1–2), is widely condemned, though of course still practiced. Newman 1887–1902 cites Isocrates *Panath.* 220, which commends three similar causes: fighting against invaders, "those in error" (τοὺς ἁμαρτάνοντας), and non-Greek "barbarians"; Isocrates too blames the Spartans for violating these precepts.

This objection is found in earlier writers, and Aristotle singles out Plato's critique in the *Laws* by name.[8] But its application to the specific question of the Spartans' own aims seems to be new. As Aristotle observes elsewhere, most writers praise the Spartan constitution out of admiration for its objective, "the aim [σκοπός] of the legislator" (*Pol.* 7.14 1333b11–14). But their admiration "is easily refuted by argument [κατὰ τὸν λόγον] and has now been refuted by the facts [τοῖς ἔργοις]" (b15–16). To be sure, the militarism of Spartan life had won them the supremacy that they sought (τὸ κρατεῖν, b14, b20–21; cf. 7.2 1324b6–9), first over their neighbors and later more widely. But even on the premise that empire is a sufficient goal, their way of life should be judged a failure since it proved ineffective for maintaining the power they sought; in short, the Spartans were "not happy" (1333b21–23). First, their despotism heightened the risk of attack from without. The Spartan tendency "to rule like masters" (δεσποτικῶς ἄρχειν) naturally made their victims eager to escape their yoke, and it made even their allies venture hostilities (b26–29). Nearer to home, the long-standing enmity of surrounding states (1269b3–5) and their brutal subjection of the helots resulted in constant menace. Moreover, their way of life also created dangers from within. Raised to honor military rule above all, Spartan leaders frequently sought to exercise supreme command even in civil society (1333b29–33). As Aristotle adds, the Spartans themselves blamed Pausanias for treason (b34–35), and his self-aggrandizing efforts and attempted coup ended in his being condemned to death by the ephors.[9] Exposed to subversion from within as well as attack from without, the Spartans themselves had reason to be dissatisfied with the priorities of their culture, for as events of the fifth and fourth centuries showed, Spartan military training might win supremacy for a time, but it proved incapable of preserving that goal for long. By their own standards, their devotion to martial prowess was a mistake.

8. See *Laws* 625c–38b (esp. 630d–31b), 660–66, 668a, 705d; cf. *Pol.* 7.14 1333b29–31. Aristotle's criticisms echo Plato's on other points as well.

9. The allusion is probably to the victor of Plataea, i.e., the grandfather of the Pausanias who authored a tract on the Spartan constitution (see *n*4 above); Aristotle also cites this elder's deeds to exemplify a source of strife to which aristocracies are especially prone (*Pol.* 5.7 1307a2–5; cf. Thucydides 1.131–35). The disgraceful conduct of Spartans abroad was notorious; Brasidas is a notable exception (Thucydides 4.81.3).

Aristotle attributes Sparta's downfall to the preoccupation with victory and the neglect of all but its means. In general, this criticism is directed against the ethos of war that pervaded Spartan life (2.9 1271b5–6): the Spartans' military training enabled them to defeat most of those they faced, and so long as they were at war, the exercise of their chosen excellence achieved their aim of victory (b3–4). Their conduct even bears some likeness to the happiness of virtuous activity: the rigors of war inspire valor and impose the self-restraint and obedience celebrated as *eunomia*. Aristotle acknowledges that the military way of life fostered "many parts of virtue" when the Spartans of earlier times were often on lengthy campaigns (1270a1–6), but he finds little evidence of the virtues in contemporary Sparta. Citing the "testimony of events," he suggests that, "like iron, they lost their mettle in the conduct of peace" (7.14 1334a5–10). Although possessing a tool useful for *acquiring* power (1271b3), they were ill prepared to *use or enjoy* its fruits. Once supremacy was won, the warriors shed the virtues induced by war, and society began to disintegrate "because they did not know how to use free time" (b4–5). In the end, their training proved worse than useless for enjoying what they won because they had no practice in "more sovereign" pursuits (b6). Although Sparta's constitution made elaborate provision for training its citizens, it focused on the wrong end, since it failed to promote the discipline useful in peace.

The problem is a common one, Aristotle thinks, for "war compels [ἀναγκάζει] people to be just and to practice temperance, but the enjoyment of prosperity and the leisure of peace tend rather to make people arrogant and violent [ὑβριστάς]" (*Pol.* 7.15 1334a25–28; cf. 5.8 1308a24–30). An army needs an enemy. When war comes to a close, the veterans lack an outlet for their habits of aggression, and they are liable to turn upon their fellow citizens. Unchecked "arrogance" then breeds fear and insecurity, as well as crime and injustice, and the whole social fabric wears thin. These consequences were aggravated by the agonistic rituals of the military training, which "brutalized" the Spartans in their youth (8.4 1338b9–38).[10] So the fault lies with their institutions, "for it is ridiculous if, when they maintain the laws of their law-

10. For the deadly hide-and-seek of the *krupteia* and other games, see Plut. *Lycurgus* 16–17.

maker and when nothing prevents them from using those laws, they have thrown away their fine life [τὸ ζῆν καλῶς]" (1333b23–26). In short, Spartan laws and education were effectively self-defeating, for the habits they fostered ultimately undermined their own aims and made life worse for all.

Roused by the presence of external ills and serving not to enjoy but only to protect present goods, courage (ἀνδρεία) is a virtue of necessity. Worse, on Aristotle's analysis, the martial prowess that was the pride of Spartan culture turns out to rest less on that virtue than on the dubious trait of "boldness" or "rashness" (θρασύτης), something which is "useful for nothing in civil life, but if at all, for war" (*Pol.* 2.9 1269b34–36). Indeed, his analysis makes boldness the vice of excessive confidence contrary to courage (*EN* 2.7 1107b2–3, 3.7 1115b24–29, *EE* 2.3 1221a17–18). And although less common than cowardice and less distant from the virtuous mean, boldness usually masks fear and rarely leads to courageous action: the courageous "are disposed toward fearful things as the bold *want* to be," but the bold are "bold cowards [θρασύδειλοι], for while given to boasting [θρασυνόμενοι], they do not stand and face fearful situations" (*EN* 3.7 1115b29–33). By contrast, the courageous see something the bold do not, and they choose to act as they do because they find something noble in their action (b11–13). To the extent that the Spartan training fostered boldness instead of courage, it failed to inculcate values higher than personal safety. And again, when the events of the fourth century showed a failure of nerve in their troops, the Spartans themselves had reason to reject their training for depriving them of their goal.

Aristotle's analysis of courage provides a basis for further criticism here. The better to mark off the precise nature of true courage, he contrasts it with five different but closely related "traits" (τρόπους) with which it is often confused (*EN* 3.8 1116a15–17), namely, forms of bravery associated with (1) citizen-soldiers, (2) professional soldiers, (3) the angry, (4) the optimistic, and (5) the ignorant. Granting that they all *act bravely*, Aristotle counts none in these groups *courageous* unless they have some noble end as well as their own safety in view. Many Spartans would presumably fall in the first group: their training often instilled a sense of civic duty, and they had a tradition of holding valor in the highest honor (a18–21).[11] This "political" bravery comes closest to true courage (a17) when it aspires to the noble aim of honor (a27–29), but Aristotle still attributes it rather to a fear of reproach or punishment. Citing the vaunts and threats of Homeric heroes (a23–26, a34–35), he claims it is not virtue but "shame" (a28) that gives most citizens reason to fight. And apart from this slight to the grand tradition of Iliadic heroism, the horrors of hoplite warfare lend credence to his doubt that most Spartans were quite the noble warriors that Tyrtaeus and later propagandists made them appear.[12] Worse, when the threat of disgrace or even flogging is needed to "compel" people to fight (a29–b3; cf. a19), bravery must seem onerous and is less than reliable; if Sybarites can be trusted, it was fear of the Spartan gruel that drove them to seek an exit from life (Plut. *Pelop.* 1). In fact, their training enabled them to win only until they faced others who had trained for combat (*Pol.* 8.4 1338b24–32). They had learned how to fight but without seeing why they should.

The demands of their training and of frequent war gave the Spartans two other traits that reinforced their civic bravery, military expertise and a boldness born of success. First, they shared the confidence of professionals that is won by "experience" and knowing how to fight (*EN* 3.8 1116b3–8). The skills they cultivated gave them a professional edge, "like athletes over amateurs" (b12–13), since they knew when to be cool in battle (b6–8), were skilled in weapons and tactics (b9–12), and had built up the strength needed for combat (b13–15). But their very expertise left them ready to flee at the prospect of serious danger, whenever they sensed their inferiority "in number or preparations" (b15–19); the contrast with genuine courage is so sharp that Aristotle calls this cowardice (b16). The basic difference is one of motive: the courageous consider the noble more "choice-worthy" than safety, but troops who fight on the basis of experience act after calculating their chances for safety, not from conviction (b19–23). Second, much of the Spartans' confidence was bound to stem from their history of success. Encouraged, as it were, by victories

---

11. If right, a scholiast's suggestion (Eustratius 165.1–3, citing Tyrtaeus fr. 9) that 1116b1 alludes to the Spartans would confirm this suggestion.

12. Cf. Thucydides' skepticism about Mycenaean heroes: "mostly from fear, not kindness [χάριτι]" (1.9.3).

over many opponents, "they are confident [θαρροῦσιν] in dangers" (1117a10–11). But the "optimistic" (εὐέλπιδες) are confident "because they believe that they are strongest and will suffer no harm" (a12–14). If their expectations are disappointed, they are eager to flee (a15–16). The difference here, Aristotle adds, can readily be seen "in sudden fear": it is a better sign of courage to stand up to unexpected danger than to be confident "in foreseen situations," because sudden danger triggers an immediate response according to character, but distant dangers allow one to make "preparations" that curb the temptation to flee "from calculation and reasoning" (ἐκ λογισμοῦ καὶ λόγου, a17–22). In the case of optimism, as in the case of expertise, bravery remains unreliable because confidence bred of high hopes can evaporate at the prospect of unexpected danger, regardless of the importance of what is at stake. Based on the wrong priorities, in short, Spartan valor fell short of courage, and it evaporated when tested by more spirited neighbors and more practiced forces from the north.

The Spartan training for war won success for a time. At home, however, life became problematic early on. The license of Spartan women, who were spared the rigors of any regimen, was notorious. Aristotle accuses them of "every form of unrestraint," including extravagance (*Pol.* 2.9 1269b19–23), and he reports that even Lycurgus was unable to bring them under the rule of law (1270a6–9).[13] But when the position of women is "ignobly arranged," the result is "a kind of indecency" (ἀπρέπειά τις) that detracts from the life of all (a11–13). Where half the population is "lawless," there is little room for happiness in the society as a whole (1269b14–19). The dissolute ways of the women infected the men as well. "Possessed" by the attractions of sex, the Spartans behaved in ways that Aristotle takes to be typical of militaristic societies—he finds the bawdy Homeric tale of Ares and Aphrodite a "reasonable" reflection of their nature—and they

13. Newman 1887–1902 on 1269b22 collects earlier versions of the charge and quotes Aristotle's list of the forms of intemperance: "wine guzzling, gluttony, lechery, gourmandizing, etc." (*EE* 3.2 1231a18–21). The custom of "childmaking" (by sharing wives) legitimized sex with handsome young men; see D. M. McDowell 1986: 82–88. The example of an early Spartan princess, Helen of Troy, was used to exaggerate the reputation, as in Peleus' tirade from Euripides *Andromache*; cf. the tale of Alcibiades seducing the wife of King Agis (Plut. *Alcibiades* 23.7–8).

ended up ruled by their women (1269b23–34). The ephors, whose supreme office made them virtually above the law, regularly succumbed to self-indulgence, and their severity toward others was so extreme that many simply ignored their edicts, "sneaking out from under the law to enjoy physical pleasures" (1270b31–35). And as the Spartans' efforts at reform show, the license fostered by the system was recognized as contrary to their own aims, not to mention the good of the city (1269b12–14). Despite their regimen, the paradigms of manly virtue were unmanned, and the very men who made "subjection" their principal aim found themselves "subjected" to the women in their own homes (γυναικοκρατούμενοι, b24–25, b31–34). In short, prudish though some of his strictures seem, Aristotle's complaints describe consequences abhorrent to his contemporaries, and not least to many Spartans and their admirers. Indeed, temperance was widely considered the distinctive virtue of women, and by common consensus, its absence would mean that the Spartans "are not happy in half their society" (*Rhet.* 1.5 1361a5–11).[14]

Family arrangements in Sparta contributed in turn to private greed and the "love of property" (φιλοχρηματία); the result was serious inequities in the distribution of wealth (*Pol.* 2.9 1270a11–18; cf. 1271b17). Since these represent injustice in individuals and in society, respectively, Sparta was seriously deficient in the virtue most necessary for political life. First, although one of the more famous "Lycurgan" reforms was the abolition of currency in favor of iron ingots (imagine the trials of retailers), private hoards were not unknown (Plato *Alcib.* I 122c, Plut. *Lycurgus* 18). Worse, the laws on property and inheritance drove many of the Spartan elite into poverty (*Pol.* 2.9 1271b4–6) and concentrated too much land and property in the hands of a few (1270a11–29).[15] Creating incentives for legacy hunting, these arrangements promoted materialism and greed at the expense of the social order. Indeed, the desire for gain lay at the heart of the regimen that encouraged "the virtues that are thought useful and more profitable [πλεονεκτικωτέρας]" (7.14 1333b8–10). But *having* more than

14. See North 1966: 206. Aristotle and Plato were not alone in bemoaning Spartan morals: cf. Democritus B214 and Cartledge 1981.

15. The relative length of Aristotle's diatribe against Spartan legacies and dowries (1270a18–b6) shows how important he thought the problem; see Lane Fox 1985: esp. 220–23.

is fair (πλεονεξία) violates distributive justice, and *wanting* more (the "love of property") is the motive to that end. Thus, by cultivating these interests and then giving them free play, the system fostered injustice.[16] Desire for the external goods of material and political superiority, or greed and ambition (φιλοτιμία), are the two major motives to crime and injustice (2.9 1271a16–18). And when there is little hope of rectifying the wrongs, corrective justice gives way to retaliation, as the case of the helots showed. Linking their oppression to similar systems elsewhere, Aristotle underscores the dangers for the oppressors by noting the constant aggression and frequent rebellions that Spartan tyranny spawned (1269a37–b12). The risks were greater for Sparta, which was surrounded by hostile states as well. When social unrest erupted into rebellion under the "brave" Cinadon (5.7 1306b34–36), the savagery with which the rebels were suppressed bespeaks dire necessity on both sides. Finally, the impoverishment of so many also had disastrous consequences for Sparta's military aims, for on Aristotle's account, the extreme disparities in wealth (2.9 1270a15–16, a38–39) combined with frequent warfare to depopulate the warrior-elite and deprive the city of its military might (a29-b4).[17] Hence, neglect of social justice and the covetous self-interest engrained by the Spartan regimen were a source of grief at home and abroad and major causes of Sparta's demise.

To survive these dangers, Sparta needed good government. But the system held military excellence in too much honor and left civil administration in the hands of officials who lacked the practical wisdom and respect for justice that Aristotle insists is required of *political* leaders. Here too distributive justice was deficient, since the holders of office were very often inept or corrupt. The highest office was the ephorate, "sovereign over the most important matters" (2.9 1270b7–8). Yet by making the office open to any and all (b8–9), the constitution ensured that it was held by men who lacked a "more sovereign training." The annual election of ephors from the people might help hold the state to-

16. For charges of greed in other sources, see David 1982–83: 75 n29. "Having more" is the hallmark of injustice, whereas "equality" is the mark of justice (*EN* 5.1 1129a32–b11, 5.2). In distributive justice, equality is meritocratic (a "geometric proportion," 5.3), but egalitarian in corrective justice (an "arithmetic proportion," 5.4); see Hardie 1980: 187–94. Sparta violated both.

17. The famous uprising of Cinadon occurred soon after the great war, ca. 398; cf. Xenophon *Hell.* 3.3. On the question of population, see Cawkwell 1983.

gether (b17–20), but since they were chosen "in an extremely childish fashion" (b26–28), there was every chance that incompetence would rule. Because many came to office "extremely poor" (b9–10), they were especially liable to bribery, and their venality had "destroyed" the city several times (b10–13). Despite their failings, the ephors exercised an authority "equal to tyranny," which brought harm to the whole: they dominated the kings (b13–16), and their power to scrutinize all other officials gave them control over the entire system (1271a6–8). Predictably, their lack of "more sovereign" training produced consistently bad policy. As if honesty could excuse incompetence, one ephor under scrutiny defended his bad judgment by boasting that he had not been bribed (*Rhet.* 3.18 1419a31–35). The ephors also sowed discontent by their corrupt administration of justice. Individual prerogative and the absence of written law are "dangerous" in any state (*Pol.* 2.10 1272a38–39), but the situation in Sparta was so bad that Aristotle cites it to confirm the advantages of laws and the dangers of leaving decisions entirely to judges (1270b28–31).[18]

Although the *gerousia* could lay claim to wider virtues, Aristotle also finds it wanting in political virtue and judgment. Composed of the "noble-good" (οἱ καλοὶ κἀγαθοί) who had won prestige supposedly on the basis of their virtue (1270b23–25), this body was in effect a sort of senior officers' club, dominated by men whose martial prowess commanded respect.[19] Had they been given adequate training for civil rule, Aristotle allows, they could have served Sparta well (b37–38), although their lifelong tenure made even that "debatable" (b39–40). But when their experience was limited to military command, good government was not to be expected. Like the ephors, they were elected by a "childish" system of popular acclamation (1271a9–12),[20] and since fighting was the principal criterion of excellence, the honor of office fell to those best in war rather than in governing. Their training left "even their lawmaker himself with no confidence in their being good men," and many succumbed to venality and fa-

18. Newman 1887–1902 compares 3.1 1275b9 and 6.2 1317b26; see D. M. McDowell 1986: 127–37.

19. "Noble-good" here is used in its conventional sense of aristocratic excellence; for Aristotle's distinctive use of the term, see *nn*28, 29 below.

20. Aristotle calls the office "a trophy for virtue" (1270b24–25), but the mode of election "imperial" (δυναστευτική, 5.6 1306a18); cf. Tyrtaeus fr. 12.

voritism, as personal interests outweighed concern for the common good (a1–5). The constitution erred in leaving the office open to any who wished but requiring it of none (a10–12), which naturally attracted those motivated most by ambition and hence willing to do wrong (a13–18). For the kings, membership in the *gerousia* was hereditary; yet if this avoided the folly of the elections for other offices, it still left the kings without a more sovereign training. In Aristotle's judgment, the constitution itself betrayed a distrust in their character, both by requiring rivals to accompany the kings on any missions abroad and by devising the twin kingship to serve as check on their military command (a19–26). Thus, as befits a traditional aristocracy of hoplites, Sparta rewarded its best warriors, its elder warriors and the kings, with a part in government. But the rivalry and self-interest of all, he concludes, only made the Spartans vulnerable, in war as in peace, to the competitive habits fostered by a regimen for war.

The root of these problems was the perverse priority given warfare in Sparta's civil life. Political understanding, the "most sovereign and most authoritative" form of knowledge (*EN* 1.2 1094a26–28), was neglected. This "more sovereign training" would have prepared Sparta's leaders to provide for a peaceful society, to formulate policies and programs to achieve those needs, and to exercise control over the economy and the military with a view to the good life of all (b1–7). The same in essence but wider in scope than "practical wisdom" (φρόνησις), "political understanding" (πολιτική) aims at the human good for all. Both are based on practical knowledge of virtuous principles together with an ability to deliberate how to pursue those virtuous ends. Although it is "nobler and more divine" to achieve the good life for a nation or city (b7–11), the sovereign position of political rule in public life has the same basis—namely, a conception of happiness that gives practical wisdom its sovereign role in private life.[21] Hence, by valuing military virtue above all else, the Spartans left themselves deficient in the most important skills. As Aristotle's critique of their public life is meant to show, that produced a government that undermined Spartan supremacy by

21. They are "the same state of character" since both are "practical" and "deliberative," but "their being is not the same" since the former plans for the individual whereas the latter plans for society as a whole (*EN* 6.8 1141b23–33); cf. 6.5 1140b7–11, 6.7 1141a20–21, b8–16, 6.8 1142a9–10.

private vices and public incompetence. No mere moralizing, his argument shows why, even by the Spartans' own standards, training for other virtues was necessary: had their culture fostered the civic virtues of justice and political leadership more, they could have avoided many of their troubles.

If Sparta really had one of the better systems, Aristotle's critique of their ethical culture would apply a fortiori to most states. The true courage he describes is never common, sexual appetites and economic motives naturally tend to excess, and rulers are rarely as wise or as just as he would have them be. But that is only to charge him with political idealism and the belief that any society lacking in these virtues will face similar problems. Indeed, one exceptional feature of Spartan society, and a major reason it attracted so much attention, was that it did have an organized system of training for some virtue, when many other states had no public system of education at all. However, a narrow focus on war, though originally occasioned by legitimate defensive concerns, had devastated the once flourishing culture of Sparta. The preceding two centuries had seen a drastic decline in the practice and enjoyment of humane arts, both literary and artistic, and the poverty of public building—the physical body of a city—was remarkable (so Thucydides 1.10.2).[22] By isolating the flaws in their system, Aristotle's critique not only unmasks its pretenses, but maps out directions for improvement. If his argument is sound, then both by Spartan standards and by others as well, a broader training for virtue was necessary, for hegemony in peace proved their reputation for virtue a sham. Instead of pervasive militarism, education should promote civic virtues that make for a good life in peace.

So the reason why a society that is going to be happy and excellent [σπουδαίαν] should have a share of the virtues is clear; for it is a sign of a disgraceful person to be unable to use good things. It is still worse to be unable to use good things in free time [ἐν τῷ σχολάζειν], and to look good when busy [ἀσχολοῦντας] with war but be servile in free time.[23]

22. Both archeology and literary evidence reveal a decline in humane culture; even traditionally noble (and warlike) athletics had become the province of a wealthy few. See Halladay 1977.

23. Aristotle's views about the good use of "free time" (σχολή) are complex. Solmsen (1964: esp. 212–18) shows that Aristotle means to include music and arts but not to require philosophy or academic study. Solmsen emphasizes the specifically ethical aims of these proposals; in addition to the goals of pleasure and

Therefore one should not train for virtue as Spartan society does. For they differ from others not in their beliefs about what are the greatest goods, but only in their belief that those goods come about more by means of some kind of virtue. But since [they believe] that these are *greater* goods [than the virtues] and that the enjoyment [of these goods] is *greater* than the enjoyment of the virtues, it is clear from these points that [people should train for virtue] also for its own sake.

(*Pol.* 7.15 1334a34–b4)[24]

Spartan society was built on the assumption that prosperity was to be won by virtue. In this it was superior to most. But in its failure to cultivate any virtues "more sovereign" than those required for war, Sparta resembled most other societies in reversing the priorities necessary for enjoying and preserving success. Training for war gave the Spartans the means to acquire power and the wealth that it brings. But they practiced their virtue *only* as a means, for the consequences that it could win. With instrumental goods as their end, they turned to pleasure and gain and soon fell from power. Hence, the course of Sparta's history gives Aristotle grounds for arguing against the view that the virtues are good only for their consequences. Implicit in their way of life, this consequentialist view of virtue was largely responsible for their demise, as he charges in the second objection at the close of his critique.

And that [holding no virtues more sovereign] is no less a mistake. For they believe that the goods people fight over are *acquired* through virtue more than through vice, and this view is fine; but their belief that these goods are *superior* [κρείττω] to virtue is not fine.   (*Pol.* 2.9 1271b6–10)

Aristotle here attributes the Spartans' downfall to their own beliefs and values: they fell because they were simply mistaken about the true value of the external goods for which they were

---

"fostering the right ethical disposition" (p. 216) that he singles out, I would add the reflective and immediate end of observing and admiring representations of good character and rational order; see 1.10 1100b19, 9.9 1169b33–70a11, and IV.iv n43 below.

24. The final sentence here may well be lacunose; see Newman 1887–1902. But sense can be achieved by (1) inserting a comma for the supposed lacuna after ἀρετῶν in 1334b4, and removing the comma after αὐτὴν, (2) understanding νομίζουσι in b3 from νομίζειν in b1 (or it may have fallen out after μείζω; the mss. betray troubles here), and (3) interpreting the elliptical last clause in the light of the argument, which aims to show why virtue is not to be practiced for the sake of external goods (the antecedent of αὐτὴν is ἀρετὴν from a40).

willing to fight. Foremost among "the fought over goods" (b8) are prestige, wealth, and power.[25] The first of these may have rewards of its own, but the value of wealth and power lies in use. Even prestige raises expectations for future performance, as foreign requests for Spartan support illustrate. Yet the pursuit of these external goods, as Aristotle's term implies, is fraught with risk. Wealth invites attack, every fight has its victims, and the struggles to retain these goods, like the struggles to obtain them, endanger society as a whole. Since success is not likely to last when virtue is practiced only for its consequences, the Spartans' system was flawed even for their own ends. For on this view, the only incentive for maintaining excellence once the end has been won is to preserve those gains, and that only interferes with enjoying the gain. Thus, once the Spartans achieved the supremacy that was their goal, they failed to maintain their rigorous discipline. Freed from the pressures of war, they lapsed into disorder, with little regard for the inequities that put everything at risk.[26] In the end, they found limits imposed on them from outside by defeat. Although they saw one use of virtue, they failed to see that the enjoyment of prosperity also requires virtue. As Solon's proverbial wisdom put it, "Abundance breeds violence." As Aristotle adds, as if with an eye on Sparta, "Lack of education combined with power breeds folly."[27]

The Spartans were not alone in their error. To explain their immense popularity, Aristotle observes that most people admire *power* because it is a source of material prosperity, because it yields "a great supply [πολλὴ χορηγία] of the goods of fortune" (7.14 1333b16–21). The value of the Spartan *training* was thought to depend on its utility in acquiring that power (b11–14). In short, Spartan virtue was admired for its consequences, and Spartan practice exemplifies, in the public sphere, the traditional aristocratic ideals of prosperity and success. In the private sphere, this ideal equates the possession of power, wealth, and prestige with the crown of personal excellence, known by the title of "noblegoodness" (καλοκἀγαθία).

25. See IV.i *n*2 above.
26. For a similar diagnosis of Sparta's demise after her victory over Athens, see Lacey 1968: 208.
27. Solon (fr. 6.3), quoted and glossed by Aristotle in the *Protrep.* (fr. 57 Rose); cf. *Ath. Pol.* 12.

There is a kind of ethical and political trait [ἕξις πολιτική] of the sort the Spartans have, or others like them might have, and this is a trait *like* that [i.e., "noble-goodness"]. For there are some who suppose one should have virtue, but for the sake of the natural goods. This is why they are *good* men [ἀγαθοὶ μὲν ἄνδρες], since the *natural goods* are theirs; but they do not have *noble-goodness*. (*EE* 8.3 1248b38–49a1)

Contrary to Aristotle's account of noble-goodness, the traditional ideal gives the highest place not to virtue but to the natural goods that are fought over (1248b26–30).[28] On this view, being good is being *good at acquiring* these goods, as the Spartans were, and being noble is being admired for *having* them; if virtue plays a part, it is primarily because of its results. Enlightened though this view may be, it is only self-interest: *having* external goods plays the dominant role in happiness, and the virtues are assigned only the instrumental value of *getting* those goods. Thus, in conventional usage, "noble-goodness" expresses an aristocratic ideal: goodness ascribes talent and the success in which it results, and nobility adds public admiration. Since most admire talent and success, this usage tends to reserve the term for the nobility who enjoy material and social superiority.[29] But not all who *have* this superiority *deserve* it, Aristotle objects; noble-goodness, he insists, belongs only to those who *merit* the prosperity they have. Acknowledging that most use the term to designate talent and status, he argues that "being good and being noble-good differ not only by name, but also by themselves [καθ᾽ αὑτά]" (b16–18), and "anyone who is going to get this title in its *true* sense clearly must have the several *particular* virtues" (b11–12). Hence, in an argument that recalls and develops his critique of Sparta, he tries to show why noble-goodness requires "all or most and the most sovereign" virtues (b15). Indeed, his failure to mention the manly virtue of courage while arguing that justice, temperance, and practical wisdom are necessary for true noble-goodness may reflect the aristocratic and Spartan view that courage is most important. His point, then, is to distinguish personal goodness from nobility by appeal to the motives with which

28. On "natural goods," see Dirlmeier 1962: 495 and Woods 1982: 186–93.

29. For a sample of instances, further references, and succinct analysis, see Dover 1974: 41–45. Warning against taking the term as a "class label," Dover claims (esp. *n25*) that its "usual application" is moral; I would add that it is *meant* to ascribe morally admirable qualities, but that in practice it is usually *applied* (by rich and poor, gentry and workers alike) to the rich and famous.

people seek and use valuable things, the natural goods of wealth, honor, power, and prosperity in general (b26–29).

The argument starts by drawing an analogy with the physical virtue of health. First, just as the whole body (or at least most of it) must be healthy for one to be healthy, so it is in other spheres (1248b13–16). In particular, for the whole person (not just the body) to be excellent, one must have all (or most) of the excellences or virtues (b12, b15). But just as "the ill, the weak, and the crippled" cannot use the diet or furnishings that the healthy enjoy, so people who are "foolish, unjust, or unrestrained" stand to gain no benefit from using the natural goods (b26–34). On the contrary, the very goods that tradition and the Spartans glorify can be "harmful" to those who lack the virtues necessary to use them well (b30). Good food can taste bad to the sick, and sometimes it aggravates their sickness. If the analogy holds, then power and prestige bring no joy to the unjust or unrestrained, and sometimes even lead them to ruin.

The difference between Aristotle's model of noble-goodness and the traditional ideal of aristocratic superiority surfaces in his critique of Spartan society. Using the term in its conventional sense, he calls the Spartan elders "noble-good" in contrast with the populace at large (*Pol.* 2.9 1270b24–26), but this is only to explain how the rise of the ephorate over the *gerousia* transformed Sparta from an aristocracy into more of a "democracy" (b15–19). In fact, he claims not only that the kings (who led the council of elders) were rarely noble-good (1271a23), but also that the elders as a whole failed to achieve "goodness" (ἀνδραγαθία, 1270b38; cf. 1271a2, a23–24) because their education was incomplete (1270b37–71a3). In short, the Spartan nobility was scarcely noble. The same contrast underlies his distinction between an admirable, legitimate form of aristocracy and rule by the wealthy, to which the title was often applied. Thus, he observes that the affluent (εὔποροι) are *called* "noble-good and distinguished [γνωρί-μους]" (*Pol.* 4.8 1293b38–40), but that is only because "education and good family more often *attend* the more affluent" (b37–38).[30] Status, of course, was no guarantee of justice or good leadership,

30. Newman 1887–1902 cites Plato's similarly anti-conventional use: "the wealthy and *so-called* noble-good" (*Rep.* 8.569a; contrast 6.489e). According to Dodds 1959 on *Gorg.* 470e9, Socrates was responsible for this "transvaluation" of the aristocratic ideal of the "gentleman."

and Aristotle claims only that the qualities required for effective public service were found "more" among the wealthy. Moreover, he insists that it is not wealth itself, but the qualities it enabled the wealthy to cultivate that underlie ordinary usage. The reason that more good public servants were well born and well off is that they *already* had the goods that others often enter public life to obtain or feel driven to pursue at public expense (b38–39). Hence, to make wealth or status rather than virtue the condition for office is to overlook the crucial difference between rule by "the few" and rule by "the best": unless excellence and merit are criteria for office, the society is only an oligarchy instead of a true aristocracy (b40–42). In short, oligarchy is not government by the noble-good (b40–42); rather, ordinary usage is misled by appearances to confuse wealth with merit.[31] Further, as Aristotle continues, a city cannot have "law and order" if it is ruled by bad leaders, and no true aristocracy lacks law and order (1294a1–3). Indeed, like "noble-good" and "aristocracy," *eunomia* has two senses: in common parlance, it means only that a society is *law-abiding*, but in the primary sense, the society must also abide by *fine laws* (a3–9).[32] Hence, to enjoy true *eunomia*, a society must have good laws and good leaders, as well as be a law-abiding community.

On this account, the Spartan banner of law and order turns out to be a mirage on all three counts. Treating virtue only as the means to acquire power, the Spartans lost the virtues required to use their gains, and in the end, the fruits of their success were no good to them. Hence, one reason not to consider them noble-good is that much more than the warrior's virtue is required to

31. Aristotle emphasizes usage: "people are wont to call" (1293b34–35), "they are considered" (b38), "they give the title" (b40), "they claim" (b42); cf. Dover 1974: 43–44. Aristotle would not, however, accept Dover's suggestion (*n22*) that "for a philosopher a majority cannot be notably good; however good most people are, the standard of goodness . . . must be pitched at a higher point on the scale." Aristotle would reject the relativism implicit in "pitching the standard" and argue that the presence of a "scale" presupposes objectivity.

32. Aristotle draws a third, parallel distinction between family status and family virtue: one is "of good family" (εὐγενής) if ancestral virtues have gained one's family honor, but one is "of noble stock"(γενναῖος) only if one upholds that tradition of virtue (*Rhet*. 2.15; cf. fr. 92). He adds that the latter is rare among the former because heredity, like land (recall Solon in Herod. 1.32.8), tends to give out over time (1390b23–25); that implies that "good families" are less noble than generally allowed. See Dover 1974: 88–95 and cf. IV.iii *nn9, 10* below on the use of γενναῖος to refer to integrity.

use natural goods well. But this is not Aristotle's only objection. On his account, noble-goodness is neither a virtue for acquiring external goods nor simply the sum of virtues for using those goods well; rather, it consists in an attitude toward the use of those goods that makes their use noble as well as good. To people who are truly noble-good, the external goods can be not only beneficial but noble; what adds nobility is using them in virtuous activity. In contrast with the conventional Spartan ideal, "complete virtue" (ἀρετὴ τέλειος, 1249a16) has its own ends over and above prosperity.

> The Spartans and those like them are *good* men, since the natural goods are theirs; but they do not have noble-goodness, because they do not have things noble because of themselves [δι' αὐτά]. But any people who have them because of themselves and who deliberately choose [προαι-ροῦνται] them are noble-good;[33] and not only are *these* things noble, but also things that are *not* naturally noble but only naturally *good* are noble for these people. That is because natural goods are *noble* whenever people do them and deliberately choose them *for the sake of* noble things. Therefore, natural goods are noble for the noble-good person.
>
> (*EE* 8.3 1249a1–7)

The crucial term in the argument here is "because of themselves": in contrast with the traditional ideal, true noble-goodness consists in doing things "because of themselves." But how is this phrase to be understood? Is it adjectival, modifying "the noble *things*" and referring to what is intrinsically noble? Or is it adverbial, describing a *way* of doing things and a distinct relation between agents and their acts? On the first alternative, the argument specifies what the Spartans lack: they do not have anything "noble because of itself," namely, the virtues and virtuous actions (1248b36–37).[34] But then the argument would be that the Spartans do not have complete virtue because they have no virtue at all, which is inconsistent with Aristotle's initial premise, in which he allows that the Spartans do have *some* virtue (1248b37–49a1). He can hardly conclude, then, that they have *no* virtue.

33. Dirlmeier (1962: 496–97) restores sense to the nonsensical Greek by inserting a clause preserved only in the Latin tradition. Instead of Susemihl's text, read: οὐ γὰρ ὑπάρχει αὐτοῖς τὰ καλὰ δι' αὐτά, <ὅσοις δὲ ὑπάρχει [sc. τὰ καλὰ] δι' αὐτὰ> καὶ προαιροῦνται, καλοὶ κἀγαθοί (1249a3). Homoioteleuton readily explains the omission.

34. See Woods 1982: 188; Woods translates "things that are fine for themselves," which he glosses as "intrinsically fine things" (his note on the text of 1249a2–4 mistakes Dirlmeier's suggestion).

On the other alternative, the crucial phrase is adverbial, which is what grammar requires.[35] The claim is not that Spartans have no virtue, but that they do not have virtue *in the right way*, a way specified as "having and deliberately choosing noble things because of themselves" (1249a3). These noble things are virtues and virtuous actions, and the difference between Spartan virtue and "complete virtue" is that only the latter involves valuing virtue and its exercise for its own sake. In contrast with the consequentialist attitude toward virtue associated with traditional ideals of noble-goodness, Aristotle requires that the noble-good deliberately choose something they see as noble, not simply something they see as good; or as he puts it, their reason for acting virtuously is "for the sake of something noble" (a5–6), not simply for the sake of results that are naturally good, such as power or prestige. Further, the difference here is not only one of emphasis, that "the truly virtuous person concentrates on the state of character first and the goods it enables one to get second."[36] Rather, the criterion for complete virtue is fundamentally moral: doing something that benefits others *is* noble, and a noble action is chosen "because of itself" if the agent *sees* it to be so. In contrast with the traditional ideal, which equates noble-goodness with *doing* noble things, Aristotle adds the requirement that one act for noble *reasons*. Although the "completely" virtuous do have their own virtue in view, it is not merely wanting to act virtuously or doing what "happens to be" noble that makes them noble-good; the decisive condition is that they choose their acts *because* of a noble end. Hence, what distinguishes true noble-goodness from its traditional counterpart is the attitude the virtuous have toward their own actions and ends, as Aristotle says in the preceding lines: "Someone is noble-good by virtue of (1) having noble things as well as what is good and (2) having them *because of themselves* [δι' αὐτά], and (3) by doing noble things and (4) doing them for *their* sake [αὐτῶν ἕνεκα]" (1248b34–36).

35. The phrase is τὰ καλὰ δι' αὐτά (1249a3), not τὰ δι' αὐτὰ καλά; as 1248b35 shows, the word order does not violate the rule for attributive position, and like κατὰ τὸ συμβεβηκός (1249a15–16), δι' αὐτά is regularly adverbial.

36. Cooper 1975: 132 *n*46. Kenny (1978: 206) spots the consequentialism Aristotle attributes to "Spartan character" but misses the crucial factor in "complete virtue" when he equates ("not really distinct") *having* all the virtues with exercising them *for their own sake*.

The first two conditions here assert that the noble-good *have* the virtues; the second pair that they *act* virtuously. But the first and third conditions can be satisfied by those who have noble-goodness in the traditional sense: they have some virtue, and they do actions that are noble. In particular, the Spartans acted with courage, temperance, and justice during the decades that led to their supremacy, since their interest in war led them to support numerous causes on behalf of other cities. Indeed, their willingness to fight and die for others won genuine and justified respect from much of the Greek world, and even beyond. As for their motives, however, the way in which success ruined them shows that their conduct was not based on virtuous reasons. Thus, the second and fourth conditions, which specify the motives and ends for which the virtuous act, deny them true noble-goodness: only those who "deliberately choose noble things because of themselves" (1249a3) act for the reasons required for "complete virtue" (a16). Hence, Aristotle sets four conditions for genuine noble-goodness: (1) the noble-good are virtuous, (2) they value the virtues as virtues, not merely for their consequences, (3) they act for ends that are noble, and (4) they value each end for what it is, not merely for what it may do for them.

Nothing here implies that the noble-good have *no interest* in the consequences of their action. Aristotle's conditions require only that the noble-good have reasons for acting that are *independent* of their interest in any external goods they may or may not obtain as a result of their actions. Of course, they also have other reasons, since the natural goods are not only noble for them but genuinely *good* for them as well (1248b26–27; cf. *Pol.* 7.13 1332a22–23 and *EN* 3.4 1113a23–31). But the decisive condition is that they consider their noble ends *sovereign* over any other ends, including prosperity and its enjoyment. Although they want and pursue natural goods, they do so only as consistent with virtuous ends. Although they act for a wide range of reasons, their *ultimate* aim is always something they recognize to be noble; the fruits of their actions are never an *ulterior* aim. From an external perspective, then, the noble-good resemble those who practice virtue for its consequences, since both do many of the same things. But from their own perspective, they differ enormously, since only the "completely virtuous" regularly choose their actions out of concern for something noble.

Aristotle does not deny the virtuous all concern for natural goods like wealth and power. On the contrary, he uses his account of noble-goodness to show the point of pursuing those goods virtuously. He first gives a prudential reason: unlike people who practice the virtues only to acquire natural goods, the noble-good use and enjoy those goods in ways that are to their benefit rather than to their harm (1248b26–34). By using wealth liberally, they minimize the dangers of resentment and antagonism, and like Solon of Athens or the Spartan Lycurgus, they benefit both themselves and others by governing for the common good instead of personal advantage. But they also reap an ethical reward: by putting their personal advantages to work for the good of others, they endow what are otherwise merely natural goods with a quality of nobility (1249a4–6), and that wins them praise. One thing that distinguishes natural goods from what is noble, Aristotle claims at the opening of his analysis, is that the latter are praised, and justice and just action are foremost among the objects of praise (1248b19–23).[37] Solon's wise and beneficent exercise of power, for example, made something that many seek for its advantages into an object of praise, and his service to his city was celebrated and admired. Likewise, the use of private resources for public liturgies turns a natural good into something noble and praiseworthy, and personal generosity wins goodwill and admiration. The pursuit of self-interest, by contrast, wins little of these: by helping others initially, the Spartans gained power, respect, and praise, but their imperious conduct in the exercise of power soon eroded their reputation and with it their power. So both in personal benefit and in public esteem, virtuous action serves the noble-good better than "Spartan character" can. As Aristotle says both to open and to close his account, "Any who suppose they must have the virtues for the sake of external goods do noble things incidentally" (1249a14–16; cf. 1248b39–40).

Aristotle also sees a third advantage in complete virtue. The just wage of virtue is honor (τιμή) and praise (*EN* 5.6 1134b6–7),[38]

37. On the intimate connections between praise and the noble, see esp. *EN* 1.12 and *EE* 2.1 1219b8–16; on their links with virtue and the good of others, see Irwin 1985*b*: esp. 127–33.

38. See Stewart 1892 on 1134b6: "The τιμή which the ruler who is nobly φιλό-τιμος, or, it may be, μεγαλόψυχος, seeks, is not an external reward, but the approval of his own 'conscience.' He gives his services to the State, because he is

and it is ambition or "love of honor" (φιλοτιμία) that draws many to public life. But to practice virtue *for the sake of* this reward is still to fall short of noble-goodness. First, to do so makes virtue dependent on an external good and subject to the judgment of others. True merit is often neglected and sometimes despised, and if a society values the wrong ends, it will honor the wrong traits. Honor, therefore, is "too superficial" to be valued for its own sake, and it makes a poor final end (1.5 1095b22–26). Further, the ambitious themselves generally want to be honored not by any and everyone, but above all by the wise and the good; respect from the foolish or corrupt satisfies few, and most want to be honored "for virtue" and "so they can confirm that they are good" (b26–29). Here again, true noble-goodness differs from the pursuit of honor: the ambitious may do what is noble, but they find little joy if they fail to win honor, and the willingness to court honor even when it is wrong is what gives their trait its bad name (4.4 1125b7–10). By contrast, the virtuous have as their aim something they themselves value and consider noble. Any honor they win only adds to their deed, and devotion to their principles can console them if they fail. Above all, they are "lovers of virtue" (φιλάρετοι) and "lovers of the noble" (φιλόκαλοι), and only secondarily are they ambitious or "lovers of honor." They find great pleasure in their actions just as "horse-lovers" and "show-lovers" find it in riding and going to plays or athletic events (1.8 1099a8–15).[39] Thus, the liberal enjoy helping friends, contributing to the community, and giving to those who need and deserve; and just rulers find satisfaction in trying to uphold justice in society. Indeed, it would be wrong to call them liberal or just unless, regardless of any rewards, they enjoy their virtuous action "by itself" (a16–21). So in holding noble ends sovereign over all other concerns, their virtuous activity is sovereign over their happiness.

'public-spirited' or 'patriotic.' . . . The final cause of his government is the public good, not his own advantage."

39. See Burnyeat 1980: esp. 76–79. "A true lover of what is noble is not simply someone with a generalized desire to do whatever should turn out to be noble, but someone who has acquired a taste for, a capacity to enjoy for their own sake, things that are in fact noble and enjoyable for their own sake" (p. 78). As Vlastos (1981: 4) points out, calling people "lovers of something" (φιλοτοιοῦτοι, 1099a9) ascribes to them a special preference for it and typically a strong emotional attachment to it: they value it over most other things and they want to spend their time with it; cf. *EN* 3.11 1118b22–24, 4.4 1125b14–17.

Aristotle argues that complete virtue is satisfying in itself, whereas the traditional ideal depends on enjoying the external goods of prosperity. But enjoyment of success is unstable at best unless its advantages can be put to good use, and few who compete for the "fought over goods" would seek them if they recognized the risks of ill use. Yet this is essentially what the Spartans did in subordinating all else to the pursuit of military supremacy: they attained their goal, but their regimen left a vacuum at the end, and they squandered their power under the pressures of success. Paradoxically, only war and loss of life could sustain their way of life. But if war is not desirable for its own sake—"it would be thought absolute savagery to make friends into enemies in order to have battles and slaughter" (*EN* 10.7 1177b10–12)—then their training is absurd. Instead, the system should have addressed another fatal flaw, the self-interest that was rife among the nobility, as Aristotle observes in the third objection, which closes his critique.

The arrangements for public property [τὰ ϰοινὰ χρήματα] are also in bad shape among the Spartan nobles: first, there is nothing in the city's public treasury [τῷ ϰοινῷ], even though they are compelled to fight great wars; and further, they are bad at paying any special taxes, for the nobles do not examine one another's payments because most of the land is theirs. The result of the lawmaker's work has been the opposite of advantageous: it has produced a city without property [ἀχρήματον], but individuals greedy for property [φιλοχρημάτους]. (*Pol.* 2.9 1271b10–17)

In effect, the self-interest of the nobility contributed to their fall, since the system of taxation allowed them to put private property before the needs of the state, even before the needs of war. Hence, by their own standards, the system was inefficient, since it left the city without the resources to finance the very wars they trained to fight (b10–13). Still worse, the constitution made it virtually impossible to improve matters. Poor finances were not an accidental condition, but the natural result of failing to have an independent check on the payment of taxes, because the nobles rendered accounts to none but themselves (b13–14). Further, if this were only a question of policy, a remedy consistent with the system could have been found, such as the audit Aristotle desiderates (b14). But a change in policy would require both a leader with the political insight to find a solution and a citizenry willing to abide by the solution. The fundamental problem was that private interests outweighed concern for the public welfare;

in Aristotle's words, the love of property (φιλοχρηματία) was pervasive. Unwilling to sacrifice private wealth for the very cause that had won them prosperity, the Spartans found themselves unable to meet the cost of war and maintain their chosen form of life.[40] They behaved in the end like merchants in a storm who would rather go down with the ship than jettison any of their precious cargo in exchange for safe passage. Few throw away their worldly goods on a whim, but as Aristotle observes, "anyone of sense" would do so to save his own skin (*EN* 3.1 1110a8–11). The Spartans, to ply the same metaphor, preferred to scuttle their state.

The survival of Spartan society, as long as it lasted, was "a work of fortune" (τύχης ἔργον).[41] In a word, its vaunted system was *constitutionally* incapable of enjoying success: institutionally averse to political or economic reform and psychologically tied to war and to wealth, the Spartans were able only to win power, not to exercise or retain it. This paradigm of a law-abiding aristocracy turns out to be a relic of long-past needs. The hoplite oligarchy, designed originally to ward off destruction in the archaic age, hastened its own demise by failing to adapt as circumstances changed their needs and by refusing to turn from the arts of war to the peaceful arts of true "law and order." Built to encourage aggression and gain, its celebrated regimen fostered habits that undermined civil society and peace. The missing link between their good fortune and the happiness they lacked was discipline in social life and care for ends to be valued for their own sake. But for that they needed "a more sovereign training," a culture that encouraged the finer uses of prosperity, not simply the power to acquire it. Devoted to the pursuit of goals entirely external to the virtues they honored, they soon discovered the perils of power exercised without "sovereign virtue."

Given that Spartan society epitomizes traditional ideals, Aristotle's critique has implications for any who share those ideals. The Spartan experience shows why, even on consequentialist

40. Cloché (1942: 301–2, 312) compares Aristotle's parallel criticism of Carthaginian society (*Pol.* 2.11 1273a37–b4). The charge of greed was an ancient one, going back to a legendary oracle to Lycurgus (reported in the Aristotelian *Const. Lac.* fr. 544); cf. Alcaeus fr. 360, Pindar *Isth.* 2.9–11, and Euripides *Andromache* 445–54.

41. Aristotle criticizes the Carthaginians, who lived under a similar constitution, for their makeshift response to endemic problems of unequal wealth (*Pol.* 2.10 1273b21–24).

grounds, pursuing noble ends for their own sake is better and more desirable than exercising virtue only for external ends and success. As Solon had seen, the self-sufficiency of happiness requires relatively few resources, and the noble action in which a good life consists has only modest needs. Or as Aristotle observes, alluding perhaps to the contrasting foundations of the Spartan and the Athenian empires, "It is possible to do fine things even without ruling land and sea"; private citizens, he adds with an eye now perhaps on the rising power of his native Macedonia, generally do better than "dynasts" (EN 10.8 1179a1–9). Hence, to summarize Solon's views, he sets only three conditions for a good life: temperate conduct in personal life, moderate resources, and fine actions (a10–13). However, that ignores the principal worry behind Solon's view, the worry that human life is prey to misfortune and happiness vulnerable to loss. Glaucon's challenge remains: How do the virtuous face adversity, failure, or loss? Can their response preserve a good life? And in particular, how do they respond if spurned or dishonored?

Honor and Dignity

THE CULMINATION of Solon's ideal lives comes, ironically enough, not in the final exploits of his happiest mortals but in the meed of honor (τιμή) each receives after dying. As Solon tells it, good fortune was but a prelude to the glory that crowns their dying deeds. Tellos was commemorated with a hero's tomb on the battlefield where he fell (Herod. 1.30.5); Cleobis and Biton survive to this day as *kouroi* dedicated by the Argives to Apollo at Delphi (1.31.5). This emphasis on posthumous honors echoes the aspirations to "glory undying" celebrated in epic and enacted in hero cult. But it also reflects a deep respect for actual perform-ance: unlike the material benefits and privileges enjoyed by the wealthy and powerful, the glory conferred for heroism testifies to great achievement. If secured by eulogies and memorials, deeds can win a sort of immortality that outlasts the hero's death. It was not enough simply to be better; the hero also had to be recognized as better, and that required actually doing better. Tel-los was fortunate to have an opportunity to win his city's ap-proval, but without that recognition, he would have been thought a lesser man. The rewards of honor, in short, were re-served for competitive excellence, and in keeping with epic ideals, it was thought that honorable men must excel in contests with others.

This public dimension gives honor a moral basis, for respect is won only by doing something that others admire. Homeric he-roes may value their honor above all, but most realize how much it depends on their upholding the welfare and safety of their fellows. The most honored warriors, from Achilles and Nestor to Hector and Sarpedon, generally do the most to deserve their privileges and prestige.[1] But honor is not always given where it is due, and deeds unsung by any Homer vanish. Moreover, honorable efforts may fail, and there can be honor in defeat but none without some kind of success. The Trojans paid great homage to the departed Hector precisely because he had long served them so well. Thus, although honor has close ties to moral concerns, it depends less on actual worth than on public perception, which looks first to performance and can be blind to desert or forget that success often hinges on chance and circumstance. In a just world, honor would go to the good and disgrace to the bad, but the wheel of fortune turns for the deserving and the undeserving alike. As Plato has Glaucon complain, the wicked are often admired, and the virtuous face scorn and abuse. Poets are free to succumb to the wishful fancies of their audience and reward the good while punishing the bad. As Aristotle insists, however, not only is that unrealistic but it makes for bad tragedy (*Po.* 14 1453a30–39). The heroic code of honor may add grandeur to poetry, but it seems blissfully out of tune with the realities of human life.

Competitive ideals retained their allure in Aristotle's day. The epics, after all, were central to education. Used to instill virtue as well as to teach letters, they continued to inspire admiration and even emulation. Competition simply took on new forms. Victorious athletes basked in the reflected grandeur of epinician odes peopled with the heroes of myth; while military exploits still won renown, generals were joined by politicians in the hunt for prestige; civic service ranging from liturgies to public office afforded avenues to glory. Indeed, the principal source of honor, it seems, was now the political arena; the very word could refer to public office as well as to respect (*Pol.* 3.10 1281a29–32). As Aristotle says, "Respectable men of action value honor first, for this is virtually the goal of political life" (*EN* 1.5 1095b22–23). Many, of course, had ulterior motives (*EE* 1.5 1216a21–27), and charges of corruption or abuse of office abound. Although politicians were distrusted as a class, however, the rewards for those who could

---

1. On this often neglected aspect of "the heroic code," see Long 1970: 123–26.

win and retain the public trust recall the perquisites enjoyed by epic heroes. Aristotle recites an impressive catalogue of the "parts of honor: sacrificial feasts, memorials in poetry and prose, rewards, shrines, front-row seats, tombs, statues, meals at public expense, foreign practices such as hand-kissing and yielding the way, and gifts" (*Rhet.* 1.5 1361a34–37).[2]

These were not the only incentives for public service, and even as politics afforded opportunities for personal advancement, it encouraged disinterested motives. Solon's heroes gave their lives for their fellows, and Sparta owed its rise in part to its early will-ingness to help other states. Likewise in Aristotle's day, aspiring Athenians could win honor for munificence in liturgical service, and those who held office had to sacrifice their time and efforts to serve the state rather than their private estates. Honor, in short, requires at least an appearance of serving some public end, whether it be the good of all or simply the interests of a significant group or class. As Aristotle puts it, "Honor is a sign of a reputa-tion for benefaction [εὐεργετικῆς δόξης], and it is given rightly and especially to those who *have shown* beneficence, although it is given also to one who is *capable of showing* beneficence" (1361a28–30). This peculiar twist, that the very disregard for per-sonal gain can be a source of honor, made politics a prime field of contest. By showing themselves superior to the pursuit of wealth or power, the ambitious could reap honors that often eluded even the wealthy, the well-born, and the powerful. Whether sought in the form of prestige and its privileges, or more ab-stractly as respect and renown, honor remained a major incen-tive for the display of competitive virtue. It was the token of a very personal success.

As the most public of the external goods, honor has an ambig-uous status. On the one hand, it has the closest ties to virtue. People pursue honor, Aristotle explains, "in order to confirm that they are good; at any rate, they seek to be honored by the wise, and by people who know them, and for virtue" (*EN* 1.5 1095b26–29). To be honored by the foolish or misled may satisfy those who seek nothing but tangible rewards. But since the dis-tinctive pleasure we find in being honored depends on the sense we get of our own excellence (*Rhet.* 1.11 1371a8–17)—just as vic-

2. This bare list comes to life with the notes on these lines in Cope 1877.

tory is pleasant because it gives us a sense of superiority (1370b32–34)—then even those interested in honor primarily for its perquisites will typically prefer to be superior rather than merely to seem so. If most want to merit a good reputation, virtue in some form must be important even for those who consider honor their end. On the other hand, honor remains heavily dependent on others and on circumstances as well: as Aristotle observes, honor is "too superficial to be the supreme end, for it is thought to depend on those who show honor rather than on the one honored" (1095b24–25). Recognition is crucial, but it must come from people whose judgment we respect. The pursuit of honor thus leads to what Bernard Williams dubs the paradox of Coriolanus, after one who ended up dependent on the very people to whom honor was supposed to show him superior.[3] Although honor surpasses other external goods in having more of the nature of an end—in being sought for itself rather than for any further ends it may serve—it still falls short of virtue, which offers its own rewards. Nonetheless, by showing how an interest in honor implies a respect for virtue and the public service that can earn it, Aristotle also justifies finding a place for it in a good life. As he does with other ends in the traditional canon, he connects honor with virtues of its own, although in ways that have proved confusing and provoked not a little distaste.

Honor is the special domain of the virtue that Aristotle ranks highest on his roster of character virtues, the virtue with the lofty title of "greatness of soul" (μεγαλοψυχία) or, as I shall call it, "dignity."[4] Here especially Aristotle has been thought to reveal elitist sympathies, and his account of this virtue has met with

3. Williams 1985: 39. Few ancients, however, spoke of public *servants*.

4. Plato never uses the word (only spurious works do); he speaks instead of the suggestively different "greatness of mind" (μεγαλοφροσύνη). Most translate Aristotle's word etymologically, but the literal "great-souled" says very little in English ("great spirited" or "high-minded," suggesting "energetic" or "arrogant," do worse), whereas the latinate "magnanimous" is too narrow and too passive in its current sense ("generous, forgiving"). "Proper pride" rightly emphasizes self-esteem but embraces humility as well. Rather than settle for transliteration and partly to clear the air, I use "dignity"; for a precedent, see Joachim 1951: 124–25. This fits Aristotle's emphasis on both objective worth and a subjective sense of worth; it captures the emotive force of his term; and although talk of "human dignity" implies a weaker sense (by ascribing a basic and purportedly inalienable minimum of worth to all human life), talk about dignity *tout court* typically refers to exceptional strength of character. As Kolnai (1976) puts it, in an essay entitled "Dignity," our response to the character trait of dignity (what he calls "the quality of dignity," pp. 257–61) resembles "our devoted and admir-

censure and even derision. The emphasis on honor has led some to suppose that he upholds traditional aristocratic ideals. In particular, the lofty sense of superiority he ascribes to dignity strikes some as cold and contemptuous and deserving of scorn rather than admiration. Others have seen a very different ideal here: his insistence that dignity presupposes "complete virtue" has led some to detect intellectualism and a portrait of the contemplative sage devoted to philosophy.[5] This confusion reflects a genuine tension in Aristotle's account, but neither extreme fits the evidence. In brief, his analysis revises traditional attitudes toward honor but retains an emphasis on action. He grants this virtue its heroic scale but transforms its basis: moral virtue replaces competitive excellence as the ground for heroism, self-respect replaces public honor as its primary reward, and an aristocracy of virtue open to merit replaces the exclusive social elites based on status and fortune.[6] Finally, as complete and sovereign virtue, dignity is sovereign over happiness. Thus, Aristotle first mentions it in connection with the virtuous response to adversity.

> When many important things go badly, they stifle and hurt one's happiness, since they bring about suffering and impede many activities. However, even in these situations, nobility shines forth when someone bears many great misfortunes with equanimity, not because of insensitivity but because of integrity and dignity. And if one's activities are sovereign over one's life, as we said, then no one who is happy would become miserable, since he will never do hateful and base things.
>
> (*EN* 1.10 1100b28–35)

The focus here falls squarely on virtuous activity and the strength of character that underlies it. Honor has a place, of course, and there are echoes of aristocratic concern for appearances: Aristotle's claim that virtue "shines forth" (διαλάμπει) evokes the imagery of conspicuous heroism used of Tellos' "most

---

ing appreciation for beauty (its 'high' forms at any rate) on the one hand, [and] our reverent approval of moral goodness (and admiration, say, for heroic virtue) on the other" (p. 252).

5. For a critical outline of the major rivals, see Hardie 1978: 65–70; cf. Dirlmeier 1956: 370–72. Aristotle's account is compatible with intellectualism but does not entail it; Rees (1971: 242) observes, for example, that Socrates would be a model of *practical* wisdom instead of theoretical knowledge.

6. Schmidt (1967: 162–68, 160 n60) details the emphasis in the *EN* on virtue instead of status; Hardie (1978: 69–72) disputes Schmidt's thesis that the *EE* differs significantly and maintains further that dignity is a virtue of heroic proportion (see below).

illustrious" end (λαμπροτάτη, Herod. 1.31.4).[7] But honor appears only as an effect in this account, not as a motivation: if the virtuous can lose their happiness under the pressure of adversity no matter how honorably they act, then they would have no reason to persevere if their only aim were the prospect of recognition or external reward. Rather, the basis for their response to misfortune is the virtue of dignity (1100b32). To act out of dignity, evidently, is to accept deprivation, failure, or loss with equanimity (b31) and yet to uphold the principles that one values most (b35). In the same vein, Aristotle insists that dignity does not depend on a mere "absence of pain" (b32); with its suggestion of Cynic detachment, that would imply insensitivity and a lack of concern that he considers alien to virtue.[8] On the contrary, some things the virtuous would hate to do (b35). The reason they "will never do anything hateful and base" (b34–35) is not that their commitments are weak but that their convictions are extremely secure. Far from the absence of concern cultivated by ascetics that would make for a paradoxically empty character, dignity rests on deep-seated convictions that earn it the title of greatness of soul.

The tenor of Aristotle's account is suggested by his reference to integrity (γεννάδας), a term that occurs only here in his corpus and rarely in extant Greek as a whole. An equivalent term (γενναῖος) is widely used to refer to the gentry or nobility: when listing the factions found in most states, for example, he sets the "nobles" (οἱ γενναῖοι) opposite the "commoners" (οἱ ἀγεννεῖς), distinguished on the basis of inherited status.[9] But Aristotle iso-

7. Cf. 4.2 1122a33, b22, 1123a22; Protrep. fr. 3.
8. In addition to finding pleasure in the right way at the right things, the virtuous also feel pain in the right way (e.g., 2.3 1104b9–16); thus Aristotle criticizes those who define the virtues as "kinds of unfeeling and quietude" precisely because they fail to say how and when it is right to remain impassive (b24–26). The virtuous not only feel physical pain (see III.iii above) but also suffer with and for family and friends (e.g., 8.6 1158a1–10), as well as experiencing the pain of emotions like fear (e.g., 3.7 1115b7–20; cf. b24–29) and anger (4.5 1126a3–8; cf. EE 3.3 1231b10–20).
9. Pol. 3.13 1283a35, 4.12 1296b22, fr. 91; cf. Dover 1974: 95. A passage from the "Divisions" (a compilation of Academic and Aristotelian views ascribed to Aristotle; see the Preface to Mutschmann 1906) shows that the Doric form has the same sense: "good family" (εὐγένεια) is first defined generically as having excellent ancestors, and then "the best kind of good family" is distinguished as entailing integrity (γεννάδας in D. L. 3.89, but γενναῖος in Marcianus 257). The Doric evokes both the steadfast Spartans and the rugged, valiant Athenians of Aeschylus' generation: see Frogs 997 (cf. Stanford 1962 on 179) and Eccles. 304

lates a stricter sense, and one he commends: in contrast to good family (τὸ εὐγενές), which denotes "excellence belonging to the family" (τὴν τοῦ γένους ἀρετήν), integrity (τὸ γενναῖον) depends on "not deviating from one's nature" (κατὰ τὸ μὴ ἐξίστασθαι τῆς φύσεως, *Rhet.* 2.15 1390b21–23).[10] Good family implies nothing more than status and a good start, for children can "deviate" (ἐξίσταται) even from the best of parents, as the notorious children of Pericles, Alcibiades, and Socrates show (b27–31). Integrity, by contrast, implies stability and fortitude. Despite its popular connotations of status and wealth, the term is used to designate the persistence of admirable traits even in those of the lowest status: arguing against the practice of torturing slaves who are to testify, Aristotle observes that they too may "endure compulsion with integrity [γενναίως]" (*Rhet.* 1.15 1377a7–7d).[11] More typical is a quip he ascribes to Iphicrates, that Harmodius and Aristogeiton, the celebrated tyrannicides who were honored as martyrs to Athens' democracy, show that "the best is what has most integrity," for whatever their family origins, they "had no integrity until they *acted* with integrity" (*Rhet.* 2.23 1398a17–20).[12] And at his last hour, Socrates is credited with exceptional integrity by the prison guard (γενναιότατον, *Phdo.* 116c). Aristotle connects integrity with misfortune, then, to highlight the steadfast resolve with which the virtuous act even under severe pressures. But if integrity implies stability rather than status or external fortune, what is its basis? And how is it connected with dignity?[13]

(see Ussher 1973, citing *Lys.* 801–4 and the "men of Marathon"), and contrast an ironic application to Cleon (*Kn.* 240).

10. Cf. *His. An.* 1.1 488b18–20, where τὸ γενναῖον is glossed as τὸ μὴ ἐξιστά-μενον τῆς αὐτοῦ φύσεως. The example, which applies the term to the "lazy and plotting fox" in contrast with the "free, courageous, good-familied lion," shows that constancy and endurance are more basic to its sense than high birth is; cf. Cope 1877 on *Rhet.* 2.15.3. The formula for "good family" is also the conclusion of an argument from the lost dialogue "On Good Family" (fr. 92 = fr. 2 Ross), where it is distinguished from two undesirable senses. Plutarch doubted the authenticity of this work (fr. 93 = fr. 3 Ross), but similar views occur in *Rhet.* 1.5; cf. IV.ii *n*32 above.

11. Whether these lines are Aristotle's or not (most editors reject them as an interpolation), they illustrate the strict sense of integrity.

12. The tyrannicides were virtually revered; see *Ath. Pol.* 18, Thucydides 6.53–59.

13. The collocation of integrity and dignity in connection with misfortune seems to have become virtually a cliché; see Lycurgus 1.100, Polybius 6.2.6, and D. L. 3.89.

To show integrity is to act on noble principles even at personal cost. The basis for this fortitude is dignity, which on Aristotle's analysis has two sides: a general lack of concern for external advantages and a great concern for goodness of character, or virtue. On the one hand, this results in the great self-confidence that many find distasteful. But in fact, their having the courage of their convictions helps explain how the virtuous are able to respond heroically to situations of great adversity. On Aristotle's argument, moreover, their confidence stems from the fact that dignity represents the pinnacle of good character, complete and sovereign virtue. Although he maintains a connection between dignity and honor, he downplays honor as a motive and emphasizes instead doing good for others. Those who show dignity *deserve* honor, but they have greater *concern* for acting as they see fit than for acting to win privilege or prestige. Just as beneficence is most valuable when help is most needed, dignity is a virtue suited especially for misfortune. Hence, it clarifies the relation of virtue to prosperity and its contrary. To see how this works requires a closer look at dignity.

At the center of Aristotle's analysis is a twofold claim, that people who have dignity "*consider* themselves worthy of great things and *are* worthy" (*EN* 4.3 1123b2). The high self-esteem here is obvious, and Aristotle concedes that it results in some disdain.[14] But dignity differs radically from pride and vanity because its self-esteem is based on genuine merit. The vain (χαῦνοι), with whom people of dignity are readily confused, have no basis for pride, but "the genuinely dignified person must be good" (b29). After all, it would be "utterly ridiculous" if people of dignity lacked any of the virtues (b31–34)—if they quaked with fear at the sight of a fly or were willing to gratify every appetite or betray their best friends for gain, as he says elsewhere (*Pol.* 7.1 1323a27–35). Indeed, since dignity deserves the *greatest* things, those who have it must be the *best* people (1123b27–28); having it entails having not only complete virtue but "what is great in each virtue" (b29–30). Far more than an "ornament" for virtue, dignity is "like an ordered system [κόσμος τις] of the virtues," and having every virtue makes them all "greater" (1124a1–3; cf. *EE* 3.5

14. Some confusion has resulted from one of Aristotle's terms: he repeatedly refers to "*considering* oneself worthy [ἀξιῶν]" of honor, which does not imply that one *wants* honor, as many assume; cf. *n*23 below.

1232a31–38).[15] It is equivalent, therefore, to noble-goodness (1124a3–4), or as Aristotle puts it here and nowhere else, it is nothing but "total virtue" (ἀρετὴ παντελής, a7–8, a28–29). Although Aristotle thinks great pride always accompanies dignity, he argues that this pride must be justified and hence must be based on genuine merit. In short, total virtue is essential for dignity.

Before we look at the role this gives honor, Aristotle's procedure here warrants comment. In keeping with his usual approach, he first presents received views and then analyzes them to construct his own account. His starting point is the word "greatness-of-soul," from which he first infers that dignity involves "great things" (1123a34–35). But that, as he immediately adds, fails to specify what these great things are (a35).[16] To answer this question, he introduces the two conditions of pride and merit (b2), in a formula that sounds definitive. But the formula serves only to locate dignity as a mean between contrary extremes and does not state its essence. Thus, the only other time Aristotle mentions the formula (*EE* 3.5 1232b29–33a3), it follows several other marks of dignity—all reputable views and none definitive. The first of these, moreover, is that dignity and "all the virtues" are mutually entailing: having this one virtue entails having every virtue, and vice versa (1232a31–38). And in the *Rhetoric*, where there is no mention of worth, dignity is defined instead as "a virtue for producing great benefits" (1.9 1366b17); since virtue is defined in the preceding lines as "a capacity for doing many great benefits" (a38), dignity turns out to be equivalent to virtue. In the *Nicomachean Ethics*, in fact, Aristotle presents the formula about worth as a reputable view (δοκεῖ, 1123b1). He endorses the formula, of course, but only as the basis for further analysis, not as the final word. After all, the formula links dignity with merit, but it fails to specify the basis for this merit or to iden-

15. It trivializes Aristotle's point to translate κόσμος as "ornament" or "adornment," as many do; translating it as "crown" (as if στέφανος), though an apt image for the sovereignty of virtue, emphasizes the reward rather than what warrants it. Stewart (1892) is near the mark when, in his notes on 4.3, he refers to the "beautiful harmony" of fully virtuous character; cf. Hardie 1978: 63. On complete virtue, which of course implies justice (5.1 1129b14–34), see II.iv–v and IV.ii above.

16. The same unclarity attends Aristotle's opening inference from the name in the *EE* (μεγέθει τινί, 1232a29); cf. the diverse ways of being "great" (b17–23).

tify its major concerns or even to mention honor. It remains to be seen what "great things" dignity deserves.

Aristotle's notion of worth is obscure, but his remarks about the two necessary conditions of dignity show that the great things of which it is worthy center on actions, not rewards. Roughly, he equates being worthy of great things with being *capable of doing* great benefit, and considering oneself worthy of great things with being *willing to attempt* those deeds. The basis for worth is thus prospective as well as retrospective: it rests on confidence rather than pride, and it implies continued willingness to act as one thinks best, not merely pride over things done in the past. This is clearest when Aristotle connects vanity, the vice of excess, with doing more than one can or should, and "meekness" (μικροψυχία, literally "smallness of soul"), the vice of deficiency, with doing less. Neither defect makes people actually "bad," since neither makes them "wrongdoers" (1125a17–19), but each is still a vice, because vanity leads to errors of commission, meekness to errors of omission. The vain are "foolish," and because they "don't know themselves," they venture beyond their abilities, only to pay when "refuted" by events (a27–29).[17] The meek, by contrast, are "reluctant" rather than "foolish" (a23–24): because they think themselves unworthy, they deprive themselves even of goods they deserve (a20–22), and "they refrain both from noble actions and from other endeavors, as well as from external goods" (a25–27).

The root of the problem in each case is ignorance and self-deception (a22, a28). But violating the Delphic injunction to self-knowledge is an ethical defect only because it affects how people feel and act. What makes vanity a vice is not *having* more than one deserves but *trying to do* more than one can achieve. If the vain did nothing, there would be no problem. All too often, however, good fortune inspires overconfidence and power corrupts: undeserved prosperity makes people "contemptuous and arrogant [ὑβρισταί]," and because they feel superior to everyone else, "they do whatever they wish [ὅτι ἂν τύχωσιν]" (1124a29–b2). Ar-

---

17. Aristotle associates foolishness with imprudence and self-inflicted ills; it affects others only incidentally. Among those he calls ἠλίθιοι are people who waste their time deliberating about matters beyond their control (3.3 1112a20), wastrels who use up their own means (4.1 1121a25–27), and people who try to do something munificent without having the means (4.2 1122b26–29).

istotle's account smacks of tragedy and recalls Solon's proverbial warning, that "surfeit breeds hubris whenever great prosperity attends people whose minds are not shrewd" (fr. 6, from *Ath. Pol.* 12.2; cf. *Protrep.* fr. 3).[18] Or as Aristotle puts it, "Without virtue, it is not easy to bear good fortune harmoniously" (1124a30–31; cf. 1.10 1100b20–21). Always a threat to themselves, their actions can have dire effects on others as well. If the vain rise to positions of power, their mistakes are magnified by their position; even if they intend nothing bad, they can wreak havoc on any number of lives. The vain, then, only "imitate" the virtuous, and although eager to attempt great things, they fail to do what they should (1124b1–5).

If the vain cause themselves grief because they think too highly of themselves, the meek lead diminished lives for the opposite reason. Like the vain, they are usually "mistaken" rather than "bad" (1125a18–19),[19] and their reluctance to act (a24) makes them less likely to cause others harm. It may seem odd that meekness is a vice at all, since it presupposes genuine worth and its basic error is only to underrate one's worth. Nonetheless, Aristotle thinks meekness a more serious defect, more opposed to dignity, as well as more common (a32–34). The decisive flaw again has to do with action, although this time on the side of omission, since meekness undermines the very will to act. The meek think so little of themselves that they are unwilling to strive for the goods they deserve (a19–23), and low self-esteem "makes them worse" because it leaves them unwilling to do the noble actions they should (a25–27). The vain come closer to dignity, then, because they are at least willing to attempt great deeds. Their ambitions show a healthy respect for honorable action, and they would have dignity if they could do well what they do. So again, the focus of Aristotle's objection is on action rather than rewards: the meek do less than they should, and their low self-esteem or "smallness of soul" is actually an ethical flaw not be-

18. On the tragic potential of vanity, cf. 1124a26–b5, 1125a27–29, and the reference to *hamartia* at a19, with 5.1 1129b31–30a8, *Po.* 13 1453a7–17, and *Protrep.* fr. 3. Armstrong and Peterson (1980: 67–70) point out some similarities between Aristotle's analysis of tragic plots and earlier reflections on the disasters that can befall powerful people who overstep the limits of their abilities; cf. Halliwell 1986: 153–54.

19. The contrast between "bad" and "mistaken" implies that their defect is cognitive rather than moral.

cause it leaves them with fewer possessions, but because it betrays a lack of serious commitment or moral aspiration and an unwillingness to act on behalf of valuable ends.[20] As he wonders at the outset (1123b10–13; cf. EE 3.5 1233a25–30), if worthy people are unwilling to do what they can, "how little would they do if they were not worthy of so much?" In contrast with vanity, then, dignity entails the ability to do great things; in contrast with meekness, it entails the confidence and willingness to attempt great deeds.

Dignity makes the virtuous worthy of doing great things, and only for that reason do those who have it deserve honor. This is primarily a matter of performance, but it is also a question of scale. Aristotle denies that being virtuous is enough for having dignity, and he argues that dignity is not the only virtue that falls between the extremes of vanity and meekness. Sketching an exhaustive schema, he distinguishes having dignity first from being worthy of only minor things and attempting nothing more (1123b5–8), and only then from attempting great things but not being capable of them (b8–9), and from being capable of great things but not attempting them (b9–13).[21] The first group deserves praise for being temperate and moderate (b5, b7), but not for dignity, since that requires great worth. This justified modesty, however, is not a contrary of dignity, since it differs only in scale and both have the same "nature": each entails knowing what one can do and acting accordingly, and unlike the meek, the modest are willing to do all they can do (EE 3.5 1233a16–27). In short, even this difference in scale depends primarily on action. Dignity and modesty both entail knowing what one should do, being willing to do it, and doing it; but those with dignity can do

20. Cf. EE 3.5 1233a12–15. Hardie (1978: 70) calls it a paradox that the meek are "both greatly deserving and vicious." But the paradox dissolves if being "deserving" means, as I argue it does, "deserving to act" rather than "deserving admiration"; the meek err by omission and refuse to act when they can and should. This highlights one reason for translating Aristotle's "small-souled" as "meek" rather than "humble": the latter can still have great self-confidence and, though reserved, still be quite willing to act. For a thorough analysis of the relations between self-assessment and action, see Taylor 1985; Nussbaum (1980: esp. 397–404) argues that self-respect is morally important because subjective feelings of unworthiness interfere with action.

21. The schema omits "average" things and those who deserve or claim nothing more or less. But since Aristotle uses "moderate" to describe those who deserve "little" (1123b7), he evidently means "little" to be equivalent to "not great" (the contradictory rather than the contrary of "great").

more, should do more, and are willing to do more. Although both are guided by practical wisdom and both fulfill the Delphic injunction to know one's limits, only modesty is advantageous prudentially, since dignity entails being willing to take great risks. But why are people with dignity willing, and what is their motive? What in particular do they want to do?

Aristotle makes honor the special domain of dignity, because dignity is worthy of great things, "especially the greatest" (*EN* 4.3 1123b15–16). As practice shows, honor is the greatest of external goods (b20): it is what people offer the best beings, the gods, it is what the eminent aim for most, and it is the prize set for the finest deeds (b18–21). Of course, honor is only the greatest external good, not the best good of all; it is simply the best anyone can offer in return. In fact, no honor can match what dignity deserves, although it comes closer than anything else (1124a7–9). In particular, the actions that deserve honor are greater goods, but they are rewarded with honor because "worth is said relative to external goods" (1123b17).[22] Does this mean that honor is the principal goal of dignity or that the virtuous want and seek honor above all? If it does, then Aristotle's paragon of virtue is basically self-interested and hardly a model of *moral* virtue. To set great store in honor and pursue it with zeal bespeaks vanity rather than dignity and a greater concern for one's reputation than one's merit.

Although Aristotle says repeatedly that dignity *deserves* honor, he says nothing about an *ambition* for honor.[23] On the contrary, he

22. The remark is obscure, but its point seems to be that external goods are the only way to *reward* worth. The explanation may be that benefaction involves external goods; if one tried to reward a benefactor in kind by returning favor for favor, one would have to offer material, physical, or social assistance. This suggestion resolves the alleged contradiction between the claim here that honor is the greatest external good (1123b20–21), and a later claim that *philoi* are (9.9 1169b10; cf. 8.1 1155a4–10): friends are better, but honor is the best anyone can *give*, since the best friendships rest on *mutual* respect and *shared life*, and all anyone can give is respect and time. For other interpretations of the inconsistency, see Jaffa 1952: 123–34, and Gauthier and Jolif 1970 on 1123b20 (they mistake δοϰεῖ at 1169b10 as a disparaging reference to "la foule").

23. It is widely assumed, on the basis of Aristotle's inference that dignity is "about great honors," that dignity entails a *desire* for great honors. But he never says that people who have dignity *want* honor, let alone that honor is their overriding end. Bywater (1892) emends the text at one point to suggest that they do: where all mss. say that "great people consider themselves worthy of honor most of all" (1123b23), Bywater excises "great people" (which would refer not to dig-

argues that people of dignity care little for most honors (1124a10–11), that they enjoy even great honor only "moderately" and only for major achievements and from others who are virtuous (a6–7), and that far from thinking honor the greatest good (a16–17), they consider it something minor or "small" (a19). In the first place, even most who are motivated by honor seek it not "for itself" but "coincidentally," either as a token of future favor and gain or to confirm their sense of self-worth by winning honor from the good and wise (8.8 1159a17–24; cf. 1.5 1095b26–29). But rather than acting to win recognition or personal gain or to assure themselves of their excellence, those who have the complete virtue of dignity act for ends they consider good by themselves. After all, they are self-sufficient (1125a11–12) and have very few needs (1124b17–18); they see no need to win approval for doing what they already value most. Moreover, although they know that they deserve honor, they have no interest in being honored merely on the basis of status or class. Others value power and wealth in part for the honor these bring them (a17–19), because success is something most people want and admire. But the virtuous know that "in truth, the good alone deserve honor" (a25). External advantages can "contribute" to dignity (a20–21) and make people more worthy of honor (a25–26), but only if the fortunate put their advantages to good use in the pursuit of good ends.[24] Prosperity adds to dignity only because the virtuous can typically *do* more with resources than without.

Far from fostering competition, dignity tends to deter the virtuous from entering the arenas of popular honor and success. Since their actions are not motivated by a desire to win praise (1125a6–7), they do not care to compete for popular honors (τὰ ἔντιμα) or to challenge others who already perform honored tasks well (1124b23–24).[25] This is not to say that dignity precludes

nity but to the prosperous; cf. 1124a21–29); even after emendation, the point is only that people with dignity know they *deserve* honor, not that they are eager for it. Indeed, "considering oneself *worthy* of honor" is hardly inconsistent with *valuing* it only slightly (a19).

24. After saying that status, wealth, and power can give the virtuous "more dignity," Aristotle explains that this wins them honor "from some" (a24); he goes on to insist that "neither is it just for people who have these [external] goods without virtue to consider themselves worthy of great things, nor is it correct to say they have dignity" (a26–28).

25. The phrase οὗ πρωτεύουσιν ἄλλοι is obscure; Aspasius (113.30–34) suggests competing in political debate or musical contests. For the awkward ἔργον

all interest in honor, but only that its motives involve much more than ambition. As Aristotle observes, "ambition" (φιλοτιμία, literally "love of honor") generally refers to an excessive interest in honor (4.4 1125b8–10). Of course, he uses the same term also for the virtuous desire for honor, but only because ordinary usage has no other name for the mean-state (b17–21). As its name suggests, this virtue views honor as an end (b7, b19): it consists in wanting and pursuing honor in the right amount, in the right circumstances, and in the right way (b7–8). To be virtuous, then, the ambitious must know the true value of what is at stake in any given situation: minor deeds deserve little honor and should rouse little ambition, and only great things warrant much honor or ambition (cf. *EE* 3.5 1232a31–38). Even great honors, moreover, must be pursued "in the right way" (*EN* 4.4 1125b8, b20). Rather than harboring ulterior motives or being attracted to honor by itself, the virtuous want to do honorable things when— and only when—they see that other valuable ends are at stake. For an action to deserve honor, after all, it must promote some valuable end, and for the virtuous to deserve honor, they must aim at that end and not only at honor itself. The major difference between dignity and ambition is not that dignity involves greater honors (a35–b5), for the overly ambitious want those most of all. Nor is it that the ambitious seek more honor than they deserve; that merely distinguishes excessive ambition from the virtuous mean (b7–10, b15–21). The decisive difference is rather that honor is not the chief aim of dignity in the first place. Although dignity is worthy of great honor, that is only because it is worthy of *doing* great things. Dignity includes the correct ambition and desire for honor, but as "total virtue" it embraces much more. The ambitious seek honor in what they do, but those who have dignity choose each of their actions for itself, regardless of whether they expect any honor to ensue. Honor, of course, cannot be the sole end for any virtue, since all virtuous actions are chosen at least in part "for themselves."[26] But whereas even virtuous ambition is aroused only by the prospect of honor, dignity entails being willing to do what is right even at the risk of public disgrace.

---

of the mss. (1124b25), he evidently read ἔρως (114.5–8), which would be a remarkably personal motive for great deeds (but cf. 1124b31–25a2 on friends).

26. See II.iv–v and IV.ii above.

Honor is the special province of dignity because that is its just reward, not because that is its chief concern. The virtuous deserve honor, as they deserve to fare well on the whole. But life is not always fair, and dignity entails having the right attitude and response to dishonor too (1123b21, 1124a5). People who have dignity "think very little" of minor honors, Aristotle claims, and they have no more concern for dishonor (a10–11). This point has a basis in reputable views. To illustrate an inductive approach to definition, for example, Aristotle lists two sets of men who received less than their due: heroic men of action, like Achilles, Ajax, and Alcibiades, are offered as exemplars of dignity for refusing to endure injury to their honor; Lysander and Socrates are credited with dignity for being "indifferent" (ἀδιάφοροι) to fortune, whether good or bad (*An. Pos.* 2.13 97b17–24). The examples are provisional, of course, and the initial explanations may need revision: the former may put too high a price on honor, and the latter may be too dispassionate. But the aim is to find what is common to all these cases (b15–17, b22–23), and although Aristotle offers no solution here, his analysis in the ethical works shows how to reconcile the two divergent groups. The common denominator, though obscured by popular usage, is upholding principles that one has adopted as one's own, regardless of the consequences: the former show dignity, not because of wounded pride, but because they refuse to endure what they consider wrong (b19–20; note ὑβριζόμενοι); and the latter have dignity, not because they have no feelings at all, but because of their "impassivity toward fortune" (b23), which enables them to act as they think best without regard to honor or reward. All thus act as they do for the twin reasons that they think themselves worthy of great acts, and they are.

If honor is not their chief end, what do people who have dignity want and pursue? On the one hand, Aristotle concedes, their lack of ambition can make them look "lazy and hesitant" (*EN* 4.3 1124b24). But this inactivity is limited, and its basis is specifically moral. Thus, he does not say that they do nothing at all; he argues rather that they are quite willing to act for the benefit of others. Although they have little ambition for wealth or public life (a16–19), they accept them and use them well when a good cause requires. In particular, they like to "cause good [εὖ ποιεῖν], but are ashamed to receive benefit [εὐεργετούμενος]" (b9–10); if others help them, they do more in return (ἀντευεργετικός, b11). Since their own needs are few, they "help [ὑπηρετεῖν] others gladly" (b17–18). The aim here is not to earn a return; citing Homeric gods (*Il.* 1.498–516) and Spartan history as exempla, Aristotle insists that people who have dignity "remember whom they help, but not by whom they are helped" (1124b12–17). Their motive for helping, then, is not to serve their own advantage, but simply to do something they consider good.[27]

Aristotle shows what sort of help he has in mind in the *Rhetoric*. After linking honor with doing benefit, he says that beneficence involves helping others "in survival and the causes of life, or in wealth, or in any other goods that are not easy to acquire, either in general or at a particular place and time" (1.5 1361a30–32). The point is not that beneficence always involves hardship or sacrifice, although his examples suggest that it often does. Nor does he say that it is right to offer help indiscriminately to all who want it; presumably, the virtuous act only when there is genuine need and their help is deserved. But the examples do show that beneficence is an expression of *moral* virtue, because benefaction involves doing for others something genuinely good, even at some personal risk or expense. Saving others' lives takes courage and often endangers the savior's own life, offering material assistance shows liberality and detracts from the giver's own property, and in general, helping others usually requires putting their needs and interests ahead of at least some of our own.[28] Help is often given with ulterior motives, of course, in the hope of return, but to the extent that it is given for the benefit of others, it is an exercise of moral virtue. Thus, Aristotle singles out justice, courage, and liberality, on the ground that "necessarily, the greatest virtues are those most useful to others, if indeed virtue is a capacity for doing benefit" (1.9 1366b3–9). Dignity, then, is simply great virtue, for as he goes on to say, it can be defined as the virtue "for producing great benefits" (b17).

Magnificence, the other grand moral virtue in Aristotle's

27. Aristotle sketches an intriguing but obscure psychological account of why anyone would be willing to benefit others without regard for any return: people are fond of what they do and achieve, because "existence is desirable and loved, and we exist in activity (for we exist in living and doing), and in actuality [ἐνεργείᾳ] the maker in a way is his work [ἔργον]" (9.7 1168a5–7). The product is simply a realization of the producer's activity; cf. Price 1989: 164–65.

28. Aristotle considers it a commonplace that "benefactors" *care* more for those they benefit than vice versa (9.7 1167b17–18). Some found this paradoxical (b18–28), but to show how it can make sense, he argues that liking and caring are expressed primarily in *doing* good, not in receiving it (b28–68a5).

canon, requires great resources to underwrite its largesse. Greatness of character, however, is the essence of dignity (literally "greatness of soul"), and it can be exercised even without great means.[29] Beneficence takes many forms, only some of which provide material aid; lives can be saved, justice upheld, and the social welfare enhanced simply by timely action. In fact, dignity implies a certain disregard for all external resources, not only honor and dishonor but "wealth and power and every kind of success and failure" (*EN* 4.3 1124a11–15). Anyone who considers honor "something small," Aristotle claims, is not likely to be very concerned about other external advantages (a19); others may expect to be honored for their status, rank, or wealth (a17–22), but people with dignity hold only the virtuous in high honor (a25). Aristotle's claim is not that people who have dignity are wholly uninterested in external goods; to consider honor "small" is not to deny it has any value, and other things being equal, they too prefer honor to public disgrace. All he claims is that success and personal advantage are not among their priorities.

This relative lack of concern for the most honored external goods is a major source of the bad name that Aristotle's account of dignity has acquired. This disregard, however, has a specific focus and definite limits, and it rests on knowing what is most valuable and what deserves respect: just as the virtuous respect only genuine merit, so they have disdain only where it is "just" and due (b5–6). In their own affairs, those who have dignity "behave moderately with wealth and political power and every kind of success and failure, however things may turn out" (a12–15),

29. On the material requirements for magnificence, see IV.i above. A parallel requirement for dignity is widely assumed, but Aristotle never makes one explicit. Nor is any implicit, though adapting the argument of Irwin 1988: 62–64, one might infer that the virtuous need firsthand experience and practice in doing great deeds before they can *know* which deeds are great and when to attempt them. But the examples of benefaction listed in the previous paragraph show why it would be wrong to assume that we need any special expertise to recognize *great* deeds. The argument seems to rest on a "fallacy of antecedents" (*hoc ergo aliquid ante hoc*): some great deed must come first, and if the "total virtue" differs from lesser virtue primarily in strength of conviction rather than in "scale" of deeds, it can result gradually from sustained exercise of lesser virtue. Myth and history, ancient and modern alike, are full of stories of minor characters (e.g., Solon's heroes) who respond to crises with great virtue and dignity; thus, Socrates thought himself unfit for most great deeds in politics, but it did not prevent him from showing dignity in battle (*Symp.* 220d–21b), on trial for his life (*Apol.* passim), and even as a member of Athens' presiding council (*Apol.* 32a–d).

and they are "neither overjoyed at prosperity nor distraught at failure" (a15–16).[30] Dignity cannot make anyone immune to suffering or induce emotional anesthesia, but those who have it are "least given to mourning the loss of necessities and minor things" (1125a9).[31] Likewise in their relations with others, they measure their manners to suit their company. Not easily impressed by the trappings of prosperity (a2–3; cf. a30–32), they are "grand" toward the prosperous, but modest toward others, especially the lowly (1124b18–23); they are "frank" (b29) and "honest" (b30), and they care more for truth than approval (b27–29); they are open about whom they like or dislike (b26–27); they bear no grudge and readily "overlook" their own ills (1125a3–5); and though sparing with praise, they are also sparing with reproach, even toward enemies (a7–8).

Misconceptions about dignity are abetted by its superficial resemblance to vanity on some of these behavioral points. The difference between them, however, though not always apparent to observers, is actually quite stark. Both the vain and the virtuous believe themselves worthy, and confident of their excellence, both are willing to do great things. But the vain at best only "imitate" the virtuous (1124b2). The basis for their confidence, of course, is quite different. Dignity rests on total virtue, but vanity only on presumption and their external advantages (a21–24). Dignity inspires disdain for the mere trappings of success (b18–23); the vain want their own success to be conspicuous and preen themselves on their good fortune (1125a30–32). This usually leads to different results: trying to do more than they can or should, the vain misuse and abuse their advantages (1124a29–31, b4), and in the event, their inabilities are revealed (a31–b2; cf. 1125a29). But it also promotes different attitudes toward others: dignity inspires compassion for those in need and modesty toward all but the proud and the great (1124b18–23), but the vain

30. A similar saying is ascribed to Periander by one of Aristotle's younger colleagues, Demetrius of Phaleron, who collected the sayings of the Seven Sages; see Stobaeus 3.124.

31. Aristotle restricts his claim here to instrumental goods, and in the passage quoted at the outset, he implies that misfortune can cause even people with dignity to suffer (μὴ δι' ἀναλγησίαν, 1100b32); cf. *n*8 above. Grieving for the loss of loved ones, for example, he thinks generally admirable; it is excessive only when paralyzing, as in the case of Niobe whose legendary sorrow turned her to stone (7.4 1148a31–34).

feel contempt for people less fortunate (a29–b2), and in acting as they wish, they have disdain for everyone else (b4–5).[32]

Dignity inspires disregard for one's own fortunes, but not for all the misfortunes of others. It inspires disdain for undeserved success and people who expect to be honored merely for what they have, and it makes the virtuous willing to resist injustice and to help others in grave crises. Thus, while those who have dignity meet their own misfortunes with equanimity, they are not impassive in the face of violence and arrogance (ὕβρις, 1124a8–9) or willing to accept injustice (Pol. 7.7 1328a8–10). Dignity, in fact, is compatible not only with "resentment" (νέμεσις), which Aristotle defines as pain at the undeserved success of others (Rhet. 2.9 1386b8–11; cf. 1387b5–15), but also with "pity," which he defines as pain at the undeserved suffering of others (2.8 1385b13–14; cf. b27).[33] Both feelings, after all, belong to "a good character" because each is aroused by injustice (1386b11–15, cf. b25–34). People who have dignity may experience these feelings less than most, since their judgment is governed by fairness and there are fewer losses they consider serious. They feel pity, for example, not for everyone who feels hurt, but only for those whose lives are seriously and unfairly damaged, by physical trauma or loss of family or friends (1386a4–16). It should be emphasized, however, that when they help people who need and deserve it (EN 4.3 1124b9–18), they act not out of indifference to others but out of principles of fairness and respect for their lives. This "total virtue," then, rests not on contempt for human life or a wholesale disregard for fortune, but on the belief that people should be measured by their character and conduct rather than by what they happen by fortune to have or to lack.

The concern for fairness is part of the moral aspect of dignity, but the concern for doing "great things" gives this a heroic di-

32. Paris, the Trojan prince, offers an instructive case: some evidently thought he had dignity, since he spent his youth alone on Mount Ida out of disregard for society (Rhet. 2.24 1401b20–23). Aristotle, however, thinks the case misleading and uses it to illustrate the fallacy of the consequent, i.e., disregard for popular approval follows from dignity, but not vice versa (cf. SE 5 167b1–20). According to myths dating back at least to fifth-century tragedy (see Apollodorus 3.12.5 and Cicero de Div. 1.42), the reason he lived alone had nothing to do with dignity; he was simply a foundling.

33. Since the situations that should arouse pity and resentment are undeserved, each emotion is connected essentially to fortune; see esp. 1386a6–7, 1387a10–15, b16–17.

mension. The greatest deeds are those that do the greatest good, and although those who have dignity do little of what is popularly honored, they do undertake "great actions worthy of renown" (1124b23–26). Aristotle's point is not that they seek out opportunities for doing great deeds; he denies that they are "risk-lovers," since they consider few things worth much risk (b6–7). But if a cause is deserving, they are ready to risk all, even their lives, in the firm belief that life under some conditions would not be worth living (b8–9). Others often run risks to win wealth, influence, or political office, but those who have dignity use such external advantages only to achieve some good, and they are interested "more in what is noble but fruitless than in what is fruitful and advantageous" (1125a11–12). If they engage in politics, for example, their aim is not to advance their own fortunes or to win public acclaim but to preserve or restore justice and to further the good of society.[34] But great benefaction is not exclusively public or political. Saving someone's life in battle or sustaining a group of exiles, though each an act of personal courage or liberality, still confers benefits of a very great order. The greatness of dignity, in short, is a function not of rank or prestige but of the benefits conferred.

The greatest demand for dignity, in fact, occurs in adversity, and moral heroism is its chief expression. Aristotle thus singles out moderation as admirable in the use of prosperity, but dignity as noble in response to misfortune (*Rhet.* 1.9 1367b15–16; cf. *EN* 1.10 1100b28–33). This is not to say that dignity has no place in the absence of grave injustice or serious need, but simply that it is most needed and most clearly shown not when life goes well but when it is harsh or unfair. The greatest test of virtue comes not if the virtuous are tempted by more goods but if they are threatened by loss. As Aristotle puts it when he explains why courage is especially painful, "It is more difficult to endure painful things than to hold back from pleasant things" (3.9 1117a33–35). Since further goods can at best only add to an already good life, it may not be hard to resist reaching for more. But imminent

34. Although Aristotle disapproves of most forms of monarchy, he commends the form "in heroic times" when kings were "benefactors" in technology, war, political organization, and justice (*Pol.* 3.14 1285b3–11). Hardie (1978: 70–73) also associates dignity with heroic virtue; he refers to Aristotle's argument in *Pol.* 3.4–5 that the virtuous are "sovereign or able to be sovereign, either alone or with others, over caring for common affairs" (1278b1–5).

danger and the threat of grave loss compel us to choose not merely between having more or remaining the same, but between giving up or holding on to things we already have and value; the tempting alternative in some cases, far from offering more than we have, is simply survival. For the virtuous, one side of the choice is the same in either case, and although it is harder to resist the fear of loss than the prospect of gain, giving in to either is for them giving up on their virtue and what they value most. But that shows only that the exercise of rational virtue is their sovereign concern, not that they have the strength of character always to act on that concern. What sets dignity or "total virtue" apart, then, is its capacity for action: it is sovereign virtue in the highest degree.[35]

All who have noble-goodness or "complete virtue" value rational virtue more than anything else, and all want to exercise it at any cost, but some situations pose challenges that can be met only by those who have the exceptional capacities implied by dignity. Some actions, in short, are too difficult or demanding even for many of the virtuous to perform; then, whether the deficiency is in talent or in courage and conviction, it would be vain and foolish for them to attempt what they cannot reasonably expect to achieve. It takes an Ajax to rescue someone from the onslaught of a Hector and lesser warriors should withdraw to defend their cause another day; or it takes a Socrates to confront a Callicles with the profound errors of his life and those less adept in argument or more vulnerable to reprisal would do both themselves and the cause of justice a disservice in provoking the ire of the vindictive and powerful. People who have dignity, then, excel even among the virtuous: not only is virtuous activity their sovereign concern, but they can also uphold that concern in action even when confronted by grave challenge or misfortune. This capacity to meet the special demands imposed by adverse circumstances raises dignity to the pinnacle of moral virtue.

Risk is implicit in the sovereignty of virtue. No life is free of failure, injustice, and loss, and in the normal course of events,

35. See II.v above. Cf. Irwin 1985d: 118–22; Irwin also connects dignity with the virtuous response to misfortune. As Kolnai (1976: 270) puts it, people with dignity are *"penetrated*—rather than merely commanded, controlled, governed, or interested—by Morality to the point of being *personally inseparable* from it" (his italics). Taylor (1985: 109–11) describes "integrity" in very similar terms.

everyone faces painful choices and grief. But much depends on how we respond. We always have to select from the available options, and even in the best of circumstances, we can aim only at part of the overall good, never at all of it at once. Adversity diminishes our options, but it rarely eliminates them all, and although it leaves us wishing for better alternatives, we are free to follow the option we value most. In his account of dignity, Aristotle simply extends this truism to those who have sovereign virtue: they want to prosper in doing what is right, but if forced to choose between the exercise of virtue and the enjoyment of prosperity, they are prepared to risk life itself rather than forsake the values and priorities that give their life its meaning and point. In some respects, this is true of nearly everyone. Most people, and animals as well, have something they want so much that they are willing to die for it and unwilling to live without it.[36] Where the virtuous differ is in what they want most and in the strength of their devotion to it. People who have dignity, although they want many of the same things others do, have different priorities. They value health, resources, honor, and family and close friends, but only in ways consistent with rational virtue; although virtue is not their only end, they view it as outweighing all other claims if its exercise is ever at stake. First, whereas others are willing to take great risks to gain wealth or win honor, they are willing to take risks for justice or the good of friends or city and others, although only as accords with correct reason. And second, rather than acting in order to win approval from others, the virtuous heroically uphold standards they consider their own. In its motives, then, dignity differs sharply from traditional forms of heroism associated with the warrior's code of honor. There the decisive norms remain essentially public and external, even when internalized by the warrior; even if he acts as he wishes and chooses, his aim is to win honor or rewards from others or to avoid disgrace in their eyes.[37] But the primary motive for

36. Aristotle thinks this claim uncontroversial (*EE* 1.5 1215b18–26); in particular, "no one" would want to live without friends (8.1 1155a5–6) or by himself (9.9 1169b16–19), and even animals are willing to die for their young (*EE* 7.1 1235a33).

37. Cf. 3.8 1116a17–29, where Aristotle refers to Homeric heroes in connection with "civic bravery," which comes closest to his account of courage because its motive is "a desire for something noble, viz. honor, and avoidance of reproach, which is ignoble" (a28–29). He thinks that this still falls short of complete

dignity is to do something one sees to be noble and to uphold the principles by which one lives and which one values more than any public approval or dishonor.

In his analysis of dignity, Aristotle transforms traditional conceptions of honor and heroic action. In place of competitive ideals based on status that exalt external success, he proposes a cooperative ideal based on self-knowledge and rational virtue that finds its highest expression in beneficence. In his model of heroism, then, the end of dignity is not any reward for benefaction but great benefaction itself, which the virtuous see as an expression of their being and of what they value most. The heroic dimension of dignity, however, does not require any moral crusade or imply that people who have dignity are moral saints. Like the philosophers in Plato's cave, they may prefer to live for themselves and their friends and to engage in private activities. This involves an element of conservatism but not of moral complacency. Although they are not eager to risk their good life, neither are they unwilling to be disturbed if the need is real or the cause great. The extent of their conservatism depends on how much injustice they are willing to accept. Aristotle no doubt acquiesced in more than most today think we should. But quite apart from any worry about moral indolence or apathy, there is an important question for theory here. It is one thing not to engage in immoral practices, but something else to prevent others from engaging in them; it is easy to condemn ancient injustices such as slavery and to wish for their elimination, but it is questionable whether any ethical theory can or should *require* action to eliminate them. We can admire those who do attempt to improve society, but it would be harsh to condemn all who do not. Obligation is different from supererogation, and it would need to be shown that morality can require nearly as much as it extols.

The threat here is not simply that morality may become pervasive, but that the boundary between obligation and supererogation may disappear and moral heroism end up morally required. Or in Aristotle's terms, justice threatens to *require* dignity. It would not be enough to be generous; one would have also, should the occasion arise, to sacrifice everything including life

___

courage, however, because its ends are determined externally ("from the laws," b19).

itself. But "total virtue" is an ideal, and unless mortal sacrifice is to be a moral imperative, the commands of virtue must be less rigorous than its acme. There is even something ennobling in leaving room for action "beyond the call of duty." Arguably conservative in some respects, Aristotle's position here is actually quite humane. As he observes in connection with "mixed actions," people who take great risks or endure great pain or loss for a noble end deserve praise, and those who succumb sometimes deserve reproach; but although there are some things we should never consent to do, there is also room for "compassion when, because of things that surpass human nature and no one would endure, someone does what he should not" (*EN* 3.1 1110a19–27). The place of dignity in Aristotle's theory is to sketch a model not of how the virtuous must act but rather of how nobly they can and might act if the exercise of rational virtue is wholly their sovereign concern. But occasions for great sacrifice occur rarely in most lives, and the risks the virtuous are willing to take, though generally greater, are also far fewer. In this way, dignity leaves life relatively secure for the virtuous. Still, the devotion to principle that makes some ready to risk all leaves some exposed, and a serious question remains. Why are people who have dignity willing to sacrifice their own interests to help others, and why are those who lead the best lives ready to risk all? How do they view this seemingly selfless action?

The Sovereign Self

PLATO'S GLAUCON asks to be shown why we should want to be just and why we should ever be willing to sacrifice our own advantage or welfare for the benefit of others. Traditional wisdom, he complains, promises rewards for justice, but even if everyone prefers virtue *and* prosperity to vice *and* misfortune, the choice is rarely so clear. It is harder to see the value of justice when being just adds nothing to prosperity, when success can be won unjustly as well, or when misfortune is the prospect no matter what we do. Hardest of all is seeing why we should do what is just even at great cost, when even a short lapse or a few misdeeds can fend off serious loss or bring major gain. In these cases, the sovereignty of virtue faces its severest tests and Glaucon's worries take on added urgency. This is what gives adversity and misfortune their special importance for ethics: the choices we make under great pressures reveal our priorities. By posing the problem of moral motivation in its starkest form, misfortune can show what we might gain by holding virtue sovereign in our lives. No reasonable person wants to face these hard choices, and even the "total virtue" of dignity does not demand constant sacrifice or a moral crusade. But should the occasion arise and the virtuous face an unfortunate choice, what reason do they see to uphold their values and principles? Why are the virtuous willing to make great personal sacrifice? How can those who lead the best lives be willing to relinquish everything, including life itself?

Aristotle sketches part of an answer in his account of courage, the virtue shown in responding to danger of the worst sort.[1] Courage, like dignity, implies a willingness to risk life itself for the sake of larger causes, and it raises similar questions about the motives for sacrifice.[2] In his account of courage, Aristotle tries to explain why the virtuous, who have more to lose than anyone else, are nonetheless willing to risk their lives for something else. Fearlessness, he argues, is not the reason: that is a sign not of virtue but of madness (*EN* 3.7 1115b24–29); true courage involves fearing the right things, to the right degree, and so on (b7–20). The virtuous actually "suffer more" at the prospect of death, because they know they have the most to lose (3.9 1117b11–13); the greater their virtue and the happier their lives, the more painful their risk (b10–11). Despite their fear, however, the courageous retain their equanimity and feel no terror (ἀτάραχος, a19, a31, 1115b11; cf. 1116a9).[3] Without eliminating all fear, that enables them to "endure" even what they rightly fear, and to persevere in their chosen course of action in spite of any pain or harm they expect (1117a29–35). But how do the virtuous find the mean in fear, and why are they ready to act in spite of fear?

As in the case of dignity, the key here is the nature of their ends and the way they view them.[4] Courage, on Aristotle's analysis, consists in correctly evaluating both the danger to oneself and the danger to something else, and in accepting the former, even

1. Aristotle restricts courage to facing life-threatening danger (3.6). This makes its range considerably narrower than Socrates proposed (*Laches* 191d), but Aristotle's proposal rests on a more precise analysis of virtuous motives. Every virtue entails being willing to accept some loss in the field of its concern; the temperate, for example, are glad rather than afraid to avoid some physical pleasures. In general, unless the loss envisioned is terrible in the first place, the "courage of one's convictions" is courage only in a weak and derivative sense.

2. The Stoics later emphasized this similarity by counting dignity as a species of courage; see *SVF* 3.264, 269. Cicero often uses *magnanimus* and *fortis* as virtually equivalent (e.g., *TD* 2.43, 4.61, *Off.* 3.99).

3. Aristotle's *ataraxia* corresponds to what Pears (1980: 178–79) calls "behavioral fearlessness."

4. For a more thorough analysis, see Pears 1980: esp. 183–87, to whose discussion my cursory account is indebted. My distinction between the ends of personal safety and of protecting others corresponds to what he calls "the counter-goal" and "the external goal." Pears also distinguishes a third factor, an "internal goal," to cover Aristotle's references to "the noble." I would argue rather that "noble" refers to the external ends that we seek by and for themselves (e.g., protecting others), in contrast with those we seek for ourselves (victory or honor); for the virtuous, noble external goals are "sovereign" in that they always tip the balance, to borrow Pears's image.

though it inspires fear, in order to minimize the latter. The end sought by the courageous, then, is twofold: to protect others—be they family, friends, or an entire community—and to survive. Everyone seeks both of these ends, though in very different proportions; we all wish well to ourselves and at least to some others. When survival is the only thing at stake, it is foolish not to flee; the only good reason for endangering our lives is to protect some larger good. Where courage comes in is in the order of our priorities and the choices we make when the pursuit of other ends endangers our own safety. Cowards seek their own safety more than they should, and the rash risk their own safety more than they should; only the courageous take the right risks for the right ends (3.7). The end the courageous have in view is the safety and well-being of something else besides themselves. Although their concern for its safety does not eliminate their desire to live, it outweighs that desire and moves them to risk their own safety. The basis for courage, then, is a conviction that some other ends are more valuable than our own safety, and courage is shown in choosing to protect those in spite of the fear we feel for ourselves. The courageous differ from others in knowing which ends are more valuable than their own survival, and in acting on behalf of those ends even at the risk of death. That is not to say that they are reckless—that they reckon danger to themselves as naught—but only that they are ready to risk their lives for ends they value more than saving their skin.[5]

Courage is necessary only when the pursuit of other ends interferes with our own safety, only when the best ways to protect those other ends are incompatible with the best means to survival. It thus requires choosing among our ends and sacrificing some for the sake of others. Cowards also make a choice; they too typically sacrifice something they want or value. But whereas cowards forsake and forgo something else in order to protect themselves, the courageous risk their own safety to protect something they value more. Both are motivated by something they value; their choice simply reveals what they value more. In acting to protect others, the courageous are motivated by ends they consider attractive, even if the attraction is "obscured by circumstances" (3.9 1117b1–2). Some attractive reason lies behind

5. Cf. what Williams (1976b: esp. 12–13) calls "ground projects": if G is a ground project for S, then life without G would seem meaningless to S.

every acceptance of risk; the courageous simply take the right risks for the right reasons. To illustrate, Aristotle draws an analogy with athletes. Boxers, although they are sure to get hurt and risk even death, are willing to pay the price in the hope of prizes and honor if they win (b2–6); likewise, the virtuous know their lives are at stake, but they endure their fear and accept the risk "because it is noble or because it is ignoble not to" (b9).[6] If others expose themselves to danger and harm even for fairly insignificant gain (b6), it is easier to see why the virtuous risk death, since the exercise of rational virtue is what they value most. For them, though not for everyone else, it is enough to see their end as noble; even though they risk losing life and happiness itself, which is more than anyone else risks (b10–13), they are willing to continue living only if they act as they think best. Far from refusing to risk their lives, then, the virtuous show courage "presumably even more, because they choose something noble in war instead of the alternative" (b13–15).[7] In doing something they themselves consider noble, they uphold what they prefer over everything else, and not merely because it is admired by others, but because acting nobly is the single end they themselves value most.

Aristotle recognizes that "pleasant activity is not found in all the virtues" (b15–16). Yet he adds that the virtuous find pleasure in courageous action "to the extent that they attain their end" (b16). If their end is wholly external, or if their aim is only to survive, then they will find pleasure only in success or survival; if the only end is winning or protecting others from harm, then defeat or failure removes all room for pleasure. But to the extent that their end is internal to their action and they see their act as valuable because of itself, they can find satisfaction in doing what they want even if their action is painful and they fail. If their end includes, for example, not only victory and success but also

6. Aristotle repeatedly insists that a noble end is the basic motive of courage (1115b12–24, 1116a11–12, b2–3, b18–23, b30–31, 1117a17); cf. IV.ii above, on Spartan bravery.

7. The choice here is between risking one's life for something noble and forsaking that to save one's life; or to put it another way, the antecedent of ἐκείνων is "great goods" (b12), including life itself. The translation of ἀντ' ἐκείνων (b14) is problematic; but the point is the same if it is translated as "choosing the noble *in exchange for* (or at the cost of) life and everything else." On the heroism in this kind of choice, see Hardie 1980: 372–73, 401–4.

doing the best they can to achieve those ends, and if in striving to protect others they also strive to uphold the values on which their way of life is based, then they can be glad of their choice even if they know they are unlikely to enjoy victory or even survive. They know that death is bad in general, or intrinsically bad, but they still are willing to risk it to avoid some alternatives. And although they accept their loss "unwillingly" (ἄκοντι, b8), they do what they prefer in the given situation. Thus, by Aristotle's analysis of "mixed actions," their choice is voluntary as a whole: "for their action is desirable then *when* they act, and the end of an action depends on the occasion [κατὰ τὸν καιρόν]" (3.1 1110a11–14).[8] Socrates, for example, could have avoided condemnation had he agreed to abandon his ethical investigations, but convinced that an unexamined life is not worth living, he refused to change his ways, even to save his life. What he wanted most was to continue living as he had; when that was no longer possible, he chose to continue his ways even at the risk of death, rather than live on without doing what he valued more than any other single end.

Aristotle explores the phenomena of sacrifice from a different angle in his analysis of self-love. Focusing on the perspective of the virtuous themselves, he tries to show more clearly how they see themselves as choosing the greater good. Loving oneself, he concedes, is widely criticized because it is usually equated with seeking one's own good first and foremost, and even at others' expense (*EN* 9.8 1168a29–35). According to some very basic beliefs about friendship, however, we each love and should love ourselves most of all (b1–10). To resolve this dispute, Aristotle distinguishes two forms of self-love, one objectionable and one commendable, according to the sort of ends people seek for themselves.[9] The crucial difference, on his account, lies not in

8. Something that would be involuntary "by itself" and "intrinsically" may be voluntary (3.1 1110a18–21), and something undesirable "by itself" may be desirable "now and instead of these [alternatives]" (b3–7). Hursthouse (1984) uses a notion of "internal compulsion" to show that *what* we feel compelling, not *that* we feel compelled, makes the ethical difference here. Aristotle's account rests on his idea of "intrinsic goods": what is usually or "intrinsically" good (i.e., "by itself") can still be "conditionally" bad in some conditions, and conversely; cf. I.i above, esp. *n*15.

9. Aristotle introduces the topic as a puzzle (1168a28, b10); as Annas (1988b: 4–5) points out, dispute arises only because it seems both that we should love ourselves most and that we should not (note δεῖ, a28, b1). To resolve it, Aristotle

whose good we seek, but in *what* we conceive that good to be: both
forms of self-love consist in assigning oneself what one believes
to be the greater good; people simply disagree about what is best.
People who criticize self-love, he argues, equate it with "assigning oneself more of property, honors, and physical pleasures"
(b15–17). No one is blamed, however, "if he is always concerned
himself [αὐτός] to do what is just or temperate or any other virtuous acts more than anything else, and if in general he always
secures for himself what is noble" (b25–28).[10] Self-love, then,
while often objectionable, can also be virtuous.

Since the first form is much more common, Aristotle claims, it
is what most people mean by self-love (b21–22). Such conduct, he
continues, is rightly criticized, but what everyone finds objectionable is the way in which most people love themselves, not
their self-love itself (b22–23). The second form, although few if
any would call it self-love (b28), not only wins praise but is actually "more self-loving" (b29). Both qualify as love, since each consists in wishing and doing for ourselves things that we believe to
be good, which is Aristotle's standard analysis of loving (b1–5).[11]
We differ, however, in what we take to be best, and hence in what
we wish and do for ourselves: most people are most interested in
pleasure and external goods "in the belief that those are best"
(b17–18), whereas self-lovers of the second kind "assign themselves the noblest and best goods" (b29–30). Although we all are
right at least sometimes and seek things that really are good,
most of us sometimes also seek what is bad, mistaking it for
something good. Money and honor are generally good, but we
often seek them more than we should, even when they are use-

adds precision by distinguishing (b12–13) two forms of self-love in terms of their
ends (see following note), as in the method of reputable views.

10. Translation is crucial here: πάντων (1168b26) refers to kinds of actions,
not to other people (as widely assumed); the preceding lines contrast two sets of
interests and ends without any mention of interpersonal comparison (which follows in b29 only after the two groups have been defined by their ends). Hence,
μάλιστα πάντων means "more than *any other things*," not "more than *anyone else*";
for the problems this reading can generate, see Kraut 1989: 116–23. Cf. b29–30
and 1169a22–32, where the only terms of comparison are options for action; see
also nn13 and 20 below.

11. See, e.g., 8.2 1155b29–56a5 (adopting a reputable view) and 8.3 1156b7–
11 (on perfect love). The precise meaning of this formula has occasioned much
debate; see nn26 and 28 and further below. Aristotle sometimes adds a proviso
"things that we *believe* good" (as in *EE* 7.6 1240a24, *Rhet.* 2.4 1380b36–37; cf.
1155b21–27); it is crucial here.

less, harmful, or wrong. The second group, on the other hand, is right about what is really good, and they always wish and do for themselves what really is good: the virtuous value external goods as they should, and they use them well in accord with justice and the other virtues. Both groups are engaged in actions involving external goods; but whereas most people value such goods as their principal end, the virtuous value them for their use in virtuous action most of all. Finally, since these different interests in the same things involve different forms of desire, Aristotle draws a parallel contrast in terms of the different "parts" of ourselves we favor: those in the first group "favor their appetites and generally their passions and the irrational side of their soul" (b19–21), whereas the virtuous "favor what is most sovereign in them" (b30), which is their mind (b35) and reason generally (1169a1). By favoring the judgments of reason, the virtuous favor their sovereign self, which is who and what they most fully are (1168b30–69a3).[12] The difference between the two forms of self-love is thus twofold, depending both on what ends a person desires most, and on what kinds of desire he or she favors.[13]

Throughout this account, Aristotle emphasizes the self-lover's own perspective rather than any effects either type has on others.[14] But in practice, the virtuous form of self-love also tends to be cooperative and beneficial to others, and the more common form tends to be competitive and harmful to others (a11–14). This is a consequence of his distinction, however, and not the basis for it. For whether self-love leads to conflict between self and others,

12. For some of Aristotle's reasons for equating our rational life with human life, see III.i above. His focus here is on practical reason (note the references to "self-control"), and it is unclear whether he intends to include or require activities of theoretical reason; see Cooper 1975: 169–75 and Kraut 1989: 128–31. The same psychic faculty is at work in either case, though on different objects or in different ways. As Annas (1988b: 4) puts it, "to identify with your practical reasoning . . . is simply to make decisions and commitments based on what developed practical reasoning has worked out, and to regard these as *your* decisions and commitments."

13. Aristotle summarizes the difference in the same two ways: the two groups differ "as much as living by reason differs from living by passion, and desiring what is noble differs from desiring what one believes advantageous" (1169a4–6; cf. a13–18: πάθεσιν as opposed to νοῦς).

14. There is hence no need for Annas (1988b: 11–14) to isolate motive from explanation; that would leave the virtuous a moral "blind spot" and require that their reasons be opaque; they would then know only *that* what they do is right, without knowing *why* it is. See II.iv above, on sovereign virtue.

he argues, depends on one's ends. Those who try to increase their supply of external goods can harm others, since the goods they seek are "fought for" and acquired by competition (1168b19), but those who are most concerned to do what is virtuous are beneficial, because "when everyone strives for the noble and strains to do what is noblest, everything will be as it should be in common, and the greatest goods will belong to each individually" (1169a8–11).[15] Part of the reason for these different effects is scarcity. External goods are typically in limited supply and sought by more people than can have them. To be or become wealthy, we must keep others from using what we have, even if we are productive and increase the supply; for one person to win the honor of a contest or official post, others must lose and do without. The opportunities for virtuous action, however, are not limited in this way, and we can all do what we should without interfering with others doing what they should. Unlike gold, virtuous activity is what Julia Annas calls a "Shelleyan good where to divide is not to take away."[16] But this difference is only incidental: it explains neither why virtuous action would never be scarce nor why the virtuous would not compete with one another for some virtuous actions. Even when the supply of property or honor is abundant, for example, people still compete for it, and some even hoard.

The essential difference depends on how we want "more." Most people want to have more pleasure, wealth, and honor *than they have*; the virtuous simply want to do what is virtuous more *than anything else*. The latter desire rests on qualitative comparison, since it expresses a preference *among options*. But the former desire, although it too rests on a preference for certain things over others, is necessarily quantitative and inherently maximizing.[17] That is why it affects others directly: acquiring more than

15. Translation again risks being prejudicial: I say "strives" (ἁμιλλωμένων) because the word does not *mean* "compete" (see LSJ s.v. II, and note πρός; cf. 8.13 1162b8), although it is often used in connection with contests. Aristotle uses the word partly to underscore this contrast; as Annas (1988b: 8) puts it, he "is reinterpreting the notion of competition." Similarly, the superlative "noblest" is measured by comparison not with other people, but with other options for action. See further below.

16. See Annas 1988b: 8–10, n12 (quoting *Epipsychidion*), and n16.

17. It might seem that the virtuous would also want to maximize virtuous activity, always doing the very best they can and not settling for what is merely good enough. Thus, Aristotle allows that some virtues are less good than others:

one has typically leads to having more *than others have*, and in the event of scarcity, it is bound to leave others with less than they had or might have had, or less than they want, or even less than they deserve. In striving to do what is noble, on the other hand, the virtuous have no desire to outdo anyone else. On the contrary, they would rejoice if everyone else acted as well or better, for then society would function as well as it could and everyone would benefit (a8–11). In one sense, of course, the virtuous always act better than others do: necessarily, those who do what is virtuous do better than those who do not. But their doing better than others, though not an accidental result of their choices, is not the way they see or measure their aim. Rather, they simply choose what they judge best (a17), and the standards by which they decide what is best are not interpersonal comparisons but their own judgment of what is good and right—what it is good for a reasonable human to do. In assigning themselves "more of what is noble" (a35; cf. a28), their aim is not to outdo anyone else, but only to do better than they themselves would do by acting otherwise. For them, this personal best implies doing *better than others* only if those others act otherwise; they always do only *as well as* others who do what is right. This is only as they wish, for the end at which the virtuous aim is not to outdo others but to uphold internal standards of their own. The good life is an object of emulation, not of competition.

To underscore this contrast, and to forestall the objection that the virtuous might compete for the same action, Aristotle adds not only that it can be noble and virtuous to refrain from a virtuous action so that others may do it, but that such omissions can actually be more noble, since "being responsible for a friend's action can be nobler than doing it oneself" (a32–34).[18] Charges of "moral competition" are ill-founded, however, and rest on a myopic view of virtue. When we focus on a single action, there may

---

a temperate diet is not as admirable as courageous heroism or wise leadership, and reflection can make practical virtues look "silly" (10.8 1178b7–18). But this is still a qualitative contrast, and even better types of action are bad if overdone: it is wrong to maximize philosophy if it leads to cowardice or injustice by omission. Thus, the contrast remains: there can be no "excess" in virtuous activity (2.6 1107a20–27), because every virtuous act is good, but the pursuit of pleasure and external goods is always liable to excess.

18. Aristotle here speaks only of yielding to friends, but in his account of dignity, he also claims that the virtuous refrain from doing things when others are already doing them well (4.3 1124b23; see IV.iii *n*25 above).

seem to be room for competition. Once someone saves another's life, there is no chance for anyone else to do exactly the same act; if Crito properly supplies the material needs of Socrates and his family, then it might even be wrong for another to give them more. But once the frame of reference is expanded to include other actions, it is obvious that there is always *something else* for others to do. Both the savior and the saved may need and deserve care, and other lives may still need to be saved; if Crito monopolizes liberality toward Socrates, there is still room to be generous to others as well as to exercise other virtues with him. Thus, although refraining from an action deprives one of doing that act, it can also itself be a form of noble action. If Crito steps aside to let Plato help Socrates, they both do something noble; if the act of omission is nobler for Crito here, then he actually does better than if he had acted by himself.

Virtuous action is a "Shelleyan" good because it is not something we have or acquire but something we do.[19] The supply of resources like gold is externally given, but virtuous activity is creative and productive: instead of taking from the available goods, it adds to the supply. Just as farmers use seed to transform soil into food, so the virtuous put their resources to use in ways that produce the additional good of virtuous activity. This often involves a transfer or exchange of external goods, but it also effects a net gain: although a just return or liberal gift adds nothing to the supply of external goods, it yields the further good of virtuous action. All self-lovers do more of what they want than they would otherwise, but the virtuous never interfere with others by doing more of what they want, since rational virtue is their standard.

It is true that the virtuous do many things for their friends and their city, even if they have to die for them. For they will yield property, honors, and the fought for goods in general, though securing for themselves what is noble. For they would much rather choose to enjoy life intensely for a brief time than mildly for a long time, and to live nobly for a year rather than many years as fortune has it, and to do one great and noble action rather than many minor actions.[20] (*EN* 9.8 1169a18–25)

19. Cf. the argument that happiness (which is virtuous activity) is not a "possession" or "having" (1.8 1098b31–99a7); cf. J. M. Cooper's suggestion, reported in Annas 1988*b*: 18 *n*7.

20. The point of the final sentence is not that the virtuous dislike the routines of normal daily life and long for a noble escape, but that if faced with a choice between risking life for something important and remaining secure by avoiding

In doing this, they "assign themselves the greater good" (a28–29). To be sure, they end up with fewer external goods than they might have had, as they expend their property to help others and forgo opportunities for rewards, honors, and power. But if they put their advantages to good use, Aristotle claims, they actually end up with something better, "since their friends get money [and honors and offices], but they get something noble" (a26–30). Their loss is actually a gain, since they give themselves "more of what is noble" (a35): they act more nobly than they would have otherwise. If their generosity involves external goods, they may also act more nobly than their friend, since it is noble to give but only advantageous to receive (9.7 1168a10–12). But if the friend also goes on to use the gifts well, or if the "gift" is an opportunity for virtuous action in the first place, then the friend may act just as nobly or even more nobly than the giver.[21] In any case, all parties end up with a greater good than they would have had otherwise, and all do what they prefer over *anything else*. Of course, as Aristotle indicates by limiting the case to "everything admirable" (a34–35), the "moral generosity" of yielding virtuous actions to others works only if it really is virtuous to be responsible for someone else doing a given act; if it is cowardly to induce another to take one's place, one ends up with less of the noble than otherwise, and there is no net gain.

When the sacrifice is minor, when all the virtuous lose is some of their property or the duties of public office, their gain is relatively clear. But Aristotle uses the same analysis to explain and justify the phenomenon of mortal sacrifice. Pressing his account to its logical extreme, he argues that in dying for friends or country, the virtuous "choose something *great* and noble for themselves" (a26). On the principle that noble action is a greater good than any external goods, even life itself, making the ultimate sac-

---

needed action, they would rather do what is right than compromise their principles. Without *seeking* opportunities for great acts, they simply refuse to steer their course "as fortune has it" (τυχόντως, 1169a24): they do not depend on fortune, and whatever comes their way, they do as they think best.

21. This is underscored by αὐτόν in a34: the contrast is only between "A doing X" and "A letting B do X," not "B doing X," which may be more, less, or as noble as the first. This is also why Aristotle says "a greater share" (πλέον, a35) rather than "*the* greater share" of noble action. I agree with Price (1989: 111–14) that the notion of "moral generosity" is "radically faulty" if the basis for comparison is interpersonal (getting more than others); it is not incoherent, however, if the comparison is intrapersonal.

rifice turns out to be choosing the greatest good. But how can anyone who dies have a greater good or any good at all?

Aristotle's conclusion has an air of paradox, but its plausibility increases if his view of virtuous choice is accepted. In fact, cases of ultimate sacrifice highlight some common and basic misconceptions about the ends of virtuous action. The key here is that even if those who sacrifice themselves lose everything else, they still do what they themselves want and value most, if virtuous action is their sovereign concern. Obviously, it would be foolish to die for anything that could be enjoyed only after the event. It makes sense to risk life for honor only if we expect to be able to experience the honor we win. The same holds true for external goods in general; if they are our only end, then death precludes us from having or enjoying them, no matter how much our dying actions win. But if our end is not exclusively external, then we attain at least some of what we want even if we die. And if we act not only to effect some change in the world but also to uphold the values that make us who and what we are, then we realize ourselves in our action, no matter what the outcome, and we express our sovereign self in living as we wish and as we choose right through to the end. In dying for what they think right, this is what the virtuous do, for doing what is right is what they prefer more than any other single end. Or as Aristotle puts it, they "choose what is noble over everything else (ἀντὶ πάντων)" (a32).[22] From their perspective at least, which Aristotle thinks the correct one, they actually do better by dying than they would have done by choosing to remain alive. Though giving up what others would prefer, they still do what they want most and get the greater good. Of course, they would prefer not to have to make the ultimate choice, but in the face of some alternatives, sacrifice is what they prefer. Hence, although it is wrong to love oneself as most people do (b2) by seeking and taking a greater share of external goods (1168b16, b19), it is right to love oneself as the virtuous do, since their getting a greater share of virtuous action not only does not interfere with the well-being of others but actually improves, materially and socially and ethically, both their own and others' lives.

22. An alternative translation would be "they choose what is noble at every [hence any] cost"; cf. *n7* above, on the courageous choosing what is noble ἀντ' ἐκείνων (1117b14–15).

The significance of Aristotle's distinctions will appear more clearly if they are compared to the notorious contrast between egoism and altruism. Both terms are used in many different senses, and it is difficult to define either precisely. One distinction that is crucial here is between psychological egoism as a claim about what people actually do and ethical egoism as a claim about what they should do. My interest here is in how the virtuous themselves view their choices when they sacrifice what most people would call their own interests.[23] In one sense, my question is whether psychological egoism is true of them; my aim is to clarify how the virtuous view their choices, not to define the criterion by which they decide what to do. However, since their choices are governed by their views on how people should act, my question is also whether they endorse ethical egoism. Since Aristotle thinks their views correct, that implicitly raises the question whether he endorses ethical egoism. My primary question is how the virtuous view their own choices, but the answer has implications for Aristotle's ethical theory.

For the present argument, let egoists be understood as those who always act in pursuit of their own good, regardless of how they think their actions may affect others. Their actions may benefit others, but they see no independent value in such results. Altruism could be equated with the simple contradictory, having some regard for how our actions affect others at least sometimes. But it will be helpful to equate it rather with the contrary: altruists act at least sometimes for the benefit of others, *regardless or even in spite of what they themselves want*.[24] My question, then, is whether Aristotle considers the virtuous egoists or altruists. The self-lovers he and others criticize—those who favor their appetites and passions—look very much like egoists: they are selfish about

23. Putting the point in terms of interests can mislead unless subjective interests (what one wants and is interested in) are distinguished from objective interests (what is in fact good for one): as I distinguish them, egoists pursue the former without regard for the latter, altruists sacrifice the former for the latter, and only for the virtuous do the two regularly coincide. Some of the difficulties in defining these contrasts are analyzed in Williams 1973.

24. It is questionable whether altruism as here described is psychologically possible, whether anyone can do anything without seeing it as good in some way. If not, the contrast could be drawn as follows: altruists are motivated to help others only by an entirely general desire to do the right thing, and they see no gain at all for themselves in their action, whereas the virtuous see their action as "giving them a greater good" than any they lose.

external goods, and they seek to have more of them, often without regard for what their actions may leave for others. The self-love he praises, however, is not a form of altruism, for the virtuous are not selfless or meek, and the acts they do for others are still what they themselves want most to do. Rather, they fit the contradictory of egoism, which I shall call egocentrism: they forgo some of the things they want, but in doing so, they see their actions as part of doing what they value more.[25] Unlike egoists they sometimes act for others, but unlike altruists they do this at least in part because they see it as one aspect of leading the sort of life they want to live and as necessary for being the sort of people they want to be. In acting for others, altruists sacrifice what they would rather have, but the virtuous, far from sacrificing what they think best, still do what they value most. They often choose the same actions as altruists, but only they make their choices on the basis of what they want most. And although their action is always an expression of their regard for themselves, it is only self-centered, since the circle of their interests also embraces the good of others. Egoists and altruists, then, though they usually act very differently, agree that external goods are the best they can have: the selfish and the selfless alike view their choices in terms of external ends, and they differ only in how much they seek these ends for themselves. The virtuous seek different ends from the start: the exercise of rational virtue is what they think best, and since that is their sovereign concern, their reasons for action are self-centered rather than selfless.

The clearest example of egocentrism is Aristotle's analysis of love and friendship. Loving someone, as he regularly puts it, consists in wishing good things to another for his or her sake (ἐκείνου ἕνεκα).[26] But this formula exploits his standard phrase

25. Egocentrists always choose to act for *some* end of their own and for *something* they value. Irwin (1977: 254–59) uses "egocentrism" in a similar way to name an *ethical* thesis; what I call egoism is a *psychological* version of what he calls "moral solipsism." Kraut (1989: 78–86) distinguishes three varieties of egoism, but his taxonomy does not easily map onto mine, since he does not define them by the kinds of ends they prefer. Thus, my "egocentrists" differ from his "pure egoists" in attaching some weight to the good of others, though not any "independent weight," since action for the good of others is one of their own ends; and egocentrists are neither "combative" nor "benign" egoists since they value others' *material* welfare independently of their own material welfare, but not independently of their own happiness and virtuous activity.

26. Aristotle's analysis is notoriously obscure; see n28 below. For present purposes, I distinguish only two elements: viewing the friend as a recipient of good

for specifying the final ends for which we act and which we value "by themselves." It thus implies that we view the well-being of each of our friends as ends of our own. In many of our interactions with others, of course, we wish them well only or primarily because they serve some other end of our own, and we harbor ulterior motives for valuing their well-being. Aristotle singles out relations of utility and enjoyment, in which we wish others well primarily because we expect them to help us in some way or because we enjoy their company. Here, the primary "objects of liking" (φιλητά) are the particular advantages or enjoyment we expect from our friends, not the friends themselves; our end in these cases is something we acquire or feel, not something beyond us such as the good of another person (EN 8.2 1155b17–21). In at least some of our personal relations, however, we want others to fare and do well no matter what we might gain if our wishes are fulfilled, and we want this so much that we regularly act to realize this end. In these paradigmatic cases of love and friendship, we value the well-being of another person primarily because we see both the other person and his or her well-being each as something good by itself. When we act for the sake of these ends, therefore, our motive is not egoistic, for our primary aim is not to obtain any pleasure or external good for ourselves. Nor is it altruistic, since the other's well-being is something we value and want very much. Rather, it is egocentric, since we count the other's good as an end of our own for which we want to act, and we view the pursuit of this end as a major part of leading the life we most want to live. Our own happiness is still our ultimate end and virtuous activity our central or sovereign end, but the full circle of our ends also encompasses the other's well-being.[27]

The egocentric basis for love and friendship is in some ways so clear that moral concerns may seem to have no place. In particular, our intimate relations are so clearly part of *our lives* that they may seem not to rest on concern for *others*. In some cases, how-

---

and the beneficiary of our action (ἐκείνῳ), and viewing the friend's welfare as the purpose for which we act and an end of our own (ἐκείνου ἕνεκα).

27. For a detailed analysis of how this works in practice, see Price 1989: 114–30. After concluding that "notional egoism, directed at my own *eudaimonia*, becomes practical altruism, since my *eudaimonia* and [my friend's] overlap," Price states what in effect is a version of egocentrism: "Your activity may at the same time be myself in action, and your acting well part of my own *eudaimonia*" (p. 124).

ever, moral concerns are part of the basis for love. Aristotle argues that the best friendships are found among the virtuous, who love their friends for who they are and what they do—in short, for their good character. And presumably, we all approach this kind of love to the extent that we like other persons not only for what we get from them but also for who each of them is and because we admire the good talents or traits each has.[28] Unlike relations based primarily on what others can do for us, these relations do have a moral element: they rest on judgments about character, and they involve concern for another's good. But all friendship, virtuous or not, remains personal, and it is linked to our concern for our own lives in such a way that any impartial moral concern must remain limited in extent. In particular, this account of love offers no reason to think that the virtuous would ever act for anyone outside their circle of friends. For anyone to have broader moral concerns, their egocentrism must extend further.

Aristotle's analysis of "goodwill" (εὔνοια) shows part of what is missing. Goodwill "resembles" love because it consists in wishing good to people we know only slightly or distantly (*EN* 9.5 1166b30–67a5), whom we admire without regard for anything we expect to get from them (a12–18). Although inspired by ethical judgments and a recognition of some sort of virtue in others (a18–21), this still falls short. Goodwill is only "idle love" because it does not extend to action: "People only wish good to those for whom they have goodwill, but they would not do anything with them or take any trouble for them" (a8–12). Admiring others and wishing them well is one step, but the question is whether the virtuous also act on others' behalf. Only if they are willing in at least some cases to limit their own pursuits in order to serve the good of others, only then do moral obligations fall within the circle of their egocentrism.

The question here is about nothing less than the limits of moral obligation. But since detailing Aristotle's views on this

28. It is unclear how exactly Aristotle thinks "virtue-friendship" is related to the more general class of "character-friendship"; see Cooper 1977 and Price 1989: chap. 5. The three forms of friendship correspond loosely to the tripartition of goods (see II.iii *n*5 above): external goods such as property and prestige are the basis for "utility-friendship," physical and sexual appetites are common motives for "pleasure-friends" (cf. 9.12 1172a1–4), and goods of the soul attract "character-friends."

huge topic would distract from my central question about the
motives for virtuous action, I shall illustrate his position by looking at one area in public life where he locates specifically moral
concern. The virtues of liberality, magnificence, dignity, and
courage require sacrificing some of our own resources and advantages in order to help others, and not only for friends and
close relations. But one of the widest forms of concern for others
appears in Aristotle's brief account of "unanimity" (ὁμόνοια),
where we find not only action for others but also the sort of moral
concern associated with friendship, although without its intimacy or personal attachment. Unanimity is implicit among
friends (EE 7.7 1241a15–16), but it can also extend to larger
groups and, ideally, to entire communities: "Cities are said to
have unanimity when they have the same *judgments* about what
is advantageous, when they *decide* on the same things, and when
they *do* what they have jointly decided" (EN 9.6 1167a26–28).
Even in this extended form, then, it resembles love enough to be
dubbed "civic friendship."²⁹ As Aristotle's sketch shows, this
threefold conformity of judgment, decision, and action involves
much more than civility: it supplements goodwill with both a
willingness to act and actual performance. Although it requires
none of the intimacy of friendship or love, it consists in a similar
broad agreement about practical affairs and the good life (cf. a22–
26). Civic friends do not share all the same interests, of course,
but they must at least agree about the distribution of important
but limited public goods, civic posts above all (a28–b2, EE 7.7
1241a27–32). But to agree about the common good and control
over public policy is to agree about the relation of political authority to private life and hence in turn about the limits on private
pursuit of external goods (note πλεονεξίας, EN 9.6 1167b10) and
the scope of private obligations toward others (such as public
works, b11–12). Unanimity, in short, consists in agreement about
the nature of political and social justice (b8–9). This ethical consensus, however, occurs most among the virtuous, who "both

29. The title is not Aristotle's invention (φαίνεται . . . καθάπερ καὶ λέγεται,
9.6 1167b2–3); cf. φιλικόν (a22–25), 8.1 1155a22–28, EE 7.7 1241a32–33, and Xenophon Mem. 4.4.16. Unanimity qualifies as a form of friendship by meeting four
accepted criteria, though only in diminished degree: citizens who have unanimity value one another's well-being and lives, they live together, and they share
some joys and sorrows (EN 9.4 1166a2–8; see below). For a more thorough analysis of civic friendship and related topics, see Price 1989: 193–205.

value what is just and advantageous and seek these together" (b4–9), and least among the bad, who "seek more than their share of benefits but fall short in labors and liturgies" (b9–12; cf. *EE* 7.7 1241a21–27). By implication, then, the virtuous have greater concern for the good of others than anyone else does, and they have sufficient "friendship" toward the rest of the community both to claim only the goods they need and should have, and also to support the interests of other members and to defend those whose claims are threatened or harmed.

The motives for unanimity are far from selfish because it requires some sacrifice of one's own external resources. But its close connection with friendship shows that it is not purely altruistic either. Rather, Aristotle's account illustrates egocentrism because, in acting from unanimity, we show sufficient care for others to value their good as an end of our own. Among the virtuous especially, this community of values and action links egocentrism to morality in ways that extend beyond dispassionate belief to action and feeling. The unanimity of the virtuous also shows how their egocentrism is impartial without being impersonal. Unlike friendship, it requires no personal ties, precludes any favoritism, and decides always on what is just. Like the best friendship, however, its concern for others is personal as well as moral, and although typically less intense than love, its care extends to action in the same way that love does. Whereas egoists show partiality in seeking their own good and altruists see no personal gain in upholding the good of others, the virtuous are personally attracted to others' good but seek it only impartially. More than any enlightened self-interest, which acquiesces in present losses only in the essentially selfish hope of future gains, this impartial but personal egocentrism highlights the distinctive motives for virtuous concern: like the temperate, the self-centered do what they want most in doing as they should. The selfish, by contrast, resemble the unrestrained in doing what they want but not as they should, and the selfless, who do what they know to be right but still prefer what they lose, are at best only continent. Only altruists, then, sacrifice what they think is their own best interest. Egoists and egocentrists, though they have radically different views about where their best interest lies, both seek what they take it to be.

The self-love of the virtuous is egocentric. The exercise of ra-

290 VIRTUES IN ACTION

tional virtue is what they think best, and since that is their sovereign concern, their reasons for action are self-centered rather than selfless. But since the virtuous are right, Aristotle's theory is a version of ethical egocentrism. That is only natural, given the sovereignty of virtue. Virtuous activity, which includes but is not limited to moral action, is the best single good, though not the only good, in human life. Because the virtuous know this, they value the exercise of rational virtue more than anything else. That is not to say that all egocentrism is right. Most of us, quite likely, are neither selfless nor purely selfish, and we see the good of some others as part of our own, although we may act for them too rarely and for the good of too few. Egocentrism itself says nothing about the limits of moral obligation, and how to balance using external goods for ourselves and for others. Although major questions of practical morality remain open, Aristotle's account of self-love does show that the line between our own good and the good of others is rarely as sharp as contrasts between egoism and moral altruism suggest. By showing how the virtuous view acting for the good of others as *part* of their own happiness, he finds a place in eudaimonism for moral virtues and provides a way to see acting for others as an integral part of our own good.

Aristotle's analysis of virtuous action, even with his detailed remarks about the several virtues, fails to provide a complete picture of ethical life. But this may be an inevitable shortcoming of theory. After all, to gain understanding from ethical theory, as he is wont to say, we must already have fairly wide and detailed knowledge about ethical life and what is good and bad. That is where Aristotle thinks we should turn to settle questions of application, of when to act for the good of others as part of our own, and of when to risk our lives for what ends. But if the criteria for deciding what to do when for whom remain unclear, his account of self-love does map out the psychology of virtuous choice in ways that clarify the paradox of heroism and self-sacrifice. By looking at the lives of the virtuous from their own perspective, he shows how the virtuous can be happy even when everyone else would doubt they could. By pointing to some of the good they expect to retain even when their actions are not successful, he shows how they can maintain what they value most even when they live without the favor of fortune, even when traditional views would count them miserable. How then does sovereign virtue bear on happiness, and what basis does it leave for a continued good life even in the event of misfortune?

The continued exercise of rational virtue is the basis of the virtuous response to fortune. Anyone who ceased to exercise virtue, of course, would no longer meet Aristotle's criterion for happiness. But the motives on which the virtuous act are the basis for calling them happy in a more conventional sense as well. Aristotle offers a craft analogy to clarify his point: artisans of all sorts, if their talent is great, can continue doing fine work even when deprived of their preferred resources (*EN* 1.10 1101a3–6). In the same way, "the truly good and wise" retain the beliefs and values to which their actions give expression; if they continue to act for some of what they value most, they may still find joy in their life even when left with meager resources or struck by grievous loss. Aristotle concedes that disaster can ruin a life (a9–11). But his aim is only to show how it is *possible* to remain happy by upholding one's sovereign concerns; happiness is never invulnerable, but sovereign virtue and dignity, which are more secure than anything else in human life, make a good life as secure as any can be (1100b7–22). It lies beyond the compass of theory to say precisely how much misfortune and grief anyone can endure. In the end, only the virtuous can say whether they are happy or not, for only they can say whether they find sufficient joy in their lives. But whatever their answer, they remain clear of the depths of unhappiness and despair. "If one's activities are sovereign over one's life, as we said, then no one who is happy would become miserable, since they will never do hateful or base things. For we think that truly good and thoughtful people bear all their fortunes gracefully and always do the finest out of what is available" (1100b33–1101a3).

Aristotle's reason for denying that those who have complete and sovereign virtue ("the truly good and thoughtful") ever reach a state of "misery" is initially puzzling: they never do anything "hateful or base" (τὰ μισητὰ καὶ τὰ φαῦλα).[30] If this is an exclusively ethical reason, it begs the question about happiness;

---

30. In conventional usage, "misery" is not the absence of happiness but its contrary, and although it was thought that anyone, even the happiest, could end up "miserable" (ἄθλιος, 1100b34), no one could be happy at the same time; cf. Irwin 1985a: 415.

if it refers only to actions, it fails even to address the possibility that people who *do* nothing bad can still *feel* miserable. The scope of his claim, however, is limited to the virtuous; since they know what is bad, they can recognize bad actions as bad and respond with aversion accordingly. As his reference to "hateful" suggests, the reason why the virtuous can never end up miserable has a psychological dimension as well: they never do anything they themselves "hate" and despise. Of course, since the basis for hate is a judgment that something is bad—that it is of a bad sort (*Rhet.* 2.4 1382a3–7)—hate has an ethical dimension too. But hate is a passion, and although it does not entail constant pain (a12–13), it does entail desire, or rather aversion. Just as love consists in wishing good for others and acting for them, so hate consists in wishing ill for them and acting against them.[31] Hence, people who do something they themselves hate are sure to wish themselves ill, or at least to experience a sort of divided self, resenting the side of their self that did what they hate. So if the virtuous were to do anything hateful, they would hate their action and themselves.

Aristotle's point here is not limited to what the virtuous do; it also characterizes their attitudes toward themselves. To show that shame (αἰδώς) is not a virtue, for example, Aristotle denies that being ashamed of doing something "bad" (φαῦλον) or "shameful" (αἰσχρόν) is a sign of virtue (*EN* 4.9 1128b19–34), since the virtuous "will never willingly do bad things [τὰ φαῦλα]" (b28–29). And since shame is felt only in response to actions done willingly (b28), that implies further that the virtuous have no occasion for shame. Similarly, whereas the low self-esteem of the meek exposes them to shame and self-reproach by causing them to refrain from doing even things they see to be noble, the virtuous have sufficient self-confidence to do as they know they should and hence to avoid the potentially debilitating pain of self-reproach.[32] Thus, Aristotle's claim that the virtuous never become miserable as a result of bad fortune has both an active and an emotive side. First, they never become corrupt or do anything vicious. Second, by always acting willingly for what they value most, they retain their self-respect and re-

31. Aristotle nowhere offers an explicit analysis of hate, but my formulation is implied by his analysis of love.

32. On self-respect, see IV.iii above; on shame, see II.iv n24 above.

main free of the unhappiness of shame and remorse. Their continued pursuit of virtuous ends, in fact, can sustain their happiness not only by sparing them self-hatred, but also by securing them the self-love that comes from doing as they think best. There is a close link, then, between the way we evaluate our own actions and the satisfaction or happiness we find in our lives. Aristotle analyzes this link in his discussion of self-love. Drawing a sharp contrast between the love the virtuous have for themselves and the feelings of self-regard everyone else has, he argues that people love themselves if and only if they respect themselves as good. Several features of love show, he claims, that most people—with the exception of the utterly wicked—display some degree of self-love, but only "to the extent that they are content with themselves [ἀρέσκουσιν ἑαυτοῖς] and believe themselves respectable [ἐπιεικεῖς]" (*EN* 9.4 1166b2–6).[33] Although virtually everyone loves himself, the virtuous actually do so most of all; or to give the claim an air of paradox, egocentrism involves greater care for oneself than egoism does. More to the point, virtuous self-love is inherently more fulfilling, and the virtuous maintain a sort of reservoir of satisfaction to sustain them come what may. Before looking at Aristotle's defense of his claim, however, the scope of his contrast needs to be clarified. Unlike Plato, who typically draws his contrast in extreme terms and argues at length that tyrants are actually "miserable,"[34] Aristotle contrasts the virtuous with "most people," who are neither wholly good nor wholly bad. But to dismiss the utterly wicked without further argument seems to beg part of the question, for contrary to his allegation that "the utterly bad and impious neither have *nor are thought to have*" any self-love (b5–6), it was a common worry that tyrants, who were widely thought to exemplify the worst vices, lead the best life because they are free to do whatever they wish. Or in Aristotle's terms, the wholly vicious seek the wrong ends and act on the wrong values, but rather than feeling any qualms about their actions, they seem likely to rejoice because they wholly endorse their choices. So in some ways, it simplifies Aris-

33. Aristotle presents his account as based on reputable views ("they define," a2, a10; "they posit," a3; "others say," a6; δοκεῖ, a32, a34; φαίνεται, b2, b6).

34. Most of the *Gorgias* is an attempt to refute the grandiose claims made by Polus and Callicles for the tyrant Archelaus and his ilk (see esp. 470c–72e), and the *Republic* is a response to similar claims given their sharpest contours by Glaucon.

totle's argument to exclude the wicked; by focusing on "the many," he can cite their psychic conflict and the internal strife they suffer when torn between better and worse impulses. But this focus also enables him to defend stronger claims, that everyone but the virtuous suffers from some form of self-reproach, and that all flaws of character interfere with self-love and happiness. And although part of his argument appeals to the phenomena of incontinence and weakness of will, he also argues that all but the virtuous are bound to experience conflict within desires even of the same kind.[35] It could then be argued, a fortiori, that the wholly bad suffer much worse, although Aristotle does not develop this thesis here. Rather, the picture he draws of "the bad" is of people with some ethical failings who still have some knowledge of what is good and feel some attraction toward it.

To defend his picture, Aristotle examines four common marks of love and argues that all of them are found in virtuous people's relations with themselves but none occur in the bad.[36] First is his standard formula for friendship, "wanting and doing things for the friend's sake" (1166a3–4). By this criterion, self-love requires wishing and doing good for oneself. The good and the bad do both, but in very different ways and favoring different parts of themselves: the former are egocentrics, the latter egoists. Thus, it is a major source of reproach, as Aristotle observes later, that the bad "do everything for their own sake" (9.8 1168a31–33), that is,

35. Observing that much of Aristotle's argument seems aimed at incontinence, Irwin (1985a: 367–68) argues that prudent intemperance is bound to cause conflict and regret. But this defense of Aristotle also explains why he excludes "the utterly bad," for it rests on the conflict between a vice and the virtue at least of "good planning." Aristotle could explain his neglect of tyrants in a similar way: even the worst are likely to have some traces of virtue, since it takes courage, self-control, and cleverness to acquire power in the first place and some justice toward their cronies to keep them on their side. Socrates, for example, tries to convince Thrasymachus that even a band of villains needs enough fellow feeling to remain a band (*Rep.* 1.351c–52a; cf. 1167b10 on unanimity).

36. Irwin (1985a) distinguishes five marks by dividing the third; cf. Stewart 1892 on 1166a1. This upsets the order in an otherwise entirely systematic presentation: Aristotle first lists the marks, then argues that the virtuous have them but others do not, each time in the same order, whereas Irwin's fourth mark appears first in each half of the following argument. Nor does the parallel discussion in *EE* 7.6 distinguish Irwin's further criterion, though it lists the same four marks in the same order. Rather, as grammar confirms (note δή in a15, γάρ in b8; τόν in a7 links Irwin's third and fourth criteria), Aristotle presents the inner unity or conflict mentioned at the opening of each series (a13–14, b6–7) as part of the first mark (wishing and doing well) and counts "choosing the same" as an expression of the third (cf. *n*42 below).

they favor their appetites and passions (9.4 1166b7–10, 9.8 1168b15–21). The good, however, favor the values approved by their sovereign reason (9.4 1166b16–17, 9.8 1168b30–69a6). Since Aristotle's pluralistic model of the soul ensures some potential for conflicting desires, it may be that neither group does all and only what they want. He would argue, of course, that reason and rational desire are what we are most of all (9.4 1166a17; cf. 10.7 1178a2–8); even if the virtuous have conflicting desires, they do what their true or sovereign self wants. But instead of relying on this move here, he also argues that the virtuous are free of conflicting desires in the first place, because they are fully integrated: they "are of one mind with themselves and want the same things with all their soul" (9.4 1166a13–14). Only the bad are divided and in conflict with themselves: they "differ with themselves, and they have an appetite for one thing but value something else" (b7–8). The source of competing desires here is not any change over time, but simply a division within the self: the bad follow their appetites (ἐπιθυμοῦσιν) rather than their reasoned desires (βούλονται), and "instead of choosing what they think is good, they choose pleasures that actually harm them" (b7–10). So far as they see what is good and what they should do, they are weak-willed and "like the incontinent" (b8) rather than mistaken. Even if they decide to do what they think is good, they often lack the conviction to carry through because they have opposing appetites. This internal conflict can be so painful that whereas the virtuous "persevere" in their pursuits (a16), the bad regularly "refrain from doing even what *they suppose* to be best" (b10–11). Or as he adds further on, "their soul is in revolt [στασιάζει],[37] and one part suffers because of vice as it holds back from some things, while the other is pleased; and while one part drags them this way, the other drags them that way as if tearing them apart" (b19–22). Whether they choose something harmful in the first place or abandon their good choices later, they cause themselves dissatisfaction and regret by wanting something other than what they do or have. The virtuous, in contrast, do as they think best; whether or not they achieve their external ends, they have a steady inner source of satisfaction in their constant integrity and unity of purpose.

37. The image of internal revolt or *stasis* refers to a struggle for control within a single individual or collective body; cf. 9.6 1167a33–b16.

A second criterion of love, closely related to the first, is valuing the survival and well-being of the beloved (9.4 1166a4–5). Aristotle's examples emphasize a deep concern and care, such as mothers feel for their children (a5–6),[38] and he develops the contrast in ways that highlight both the dignity of the virtuous, and the paradoxical disregard for life that many others often have. He claims, of course, that the virtuous have this form of self-love in the highest degree. But remarkably, he explains his point in a way that alludes to self-sacrifice, which seems a very odd way to illustrate their love of life.

> The virtuous want themselves to live and to survive, and especially that by which they think. For existence is good for the virtuous, and each wishes good things for himself. But no one chooses to have everything by becoming someone else—for a god has a good life even in the present—but by being what it is. And each is thought to be, or to be especially, what does the thinking.   (9.4 1166a17–23)[39]

The example of a god points in more than one direction, but the principal point has to do with a problem of personal identity. Having just argued that the virtuous act "on behalf of their thinking part" (a17), he now extends the claim to show why they are unwilling to save their skin at any cost. Although they love life and want very much to live, they love *their* life—their *way of life* or "what living is for them" (9.12 1172a1–2)—still more. Since rational activity is the essence of their life and what they value most of all, they have no desire to stay alive if it means violating the very nature of their life, even if they could then have every other good ("everything," 1166a21). Moreover, just as the gods always enjoy a good life because of their constant rational activity, so the

38. Aristotle often cites maternal love as a paradigm of deep and unselfish love, as again in the following lines (1166a8–9); cf. 8.8 1159a28–33, 8.12 1161b18–29, 9.7 1168a23–26, and *EE* 7.8 1241b4–9.

39. The text here is problematic, partly for want of punctuation: Bywater's (1894) parenthesis should include the following six words (as in Michael of Ephesus, 481.17–25); τἀγαθόν (1166a22, rather than τἀγαθά, as in a20) refers to happiness (cf. 1094a22, 1098a20); and there is no need to remove the phrase bracketed by most editors, since it makes no difference in sense (it would be the subject of ἔχειν): "no one wants [after becoming someone else] *that thing he has become* [ἐκεῖνο τὸ γενόμενον] then to have everything" (1166a20–21). Finally, although the example of a god recalls 8.7, the point is rather different here: there we do not wish our friends to become as good as gods (1159a3–12), but here we do not wish to give up what semblance of divine life we have by yielding to lower impulses. Thus, despite modern doubts, it is wrong to dismiss the ancient commentators here, esp. Michael, 480.23–481.28.

virtuous can find happiness "even in the present" (a21) because of the kind of life they lead. But if their activity is like the activity of the gods, which is the best life of all, they see no reason to stay alive by doing and becoming something less and worse. So when the survival of their reason and virtue is at stake, they refuse to save their lives by changing who they are.

Like rational virtue in this respect, the values of "most people" can also make them willing to die. In every other way, however, the contrast here could not be sharper. Whereas the virtuous love their life, the bad can drive themselves to despair: "Those who have done terrible things and are hated because of their vice both shun life and destroy themselves" (b11–13).[40] In contrast with the virtuous, who love themselves and wish to continue living as they do, the bad hate themselves and wish their lives would either change or end. Whether or not Aristotle's words refer to suicide, they imply acting in ways that are virtually suicidal, as well as at least a rashness based on slight concern for one's own life. In one sense, then, the virtuous and the bad both act for what they value most: the virtuous uphold their life of rational virtue; the bad pursue the pleasures or gain they value most, or they flee the pains they think are worse than death. There remains, however, a vast difference between virtuous self-sacrifice and reckless self-destruction. The virtuous risk their lives only to preserve the life they always want to lead, but the bad risk death merely for temporary pleasures or to gratify their passing desires. Whereas the virtuous are only "willing" to die and do their best to fend off death, the bad seem sometimes eager for death or even embrace it as an escape.[41] The bad still love something of

40. I follow Bywater's (1894) punctuation, which would be guaranteed if M and the Latin are correct (L would guarantee a comma after πέπρακται, but leave the first καί in b12 unexplained), not only for sense (acts and self-hatred lead to self-destruction), but also to balance the clauses. The verb μισοῦνται, though passive in form and sense, implies self-hatred as well: people who are hated end up destroying themselves only if they also hate themselves; cf. ἐχθρὸν εἶναι ἑαυτῷ (Rep. 1.352a) as opposed to εὐκόλως ἑαυτῷ (330a). On the bad wishing they could change their ways, even when it takes more than wishing to change, see EN 3.5 1114a11–21 and White 1988: 227–28.

41. Aristotle indicates elsewhere some of the external goods that he thinks absurd to value more than life itself: people who recklessly go to any length to gratify their lust display "the courage of asses," which stubbornly refuse to stop eating even if flogged (EN 3.8 1116b34–17a2); courage requires a noble end, and it is cowardice rather than courage to die merely to escape poverty, erotic passion, or pain (3.7 1116a12–15).

themselves, but there is also much they hate both in what they have done and in what they have become (b11–12)—sometimes so much that they detest their very lives. Self-hatred or self-resentment is the rationale Aristotle gives for their self-destructive ways: in their misery, the bad may decide that the ends they have sought are not worth pursuing, and hence their own lives not worth continuing. Worse than miserable, they can end up dead. As in his response to Solon, where he argues that the virtuous never become miserable because they never do anything they hate (1.10 1100b30–35), the contrast he draws here shows why happiness depends on our own actions rather than on our fortunes, and why our evaluations of our own character and deeds can decide whether we are happy or miserable, or somewhere in between.

Aristotle uses the remaining two marks of love to show how the virtuous retain integrity and equanimity and how, even in the absence of the divided self and chronic inner conflict of incontinence, the bad suffer for doing what they want. First, the virtuous exemplify the kind of intimacy many consider "most characteristic of love" (μάλιστα φιλικόν, 8.6 1158a1–10; cf. 9.10 1171a2), namely, sharing time and activities with the beloved (9.4 1166a7).[42] In self-love, this reduces to spending time alone with oneself. That leads to the paradox that the bad, who "search for people with whom to share their days and try to escape themselves" (b13–14), seem more sociable than the good, who "value spending time by themselves, since they do it with pleasure" (a23–24). But the paradox rests on confusion, as Aristotle shows by explaining the motives at work in each case. The virtuous enjoy recalling what they have done, their expectations for a continued good life give them pleasure, and in a word, "they are well supplied with things to think about" (a24–27).[43] One benefit they

42. Aristotle concludes his lengthy discussion of love and friendship with an attempt to explain why this is the surest sign (9.12): "the exercise [ἐνέργεια] of love occurs in living together" (1171b35, summarizing 9.9), and "people want to engage together with their friends in whatever existence is for them and in the things for which they choose to live" (1172a1–3). As his examples show, this is what he means by "choosing the same things" (1166a8): drinkers drink together, philosophers think together. Cf. Pol. 3.9 1280b35–39.

43. The terms here (θεωρημάτων εὐπορεῖ, a26) recall the claim that "the truly good man, four-square without blame, will always—or more than anything else—do and think about [πράξει καὶ θεωρήσει] virtuous things" (EN 1.10 1100b19–22). This includes, but is not limited to, the claim that the virtuous can

derive from being self-centered, then, is that having done what they should is always a source of satisfaction. Moreover, their sustained concern for their ends pulls them forward to further self-expression and the further exercise of their virtues. The bad, on the other hand, seek company to "forget themselves," so bad do they find both their memories and their prospects (b15–17). Dislike of themselves for how they have acted in the past and for what they expect, rather than any care for others, is what drives them into the company of others. The point of Aristotle's contrast, then, is not that the virtuous enjoy solitude more than they enjoy their friends, but that they can enjoy solitude more than others do. The initial paradox has been replaced by another, and one that is inescapable: the bad love themselves in ways that drive them away from themselves. A major cost of egoism, it turns out, is alienation, for in addition to anxiety over both their past and their future, the bad, "having nothing likable [φιλητόν], feel nothing characteristic of love [φιλικόν] toward themselves" (b17–18).

In his discussion of the fourth mark of love, Aristotle develops this paradox of egoism further. If sharing the joys and sorrows of someone else indicates love for that person (9.4 1166a7–8), then self-love entails a similar unity of emotional response within ourselves. Since he has already argued that the virtuous enjoy an effective unanimity of desire at any one time, Aristotle focuses here on unanimity over time. Stability of character entails stable values, hence a consistent emotional response, and the virtuous are pleased or pained always by the same sorts of things (a27–29). They are, in short, "virtually without regrets" (a29). The contrast with the bad, according to Aristotle, could scarcely be more stark. Even apart from any conflict they may experience in the present, the bad "teem with regret" (b24–25). Typically, they are "torn" in opposite directions as they deliberate and act (b21). But even if they are wholly committed to their actions, even if they achieve temporary unanimity, they eventually come to regret

---

reflect or "withdraw into themselves"; cf. Nussbaum 1986: 325–26. In addition to thinking about what is somehow absent (memories, plans, remote people and events, literature, theories), the virtuous also "observe" (one sense of θεωρεῖν) and think about people and events around them; cf. the argument that the virtuous need friends in part in order "to observe [θεωρεῖν] fair and familiar actions" (9.9 1169b28–70a4).

their choices. Even if simultaneous pain and pleasure are impossible and one can succeed the other only "after a little bit," they are often "pained *because* they had pleasure, and they wish they had not found those things pleasant" (b22–24). It is one thing to wish that fortune had been kinder, that events had gone better, or that others had acted otherwise; the virtuous are not entirely immune to such "external regret."[44] But it is something quite different to wish that one had chosen and acted otherwise, to reproach oneself, and to condemn the very values and desires by which one was motivated. To feel resentment toward oneself for one's own past actions implies a sense of self-betrayal, and this "internal regret," which amounts to the guilty conscience of remorse, verges on self-hatred rather than self-love.[45] The virtuous, by contrast, not only avoid the pain of remorse at having betrayed themselves and their basic values or ends but also find constant satisfaction in upholding the essential and sovereign concerns of their lives. If they also survive, they can enjoy the retrospective satisfaction of their having upheld those concerns.

If Aristotle fails to show that the bad are "extremely miserable" (1166b27), he has shown at least why they often dislike major parts of their lives and themselves. This shortage of self-love, which sometimes verges on self-hatred, still gives good reason to "flee vice strenuously and try to be fair," as he concludes in a hortatory tone, "since in this way one would both be loving toward oneself and become friends with others" (b27–29). Misery, on his account, stems not from misfortune and faring poorly in external affairs but from thinking ill of oneself and one's actions. Alongside his account of happiness as virtuous activity, then, he isolates an active form of unhappiness. And since his argument centers on love and hatred and the complex beliefs and values behind these attitudes, the contrast he draws is not narrowly

44. Aristotle's description of the regret felt by the vicious turns on a division between rational desires or values (ἐβούλετο, 1166b24) and the appetites and passions. Although this source of regret is alien to virtue, even the best people are all but certain to experience some regret, since the reasons on which they act can "silence" many but not every competing claim: "every sensible person" performs at least some mixed actions "unwillingly" (3.1 1110a9–b9, esp. a29–31, b7–9); and acts done out of ignorance are involuntary rather than "non-voluntary" only if the agent regrets doing them (b18–24, 1111a15–21).

45. Although Aristotle has no single words equivalent to some of these terms, his picture outlines many of the central features of self-love and self-hatred that recent work in ethics has explored; see esp. Williams 1976a.

moral but rooted more broadly in our own interests and concerns. The bad are not unhappy simply because they fail to satisfy a definition; rather, their habits, conduct, and character make them resent themselves and their circumstances and cause them suffering that they too can recognize as bad. Likewise, the virtuous are happy not simply because they do what they should but also because this activity is what they value most; the sustained exercise of their sovereign end makes them love themselves and their lives. Even in the worst misfortune, they retain at least themselves as friends. This self-respect cannot eliminate all suffering from their lives, but it explains why the virtuous never become miserable, why they find their lives enjoyable, and why they may remain happy by conventional standards as well.

Is this picture realistic, or does it exaggerate its contrasts? Even granting Aristotle his claims for sovereign virtue, does he not overstate the costs of egoism and draw too dark a portrait of life for "most people," not all of whom are "bad"? Many who go wrong never recognize their errors or feel any remorse. Heroes like Achilles and Oedipus who do come to see and regret their actions are all the more admirable for their moral courage, but utterly wicked tyrants like Phalaris or immoralists like Callicles feel few scruples and no compunction. Similarly, most of us never do very terrible things, and even the regrets we have are rarely crushing or ruinous. Or those who build their lives singlemindedly around a few lofty but self-centered goals may be fair and caring on most matters but psychologically incapable of regret for any undue suffering they end up inflicting on others. Countless people, from Odysseus to Gauguin, forsake their friends and loved ones to seek glory or answer the call of a distant muse, and even if we should condemn their choices, it is not clear either that they could or that they should if it would ruin everything else in their lives. Finally, people who meet with sustained good fortune rarely feel much regret for their actions, intemperate or unjust or ill-considered or not: most possessors of Gyges' ring would rejoice and congratulate themselves on their luck, as no doubt did the usurper himself, who was widely counted happy for his great prosperity.[46]

46. On Gyges, see II.ii n7 above; I adapt the now familiar case of Gauguin from Williams 1976a. Aristotle might well number the painter among the many rather than the virtuous: some things his vocation cannot justify, and no matter

Some of these worries stem from confusions about incontinence and vice.[47] The former refers primarily to states of indeci-
sion resulting from having incompatible desires at more or less
the same time: having the appetite for drinking more but thinking it better to stop. Nonetheless, although the vicious are generally decisive, they too may come to regret their decisions, not
because they change their mind about their priorities, but precisely because they are sure of what they want. The unrestrained
"wholeheartedly" drink more, only to wake up with the sort of
pain they like least; if deprived of their drink, they may long for it
all the more. The potential for conflict between prospect and ret-
rospect, between acting as one chooses and evaluating one's actions after the event, is the key to Aristotle's argument here. Only
the virtuous are sure to continue to approve their past conduct,
whereas the bad or vicious are very likely to reproach their own
past actions and thus to resent themselves. Quite apart from any
weakness of will, then, the vicious are liable to regret their acts
and their character. What is more, if the source of their regret is
central to the lives they lead, they also have reason to regret living the way they do. So in contrast to the virtuous, whose self-
love is all but self-fulfilling, the bad act in ways that often lead to
self-condemnation.

As it stands, Aristotle has shown how the virtuous can be
happy and love their lives and themselves, but not that no one
else ever can. What if the bad never have cause for regret? What if
they always succeed in getting all and only what they want?
From an external perspective, they do what is wrong and violate
objective norms; but from their own perspective, there may be
nothing they would change, especially if they find satisfaction
and enjoy their success. Should Aristotle then concede not only
that the exercise of virtue is not sufficient for a good life but also
that it is unnecessary? Can he really maintain that no one is

---

how successful or otherwise noble his pursuit of art, he would be wrong to do
things that no one should ever do; he might never feel any regret, but that would
add to his errors, not detract from his guilt. Cf. the remarks on Alcmaeon (3.1
1110a26–29) and II.v n31 above.

47. The internalist perspective sketched in Burnyeat 1980: 84–88 is helpful
here; on incontinence, see III.iii above. I ignore a number of problems that would
complicate the picture, e.g., the distinction between "dispositional" and "occur-
rent" continence (or its contrary), i.e., between settled habits and occasions of
resistance to temptation (or of indulgence).

happy who lives immorally? Aristotle can argue that the possibility of such thorough success is extremely remote, and traditional views about the vicissitudes of human life lend him much support. But not everyone will be convinced not to gamble on fortune and success, especially when the stakes are so high and happiness rides in the balance. To the fortunate in particular, and to the adventurous in general, he offers no certainly persuasive argument. To those who seek exhilaration in the thrill of the chase and in abdicating autonomy and sovereignty over their own life, Aristotle can argue only that the risks remain considerable, and that even if their boldness is rewarded, such people lose their sovereign self by putting their own reason and rational choice at the service of external forces beyond their control and beyond any reliable prediction.

Better by far, Aristotle would argue, to model our lives on Socrates', a man of modest fortune and little pretension, but whose friends thought him "the best, the wisest, and the most just" of anyone they knew (*Phdo.* 118a). Although abused by many and condemned unjustly by his own city to die, he never forsook the virtuous way of life he valued most. Never entirely free from the influence of fortune, he prayed at the end that his "migration from here to there be fortunate" (117c). But always free to act as he judged best, he drained the hemlock "with extreme calmness and equanimity" (117c), and acting "fearlessly and with integrity" to the end, he died a happy man (58e).[48] Socrates might have prolonged his life by acting otherwise, but that would have been to sacrifice his good life. Instead, he always chose what he valued most among the options available, and in upholding his sovereign concern to the end, he lived a complete and happy life.

48. Aristotle's summary account of the virtuous response to adversity (*EN* 1.10 1100b30–1101a3) could stand as a synopsis of his teacher's portrait of Socrates' last hours in the *Phaedo*, which it even echoes at some points: εὐκόλως (117c), γενναιότατον (116c, cf. 58e), ἄριστον καὶ φρονιμώτατον (118a, cf. τὸν ὡς ἀληθῶς ἀγαθὸν καὶ ἔμφρονα).

Reference Matter

Works Cited

For the conventions followed in citing the works listed below, see the Note on Citation, p. xv.

Ackrill, J. L. 1974. "Aristotle on Happiness." *Proceedings of the British Academy* 60: 339–59. Reprinted in Rorty 1980: 15–34.

Adkins, A. W. H. 1960. *Merit and Responsibility*. Oxford.

Andrewes, A. 1938. "Eunomia." *Classical Quarterly* 32: 89–102.

Annas, J. 1980. "Aristotle on Pleasure and Goodness." In Rorty 1980: 285–99.

———. 1981. *An Introduction to Plato's "Republic."* Oxford.

———. 1986. "Doing Without Objective Values: Ancient and Modern Strategies." In Schofield and Striker 1986: 3–29.

———. 1988a. "Naturalism in Greek Ethics: Aristotle and After." *Proceedings of the Boston Area Colloquium in Ancient Philosophy* 4: 149–72.

———. 1988b. "Self-love in Aristotle." *Southern Journal of Philosophy* 27 suppl.: 1–18.

Anscombe, G. E. M. 1957. *Intention*. Oxford.

———. 1958. "Modern Moral Philosophy." *Philosophy* 33: 1–19.

Armstrong, D., and C. W. Peterson. 1980. "Rhetorical Balance in Aristotle's Definition of the Tragic Agent: *Poetics* 13." *Classical Quarterly* 30: 62–71.

Austin, R. D., ed. 1964. *Virgil, Aeneid 2.* Oxford.

Balme, D. M. 1939. "Greek Science and Mechanism: I. Aristotle on Nature and Chance." *Classical Quarterly* 33: 129–38.

———. 1987. "Teleology and Necessity." In *Philosophical Issues in Aristotle's Biology*, ed. A. Gotthelf and J. G. Lennox. Cambridge, Eng., 275–85.

Barker, E., trans. 1946. *The Politics of Aristotle*, with notes. Oxford.

Barnes, J. 1980. "Aristotle and the Methods of Ethics." *Revue Internationale de Philosophie* 34: 490–511.

———. 1982. *The Presocratic Philosophers*. London.

———. 1987. "An Aristotelian Way with Scepticism." In *Aristotle Today*, ed. M. Matthen. Edmonton, 51–76.

———, ed. 1984. *The Complete Works of Aristotle, Revised Oxford Translation*. Princeton, N.J.

———, et al., eds. 1977. *Articles on Aristotle*, vol. 2. London.

Berry, E. 1940. "The History and Development of the Concept of θεία μοῖρα and θεία τύχη down to and Including Plato." Ph.D. diss., University of Chicago.

Boer, W. den. 1954. *Laconian Studies*. Amsterdam.

Bonitz, H. 1870. *Index Aristotelicus*. Berlin.

———. 1886. *Platonische Studien*. 3d ed. Berlin.

Bostock, D. 1988. "Pleasure and Activity in Aristotle's Ethics." *Phronesis* 33: 251–72.

Bowra, C. M. 1938. "Aristotle's Hymn to Virtue." *Classical Quarterly* 32: 182–89.

Braun, E. 1956. *Die Kritik der Lakodaimonischer Verfassung in den "Politika" des Aristoteles*. Kärntner Museumsschriften 12. Klagenfurt.

Broadie, S. 1987. "The Problem of Practical Intellect in Aristotle's Ethics." *Proceedings of the Boston Area Colloquium in Ancient Philosophy* 3: 229–52.

Brunschwig, J., ed. 1967. *Aristote: les Topiques 1–4*. Paris.

Burkert, W. 1960. "Pythagoras oder Platon? Zum Ursprung des Wortes 'Philosophie.'" *Hermes* 88: 159–77.

———. 1985. *Greek Religion*. Trans. J. Raffan. Cambridge, Mass.

Burnet, J., ed. 1900. *The Ethics of Aristotle*. London.

———. 1930. *Early Greek Philosophy*. London.

Burnett, A. 1971. *Catastrophe Survived*. Oxford.

Burnyeat, M. F. 1980. "Aristotle on Learning to Be Good." In Rorty 1980: 69–92.

———. 1986. Review of Barnes 1984. *London Review*, Nov. 6.

Bywater, I. 1892. *Contributions to the Textual Criticism of Aristotle's "Nicomachean Ethics."* Oxford.

———, ed. 1894. *Aristotelis Ethica Nicomachea*. Oxford.

Cartledge, P. 1981. "Spartan Wives: Liberation or License?" *Classical Quarterly* 31: 84–105.

Cartledge, P., and F. D. Harvey, eds. 1985. *Crux*, festschrift for G. E. M. de Ste. Croix. *History of Political Thought* 6. Exeter.

Cawkwell, G. L. 1983. "The Decline of Sparta." *Classical Quarterly* 33: 385–400.

Charles, D. 1984. *Aristotle's Philosophy of Action*. Ithaca, N.Y.

Clark, S. R. L. 1975. *Aristotle's Man*. Oxford.

Cloché, P. 1942. "Aristote et les institutions de Sparte." *Etudes Classiques* 11: 289–313.

Cope, E. M., ed. 1877. *The Rhetoric of Aristotle*. Cambridge, Eng.

Cooper, J. M. 1975. *Reason and Human Good in Aristotle*. Cambridge, Mass.

———. 1977. "Aristotle on the Forms of Friendship." *Review of Metaphysics* 30: 619–48; and "Friendship and the Good in Aristotle." *Philosophical Review* 86: 290–315. Reprinted jointly in Rorty 1980: 301–40.

———. 1982. "Aristotle on Natural Teleology." In *Language and Logos,* festschrift for G. E. L. Owen, ed. M. Nussbaum and M. Schofield. Cambridge, Eng., 197–222.

———. 1985*a.* "Aristotle on the Goods of Fortune." *Philosophical Review* 94: 173–96.

———. 1985*b.* "Hypothetical Necessity." In Gotthelf 1985: 151–67.

———. 1987. "Contemplation and Happiness: A Reconsideration." *Synthese* 72: 187–216.

———. 1988. Review of Nussbaum 1986. *Philosophical Review* 97: 543–64.

Cornford, F. 1907. *Thucydides Mythistoricus.* London.

David, E. 1982–83. "Aristotle and Sparta." *Ancient Society* 13/14: 67–103.

Davies, J. K. 1971. *Athenian Propertied Families, 600–300 B.C.* Oxford.

———. 1981. *Wealth and the Power of Wealth in Classical Athens.* Salem, N.H.

Defourny, M. 1932. *Aristote: Etudes sur la "Politique."* Paris. Reprinted in part in Barnes et al. 1977.

Deman, T. 1942. *Le Témoignage d'Aristote sur Socrate.* Paris.

Denniston, J. D. 1954. *The Greek Particles.* 2d ed. Oxford.

De Ste. Croix, G. E. M. 1981. *The Class Struggle in the Ancient Greek World.* Ithaca, N.Y.

Devereux, D. 1981. "Aristotle on the Essence of Happiness." In O'Meara 1981: 247–60.

Diels, H., and W. Kranz, eds. 1951. *Die Fragmente der Vorsokratiker.* 6th ed. Berlin.

Dirlmeier, F., trans. 1956. *Nikomachische Ethik,* with notes. Berlin.

———. 1958. *Magna Moralia,* with notes. Berlin.

———. 1962. *Eudemische Ethik,* with notes. Berlin.

Dodds, E. R. 1951. *The Greeks and the Irrational.* Berkeley, Calif.

———. 1966. "On Misunderstanding the *Oedipus Rex." Greece and Rome* 13: 37–49.

———, ed. 1959. *Plato, Gorgias.* Oxford.

———, ed. 1960. *Euripides, Bacchae.* 2d ed. Oxford.

Dover, K. J. 1974. *Greek Popular Morality in the Time of Plato and Aristotle.* Berkeley, Calif.

———. 1978. *Greek Homosexuality.* Berkeley, Calif.

———. 1983. "The Portrayal of Moral Evaluation in Greek Poetry." *Journal of Hellenic Studies* 103: 35–48.

Dybikowski, J. 1981. "Is Aristotelian *Eudaimonia* Happiness?" *Dialogue* 20: 185–200.

Edmonds, A. L. 1975. *Chance and Intelligence in Thucydides.* Cambridge, Mass.

Engberg-Pedersen, T. 1983. *Aristotle's Theory of Moral Insight.* Oxford.

Finley, M. I. 1970. "Aristotle and Economic Analysis." *Past and Present* 47: 3–25. Reprinted in Barnes et al. 1977.

———. 1973. *The Ancient Economy.* Berkeley, Calif.

Forrest, W. G. 1968. *A History of Sparta, 950–192 B.C.* London.

Fortenbaugh, W. W. 1975. *Aristotle on Emotion.* London.

Foucault, M. 1985. *The Use of Pleasure.* New York.

Fraenkel, E., ed. 1950. *Aeschylus, Agamemnon*. Oxford.
Fränkel, H. 1946. "Man's 'Ephemeros' Nature According to Pindar and Others." *Transactions of the American Philological Association* 77: 131–45.
————. 1973. *Early Greek Poetry and Philosophy*. Trans. M. Hadas and J. Willis. New York.
Frede, D. 1985. "The Sea-Battle Reconsidered: A Defence of the Traditional Interpretation." *Oxford Studies in Ancient Philosophy* 3: 31–87.
Frede, M. 1980. "The Original Notion of Cause." In *Doubt and Dogmatism*, ed. M. Schofield et al. Oxford, 217–49.
Furley, D. 1981. "Antiphon's Case Against Justice." In *The Sophists and Their Legacy*, ed. G. B. Kerferd. Hermes Einzelschriften 44. Wiesbaden, 81–91.
————. 1986. "Nothing to Us?" In Schofield and Striker 1986: 75–91.
Gagarin, M. 1987. "Morality in Homer." *Classical Philology* 82: 285–306.
Gallop, D. 1988. "Aristotle on Sleep, Dreams, and Final Causes." *Proceedings of the Boston Area Colloquium in Ancient Philosophy* 4: 257–90.
Gauthier, R. A., and J. Y. Jolif, trans. 1970. *L'Ethique à Nicomaque*, with commentary. 2d ed. Louvain.
Geddes, A. G. 1987. "Rags and Riches." *Classical Quarterly* 37: 307–31.
Gildersleeve, B. L., ed. 1885. *Pindar, The Olympian and Pythian Odes*. New York.
Gomme, A. W. 1954. *The Greek Attitude to Poetry and History*. Berkeley, Calif.
Gosling, J. C. B., and C. C. W. Taylor. 1982. *The Greeks on Pleasure*. Oxford.
Gotthelf, A., ed. 1985. *Aristotle on Nature and Living Things*, festschrift for D. Balme. Pittsburgh.
Grant, A., ed. 1885. *The Ethics of Aristotle*. 4th ed. London.
Greenwood, L. H. G., ed. 1909. *Nicomachean Ethics, Book Six*. Cambridge, Eng.
Halladay, A. J. 1977. "Spartan Austerity." *Classical Quarterly* 27: 11–26.
Halliwell, S. 1986. *Aristotle's "Poetics."* Chapel Hill, N.C.
Hardie, W. F. R. 1978. " 'Magnanimity' in Aristotle's Ethics." *Phronesis* 23: 63–79.
————. 1980. *Aristotle's Ethical Theory*. 2d ed. Oxford.
Harvey, F. D. 1965. "Two Kinds of Equality." *Classica et Mediaevalia* 26: 101–46.
Heer, C. de. 1968. Μάκαρ, εὐδαίμων, ὄλβιος, εὐτυχής. Amsterdam.
Hellman, F. 1934. *Herodots Kroisos-Logos*. Neue philologische Untersuchungen 9. Berlin.
Hermann, G., ed. 1852. *Aeschyli Tragoediae*. Leipzig.
Herzog-Hauser, G. 1948. "Tyche." In *Real-Encyclopädie der klassischen Altertumswissenschaft*, ed. A. F. von Pauly and G. Wissowa, vol. 7A:2. Munich, 1643–89.
Huby, P. 1983. "Peripatetic Definitions of Happiness." In *On Stoic and Peripatetic Ethics: The Work of Arius Didymus*, ed. W. Fortenbaugh. New Brunswick, N.J., 121–34.
Humphreys, S. C. 1969. "History, Economics, and Anthropology: The

Work of Karl Polanyi." *History and Theory* 8: 165–212. Reprinted in idem, *Anthropology and the Greeks.* London, 1978: 31–75.

Hursthouse, R. 1981. "A False Doctrine of the Mean." *Proceedings of the Aristotelian Society* 81: 57–72.

———. 1984. "Acting and Feeling in Character: *Nicomachean Ethics* 3.1." *Phronesis* 29: 252–66.

Hutchinson, D. S. 1986. *The Virtues of Aristotle.* London.

Irwin, T. 1977. *Plato's Moral Theory.* Oxford.

———. 1980. "The Metaphysical and Psychological Basis of Aristotle's Ethics." In Rorty 1980: 35–53.

———. 1981a. "Aristotle's Methods of Ethics." In O'Meara 1981: 193–223.

———. 1981b. "Homonymy in Aristotle." *Review of Metaphysics* 34: 523–44.

———, trans. 1985a. *Nicomachean Ethics,* with notes. Indianapolis.

———. 1985b. "Aristotle's Conception of Morality." *Proceedings of the Boston Area Colloquium in Ancient Philosophy* 1: 115–43.

———. 1985c. "Moral Science and Political Theory in Aristotle." In Cartledge and Harvey 1985: 150–68.

———. 1985d. "Permanent Happiness: Aristotle and Solon." *Oxford Studies in Ancient Philosophy* 3: 89–124.

———. 1986. "Stoic and Aristotelian Conceptions of Happiness." In Schofield and Striker 1986: 205–44.

———. 1988a. *Aristotle's First Principles.* Oxford.

———. 1988b. "Disunity in the Aristotelian Virtues." *Oxford Studies in Ancient Philosophy* suppl.: 61–78.

Jacoby, F., ed. 1923–58. *Die Fragmente der griechischen Historiker.* Berlin.

Jaffa, H. 1952. *Thomism and Aristotelianism.* Chicago.

Joachim, H. H. 1951. *Aristotle, The Nicomachean Ethics.* Oxford.

Joly, R. 1956. *La Thème philosophique des genres de vie.* Brussels.

Jowett, B., ed. 1885. *The Politics of Aristotle.* Oxford.

Kenny, A. J. P. 1966. "Aristotle on Happiness." *Proceedings of the Aristotelian Society* 66: 93–102. Reprinted in Barnes et al. 1977.

———. 1978. *The Aristotelian Ethics.* Oxford.

Kerferd, G. B. 1976. "The Wise Man in Greece Before Plato." In *Images of Man in Ancient and Medieval Thought,* festschrift for G. Verbeke, ed. F. Bossier et al. Louvain, 17–28.

———. 1981. *The Sophistic Movement.* Cambridge, Eng.

Keyt, D. 1983. "Intellectualism in Aristotle." In *Essays in Ancient Greek Philosophy* 2, ed. J. P. Anton and A. Preus. Albany, N.Y., 364–87.

Kirkwood, G. M. 1975. "*Nemean* 7 and the Theme of Vicissitude in Pindar." In *Poetry and Poetics,* festschrift for James Hutton, ed. G. M. Kirkwood. Cornell Studies in Classical Philology 38. Ithaca, N.Y., 56–90.

Kolnai, A. 1976. "Dignity." *Philosophy* 51: 251–71.

Korsgaard, C. 1983. "Two Distinctions in Goodness." *Philosophical Review* 92: 169–95.

Kosman, L. A. 1980. "Being Properly Affected: Virtues and Feelings in Aristotle's Ethics." In Rorty 1980: 103–16.

Kraut, R. 1976. "Aristotle on Choosing Virtue for Itself." *Archiv für Geschichte der Philosophie* 58: 223–39.

———. 1979a. "The Peculiar Function of Human Beings." *Canadian Journal of Philosophy* 9: 467–78.

———. 1979b. "Two Conceptions of Happiness." *Philosophical Review* 88: 167–97.

———. 1983. "Comments" on Vlastos 1983. *Oxford Studies in Ancient Philosophy* 1: 59–70.

———. 1988a. "Comments" on Irwin 1988b. *Oxford Studies in Ancient Philosophy* suppl.: 79–86.

———. 1988b. "Comments" on Annas 1988b. *Southern Journal of Philosophy* 27 suppl.: 19–23.

———. 1989. *Aristotle on the Human Good*. Princeton, N.J.

Kullman, W. 1985. "Different Concepts of the Final Cause in Aristotle." In Gotthelf 1985: 169–75.

Kurke, L. 1989. "Καπηλεία and Deceit: Theognis 59–60." *American Journal of Philology* 110: 535–44.

Lacey, W. K. 1968. *The Family in Classical Greece*. Ithaca, N.Y.

Lane Fox, R. 1985. "Aspects of Inheritance in the Greek World." In Cartledge and Harvey 1985: 208–32.

Lang, M. 1984. *Herodotean Narrative and Discourse*. Martin Classical Lectures 28. Cambridge, Mass.

Lear, J. 1984. "Moral Objectivity." In *Objectivity and Cultural Divergence*, ed. S. C. Brown. Cambridge, Eng., 135–70.

Lennox, J. G. 1985. "Are Aristotelian Species Eternal?" In Gotthelf 1985: 67–94.

Leutsch, E. and F. G. Schneidewin, eds. 1839–51. *Corpus Paroemiographorum Graecorum*. Göttingen.

Lloyd, G. E. R. 1968. "The Role of Medical and Biological Analogies in Aristotle's Ethics." *Phonesis* 13: 68–83.

Lloyd-Jones, H. 1983. *The Justice of Zeus*. 2d ed. Berkeley, Calif.

———. 1985. "Pindar and the After-Life." In *Pindare*, ed. A. Hurst. Entretiens de la Fondation Hardt 31. Geneva, 245–79.

Long, A. A. 1968. "Aristotle's Legacy to Stoic Ethics." *British Institute of Classical Studies* 15: 72–85.

———. 1970. "Morals and Values in Homer." *Journal of Hellenic Studies* 90: 121–39.

———. 1988. "Socrates in Hellenistic Philosophy." *Classical Quarterly* 38: 150–71.

Lord, C. 1982. *Education and Culture in the Political Thought of Aristotle*. Ithaca, N.Y.

MacDonald, M. 1978. *Terms for Happiness in Euripides*. Hypomnemata 54. Göttingen.

McDowell, D. M. 1986. *Spartan Law*. Edinburgh.

McDowell, J. 1980. "The Role of *Eudaimonia* in Aristotle's Ethics." *Proceedings of the African Classical Association* 15. Reprinted in Rorty 1980: 359–76.

MacIntyre, A. 1981. *After Virtue.* Notre Dame, Ind.

Mansion, S., ed. 1961. *Aristote et les problèmes de méthode.* Louvain.

Markle, M. M. 1985. "Jury Pay and Assembly Pay at Athens." In Cartledge and Harvey 1985: 265–97.

Martina, A. 1968. *Solone.* Rome.

Meikle, S. 1979. "Aristotle and the Political Economy of the Polis." *Journal of Hellenic Studies* 99: 57–73.

Morrison, J. S., and R. T. Williams. 1968. *Greek Oared Ships.* Cambridge, Eng.

Morrow, G. 1960. *Plato's Cretan City.* Princeton, N.J.

Murdoch, I. 1970. *The Sovereignty of Good.* London.

Mutschmann, H. 1906. *Divisiones quae vulgo dicuntur Aristoteleae.* Leipzig.

Nagel, T. 1972. "Aristotle on *Eudaimonia.*" *Phronesis* 17: 252–59. Reprinted in Rorty 1980: 7–14.

———. 1976. "Moral Luck." *Proceedings of the Aristotelian Society* suppl. 50: 137–51. Reprinted in idem, *Mortal Questions.* Cambridge, Eng., 1979: 24–38.

Newman, W. L., ed. 1887–1902. *The Politics of Aristotle.* Oxford.

North, H. 1966. *Sophrosyne: Self-knowledge and Self-restraint in Greek Literature.* Cornell Studies in Classical Philology 35. Ithaca, N.Y.

Nussbaum, M. C. 1980. "Shame, Separateness, and Political Unity: Aristotle's Criticism of Plato." In Rorty 1980: 395–435.

———. 1986. *The Fragility of Goodness.* Cambridge, Eng.

———. 1988. "Nature, Function, and Capability: Aristotle on Political Distribution." *Oxford Studies in Ancient Philosophy* suppl.: 145–84.

Ollier, F. 1933. *Le Mirage Spartiate: Etude sur l'idealisation de Sparte dans l'antiquité Grecque.* Paris.

O'Meara, D., ed. 1981. *Studies in Aristotle.* Studies in Philosophy and the History of Philosophy 9. Washington, D.C.

Owen, G. E. L. 1957. "A Proof in the *Peri Ideon.*" *Journal of Hellenic Studies* 77: 103–11.

———. 1960. "Logic and Metaphysics in Some Earlier Works of Aristotle." In *Aristotle and Plato in the Mid-Fourth Century,* ed. I. Düring and G. E. L. Owen. Göteborg: 163–90.

———. 1961. "Tithenai ta Phainomena." In Mansion 1961: 83–103.

Page, D., ed. 1962. *Poetae Melici Graeci.* Oxford.

Pears, D. F. 1980. "Courage as a Mean." In Rorty 1980: 171–87.

Phillips, E. D. 1973. *Aspects of Greek Medicine.* London.

Pincoffs, E. 1971. "Quandary Ethics." *Mind* 80: 552–71.

Polanyi, K. 1957. "Aristotle Discovers the Economy." In *Trade and Market in the Early Empires,* ed. K. Polanyi et al. Glencoe, Ill., 64–94.

Price, A. W. 1989. *Love and Friendship in Plato and Aristotle.* Oxford.

Rabinowitz, W. G. 1961. "*Ethica Nicomachea* II 1–6: Academic Eleaticism and the Critical Formulation of Aristotle's Discussion of Moral Virtue." In Mansion 1960: 273–301.

Ramsauer, G., ed. 1878. *Aristotelis Ethica Nicomachea.* Leipzig.

Rassow, H. 1874. *Forschungen über die "Nikomachische Ethik."* Weimar.

Rawls, J. 1971. *A Theory of Justice.* Cambridge, Mass.

Rees, D. A. 1971. "Magnanimity in the *EE* and *NE*." In *Untersuchungen zur "Eudemischen Ethik,"* ed. P. Moraux and D. Harlfinger. Berlin, 231–43.

Regenbogen, O. 1961. "Die Geschichte von Solon und Kroesus." In idem, *Kleine Schriften,* ed. F. Dirlmeier. Munich, 101–24.

Renehan, R. 1982. "Aristotle as Lyric Poet: The Hermias Poem." *Greek, Roman, and Byzantine Studies* 23: 251–74.

Rhodes, P. J. 1981. *A Commentary on the Aristotelian Athenaion Politeia.* Oxford.

———. 1986. "Political Activity in Classical Athens." *Journal of Hellenic Studies* 106: 132–44.

Roche, T. 1988. "On the Alleged Metaphysical Foundation of Aristotle's *Ethics*." *Ancient Philosophy* 8: 49–62.

Rorty, A. O., ed. 1980. *Essays on Aristotle's Ethics.* Berkeley, Calif.

Rose, V., ed. 1886. *Aristotelis qui ferebantur librorum fragmenta.* 3d ed. Leipzig.

Ross, W. D. 1923. *Aristotle.* Oxford.

———, ed. 1955. *Aristotelis Fragmenta Selecta.* Oxford.

Schmidt, E. A. 1967. "Ehre und Tugend: Zur Megalopsychia der aristotelischer Ethik." *Archiv für Geschichte der Philosophie* 49: 149–68.

Schmitt, C. B. 1979. "Aristotle's Ethics in the Sixteenth Century: Some Preliminary Considerations." In *Ethik im Humanismus,* ed. W. Ruegg and D. Wuttke. Boppard, 87–112. Reprinted in idem, *The Aristotelian Tradition and Renaissance Universities.* London, 1984.

Schofield, M., and G. Striker, eds. 1986. *Norms of Nature.* Cambridge, Eng.

Shiner, R. 1987. "Aristotle's Theory of Equity." In *Justice, Law, and Method in Plato and Aristotle,* ed. S. Panagiotou. Edmonton: 173–91.

Smyth, H. W. 1956. *Greek Grammar,* rev. G. M. Messing. Cambridge, Mass.

Solmsen, F. 1960. "Hesiodic Motifs in Plato." In *Hésiode et son influence,* ed. O. Reverdin. Entretiens de la Fondation Hardt 7. Geneva, 171–211.

———. 1964. "Leisure and Play in Aristotle's Ideal State." *Rheinische Museum* 107: 193–220.

Sorabji, R. 1974. "Aristotle on the Role of Intellect in Virtue." *Proceedings of the Aristotelian Society* 74: 107–29. Reprinted in Rorty 1980: 201–20.

———. 1980. *Necessity, Cause, and Blame.* Ithaca, N.Y.

Spoerri, W. 1958. Review of Joly 1956. *Gnomon* 30: 186–92.

Stanford, W. B., ed. 1962. *Aristophanes, The Frogs.* London.

Stewart, J. 1892. *Notes on the "Nicomachean Ethics" of Aristotle.* Oxford.

Strohm, H. 1944. *Tyche: Zur Schicksalsauffassung bei Pindar und den frühgriechischen Dichter.* Stuttgart.

Taylor, G. 1985. *Pride, Shame, and Guilt: Emotions of Self-Assessment.* Oxford.

Urmson, J. O. 1973. "Aristotle's Doctrine of the Mean." *American Philosophical Quarterly* 10: 223–30. Reprinted in Rorty 1980: 157–70.

Ussher, R. G., ed. 1973. *Aristophanes, Ecclesiazusae.* Oxford.

Vlastos, G. 1981. "The Individual as Object of Love in Plato." In idem, *Platonic Studies*. 2d ed. Princeton, N.J., 3–34.

———. 1983. "The Socratic Elenchus." *Oxford Studies in Ancient Philosophy* 1: 27–58, 71–74.

———. 1984. "Happiness and Virtue in Socrates' Moral Theory." *Proceedings of the Cambridge Philological Society* 210: 181–213.

———. 1985. "Socrates' Disavowal of Knowledge." *Philosophical Quarterly* 35: 1–31.

Wehrli, F. 1951. "Ethik und Medizin: zur Vorgeschichte der aristotelischen Mesonlehre." *Museum Helveticum* 8: 36–62.

Weil, R. 1965. "Philosophie et histoire: la Vision de l'histoire chez Aristote." In *La "Politique" d'Aristote*, ed. O. Reverdin. Entretiens de la Fondation Hardt 11. Geneva, 159–97. Reprinted in Barnes et al. 1977.

West, M. L., ed. 1971. *Iambi et Elegi Graeci*. Oxford.

———. 1978. *Hesiod, Works and Days*. Oxford.

White, S. 1988. "Reasons for Choosing a Final End." *Southern Journal of Philosophy* 27 suppl.: 209–32.

———. 1990. "Is Aristotelian Happiness a Good Life or the Best Life?" *Oxford Studies in Ancient Philosophy* 8: 97–137.

Whitehead, D. 1975. "Aristotle the Metic." *Proceedings of the Cambridge Philological Society* 201: 94–99.

———. 1982–83. "Sparta and the Thirty Tyrants." *Ancient Society* 13/14: 106–30.

Whiting, J. 1986. "Human Nature and Intellectualism in Aristotle." *Archiv für Geschichte der Philosophie* 68: 70–95.

———. 1988. "Aristotle's Function Argument: A Defense." *Ancient Philosophy* 8: 33–48.

Wiencke, M. I. 1954. "An Epic Theme in Greek Art." *American Journal of Archaeology* 58: 285–306.

Wiggins, D. 1974. "Deliberation and Practical Reason." *Proceedings of the Aristotelian Society* 74: 107–29. Reprinted in Rorty 1980: 221–40.

Wilkes, K. V. 1978. "The Good Man and the Good for Man in Aristotle's Ethics." *Mind* 87: 553–71. Reprinted in Rorty 1980: 341–57.

Will, E. 1954. "De l'aspect éthique des origines de la monnaie." *Revue Historique* 212: 209–31.

Williams, B. 1962. "Aristotle on the Good: A Formal Sketch." *Philosophical Quarterly* 12: 289–96.

———. 1973. "Egoism and Altruism." In idem, *Problems of the Self*. Cambridge, Eng., 250–65.

———. 1976a. "Moral Luck." *Proceedings of the Aristotelian Society* suppl. 50: 115–35. Reprinted in idem, 1981: 20–39.

———. 1976b. "Persons, Character, and Morality." In *The Identities of Persons*, ed. A. O. Rorty. Berkeley, Calif., 197–216. Reprinted in idem, 1981: 1–19.

———. 1980. "Justice as a Virtue." In Rorty 1980: 189–99.

———. 1981. *Moral Luck*. Cambridge, Eng.

———. 1985. *Ethics and the Limits of Philosophy*. Cambridge, Mass.

Winch, P. 1972. *Ethics and Action*. London.

Woods, M. J., trans. 1982. *Aristotle's Eudemian Ethics, Books I, II, and VIII,* with notes. Oxford.

Young, C. 1988. "Aristotle on Temperance." *Philosophical Review* 97: 521–42.

Index of Passages Cited

The first part of this index lists citations of works by Aristotle; the ordering of the titles follows that of the standard edition. The second part lists citations of works by other ancient authors, arranged alphabetically first by author name and then, under each author, by title. In this index an "f" after a number indicates a separate reference on the next page, and an "ff" indicates separate references on the next two pages. A continuous discussion over two or more pages is indicated by a span of page numbers, e.g., "57–59." *Passim* is used for a cluster of references in close but not consecutive sequence.

General Index

In this index an "f" after a number indicates a separate reference on the next page, and an "ff" indicates separate references on the next two pages. A continuous discussion over two or more pages is indicated by a span of page numbers, e.g., "57–59." *Passim* is used for a cluster of references in close but not consecutive sequence.

Achilles, 51–55 *passim*, 65, 90, 248, 262, 301
Ackrill, J. L., 18*n*
Adkins, A. W. H., 50*n*
Afterlife, 57–58, 89–91
Altruism, 263*n*, 284–86, 289. *See also* Supererogation
Ambition, 230, 242–43, 259–61
Anaxagoras, 28, 64*n*, 68ff, 73
Anaxarchus, 115*n*
Animals, 73*n*, 100–101, 150ff, 159f, 165f, 182f
Annas, J., 25*n*, 276*n*, 278*n*, 279
Anscombe, G. E. M., 18*n*, 35*n*, 73*n*
Appetite, *see under* Desire
Aristides, 51
Aristippus, 4, 201*n*
Aristocracy: Aristotle's objections to, 115, 191–92, 195, 214–16, 237–44; oligarchic, 220, 237–38, 245
Aristotle: and internalism, 3–6, 15–23 *passim*, 158f; and Plato, 6*n*, 7*n*, 23–24, 55*n*, 143*n*, 164*n*, 180*n*, 196*n*, 202*n*, 224; on knowledge, 31–32, 94–95

Barnes, J., 26*n*, 33*n*
Benefaction, 212f, 218, 249, 255, 262–64, 270, 278f. *See also* Gifts
Bostock, D., 162*n*, 167*n*
Burnyeat, M., 104*n*, 243*n*, 302*n*
Business, 194, 196, 198, 201–10 *passim*, 215–16; and retail, 202, 204–10. *See also* Economics; Wealth
Bywater, I., 69*n*, 259*n*, 296*n*, 297*n*

Carthage, 245
Certainty, 44–45, 91–95
Chance, *see under* Fortune
Children: immaturity of, 17*n*, 27*n*, 100–101, 106, 159, 216f; importance of, 61, 64, 76, 115, 120, 128*n*
Choice, *see* Desire: deliberative
Clark, S. R. L., 18*n*, 150*n*
Coincident, 84–87 *passim*, 162, 167, 210*n*, 260
Competition, 50, 65, 192–93, 234–36, 247–50, 279–82
Continence, *see* Incontinence
Cooper, J. M., 28*n*, 73*n*, 101*n*, 111*n*, 114*n*, 128*n*, 172*n*, 240

Library of Congress Cataloging-in-Publication Data

White, Stephen A. (Stephen Augustus)
    Sovereign virtue : Aristotle on the relation between happiness
and prosperity/Stephen A. White.
      p.   cm. — (Stanford series in philosophy)
    Includes bibliographical references and indexes.
    ISBN 0-8047-1694-3 (alk. paper) :
    1. Aristotle—Ethics. 2. Happiness. I. Title. II. Series.
    B491.H36W45 1992
    171'.3—dc20   91-26348
                                               CIP

 This book is printed on acid-free paper.